TOTAL GLOBAL STRATEGY II

TOTAL GLOBAL STRATEGY II
Updated for the Internet and Service Era

George S. Yip

London Business School

Upper Saddle River, New Jersey 07458

Library of Congress Cataloging-in-Publication Data

Yip, George S.
   Total global strategy II : updated for the internet and service era / George S. Yip.
      p. cm.
   Includes bibliographical references and index.
   ISBN 0-13-017917-5
      1. International business enterprises—Management. 2. Strategic planning. 3. Electronic commerce. 4. Service industries. I. Title: Total global strategy 2. II. Title: Total global strategy two. III. Title.

HD62.4 .Y565 2003
658'.049—dc21

2001059343

Executive Editor: David Shafer
Editor-in-Chief: Jeff Shelstad
Managing Editor (Editorial): Jennifer Glennon
Assistant Editor: Melanie Olsen
Editorial Assistant: Kevin Glynn
Media Project Manager: Michele Faranda
Marketing Manager: Shannon Moore
Marketing Assistant: Christine Genneken
Managing Editor (Production): John Roberts
Production Editor: Renata Butera
Production Assistant: Dianne Falcone
Permissions Coordinator: Suzanne Grappi
Associate Director, Manufacturing: Vincent Scelta
Production Manager: Arnold Vila
Manufacturing Buyer: Michelle Klein
Design Manager: Jayne Conte
Cover Design: Bruce Kenselaar
Cover Illustration/Photo: Tony Craddock, Photo Researchers, Inc.
Manager, Print Production: Christy Mahon
Composition: Carlisle Communications
Full-Service Project Management: Carlisle Communications
Printer/Binder: Courier-Westford

Credits and acknowledgments borrowed from other sources and reproduced, with permission, in this textbook appear on appropriate pages within text.

Pearson Education LTD.
Pearson Education Australia PTY, Limited
Pearson Education Singapore, Pte. Ltd
Pearson Education North Asia Ltd
Pearson Education, Canada, Ltd
Pearson Educación de Mexico, S.A. de C.V.
Pearson Education–Japan
Pearson Education Malaysia, Pte. Ltd

10 9 8 7 6 5 4 3 2 1
ISBN 0-13-017917-5

To my students

BRIEF CONTENTS

CONTENTS

LIST OF EXHIBITS

PREFACE TO THE SECOND EDITION

M uch has changed in the 10 years since I wrote the first edition of *Total Global Strategy*. Back then, many companies were still debating whether they should globalize or stay home. For those who were already operating internationally, many questioned the wisdom of moving away from multilocal strategies to global strategies. Would such strategies work? Would they be too difficult to implement? In 10 years we have seen the end of the debate on whether companies should go outside their home markets. We have also seen many successful applications of globally integrated strategies, some of them described in this second edition. Indeed, companies have embraced globalization so successfully that we now see a social and political backlash against it.

With experience, global companies have developed more sophisticated and flexible versions of the strategies and organizational processes described in the first edition. This second edition reflects that greater sophistication and flexibility.

We have also seen in the last 10 years the dramatic rise of the Internet. Despite the stumbles of the first round of dot-coms in the so-called new economy, it is clear that the Internet is affecting virtually all businesses, including how they globalize. In most chapters this second edition explicitly addresses the effects of the Internet on globalization, global strategy, and organization. While not a new phenomenon of the last 10 years, the service aspects of business have continued to grow in importance. Many executives from service businesses have asked me for more guidance and examples. This edition answers that call. There are no separate chapters on the Internet or service businesses, but concepts and examples on both are threaded throughout the entire book.

In the last 10 years, many managers and academics have debated the possibility of regional rather than global strategies. My view in the first edition was that *regional strategy* is a subset of global strategy. But in the intervening period I have worked on two book projects looking at global strategies for particular regions of the world—Asia-Pacific and Central and Eastern Europe.[1] These projects have informed my views on regional strategy. So this edition has a new chapter on that topic.

Perhaps the strongest call has been for more on *implementation*. I have tried to meet this demand by greatly increasing the length of Chapter 8 on global organization, while recognizing the limits for a book focused on strategy.

Between the two editions I have had the opportunity to work closely with many companies, in either consulting or executive education situations, in helping them to apply the concepts in this book. The second edition has greatly benefited from this experience. I have also had the opportunity to test and confirm many of the concepts in various academic studies. These studies have been published in numerous journals, referenced in this second edition. Other scholars have also worked in this area in the intervening time. I have learned from their efforts, and from their works that are referenced here.

In addition to readership among executives, many business schools have adopted the first edition to use in courses on strategy, international/global business, or international/global marketing. I myself have learned much from the students whom I have taught using this book. Hence I am dedicating this second edition to all my students, young and old.

With all the additions, the second edition weighs in about 50 percent longer than the first one. I hope the reader will find the extra information worthwhile.

GUIDE TO THE CHAPTERS

Chapter 1 describes the globalization changes that face companies, then sets out the framework that the rest of this book elaborates. Chapter 2 describes in detail the operation of industry globalization drivers and finishes with an application of globalization drivers to European integration. The next five chapters focus on each global strategy lever in turn: Chapter 3 on the use of global market participation, Chapter 4 on the use of global products and services, Chapter 5 on the use of global activity location, Chapter 6 on the use of global marketing, and Chapter 7 on the use of global competitive moves. Chapter 8 addresses the organization and management issues in implementing global strategy. The chapter presents a framework of the organization and management factors that determine a business's ability to implement global strategy. Chapter 9 discusses regional strategy—how companies can develop intermediate strategies that are part of global ones. Chapter 10 provides operational measures for all the industry globalization, global strategy, and global organization concepts discussed earlier. The chapter is particularly helpful for those undertaking a global strategy analysis of the type described in the last chapter. Chapter 11 pulls together the concepts of the book into a systematic, step-by-step approach to conducting a global strategy analysis.

ACKNOWLEDGMENTS

I wish to first thank David Shafer, my editor at Prentice Hall, for his persistence and patience in encouraging me to bring out a second edition.

Many coauthors have helped me to refine my thinking on this topic. They particularly include Johny Johansson, Christopher Lovelock, David Montgomery, Andrzej Kozminski, Kulwant Singh, Diana Day, and Johan Roos. I have also learned from co-teaching with José de la Torre and Richard Rumelt, and debating in conferences with Alan Rugman.

Several research assistants helped to gather new material for this edition. They include Christine Blanchet, Dominique Litmaath, and Scott Tredennick of the Anderson School at UCLA, and Anna Dempster of Cambridge University. I thank them all.

I benefited from my association with the Deloitte & Touche research program in 1998–1999 on "Innovative Leaders in Globalization," for which I thank Barry Hedley, then Chairman of Braxton Associates, the strategy consulting arm of Deloitte & Touche.

Jon Ashton, my secretary at London Business School, has helped with the production of the manuscript, as did Kim Adams.

I thank my wife, Moira, for her forbearance and support while I worked on this edition, often on weekends.

George S. Yip

PREFACE TO THE FIRST EDITION

This book argues that most multinational companies lack an adequate global strategy. These firms may have learned how to operate in foreign countries by adapting their core business strategy to international environments. But the rapid changes creating more open world markets are rendering that approach inadequate and increasingly obsolete. Companies now need a total global strategy that includes a globalization component. Such a globalization strategy seeks to manage multinational businesses on an integrated, worldwide basis, not as a loosely knit federation of subsidiaries. But the extent of integration needed varies by industry and company situation. A central theme of this book is that almost all industries have global potential in some aspects and not others. So this book provides a systematic framework for evaluating which elements of strategy to globalize and by how much. I do not advocate any one solution, but instead a methodology for arriving at the right solution for a particular company or business. Perhaps most important, this book provides a practical guide on *how* to implement a globalization strategy in order to achieve a successful, total global strategy.

WHO SHOULD READ THIS BOOK

I have written this book for several types of managers (and aspiring managers) as well as for those who teach, study, and research global strategy.

WORLDWIDE BUSINESS MANAGERS

This book is addressed first to the manager responsible for the performance of a worldwide business. This responsibility may not be direct, and there may not be a single executive with worldwide responsibility. One of the topics of this book is how to organize that responsibility. Addressed to the worldwide business head, this book is also relevant for those to whom he or she reports and for those who report to or work with him or her.

CORPORATE MANAGERS

The corporate-level executive will find this book helpful in dealing with the business-level executives who run worldwide businesses, and in understanding what corporate management can expect and should provide. But because of its focus on businesses this book does not address corporate-level global issues such as raising financing on a global scale or setting corporate objectives in relation to global societal considerations. The book touches on, but does not emphasize, the role of the corporate chief executive in global strategy.[2]

NATIONAL MANAGERS

The manager in a single country will find this book helpful in better understanding the role of his or her business in the global strategy of the worldwide business. In some ways, this is a book that a national manager will not want to read, but should. The book concerns the new trend that is curtailing the autonomy of national managers. These managers will find that the reduction in autonomy will be greater and more painful without an understanding of its global strategic imperatives. (This book does not cover how to develop a business in a foreign country or how to be a manager of a foreign subsidiary. Many other books exist on those topics.[3])

MANAGERS IN DOMESTIC COMPANIES OR BUSINESSES

Today very few industries are free from foreign competition or the threat of it. Even when competitors are not foreign, they are often subsidiaries of multinational companies, and their local strategies can be affected by their parents' global strategies. So managers of purely domestic companies or businesses will find it worthwhile to understand the global forces and competitive developments that may come to affect their own prospects.

SUPPLIERS TO MULTINATIONAL COMPANIES

Because a major theme of this book concerns where multinational companies should locate their activities and where they should source their supplies, this book is also highly relevant to managers of their suppliers. Multinational suppliers to multinational companies need to learn how to deal with the new breed of "global customers." And purely local suppliers need to understand the new global strategy also. A local supplier to a local subsidiary of a multinational company can find that its business dries up quickly when the customer's parent company switches to a global sourcing strategy.

EDUCATORS OF FUTURE MANAGERS

Educators should find useful this book's systematic integration of many ideas on global strategy. The explicit framework of this book readily lends itself to both classroom exposition and support of case discussions. *Total Global Strategy* can be assigned as a supplementary text in courses on international management or as the prime text in conjunction with the type of casebooks that are beginning to be written on the topic of global strategic management.[4] This business school edition includes assignment questions at the end of each chapter and is accompanied by a teacher's manual.

RESEARCHERS

The framework presented in this book might be characterized as taking a *contingent and continuum* approach to global strategy. The contingent approach of this book builds on the pioneering work of Michael E. Porter on the role of industry conditions.[5] The main ways in which this book differs from Porter's work is that, first, I spell out in detail the interaction between industry globalization drivers and the appropriate global strategy response, and second, I devote great attention to the implementation of global strategy, an issue largely unexplored by Porter and others. This book also differs from the excellent work of Kenichi Ohmae by providing a more systematic framework to the analysis of global strategy. Compared with the insightful works of Christopher A. Bartlett and Sumantra Ghoshal[6] and C. K. Prahalad and Yves L. Doz,[7] I place much more stress on business-level as opposed to corporate-level global strategy.

RESEARCH, CONSULTING, AND TEACHING BASE OF THIS BOOK

This book is based on extensive research, consulting, and teaching about global strategy, mostly concentrated over the last five years, as well as on my broader business experience of having worked for 10 years in a variety of multinational companies and their service providers.

From 1989 to 1991 I conducted studies of the use of global strategy by American, European, and Japanese companies, sponsored by the Marketing Science Institute.[8] These studies involved my personally visiting the head offices of 23 of the world's largest multinational companies and interviewing over 50 senior executives at these companies about the global strategies of over 30 of their worldwide businesses. In total I studied 18 worldwide businesses belonging to U.S. companies (including Armstrong World Industries, Bausch & Lomb, Citicorp, Chrysler, Colgate-Palmolive, Eastman Kodak, E. I. du Pont de Nemours, Honeywell, IBM, and McDonnell Douglas); six worldwide businesses belonging to European companies (including Beecham, Nestlé, Royal Dutch/Shell, Thomas Cook, and Volkswagen), and seven worldwide businesses belonging to major Japanese multinational companies. The interviews covered each of the elements in my framework: industry globalization drivers, global strategy levers, and global organization. So the interviews provided mini-case histories of how different businesses rated globalization forces in their industries, how they responded to these forces in terms of the use of global strategy, and how they were organized and managed in regard to being able to implement global strategy. I have included findings from these studies throughout the book, although for reasons of confidentiality, I have not identified individual companies. I have already reported the results of the study on the American companies in a Marketing Science Institute report.[9]

I was also able to test most of the concepts and measures in this book in working with member companies of the Profit Impact of Market Strategy (PIMS) program from 1987 to 1989.[10] This effort involved extensive, in-depth data collection and analysis, working with a large team of senior executives in each of four worldwide and two Europewide businesses. In each case I was involved with the business for about six months. This work was in the context of a pilot study for setting up a PIMS global strategy program. Working with the Strategic Planning Institute (SPI), I developed a global strategy questionnaire from my frameworks. This questionnaire was structured to collect matching information from the six to eight largest country-subsidiaries in a given multinational business, as well as information about the worldwide business, its markets, and its competitors. Because this was a pilot study and because of a desire to preserve confidentiality, I have not reported any data from these studies. But the insights I gained are used in many parts of this book.

I have consulted to over a dozen major multinational companies in the United States and Europe on issues of global strategy and global organization during the last five years. This consulting experience has greatly helped me to develop and test my ideas. I have also used the frameworks and ideas in this book in several executive education programs both in individual companies (in the United States, Mexico, Europe, and the Pacific Rim) and in programs offered by Georgetown University and UCLA. Last, I have tested the concepts with nine sections of three classes of M.B.A. students at Georgetown University.

ACKNOWLEDGMENTS

Many people and organizations have helped me with the development of this book. I first began work on the topic of global strategy in collaboration with Mike Yoshino of Harvard Business School and Pierre Loewe of The MAC Group. MAC's development budget, directed by Larry Bennigson, supported my early work. The Marketing Science Institute (MSI) has been very generous in supporting my interview studies in the United States, Japan, and Europe, as well as in providing access to its member companies. I am particularly grateful to George Day, Paul Root, and Katherine Jocz at MSI. The Strategic Planning Institute has also been very helpful in setting up the pilot PIMS global strategy program. Of the many SPI and PIMSA staff who helped me I particularly wish to thank Brad Gale as well as Bill Jones, Brian Keidan, Bob Luchs, Keith Roberts, Joel Rosenfeld, Catherine Roy, Don Swire, and Marinus Zyta. Koji Tsubaki of Waseda University has been very generous in both getting me access to Japanese companies as well as helping me at many of the interviews. Bob Fulmer of Columbia University and The College of William and Mary has made it possible for me to test my ideas in executive education programs, as have José de la Torre and Victor Tabbush at UCLA and Wayne Cartwright of the University of Auckland.

But it is to the School of Business Administration at Georgetown University that I owe the greatest thanks, and particularly to Dean Robert Parker and Associate Dean Robert Thomas for their encouragement and support almost from the day I first conceived of this book. Georgetown gave me an intellectual home as I conducted the research for this book and wrote it, as well as financial and research support. Georgetown's commitment to global business provided a very fruitful environment for my efforts. My new home, UCLA's Anderson Graduate School of Management, has supported me in the creation of this business school edition of *Total Global Strategy*.

Many other colleagues have given generously of their time and thinking in helping me develop my ideas and in reading my manuscripts. These include Johny Johansson, Bob Thomas, and Elizabeth Cooper-Martin of Georgetown; Bob Buzzell and John Quelch of Harvard Business School; Ruth Raubitschek of New York University; Charles Baden Fuller of London Business School and the University of Bath; Carol Franko of Harvard Business School Press; George Cressman of DuPont; Will Rodgers of Hamilton Consultants; and Bruce Orr and John Campbell of Union Carbide. Three reviewers provided by Prentice Hall have been very helpful: Alan Cody of Arthur D. Little, Ed Davis of the University of Virginia, and Allen Morrison of the University of Western Ontario. I greatly appreciate their thorough and frank suggestions. I am also grateful to my editors at Prentice Hall—John Willig, Phil Ruppel, Drew Dreeland, and Eve Mossman—for their encouragement, ideas, and support for the 1992 professional edition of this book; and to Natalie Anderson and Frank Lyman for their support of this business school edition.

I wish to thank also all those executives who gave generously of their time for my research. This kind of work would not be possible without the cooperation of companies.

Many research assistants at Georgetown helped me. These include Tapan Bhat, Rodanthe Hanrahan, George Coundouriotis, Manoj Varma, Niels Nielsen, Steve Pearson, Jeff Lander, and David Williams. Lan Nguyen has skillfully and patiently produced the many exhibits in this book. I must also thank the M.B.A. students in my Global Environment of Business course at Georgetown for their enthusiasm and application in working with my concepts and frameworks and also Tom Brewer, with whom I shared the course, for his cooperation.

Last, but most important, I thank my wife Moira and my children, Andrew and Sarah, for their patience, understanding, and forbearance while I was away on my many trips or hidden away in my study.

George S. Yip

Notes

1. See George S. Yip, *Asian Advantage: Key Strategies for Winning in the Asia-Pacific Region (Updated Edition—After the Crisis)*, (Cambridge, MA: Perseus Publishing, 2000); and Andrzej Kozminski and George S. Yip (eds.), *Strategies for Central and Eastern Europe* (Basingstoke, England: Macmillan, 2000).

2. For a book focusing on the role of the corporate chief executive in global strategy, see C. K. Prahalad and Yves L. Doz, *The Multinational Mission: Balancing Local Demands and Global Vision* (New York: The Free Press, 1987).

3. See Michael Czinkota, Pietra Rivoli, and Ilkka Ronkainen, *International Business* (Chicago: The Dryden Press, 1989), and Franklin R. Root, *Entry Strategies for International Markets* (Lexington, MA: D. C. Heath, 1987), for how to develop a business in a foreign country; and Roderick E. White and Thomas A. Poynter, "Strategies for Foreign-Owned Subsidiaries in Canada," *Business Quarterly,* Summer 1984, pp. 59–69, for the role of international subsidiary managers.

4. See, for example, William H. Davidson and José de la Torre, *Managing the Global Corporation: Case Studies in Strategy and Management* (New York: McGraw-Hill, 1989), and Paul W. Beamish, J. Peter Killing, Donald J. Lecraw, and Harold Crookell, *International Management: Text and Cases* (Homewood, IL: Richard D. Irwin, 1991).

5. See Michael E. Porter, "Competition in Global Industries: A Conceptual Framework," in *Competition in Global Industries,* Michael E. Porter, Ed. (Boston: Harvard Business School Press, 1986), and Michael E. Porter, "Changing Patterns of International Competition," *California Management Review,* Vol. 28, No. 2, Winter 1986, pp. 9–40.

6. Christopher A. Bartlett and Sumantra Ghoshal, *Managing Across Borders: The Transnational Solution* (Boston: Harvard Business School Press, 1989).

7. Prahalad and Doz, *The Multinational Mission.*

8. There have been few studies that actually measure the use of global strategy. Two exceptions are Kendall Roth and Allen J. Morrison, "An Empirical Analysis of the Integration-Responsiveness Framework in Global Industries," *Journal of International Vol. 21, No. 4, Fourth Quarter Business Studies,* 1990, pp. 541–64; and Allen J. Morrison, *Strategies in Global Industries: How U.S. Businesses Compete* (Westport, CT: Quorum Books, 1990).

9. See George S. Yip, "Do American Businesses Use Global Strategy?" Working Paper No. 91-101 (Cambridge, MA: Marketing Science Institute).

10. The PIMS program of the Strategic Planning Institute is a long-established project by which companies share strategic information. A very large number of research studies have been conducted on the PIMS databases over the last 20 years. But although PIMS data come from a large number of countries, primarily in North America and in Europe, the data are essentially domestic in nature with no international variables. Furthermore, relationships among subsidiaries in different countries are not identified. See Robert D. Buzzell and Bradley T. Gale, *The PIMS Principles: Linking Strategy to Performance* (New York: The Free Press, 1987), for a description of the PIMS program, its findings, and a list of published studies using PIMS data.

ABOUT THE AUTHOR

George Yip is Professor of Strategic and International Management and the Andersen Research Fellow for the Network Economy at London Business School, and also Associate Dean and head of the full-time M.B.A. program. He was previously the Chair of Marketing and Strategy at Cambridge University and a Fellow of Magdalene College, and has also held faculty positions at Harvard Business School and UCLA, and visiting positions at the China-Europe International Business School, Georgetown University, Stanford Business School, and Templeton College, Oxford. He has won both teaching and research awards. He is a Fellow of the Academy of International Business, and Cochairman of Perseus Consulting, a firm that leverages a worldwide network of faculty experts. He also worked for 10 years in management positions with major multinational companies and consulting firms, and now serves on a number of corporate boards.

He is Joint Managing Editor of *Business Strategy Review,* Associate Editor of *Journal of International Business Studies,* and serves on the editorial/advisory boards of *Asia Pacific Journal of Management, Journal of International Management, Journal of International Marketing, Long Range Planning,* and *Marketing Management.* He is the author of *Barriers to Entry, Asian Advantage: Key Strategies for Winning in the Asia-Pacific Region and Strategies for Central and Eastern Europe;* and of articles in the *Columbia Journal of World Business, Harvard Business Review, Sloan Management Review,* and *Strategic Management Journal.* He holds B.A. and M.A. degrees in economics from Cambridge University, a master's degree from the Cranfield School of Management, and an M.B.A. and doctorate from Harvard Business School.

1
UNDERSTANDING GLOBAL STRATEGY

◦◦◦◦

In the 1980s and 1990s, many companies debated whether they should globalize. In the third millennium this debate has ended (or in the language of the wired generation, "game over"). Companies now assume that they should globalize unless they can find very good reasons not to. The spread of the Internet and the Web provides one compelling reason: Any company that mounts a Web site has instant global reach and overseas customers follow very quickly, with corresponding demands for delivery and service. In addition, as more and more evidence shows, companies that globalize achieve better competitive and financial performance.

But globalizing, in the sense of spreading activities around the globe, is not enough. Companies also need to be globally integrated, in the sense of using globally coherent strategies, operating global networks, and maximizing profits on a global basis. However, turning a collection of country-businesses into one worldwide business that has an integrated, global strategy presents one of the stiffest challenges for managers today. Because of its difficulties, being able to develop and implement an effective global strategy is the acid test of a well-managed company. Many forces are driving companies around the world to globalize in the sense of expanding their participation in foreign markets. Companies also need to globalize in another sense, that is, *integrating* their worldwide strategy. This global integration contrasts with the multinational approach in which companies set up country subsidiaries that design, produce, and market products or services tailored to local needs. This multinational model is now in question and may be considered a "multilocal strategy" in contrast to a truly global strategy.[1]

Many managers are asking if they are in a global industry and whether their business should have a global strategy. The better questions to ask are: *How global is the industry* and *How global should the business strategy be?* This is because virtually every industry has aspects that are global or potentially global—some industries have more aspects that are global than others and more intensely so. Similarly, a strategy can be more or less global in its different elements. An industry is global to the extent that there are intercountry connections. A strategy is global to the extent that it is integrated across countries. Global strategy should not be equated with any one element—standardized products or worldwide market coverage or a global manufacturing network. Global strategy should, instead, be a flexible combination of many elements.

Recent and coming changes make it more likely that in many industries, a global strategy will be more successful than a multilocal one. Indeed, having a sound global strategy may well be the requirement for survival as the changes accelerate. These changes include the growing similarity among countries in what their citizens want to buy.[2] Other changes are the reduction of tariff and nontariff barriers, technology investments that are becoming too expensive to amortize in one market only, and competitors who are changing the nature of rivalry from country-by-country competition to

GILLETTE'S GLOBAL STRATEGY

Gillette, the U.S. shaving products company, provides one of the most aggressive examples of globally standardized strategy.[3] Unlike many corporate strategies that recognize cultural sensitivities in their global strategies, Gillette minimizes adaptation for cultural differences. The company sells the same products, uses the same production methods, enforces the same corporate policies, and advertises the same in all countries where it conducts business. The results have been impressive, as the company now dominates the shaver market with a 70 percent share of worldwide shavers. The main advantages of this business model are scale and flexibility, most notable in research and development costs and leveraging intellectual capital across the globe. In addition, the company is more nimble, as shown during the Asian Crisis in the late 1990s. Rather than maintain advertising expenditures

in an area with flat to negative growth, Gillette chose to shift its marketing funds to Eastern Europe, where it forecasted better sales growth. Since Gillette managed the world as one region, it was able to enjoy such flexibility in operations.

To effectively implement this strategy, the company's CEO, Al Zeien, notes a few key success factors. The CEO travels to all parts of its world operation, meeting workers and discussing ideas with management. He considers his physical presence as a key to delivering the corporate global strategy to Gillette employees, as well as via new communications technology. Furthermore, Gillette managers are also expected to geographically relocate three or four times in the first 12 years. They act as "idea ambassadors," transferring concepts to different areas of the world.

global competition. In the 1990s, the world saw great convergence in customer needs and tastes, the drastic reduction of many government barriers to free trade and investment, an acceleration of globalization enablers in communications, and a surge in globally applicable new technological products and services. All this does not mean that every industry has become entirely global. But today, nearly every industry has a significant global segment in which customers prefer products or services that are much more global than they are local. Around the global segment are still regional, national, or subnational niches. The size of the global segment varies, from very large in, for example, the personal computer industry to relatively small in many parts of the food industry. But the global segment is increasing in size in nearly all cases.

Trade barriers continue to fall. The most important examples include the North American Free Trade Agreement among the United States, Canada, and Mexico; the continuing integration of the European Union; the formation of the new World Trade Organization in 1995 and China joining that body at the end of 2001; and the Asian Crisis from 1997 to 1999, which helped to open up economies such as Japan and South Korea. The rise of the NICs (newly industrializing countries such as Hong Kong, Taiwan, South Korea, Singapore, Thailand, Malaysia, Mexico, and Brazil) has also increased the number of viable sites for sophisticated manufacturing operations with low labor costs. Even India is beginning to join the industrialized world and the global market economy.

Almost every product or service market in the major world economies has foreign competitors—computers, fast food, medical diagnostic equipment—a nearly endless list that is growing rapidly. Increasing foreign competition is in itself a reason for a business to globalize in order to gain the size and skills to compete more effectively. But an even

TOYOTA'S GLOBAL SPREAD

In many industries, such as automobiles, a global strategy requires multiregional production (as will be further explained in Chapter 9). In the late 1990s, Toyota spent over $10 billion on global expansion in an aggressive effort to become the first real globally organized car manufacturer.[4] Toyota developed manufacturing hubs in the three major markets (North America, Europe, and Asia), with the ability to customize vehicles for regional markets. Such extensive coverage now allows Toyota to react quickly to local tastes, bypass regional trade barriers, and utilize locally based suppliers to increase cost efficiencies. The company had set up an assembly plant in the United States as early as 1987 and continued expansion at a number of sites there and in Canada through the 1990s. In Europe, by 2001, Toyota had a regional parts center in Belgium and manufacturing plants in the United Kingdom, France, and Turkey, as well as one that would open in Poland in 2002. This local production allows Toyota to bypass tariffs and locally produce Toyota's "Europe Car." In Asia, a local network of suppliers and assembly hubs allows Toyota to build sturdy, simply designed, low-priced cars that appeal to the Asian consumer.

greater spur to globalization is the advent of new global competitors that manage and compete on an integrated global basis. In the 1980s these global competitors were primarily Japanese. Their central approach to global competition was one of the factors that allowed Japanese companies to conquer so many Western markets.[5] In the 1990s, American and European companies responded to the Japanese challenge by focusing much more on quality. This was exemplified by General Electric's and Motorola's adoption of *six-sigma* quality. In addition, American and, especially, some European companies began to develop new models of globalization that were more flexible than the centralized Japanese one. Companies such as Asea Brown Boveri developed networked models that combine the benefits of both global integration and national responsiveness.

In addition, the communications and information revolution has made it much easier to manage in a globally integrated fashion. Improvements in air travel, computers, satellites, and telecommunications make it much easier to communicate with, and control, far-flung operations. The facsimile (fax) machine made one of the most dramatic changes. Its immediacy and completeness of communication plugged the globe into every executive's desk. The Internet and the Web completed this revolution.

KEYS TO A SUCCESSFUL TOTAL GLOBAL STRATEGY

A total global strategy has three separate components, depicted in Exhibit 1-1:

1. *Developing the core strategy,* which is the basis of sustainable strategic advantage. This is usually, but not necessarily, developed for the home country first. Without a sound core strategy on which to build, a worldwide business need not bother about global strategy.

2. *Internationalizing the core strategy,* through international expansion of activities and adaptation of the core strategy. Companies need to have mastered the basics of

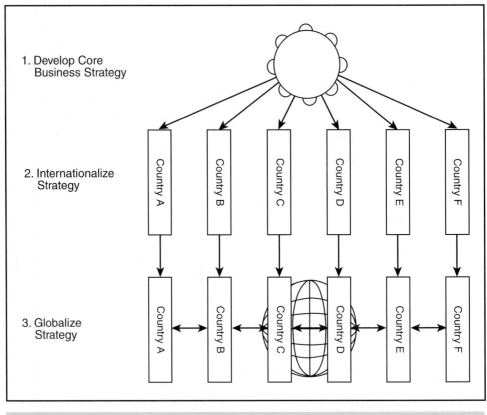

1. Develop Core
   Business Strategy

2. Internationalize
   Strategy

Country A Country B Country C Country D Country E Country F

3. Globalize
   Strategy

Country A Country B Country C Country D Country E Country F

EXHIBIT 1-1   Components of a Total Global Strategy

international business before they can attempt a global strategy (because the latter often involves breaking the rules of international business).

3.   *Globalizing the international strategy,* by integrating the strategy across countries.

Multinational companies know well the first two steps. What they know less well is the third step. In addition, globalization runs counter to the accepted wisdom of tailoring for national markets.[6] *This book focuses on the third step—global integration.*

DEVELOPING A CORE BUSINESS STRATEGY

Each separable business in a company needs its own core strategy.[7] Defining the business in the first place can be a major task. Major parameters of the definition include the types of customers served and the types of products and services offered. The type of product or service can be split into two separate dimensions—the type of need met and the type of technology used to meet that need.[8] For example, one business may be in the total packaging business, while another business may define its business more narrowly as the plastics packaging business.

A core strategy includes several key elements:

- Selection of the type of products or services that the business offers
- The types of customers that the business serves
- The geographic markets served
- Major sources of sustainable competitive advantage
- Functional strategy for each of the most important value-adding activities
- Competitive posture, including the selection of competitors to target
- Investment strategy

Strategy writers have sometimes urged the broadest possible definition of a business and criticize managers who restrictively define their business. But the breadth or narrowness of a business definition is a key element of strategic choice and directly affects sustainable strategic advantage. It is better to devote limited resources to sustaining advantage in a narrowly defined business than to overspread resources so that no advantage is sustained. In recent years the more prominent failures have come from too expansive a business definition. People Express, at one time a highly successful airline in the United States, collapsed when it expanded beyond its East Coast cut price niche. Saatchi & Saatchi, once the world's largest advertising agency group, had to reverse its expansion into the consulting business. The company had expected, wrongly, to conquer this new business as rapidly as it had conquered its traditional business. Both Matsushita and Sony redefined themselves as entertainment companies and made disastrous acquisitions of movie studios.

DEVELOPING AN INTERNATIONALIZATION STRATEGY

When a business expands outside its home market, it needs to internationalize its core business strategy. The first and most important step in internationalizing the core business strategy is to select the geographic markets in which to compete. This choice has much more importance for an international business than for a national business. In the early part of its life a national business does face issues of geographic market selection as it expands within its domestic market. These issues include identifying market attractiveness, potential competition and ways in which to adapt to local conditions, and ways in which to manage the business across a larger geographic area. For some retail or service businesses, geographic market selection continues to be vital because of the importance of site location.

But for most businesses international market selection presents issues that are much more challenging than selection within a domestic market. The sources of this challenge include the role of barriers to trade, such as import tariffs and quotas and foreign ownership rules, as well as differences from the home country in laws, language, tastes, and behavior.[9] Other aspects of internationalization strategy involve how to adapt products and programs to take account of foreign needs, preferences, culture, language, climate, and so on. *But the end result is typically that the company winds up with strategies and approaches with large differences among countries.* These differences can then weaken the company's worldwide cost position, quality, customer preference, and competitive leverage.

DEVELOPING A GLOBALIZATION STRATEGY

To overcome the disadvantages created by internationalization, companies need a globalization strategy that integrates and manages for worldwide business leverage and

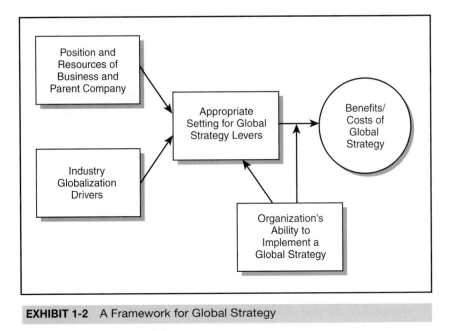

EXHIBIT 1-2   A Framework for Global Strategy

competitive advantage. *What aspects of strategy should be globalized?* Managers can answer this question by systematically analyzing industry conditions or "industry globalization drivers," by evaluating the benefits and costs of globalization, and by understanding the different ways in which a globalization strategy can be used through the use of "global strategy levers."

Exhibit 1-2 presents the framework for diagnosing and developing globalization strategy. Industry globalization drivers are externally determined by industry conditions or by the economics of the business, while global strategy levers are choices available to the worldwide business.[10] *Industry globalization drivers* (underlying market, cost, and other industry conditions) create the potential for a worldwide business to achieve the *benefits* of global strategy. To achieve these benefits, a worldwide business needs to set its *global strategy levers* (e.g., use of globally standardized products) appropriately relative to the industry drivers, and relative to the *position and resources* of the business and its parent company. The *organization's ability to implement* the formulated global strategy affects how well the benefits can be achieved.

Another way of viewing the relationship among these different forces and factors is in terms of a globalization triangle. As depicted in Exhibit 1-3, industry globalization drivers, global strategy levers, and global organization factors need to work together to achieve potential globalization benefits.

SOME DEFINITIONS AND DISTINCTIONS

Global, Globalize

The recent popularity of global strategy has caused overuse of the terms "global" and "globalize." Instead of being used to designate a particular type of international strategy, these terms are being used to replace the term "international." One reason is that "international" has come to represent, particularly in the United States, the now unfashionable

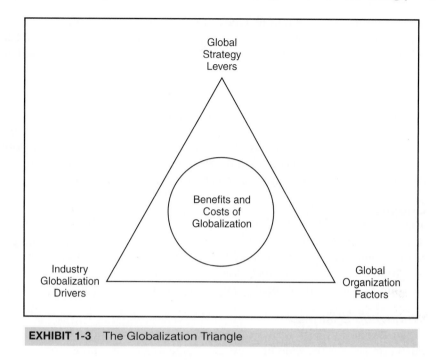

EXHIBIT 1-3   The Globalization Triangle

distinction between domestic and nondomestic business. Everyone seems to want a global strategy rather than just an international one. As a result of the widespread use of the term "global," we are losing the ability to refer to different types of international strategy. More important, executives will find it easier to delude themselves that they have a global strategy if they are careless as to what they call their worldwide strategy.

A truly global company is one that does business not only in both the eastern and western hemispheres but also in both the northern and southern ones.[11] In the process, geographic distances and time zone variations are maximized. With the rise of non-Japan Asia, Latin America, and Eastern Europe, operating in just the "triad" of North America, Western Europe, and Japan is no longer sufficient. Other differences also tend to be sharpened, such as the variety of languages, currencies, cultures, legal and political systems, government policies and regulations, educational backgrounds of managers and employees, levels of national economic development, and climates.

Simply operating globally does not mean that a company possesses a global strategy. *The global company does not have to be everywhere, but it has the capability to go anywhere, deploy any assets, and access any resources, and it maximizes profits on a global basis.*

The term "worldwide" will be used as a neutral designation. "International" will refer to anything connected with doing business outside the home country. "Multilocal" and "global" will refer to types of worldwide strategy. Much of this book will cover what these types of strategy mean. Briefly, a multilocal strategy treats competition in each country or region on a stand-alone basis, while a global strategy takes an integrated approach across countries and regions. "Multilocal" is preferable to "multinational," as the latter term has come to be associated with a type of company. Indeed, a multinational company can pursue different types of worldwide strategy for each of its different worldwide businesses. For example, as a multinational company, General Electric, may pursue a global strategy for its turbine engine business, but a multilocal strategy for some other business.

Regional
Issues of global strategy apply not just at the worldwide level but at the regionwide level. For example, companies seeking to meet the challenges and exploit the opportunities of the European Union or ASEAN are, in essence, developing a global strategy at the continental or subcontinental level. The term "regional" will be used to refer to multicountry areas, typically covering all or most of a continent.

Country
The term "country" can also be problematic. For example, is Benelux one country or three? Legally it comprises three countries, but many companies manage it as one. Management is the key. Even more ambiguous is the group of Central American countries lying between Mexico and Colombia. The term "country" will be used to refer to single countries or groups of small, contiguous countries that are managed as one country.

Worldwide Business
A worldwide business is one that has significant operations on several continents. Furthermore, a worldwide business is defined as one that produces as well as sells in multiple countries (if not continents). Thus a purely export-based business is not a worldwide business by this author's definition. A worldwide business may also not be recognized as such: The company may view it merely as a collection of similar businesses operating in different countries. One topic of this book will be how to recognize a worldwide business. Such a business may use multilocal or global strategy or some combination in between.

Transnational
Some now argue for "transnational strategy": "In contrast to the global model, the transnational mentality recognizes the importance of flexible and responsive country-level operations—hence the return of *national* into the terminology. And compared to the multinational approach, it provides for linking and coordinating those operations to retain competitive effectiveness and economic efficiency—as indicated by the prefix *trans*. The resulting need for intensive organizationwide coordination and shared decision making implies that this is a much more sophisticated and subtle approach to MNC management."[12] While this author agrees with the need to respond to country differences, *where truly* necessary, there is already plenty of advice on how to do that (in most textbooks on international business[13]). What is much harder is to achieve global integration—the focus of global strategy and of this book.

FINANCIAL BENEFITS OF INTERNATIONALIZATION AND GLOBALIZATION

Both internationalization—in terms of globally spreading activities and revenues—and globalization—in terms of globally integrating strategy—improve financial performance.

FINANCIAL BENEFITS OF INTERNATIONALIZATION

Many studies have shown that internationalization increases financial returns and reduces risk.[14] Other recent studies have shown that international spread reduces financial betas for multinational firms, but also that volatile currency markets have vastly increased the impact of exchange risk, so that the net variance in cash flows is higher today for multinational firms.[15] This empirical evidence suggests that it is premature to say that multinationals have found a way to eliminate the risk-return relationship. However, it does seem to be the case that firms can simultaneously increase returns to fixed assets and take a portfolio approach to financial risk management by increased internationalization.

While financial risk reduction seems to be less clear-cut today, business risk reduction strategies through international expansion continue to be attractive.[16] If we look at business risk as exposure to unexpected events, international markets offer several advantages. First, extended product life cycles, while perhaps less apparent than in the past,[17] still seem possible in many industries. Firms that can shift sales of outdated product in industrialized countries to developing countries can gain ongoing returns on their initial investment and may also be able to avoid sudden replacement by new technologies or innovative products. Much evidence also exists to show that strategic maneuvering in concentrated industries is most successful when used by international firms against domestic firms. Finally, political and other environmental risks can be difficult to manage for companies committed to one or a few national markets, while more internationalized firms can shift production, promotion, distribution, and even development among a number of markets to take advantage of (or avoid) local conditions or to increase bargaining power.

FINANCIAL BENEFITS OF GLOBALIZATION

Global integration is a relatively new phenomenon. So there is relatively little research on its financial benefits. Studies have provided limited evidence, all in favor of, or at least neutral toward, global strategy. A 1990 study found no significant difference in profit performance among businesses facing (1) global integration pressures, (2) local responsiveness pressures, and (3) both pressures.[18] A narrower 1989 study found that the market share and profit performance of 71 European and Japanese firms serving the U.S. market were negatively related to the extent to which products were adapted for the U.S. market; that is, businesses with globally standardized products performed better.[19] In a 1990 study of global industries, companies with a "global, combination" strategy had the best performance on measures of return on assets, and those with an "international, product innovation" strategy had the best performance on return on investment, while the companies with a "domestic, product specialization" strategy had the poorest performance.[20] More broadly, a 1994 study of American and Japanese companies found a strong positive relationship between the use of global strategy and superior performance in terms of relative market share and relative profitability.[21]

INDUSTRY GLOBALIZATION DRIVERS

Four groups of "industry globalization drivers"—market, cost, government, and competitive—represent the industry conditions that determine the potential and need for competing with a global strategy.[22] Together these four sets of drivers cover all the critical industry conditions that affect the potential for globalization. While other groupings are possible,

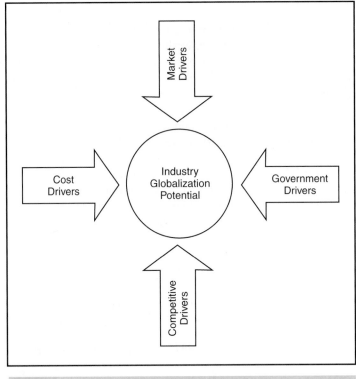

EXHIBIT 1-4   Industry Globalization Potential

these four distinguish among the sources (market or cost, etc.) of the drivers and, therefore, help managers to more easily identify and deal with them. Drivers are primarily uncontrollable by the worldwide business. As illustrated in Exhibit 1-4 each industry has a level of globalization potential that is determined by these external drivers.

Market globalization drivers depend on customer behavior, the structure of distribution channels, and the nature of marketing in the industry. Cost drivers depend on the economics of the business. Government globalization drivers depend on the rules set by national governments. Competitive drivers depend on the actions of competitors. Each group of drivers is different for each industry and can also change over time. Therefore, some industries have more globalization potential than others, and the potential also changes. A common group of changes, increasing the globalization potential of many industries, is spurring the interest of managers in global strategy.

GLOBAL STRATEGY LEVERS

Globalization strategy is multidimensional. Setting strategy for a worldwide business requires choices along a number of strategic dimensions. Some of these dimensions determine whether the strategy lies toward the multilocal end of the continuum or the global end. There are five such dimensions:

- *Market participation* involves the choice of country-markets in which to conduct business and the level of activity, particularly in terms of market share.

RECENT CHANGES IN GENERAL GLOBALIZATION DRIVERS

Although it is not the purpose of this book to examine general changes in globalization drivers, some of these common changes include:

MARKET DRIVERS

- Per capita income converging among industrialized nations
- Convergence of lifestyles and tastes (e.g., McDonald's in Moscow and Stolichnaya vodka in America)
- Increasing travel creating global consumers
- Organizations beginning to behave as global customers
- Growth of global and regional channels (e.g., by 2001, America's Wal-Mart was in 10 countries, France's Carrefour/Promodès in 31, Germany's Metro in 21, and Japan's 7-Eleven in 21)
- Establishment of world brands (e.g., Coca-Cola, Levi's, Microsoft)
- Push to develop global advertising (e.g., Saatchi and Saatchi's commercials for British Airways)
- Spread of global and regional media (e.g., CNN, MTV, Star TV in Asia)

COST DRIVERS

- Continuing push for economies of scale (but offset by flexible manufacturing)
- Accelerating technological innovation
- Advances in transportation (e.g., use of FedEx to deliver urgent supplies from one continent to another)
- Emergence of newly industrializing countries with productive capability and low labor costs (e.g., China, India, and Indonesia)
- Increasing cost of product development relative to market life

GOVERNMENT DRIVERS

- Reduction of tariff barriers (e.g., North American Free Trade Agreement)
- Reduction of nontariff barriers (e.g., Japan's gradual opening of its markets)
- Creation of trading blocs (e.g., European Union, and Euro currency in 1999)
- Strengthening of world trade institutions (e.g., formation of the World Trade Organization)
- Decline in role of governments as producers and customers (e.g., denationalization of many industries in Europe and elsewhere)
- Privatization in previously state-dominated economies, particularly in Latin America
- Shift to open market economies from closed communist systems in Eastern Europe and the former Soviet Union
- Increasing participation of China and India in the global economy

COMPETITIVE DRIVERS

- Continuing increase in level of world trade
- More countries becoming key competitive battlegrounds (e.g., rise of Japan to become a "lead" country)
- Increased ownership of corporations by foreign acquirers
- Rise of new competitors intent upon becoming global competitors (e.g., Japanese firms in the 1970s, Korean firms in the 1980s, Taiwanese firms in the 1990s, Chinese firms in the 2000s, and probably Indian and Russian firms in the 2010s)
- Rise of "born global" Internet and other companies
- Growth of global networks making countries interdependent in particular industries (e.g., electronics)

continued

continued

- More companies becoming globally centered rather than nationally centered (e.g., Stanley Works, a traditional U.S. company, moved its production offshore; Uniden, a Japanese telecommunications equipment producer has never manufactured in Japan)
- Increased formation of global strategic alliances

OTHER DRIVERS

- Revolution in information and communications (e.g., personal computer, facsimile machines, and the Internet)
- Globalization of financial markets (e.g., listing of corporations on multiple exchanges, and issuing debt in multiple currencies)
- Improvements in business travel (e.g., improved air travel and rise of international hotel chains).

- *Products/services* involve the extent to which a worldwide business offers the same or different products in different countries.
- *Location of value-adding activities* involves the choice of where to locate each of the activities that constitute the entire value-added chain—from research to production to after-sales service.[23]
- *Marketing* involves the extent to which a worldwide business uses the same brand names, advertising, and other marketing elements in different countries.
- *Competitive moves* involve the extent to which a worldwide business makes competitive moves in individual countries as part of a global competitive strategy.

For each global strategy dimension or lever, a multilocal strategy seeks to maximize worldwide performance by maximizing local competitive advantage, revenues, or profits; while a globalized strategy seeks to maximize worldwide performance through sharing and integration. Intermediate positions are, of course, feasible. A business that has a fully globalized strategy would make maximum use of each of the five global strategy levers and would therefore have fully *global market participation, global products and services, global location of activities, global marketing,* and *global competitive moves.* But, of course, not every business should use such a strategy. An overview of each lever is provided here.

MARKET PARTICIPATION

In a multilocal participation strategy, countries are selected on the basis of their stand-alone potential in terms of revenues and profits. In a global market participation strategy, countries need to be selected in terms of their potential contribution to globalization benefits. This may mean entering a market that is unattractive in its own right but has global strategic significance, such as the home market of a global competitor. Or it may mean concentrating resources on building share in a limited number of key markets rather than more widespread coverage. A pattern of major share in major markets is advocated in the concept of the USA-Europe-Japan triad.[24] In contrast, under a multilocal strategy no particular pattern of participation is required—the pattern accrues from the pursuit of local advantage.

ELECTROLUX'S MARKET PARTICIPATION STRATEGY IN APPLIANCES

The Swedish appliance giant, the Electrolux Group, is pursuing a strategy of building significant share in major world markets. The company aims to be the first global appliance maker. In 1986, Electrolux took over Zanussi Industries to become the top producer of appliances in Western Europe. Later that year, Electrolux acquired White Consolidated Industries, the third largest American appliance manufacturer. These market moves have given Electrolux a very strong global position. (Still, Electrolux has had to pay a significant price for its global position. Restructuring following the acquisitions combined with the worldwide recession from 1990 to 1991 to greatly reduce its profits.)

PRODUCTS AND SERVICES

In a multilocal product strategy, the products and services offered in each country are tailored to local needs. In a global product strategy, the ideal is a standardized core product that requires a minimum of local adaptation. Cost reduction is usually the most important benefit of product standardization. Others stress the need for a broad product portfolio, with many product varieties in order to share technologies and distribution channels; or stress the need for flexibility.[25] In practice, multinationals have pursued global product standardization to a greater or lesser extent some of the time.[26]

The nature of service delivery makes both standardization and customization equally feasible. Local elements can be easily added to a global formula such as the service provided at Club Med. The well-known chain of resorts has incorporated local adaptations to its core product. The entertainment available varies from resort to resort, such as Balinese dancing in Indonesia, and the game of mah-jongg and more group activities in other Asian resorts. Club Med steers its American customers to English-speaking clubs. They do this by printing two different brochures; the brochures featuring European resorts are primarily not available in the United States.[27]

ACTIVITY LOCATION

In a multilocal activity strategy, all or most of the value chain is reproduced in every country. In another type of international strategy—exporting—most of the value chain is kept in one country. In a global activity strategy, the value chain is broken up and each activity may be conducted in a different country. The major benefits lie in cost reduction. One type of value-chain strategy is partial concentration and partial duplication. The key feature of a global position on this strategy dimension is the systematic placement of the value chain around the globe.

To provide its global customer support service, Hewlett-Packard maintains a global chain of activity locations—its more than 30 Response Centers around the world are integrated into a global network headed by four major centers: Bracknell (United Kingdom), Atlanta (Georgia) and Mountain View (California) in the United States, and

Melbourne (Australia). Each center is staffed during extended daytime hours, seven days a week, by between 12 and 200 engineers. Problems that cannot be resolved in a smaller center may be transferred to one of the major centers. Because of time-zone differentials, at least one of the major centers is always in full operation at any time.

Citibank, one of the world's largest banks, has positioned itself as a "uniquely global consumer bank."[28] The company's objective is to allow its customers to do their banking "any way, any where, any time." To provide this service it has expanded its Citicard Banking Centers with their automated teller machines to 28 countries. These centers are globally linked, allowing 24-hour, seven days a week access. And, of course, noncash transactions can be conducted by phone.

MARKETING

In a global marketing strategy, a uniform marketing approach is applied around the world, although not all elements of the marketing mix need be identical.[29] Unilever achieved great success with a fabric softener that used a globally common positioning, advertising theme, and symbol (a teddy bear), but a brand name that varied by country. Similarly, a product that serves a common need can be geographically expanded with a uniform marketing program, despite apparent obstacles of differences in marketing environments.

For service businesses,[30] the uncertainty engendered by intangibility requires strong branding to offset it. So the primary task of the brand name or trademark for a service is to offer recognition and reassurance, rather than performing other functions such as positioning or local adaptation. McDonald's, for instance, has to be the same name around the world, so that both locals and travelers know that they will get the genuine McDonald's experience. (The author doubts, however, that the Spago and Planet Saigon restaurants in Ho Chi Minh City will provide the same experiences as the Hollywood originals after which they are named.) Travel-related services virtually require the same brand name globally. What use would an American Express card be if the brand were Russian Express in Moscow? One solution is to be both global and local. FedEx combines global and local brand names. In France the company initially used partly localized names: FedEx Priorité, FedEx Rapide, and FedEx Frêt.

Global positioning is also important. McDonald's has a globally consistent positioning and image, but this is not a globally neutral image. It is clearly American, so it stands for "us" in the United States and "them" elsewhere. Similarly, Chili's, a U.S.-based restaurant chain offering Mexican food, has its largest store in Monterrey, Mexico. But customers there go for an "American experience," not a Mexican one. In contrast, Benetton, the Italian fashion clothing concern, is one of the very few global companies that strives for a universalistic, nonnational image.

COMPETITIVE MOVES

In a multilocal competitive strategy, a multinational company fights its competitors one country at a time in separate contests, even though it may face another multinational in many of the same countries. In a global competitive strategy, competitive moves are integrated across countries. The same type of move is made in different

JAPANESE GLOBAL COMPETITIVE MOVES

Japanese companies seem to make more use than American or European companies of global competitive moves.[31] Bridgestone Company, the Japanese tire manufacturer, has tried to integrate its competitive moves in response to global consolidation by its major competitors: Continental AG's acquisition of Gencorp's General Tire and Rubber Company, General Tire's joint venture with two Japanese tire makers, and Sumitomo's acquisition of an interest in Dunlop Tire. These competitive actions forced Bridgestone to establish a presence in the major American market in order to maintain its position in the world tire market. To this end, Bridgestone formed a joint venture to own and manage Firestone Corporation's worldwide tire business. This joint venture also allowed Bridgestone to gain access to Firestone's European plants. Eventually, Bridgestone made a full acquisition of Firestone. Bridgestone had to be willing to pay the price of its increased global market participation: It had to contend with major losses at Firestone. In the same industry, Michelin also suffered losses after its 1990 acquisition of Uniroyal boosted its market participation in the United States as well as propelling it past Goodyear to become the global market share leader.

SALOMON'S RETALIATION IN SKIS

Some European and American companies do successfully integrate their competitive strategy, as U.S.-based Salomon did in the ski equipment industry. Tyrolia, an Austrian ski-binding competitor, attacked Salomon's stronghold position in its biggest market, the United States. Rather than fighting Tyrolia only in America, Salomon retaliated in the countries where Tyrolia generated a large share of its sales and profits—Germany and Austria. Taking a global perspective, Salomon viewed the whole world—not just one country—as its competitive battleground.[32]

This last example illustrates that integration of competitive moves is more than just coordination, such as simultaneous or sequenced price moves. Integration requires a concerted effort to compete on a global and not a country-by-country basis. Coordination is part of integration. Other parts include identifying and targeting global, regional, and local competitors. Having a global attack and defense plan for each major competitor is crucial. A major objective may be to limit a potential global competitor to its home country. An American company has devised a strategy to contain a Japanese competitor that has yet to move outside Japan. To prevent this competitor from using joint ventures outside Japan as stepping-stones to globalization, the American company makes preemptive joint venture agreements with the Japanese company's potential partners.

countries at the same time or in some systematic sequence, or a competitor is attacked in one country in order to drain its resources for another country, or a competitive attack in one country is countered in a different country. Perhaps the best example is the counterattack in a competitor's home market as a parry to an attack on one's own home market.

EUROPEAN HOTELS STRIKE BACK

Realizing that the competitive terrain is shifting beneath them, European hotel chains are setting out to overhaul their companies along American lines.[33] This has involved tightening management controls, creating a number of brand names instead of one, separating real estate holdings of the company from their management operations, going public, and negotiating strategic alliances with American chains. Although many European hotel companies were profitable in the 1990s, they recognize the need to go global in the twenty-first century to continue to be competitive.

With American chains competing in their market, most European hotel companies felt that they did not have much choice but to go global in the mid-1990s and follow the trail blazed by the American giants. Construction boomed, at both the high end and the low end of the market, and European hotel chains undertook many mergers and acquisitions as they sought allies to strengthen their market positions. Because the European hotel business is a fragmented market and dominated by independents—fully 75 percent of the trade compared with just 25 percent in the United States—it remains vulnerable to penetration by American chains such as Marriott International, Sheraton, and HSF. The current upheaval, though wrenching, also provides European chains like the Accor group in France an opportunity to become world players. They are seizing the opportunity largely by copying the American model. Despite the "Americanization" of the European hotel chains, they insist on not becoming American clones. The regional differences on the Continent are still too great to allow the uniformity of style and service that is possible in the United States.

BENEFITS OF GLOBAL STRATEGY

Use of the global strategy levers can achieve one or more of four major categories of potential globalization benefits:

- Cost reductions
- Improved quality of products and programs
- Enhanced customer preference
- Increased competitive leverage

Exhibit 1-5 summarizes which lever achieves what benefits. It also summarizes the major drawbacks of global strategy.

REDUCING COSTS

An integrated global strategy can save worldwide costs in several ways:

- *Economies of scale* can be achieved by pooling production or other activities for two or more countries. For example, production of large volumes of compact disc players can result in economies of scale. Realizing the potential benefit of these economies of scale, Sony Corporation at one time concentrated its compact disc production in Terre Haute, Indiana, and Salzburg, Austria.
- *Lower factor costs* can be obtained by moving manufacturing or other activities to low-cost countries. This has, of course, been the motivation of the recent surge of offshore manufacturing, particularly by American firms. For example, the Mexican

EXHIBIT 1-5 How Global Strategy Levers Achieve Globalization Benefits

Global Strategy Levers	Benefits				Major Drawbacks
	Cost Reduction	Improved Quality	Enhanced Customer Preference	Competitive Leverage	All Levels Incur Coordination Costs, Plus
Global Market Participation	Increases volume for economies of scale.	Via exposure to demanding customers and innovative competitors.	Via global availability, global serviceability, and global recognition.	Advantages of early entry. Provides more sites for attack and counterattack, hostage for good behavior.	Earlier or greater commitment to a market than warranted on own merits.
Global Products	Reduces duplication of development efforts. Reduces purchasing, production, and inventory costs.	Focuses development and management resources.	Allows consumers to use familiar product while abroad. Allows organizations to use same product across country units.	Basis for low-cost invasion of markets. Offsets disadvantage of low market share.	Less responsive to local needs.
Global Location of Activities	Reduces duplication of activities. Helps exploit economies of scale. Exploits differences in country factor costs. Partial concentration allows flexibility versus currency changes and versus bargaining parties.	Focuses effort. Allows more consistent quality control.		Allows maintenance of cost advantage independent of local conditions. Provides flexibility on where to base competitive advantage.	Distances activities from customer. Increases currency risk. Increases risk of creating competitors. More difficult to manage value chain.
Global Marketing	Reduces design and production costs of marketing programs.	Focuses talent and resources. Leverages scarce, good ideas.	Reinforces marketing messages by exposing customer to the same mix in different countries.		Reduces adaptation to local customer behavior and marketing environment.
Global Competitive Moves				Magnifies resources available to any country. Provides more options and leverage in attack and defense.	Local competitiveness may be sacrificed.

side of the U.S.-Mexico border is now crowded with *maquiladoras*—manufacturing plants set up and run by American companies using Mexican labor.

• *Focused production* means reducing the number of products manufactured, from many local models to a few global ones. Typically, unit costs fall as the number of products made in a factory declines. Such reduction in product variety cuts the costs involved in setup, downtime, extra inventory, and the like.[34]

• *Flexibility* can be exploited by moving production from location to location on a short-term basis to take advantage of the lowest costs at a given time. Dow Chemical takes this approach to minimize the cost of producing chemicals. Dow uses a linear programming model that takes account of cross-country differences in exchange rates, tax rates, transportation, and labor costs. The model comes up with the best mix of production volume by location for each planning period.

• *Enhancing bargaining power,* via a strategy that allows for switching production among multiple manufacturing sites in different countries, greatly increases a company's bargaining power with suppliers, workers, and host governments. Labor unions in European countries are now very concerned that the creation of the single European market since 1992 has allowed companies to easily switch production from country to country. This integrated production strategy has greatly enhanced management's bargaining power at the expense of unions.

IMPROVING QUALITY OF PRODUCTS AND PROGRAMS

Focus and concentration on a smaller number of products and programs, rather than many products and programs typical in a multilocal strategy, can improve the quality of both products and programs. Global focus is one of the reasons for the Japanese success in automobiles. Toyota markets a far smaller number of models around the world than does General Motors, even allowing for its unit sales being less than that of General Motors. Toyota concentrated on improving its few models while GM fragmented its development funds. For example, in the 1990s the Toyota Camry was the U.S. version of a basic worldwide model and the successor to a long line of development efforts.[35] The Camry was consistently rated as the best in the class of medium-sized cars. In contrast, General Motors' Pontiac Fiero started out in the early 1980s as one of the most successful small sports cars but was withdrawn after only a few years on the market. Industry observers blamed this on a failure to invest development money to overcome minor problems.

General Motors, in its effort to increase global efficiencies in cost and design, continues to struggle in its proliferation efforts.[36] GM has increasingly relied on Opel, GM's division in Germany, to solve many of GM's globalization problems. However, the high cost of retooling, currency volatility, and local design differences have delayed the process of reducing small car platforms and developing "world cars." Despite these delays, GM's global strategy board has approved of plans to make an upscale Saturn based on Opel's Vectra model. Opel engineers will also team up with other company technicians to assist in truck and minivan projects. Although these combined efforts may eventually be profitable, world car efforts by U.S. companies have failed in the past. As an example, the Ford Mondeo family sedan sold well in Europe but stalled in the United States due to a perceived small backseat and high price.

In contrast, most Japanese companies have successfully marketed world cars, such as the Toyota Camry and the Honda Accord. Some European companies have also succeeded, albeit with niche offerings—the Volkswagen Beetle at one end of the scale, and

Mercedes and BMW at the other end. Fiat is now making a serious attempt at a world car with its Palio model, launched in 1996.

ENHANCING CUSTOMER PREFERENCE

Global availability, global serviceability, and global recognition can enhance customer preference through reinforcement. Soft drink and fast-food companies are, of course, leading exponents of this strategy. Many suppliers of financial services, such as credit cards, have to provide global presence because of the travel-related nature of their service. Manufacturers of industrial products can also exploit this benefit. A supplier that can provide a multinational customer with a standard product around the world gains from the worldwide familiarity within the customer organization. Computer manufacturers have long pursued this strategy.

INCREASING COMPETITIVE LEVERAGE

A global strategy provides more points to attack and counterattack against competitors. In an effort to prevent the Japanese from becoming a competitive nuisance in disposable syringes, Becton Dickinson, a major American medical products company, decided to enter three markets in Japan's "backyard." Becton entered the Hong Kong, Singapore, and Philippines markets to prevent further Japanese penetration.[37]

DRAWBACKS OF GLOBAL STRATEGY

Globalization can incur significant management costs through increased coordination, reporting requirements, and even added staff. Globalization can also reduce management effectiveness in individual countries if overcentralization hurts local motivation and morale. In addition, each global strategy lever incurs particular drawbacks.

A global strategy approach to market participation can incur the drawbacks of an earlier or greater commitment to a market than warranted on its own merits. Many American companies, such as Motorola, struggled from the 1980s onward with long-term efforts to penetrate Japanese markets, mostly in order to enhance their global competitive position rather than to make money in Japan for its own sake. Similarly, many foreign companies have struggled since the 1990s in their efforts to build positions in China, attracted by the promise of future reward.

Product standardization can result in a product that fully satisfies customers nowhere.

Concentrating activities distances those activities from customers and can reduce responsiveness and flexibility. It also increases currency risk by incurring costs and revenues in different countries. Mazda, a second-tier Japanese automobile company that produced in Japan for its European sales, had great difficulty in the late 1990s as the euro fell in value relative to the yen. By 2001, Mazda, now 34 percent owned by Ford, decided to use Ford's plant in Valencia, Spain, to produce a new model for the European market, to be launched in 2003. But modern communications can offset some of the disadvantages of geographic concentration. For example, Perth, on the coast of Western Australia, is perhaps the most isolated major city in the world, with more than 2,000 miles of desert between it and other major Australian cities. But Accor Asia Pacific, the Asian arm of France's Accor, one of the world's largest hotel companies, chose Perth as the home of its global reservation center for 2,400 Accor hotels worldwide. Accor chose Perth because it is the home of Telstra, the Australian-based telecommunications corporation; it is in close

WHIRLPOOL'S GLOBAL EXPANSION IN APPLIANCES

The American appliance company, Whirlpool, is also going global aggressively, and paying the price too. Although Whirlpool's revenues have doubled since the inception of its aggressive globalization efforts, the company now faces major problems as a result of these efforts.[38] The business requires that Whirlpool offer a host of customized products that meet regional preferences and understand the logistics of local manufacturing. Whirlpool's inability to standardize these products, and the poor quality associated with Asian operations in comparison to Japanese operations, caused a reduction in profits to the company. In addition, the company saw its high start-up costs in Asia reduce profit potential.

Whirlpool had not counted on the difficulty in marketing appliances—largely homogeneous in the United States—to the fragmented cultures of Europe.[39] Because of lifestyle differences that range widely from country to country, appliance makers must target products to specific markets. For instance, clothes washers sold in northern countries like Denmark must spin-dry clothes much better than in southern Italy, where consumers often line-dry clothes in the warmer weather. Whirlpool was also caught with higher material costs, which cut into its profit margins. And the Whirlpool name, not well known in Europe, took a while to catch on with the locals. Distributors were more familiar with brands such as Electrolux, the Swedish appliance maker and Whirlpool's largest European rival. Despite the difficulties, Whirlpool remains committed to its globalization strategy.

FORD'S GLOBAL CAR

As part of its Ford 2000 plan, the company launched its first global vehicle in 1993—the midsize car known as the Mondeo in Europe and the Ford Contour and Mercury Mystique in America. The widely criticized car cost $6 billion and took six years to develop, yet has been only moderately successful. Ford defends Mondeo's prodigious start-up costs, arguing that for its money, the company completely refurbished seven plants and developed a new family of V-6 engines. It also installed a Cray supercomputer and transatlantic communication networks, which can be used for future new-car development programs. Ford was able to improve the Mondeo program with experience. Initial high costs, a longer than expected lead-

time, and sluggish American sales reduced Ford profits. Lower than expected American sales were partly due to Ford's decision to reduce rear-seat legroom in the world car. A newer version, launched in 1997, however, was greatly improved. Although similar in design, Ford made local design improvements. In the United States, more legroom was added; in Europe, the engines, suspension, and steering were improved. As a result of these minor changes, the Ford Mondeo greatly improved its appeal. By 1999, Ford had learned enough to launch an even more effective global car, the Focus. In 2001 the revised Mondeo won the coveted best car award from German automobile magazines.

geographic proximity to Asia; it offers a time-zone advantage; it is cost-effective; and it has ready access to a multilingual labor force.[40]

Uniform marketing can reduce adaptation to local customer behavior and the marketing environment. For example, the head office of British Airways mandated that every country use the "Manhattan Landing" television commercial developed by its advertising agency, Saatchi and Saatchi. While the commercial won many awards, it was criticized for using a visual (of New York City) that was not widely recognized in many countries. From the mid-1990s the firm set about transforming itself from a British airline with a global reach to an airline of the world that just happens to be based in Britain.[41] As part of a 1997 campaign, the planes took on a completely different look—with new logos and paintwork. British Airways commissioned dozens of designs from regional artists—African murals, Japanese calligraphy, and Scottish tartan plaids. Then the airline transposed these multicultural images onto ticket jackets, cabin crew scarves, business cards, and the tails of planes. Unfortunately for BA, many of its British customers objected to this transformation. Most notably, the former British prime minister, Margaret Thatcher, when confronted with a model of the new design covered the offending tail with her handkerchief. Other critics called the airline's new designs "global graffiti," and Virgin Atlantic countered by adding the British flag to its planes. By 1999, in the face of criticism and poor profits, BA began to replace the artists' designs on the tail with a new, less traditional version of the British flag.

Integrating competitive moves can mean sacrificing revenues, profits, or competitive position in individual countries. This is particularly true when the subsidiary in one country is asked to attack a global competitor in order to send a signal or to divert that competitor's resources from another country. Motorola's Japanese units played this role through the 1980s and 1990s in order to bolster the company's global battle with its Japanese rivals.

FINDING THE BALANCE

The most successful worldwide strategies find a balance between overglobalizing and underglobalizing. The ideal strategy matches the level of strategy globalization to the globalization potential of the industry. A business in an industry with low globalization potential should have a strategy that is not very global. A business in an industry with high globalization potential should have a generally global strategy. A business suffers *global strategic disadvantage* by using a strategy that is less globalized than the potential offered by its industry. The business fails to exploit potential global benefits such as cost savings via product standardization. In contrast, a business suffers *national strategic disadvantage* by being too globalized relative to the potential offered by its industry. The business does not tailor its products and programs as much as it should. While there is no systematic evidence, comments by executives generally suggest that far more businesses suffer from not enough globalization than from too much, or at least that their focus of attention is on increasing their level of globalization. In one of this author's research studies, all except one of 18 worldwide businesses had strategies that were underglobalized relative to the potential of the industries in which they competed.[42]

Managers should avoid viewing industries as global or not global, but rather as being more global or not in particular dimensions. For example, an industry may have high globalization potential for globally standardized products but low globalization potential for centralized manufacturing. The paint industry satisfies fairly similar needs around the world, particularly in interior applications where intercountry differences in weather and surfaces are less. So global paint products are perfectly possible. But the low value of paint relative to its bulk and weight renders it uneconomic for long-distance shipment. So globally centralized manufacturing is not possible for most paints.

Managers should also avoid viewing strategies as global or not global. They should focus on the extent to which different dimensions of strategy are globalized. For example, M&M Mars, the confectionery manufacturer, standardizes most of its products while maintaining different marketing approaches and even, in some cases, different brand names.

MORE THAN ONE STRATEGY IS VIABLE

Although they are powerful, industry globalization drivers do not dictate one formula for success. More than one type of international strategy can be viable in a given industry.

INDUSTRY VARIATION ACROSS DRIVERS

First, no industry scores high on every one of the many globalization drivers. A particular competitor may be in a strong position to exploit a driver that scores low on globalization. The dominance of national government customers offsets the globalization potential from other industry drivers, because government customers typically prefer to do business with their own nationals. In such an industry a competitor with a global strategy can use its other advantages, such as low cost from centralization of global production, to offset this drawback. At the same time, another multinational competitor with good government contacts can pursue a multilocal strategy and succeed without globalization advantages; and single-country local competitors can succeed on the basis of their very particular local assets. The hotel industry provides examples of both successful global and successful local competitors.

GLOBAL EFFECTS ARE INCREMENTAL

A second factor affects why globalization drivers are not deterministic. The appropriate use of global strategy levers provides *additional* competitive advantage that is *incremental* to other sources of competitive advantage. These other sources may allow individual competitors to thrive with international strategies that are mismatched with industry globalization drivers. For example, superior technology provides a major source of competitive advantage in most industries, but it can be quite independent of globalization drivers. A competitor with sufficiently superior technology can use that to offset disadvantages in globalization. At the same time, effective global strategies can leverage worldwide a technology or other advantage.

POSITION AND RESOURCES OF BUSINESS AND PARENT COMPANY

The third reason why drivers are not deterministic has to do with resources (the top left box in Exhibit 1-2). A worldwide business may face industry drivers that strongly favor a global strategy. But global strategies are typically expensive to implement initially even though there should be great cost savings and revenue gains later. High initial investments may be needed to expand within or into major markets, to develop standardized products, to relocate value activities, to create global brands, to create new organization units or coordination processes, and to implement other aspects of a global strategy.

The strategic position of the business is also relevant. Even though a global strategy may improve the business's long-term strategic position, its immediate position may be so weak that resources should be devoted to short-term, country-by-country improvements. The automobile industry has very strong globalization drivers. But Chrysler Corporation, in avoiding bankruptcy in the 1980s, had to deglobalize by selling off most of its international automotive businesses. Financial survival was more important at that point. Lastly, there may be greater returns in investing in nonglobal sources of competitive advantage, such as superior technology, than in global ones, such as centralized manufacturing.

LIMITATIONS IN ORGANIZATION

Finally, organization factors such as structure, management processes, people, and culture affect how well a desired global strategy can be implemented. Differences in organization among companies in the same industry will, therefore, constrain the extent to which the companies can, or should, pursue the same global strategy.

CHALLENGES OF IMPLEMENTATION

Implementing strategy is always difficult. Implementing global strategy is particularly challenging because of the multiple countries and nationalities involved. Furthermore, in many cases a key part of the global strategy is not so much the content of the strategy (e.g., a standardized global product) but the decision to operate with a globally integrated management process (e.g., a global product development process). Implementation can be so disruptive and difficult that there may not be enough benefit in pursuing a highly global strategy. In particular, strategy globalization often requires changes that involve one or more countries having to give up long-established strategies, products, and the like. A European consumer packaged goods business had, under a multilocal strategy, developed different versions of the same basic product. One major country marketed a product made of *opaque* plastic parts and another major country marketed the same product made of *translucent* plastic parts. There seemed to be no real reason why consumers might prefer opaque over translucent or vice versa. But the managers of each country felt committed to their version and were loathe to risk the potential marketplace disruption involved in change. It was implementation issues like this one that posed roadblocks for this business's attempt to rationalize its worldwide product lines.

Four key organization and management factors determine a business's ability to develop and implement a global strategy. Exhibit 1-6 summarizes these factors.[43]

- *Organization structure* comprises the reporting relationships in a business—the "boxes and lines."
- *Management processes* comprise the activities such as planning and budgeting, as well as information systems, that make the business run.
- *People* comprise the human resources of the worldwide business and include both managers and all other employees.
- *Culture* comprises the values and rules that guide behavior in a corporation.

Chapter 8 will elaborate on the application of these organization and management factors.

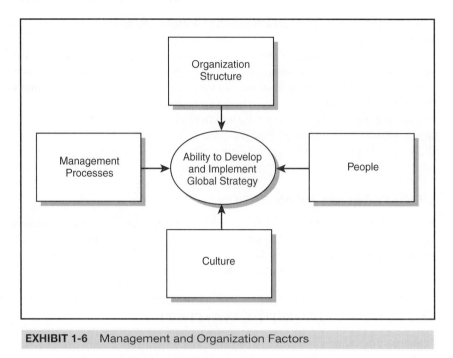

EXHIBIT 1-6   Management and Organization Factors

BACKLASH AGAINST GLOBALIZATION

Multinational companies also need to take into account the emerging backlash against globalization and multinational companies.[44] Many groups now feel threatened by the consequences of open markets and global convergence. Most of their arguments are misguided, seeking to deny the benefits of open markets to developing nations. But the actions of these groups, such as protests at meetings of the World Trade Organization and guerrilla actions against individual multinational companies, need to be taken seriously. Many of the protesters also equate globalization with Americanization—a fallacy. Globalization simply creates a level playing field for companies and individuals. Of course, many American companies start with the advantages of their large home market and the attraction of American lifestyle and culture. But companies from many other countries have shown that they can use globalization to become world leaders: Japan's Sony, Finland's Nokia, Singapore's Singapore Airlines, Taiwan's Acer Computer, France's LVMH (Louis Vuitton Möet Hennessey), and Sweden's IKEA, to name but a few. To deflect criticism, companies pursuing global strategies need to take serious account of their impacts on the economic, social, and cultural conditions of the countries in which they operate, produce, or sell. They also need to watch their public relations. Gone are the days of boasting about global standardization. Multinational companies can still "act global," but they also need to "talk local."

Discussion and Research Questions

1. In addition to those listed in this chapter, what other trends are there in general globalization drivers?
2. What forces currently work against globalization?

3. Select a company (not one discussed in this chapter) and describe its total global strategy in terms of its core business strategy, its internationalization strategy, and its globalization strategy. How successful has this company been in each aspect of its total global strategy?
4. What are the most globally successful companies from your country (region)? Why?
5. What are the social and political arguments against globalization?

Notes

1. Hout et al. (1982) coined the term *multidomestic* to apply to industries rather than strategies. See Thomas Hout, Michael E. Porter, and Eileen Rudden, "How Global Companies Win Out," *Harvard Business Review,* September–October 1982, pp. 98–108. The term *multilocal* seems better when applied to strategies, in that *domestic* implies a company competing in its home market, while a great deal of local competition occurs between companies, none of which are in their home markets.

2. See Theodore Levitt, "The Globalization of Markets," *Harvard Business Review,* May–June 1983, pp. 92–102; and Kenichi Ohmae, *Triad Power: The Coming Shape of Global Competition* (New York: The Free Press, 1985).

3. Adapted from "As Close As a Group Can Get to Global," *Financial Times,* April 7, 1998, p. 19.

4. Adapted from "Toyota's Crusade," *Business Week,* April 7, 1997, pp. 104–14.

5. See Philip Kotler, Liam Fahey, and S. Jatusripitak, *The New Competition* (Upper Saddle River, NJ: Prentice Hall, 1985). For works on Japanese management, see James C. Abegglen and George Stalk, Jr., *Kaisha: The Japanese Corporation* (New York: Basic Books, 1985); William G. Ouchi, *Theory Z: How American Business Can Meet the Japanese Challenge* (Reading, MA: Addison-Wesley, 1981); and Richard Tanner Pascale and Anthony G. Athos, *The Art of Japanese Management: Applications for American Executives* (New York: Simon & Schuster, 1981).

6. This accepted wisdom is laid out in one of the rejoinders provoked by Levitt's article; see Susan P. Douglas and Yoram Wind, "The Myth of Globalization," *Columbia Journal of World Business,* Vol. 22, No. 4, Winter 1987, pp. 19–29.

7. There are many sources of guidance on core business strategy. See, for example, Kenneth R. Andrews, *The Concept of Corporate Strategy* (New York: Dow-Jones Irwin. 1971); Michael E. Porter, *Competitive Strategy: Techniques for Analyzing Industries and Competitors* (New York: The Free Press, 1980); ——, *Competitive Advantage* (New York: The Free Press, 1985); Kenichi Ohmae, *The Mind of the Strategist* (New York: McGraw-Hill, 1982); Robert M. Grant, *Contemporary Strategy Analysis* (Oxford, England: Blackwell Publishers, 1998); and Constantinos C. Markides, *All the Right Moves* (Boston: Harvard Business School Press, 1999).

8. See Derek F. Abell, *Defining the Business: The Starting Point of Strategic Planning* (Upper Saddle River, NJ: Prentice-Hall, 1980), for an extensive framework for business definition.

9. For a complete framework on how to select and enter foreign markets, see Franklin R. Root, *Entry Strategies for International Markets* (San Francisco: Jossey-Bass, 1994). For a general review of how to conduct international business, see, for example, Michael R. Czinkota, Ilkka A. Ronkainen, and Michael Moffett, *International Business* (New York: Harcourt, 2000); and Paul W. Beamish, Allen J. Morrison, Philip M. Rosenzweig, and Andrew C. Inkpen, *International Management: Text and Cases,* 4th ed. (New York: Irwin McGraw-Hill, 2000).

10. This framework was first presented in George S. Yip, "Global Strategy . . . In a World of Nations?" *Sloan Management Review,* Vol. 31, No. 1, Fall 1989, pp. 29–41.

11. Christopher H. Lovelock and George S. Yip, "Developing Global Strategies for Service Businesses," *California Management Review,* Vol. 37, No. 3, Winter 1996, pp. 64–86.

12. Christopher A. Bartlett and Sumantra Ghoshal, *Text, Cases, and Readings in Cross-Border Management,* 3rd ed. (Boston, MA: McGraw-Hill, 2000), p. 13.

13. See, for example, Paul W. Beamish, Allen J. Morrison, Philip Rosenzweig, and Andrew C. Inkpen, *International Management: Text and Cases,* 4th ed. (New York: Irwin McGraw-Hill, 2000).

14. See, for example, Will Mitchell, J. Myles Shaver, and Bernard Yeung, "Getting There in a Global Industry: Impacts on Performance of Changing International Presence," *Strategic Management Journal,* Vol. 13, No. 6, 1992, pp. 419–32; and Peter Mason and Karl Moore, "The Impact of Globalisation on Company Performance" (Templeton College, Oxford: The Oxford Executive Research Briefings, 1998).

15. David M. Reeb, Chuck C. Y. Kwok, and H. Young Baek, "Systematic Risk of the Multinational Corporation," *Journal of International Business Studies,* Vol. 29, No. 2 1998, pp. 263–80.

16. This section on risk reduction comes from Stephen B. Tallman and George S. Yip, "Strategy and the Multinational Enterprise," in Thomas Brewer and Alan M. Rugman, Eds., *The Oxford Handbook of International Business* (Oxford, England: Oxford University Press, 2001), Chapter 12.

17. Raymond Vernon, "The Product Cycle Hypothesis in a New International Environment," *Oxford Bulletin of Economics and Statistics,* Vol. 41, No. 4, 1979, pp. 255–67.

18. Kendall Roth and Allen J. Morrison, "An Empirical Analysis of the Integration-Responsiveness Framework in Global Industries," *Journal of International Business Studies,* Vol. 21, No. 4, (Fourth Quarter), 1990, pp. 541–64.

19. Masaaki Kotaabe and Glenn S. Omura, "Sourcing Strategies of European and Japanese Multinationals: A Comparison," *Journal of International Business Studies,* Vol. 20, No. 1, (Spring), 1989, pp. 113–30.

20. Allen J. Morrison, *Strategies in Global Industries: How U.S. Businesses Compete* (Westport, CT: Quorum Books, 1990).

21. Johny K. Johansson and George S. Yip, "Exploiting Globalization Potential: U.S. and Japanese Strategies," *Strategic Management Journal,* Vol. 15, No. 8, October 1994, pp. 579–601.

22. The concept of industry conditions affecting the potential for global strategy was first developed by Michael E. Porter in "Changing Patterns of International Competition," *California Management Review,* Vol. 28, No. 2, Winter 1986, pp. 9–40; and in "Competition in Global Industries: A Conceptual Framework," *Competition in Global Industries,* Porter, Ed. (Boston: Harvard Business School Press, 1986). The concept of industry globalization drivers was first presented in George S. Yip, Pierre M. Loewe, and Michael Y. Yoshino. "How to Take Your Company to the Global Market," *Columbia Journal of World Business,* Winter 1988, pp. 37–48; and more fully developed in George S. Yip, "Global Strategy . . . In a World of Nations?" *Sloan Management Review,* Vol. 31, No. 1, Fall 1989, pp. 29–41.

23. For a full description of the value-chain concept, see Michael E. Porter, *Competitive Advantage* (New York: The Free Press, 1985).

24. Ohmae, *Triad Power: The Coming Shape of Global Competition.*

25. Gary Hamel and C. K. Prahalad, "Do You Really Have a Global Strategy?" *Harvard Business Review,* July–August 1985, pp. 139–48; and Bruce Kogut, "Designing Global Strategies: Profiting from Operational Flexibility," *Sloan Management Review,* Vol. 27, Fall 1985, pp. 27–38.

26. Peter G. P. Walters, "International Marketing Policy: A Discussion of the Standardization Construct and Its Relevance for Corporate Policy," *Journal of International Business Studies,* Summer 1986, pp. 55–69.

27. Lovelock and Yip, "Developing Global Strategies for Service Businesses."

28. Pei-yuan Chia, "Citibanking the World," *Bank Management,* July/August 1995.

29. The possibilities and merits of uniform marketing have been discussed by Robert D. Buzzell, "Can You Standardize Multinational Marketing?" *Harvard Business Review,* November–December 1968, pp. 102–13; and by John A. Quelch and Edward J. Hoff, "Customizing Global Marketing," *Harvard Business Review,* May–June 1986, pp. 59–68.

30. These examples come from Lovelock and Yip, "Global Strategies for Service Businesses."

31. See Philip Kotler, Liam Fahey, and S. Jatusripitak, *The New Competition* (Upper Saddle River, NJ: Prentice-Hall, 1985), p. 174.

32. I thank Pierre M. Loewe of The MAC Group for this example.

33. Adapted from "Room Service à la Américain, Old World Charm Bumps into New World Economics," *New York Times,* October 3, 1997, pp. C1 and C4.

34. Two very experienced consultants who worked for The Boston Consulting Group have estimated the potential cost savings in focused production. They found that if the number of products produced is halved, total factory labor costs should fall 30 percent, and total costs including materials should fall 17 percent, while breakeven should be reduced to 60 percent of capacity. See James C. Abegglen and George Stalk, Jr., *Kaisha* (New York: Basic Books, 1985), p. 87.

35. The Toyota Camry was first introduced into Japan in 1980. An export version was created in 1985. Another long-lived Japanese automobile model is the Honda Accord, first introduced into Japan in 1976. See Kiyonori Sakakibara and Yaichi Aoshima, "Company Growth and the 'Wholeness' of Product Strategy," Working Paper No. 8904, Graduate School of Commerce, Hitotsubashi University, April 1989.

36. "Can Opel Deliver the 'World Cars' GM Needs?" *Business Week,* December 4, 1995, p. 52.

37. Reported in Marquise R. Cvar, "Case Studies in Global Competition: Patterns of Success and Failure," in Michael E. Porter, "Competition in Global Industries: A Conceptual Framework," *Competition in Global Industries,* Porter, Ed. (Boston: Harvard Business School Press, 1986).

38. Adapted from "Did Whirlpool Spin Too Far Too Fast?" *Business Week,* June 24, 1996, pp. 135–36.

39. Adapted from Carl Quintanilla, "Whirlpool Seen Retrenching After Its Effort to 'Go Global,' " *The Wall Street Journal,* December 12, 1997.

40. Adapted from "Accor, World's Largest Hotel Group, Chooses Australia for Its Reservation Center," *IAC (SM) Newsletter Database (TM),* March 20, 1996.

41. Adapted from "Flying High, Going Global," *Fortune,* July 7, 1997, pp. 195–97.

42. See George S. Yip, "Do American Businesses Use Global Strategy?" Working Paper No. 91-101 (Cambridge, MA: Marketing Science Institute, January 1991).

43. This particular concept of management and organization factors affecting global strategy was first presented in George S. Yip, Pierre M. Loewe, and Michael Y. Yoshino, "How to Take Your Company to the Global Market," *Columbia Journal of World Business,* Winter 1988, pp. 37–48. Other authors such as Christopher Bartlett, Yves Doz, Sumantra Ghoshal, and C. K. Prahalad have done a great deal of work on the role of management and organization in global strategy. See Christopher A. Bartlett and Sumantra Ghoshal, *Managing Across Borders: The Transnational Solution* (Boston: Harvard Business School Press, 1989); and C. K. Prahalad, and Yves L. Doz, *The Multinational Mission: Balancing Local Demands and Global Vision* (New York: The Free Press, 1987).

44. See, for example, Anthony Giddens, *Runaway World: How Globalization Is Reshaping Our Lives* (New York: Routledge, 2000); and Naomi Klein, *No Logo* (London: Flamingo, 2001).

2
DIAGNOSING INDUSTRY GLOBALIZATION POTENTIAL

Industry globalization drivers are the underlying conditions in each industry that create the potential for using global strategy. Here we will examine each driver in more depth and, in addition, discuss how drivers affect the industry competitive forces of the threat of entry and rivalry among competitors. We will also examine possible differences in globalization drivers for service businesses,[1] and how the Internet affects globalization drivers.[2] *To achieve the benefits of globalization, the managers of a worldwide business need to recognize when industry conditions provide the opportunity to use global strategy levers.* These industry conditions are the industry globalization drivers and can be grouped in four categories—market, cost, governmental, and competitive. Each key industry globalization driver affects the potential use of global strategy levers (global market participation, global products and services, global location of activities, global marketing, and global competitive moves). The drivers are as follows:

MARKET GLOBALIZATION DRIVERS

- Common customer needs and tastes
- Global customers
- Global channels
- Transferable marketing
- Lead countries

COST GLOBALIZATION DRIVERS

- Global scale economies
- Steep experience curve effect
- Sourcing efficiencies
- Favorable logistics
- Differences in country costs (including exchange rates)
- High product development
- Fast-changing technology

GOVERNMENT GLOBALIZATION DRIVERS

- Favorable trade policies
- Compatible technical standards
- Common marketing regulations
- Government-owned competitors and customers
- Host government concerns

COMPETITIVE GLOBALIZATION DRIVERS

- High exports and imports
- Competitors from different continents
- Interdependence of countries
- Competitors globalized
- Transferable competitive advantage

Industry globalization drivers relate to, but are different from, the industry competitive forces identified by Michael E. Porter—threat of entry, rivalry among existing firms, pressure from substitute products or services, bargaining power of suppliers, and bargaining power of buyers.[3] In most cases, but not always, increases in industry globalization will increase the strength of competitive forces. Particularly for the threat of new entrants and rivalry among existing firms, increased industry globalization heightens competition by increasing its geographic scope. The specific effects on these two competitive forces vary in interesting ways depending on the specific industry globalization driver, and so will be addressed below for each of the drivers. Increased industry globalization also increases the pressure from substitutes by increasing the geographic scope of where these substitutes might come from. This effect is fairly straightforward and consistent, and so need not be discussed for individual industry globalization drivers. Lastly, the effects of industry globalization on the power of suppliers and the power of buyers can be positive in some cases and negative in others. In particular, the globalization of customers themselves (the "global customers" driver) increases their bargaining power relative to industry competitors, while the globalization of competitors reduces the bargaining power of customers. The same effects apply for the bargaining power of suppliers.

Globalization can also change the fundamental strategy required for managing competitive forces. In *Competitive Strategy,* published in 1980, Porter, in effect, recommends that companies seek to compete in markets with weak competitors and weak customers.[4] In *The Competitive Advantage of Nations,* published in 1990, Porter argues instead for participating in national markets with the strongest rivals and most demanding customers, in order to build international competitiveness.[5] The difference between his two positions is explainable by the difference between a closed, domestic industry and an open, globalized industry. In a closed, domestic industry, a company accustomed to weak competitors and undemanding customers has little to fear: There is no source of new competitors who might grow strong in more demanding competitive arenas. In an open, globalized industry, such newly strong competitors abound. *That is why it is important to understand how industry globalization drivers affect the threat of entry and rivalry among existing competitors.*

GLOBALIZATION DRIVERS FOR SERVICE BUSINESSES

How do the distinctive characteristics of service businesses affect globalization and the use of global strategy?[6] This is a crucial question for managers in numerous industries. Not only are services continuing to grow rapidly in domestic economies, but international trade in services is increasing, too. The United States, like some other developed countries, has a trade surplus in services that helps offset the deficit in merchandise trade. In contrast, Japan has been much less successful in internationalizing its service businesses.[7] So it is essential to national competitiveness that governments, as well as companies, achieve a better understanding of how to develop effective global strategies for different types of service businesses.

Service businesses have eight primary characteristics that distinguish them from manufacturing businesses.[8] These characteristics begin with the nature of the output—a performance rather than an object—and also include customer involvement in production, people as part of the service experience, greater likelihood of quality control problems, harder for customers to evaluate, lack of inventories for services, greater importance of the time factor, and availability of electronic channels of distribution. Although these characteristics provide a useful starting point for thinking about the distinctive aspects of service management, not every service is equally affected by all of them.

It is also useful to distinguish among three broad types of service businesses: people-processing services, possession-processing services, and information-based services:

People-processing services involve tangible actions to customers in person. These services require that customers themselves become part of the production process, which tends to be simultaneous with consumption. In such businesses as passenger transportation, health care, food service, and lodging services, the customer needs to enter the "service factory" (although we know it by such names as an airliner and air terminal, a hospital, a restaurant, or a hotel) and remain there during service delivery. Either customers must travel to the factory or service providers and equipment must come to the customer. In both instances, the firm needs to maintain a local geographic presence, stationing the necessary personnel, buildings, equipment, vehicles, and supplies within reach of target customers. If the customers are themselves mobile—as in the case of business travelers and tourists—then they may patronize a company's offerings in many different locations and make comparisons between them.

Possession-processing services involve tangible actions to physical objects to improve their value to customers. Examples include freight transport, warehousing, equipment installation and maintenance, car repair, laundry, and disposal. The object needs to be involved in the production process, but the customer does not, since consumption of the output tends to follow production. Again, the service factory may be fixed or mobile. A local geographic presence is required when the supplier needs to provide service to physical objects in a specific location on a repeated basis. In the case of smaller, transportable items, the vendor can provide remote service centers for servicing—although transportation costs, customs duties, and government regulations may constrain shipment across large distances or national frontiers. Modern technology now allows a few service processes to be administered from a distance, using electronic diagnostics to pinpoint the problem.

Information-based services are, perhaps, the most interesting category from the standpoint of global strategy development, because they depend on collecting, manipulating, interpreting, and transmitting data to create value. Examples include accounting, banking, consulting, education, insurance, legal services, and news. Customer involvement in production of such services is often minimal. The advent of modern global telecommunications, linking intelligent machines to powerful databases, makes it possible to use electronic channels to deliver information-based services from a single "hub" to almost any location. Local presence requirements may be limited to a terminal—ranging from a telephone or fax machine to a computer or more specialized equipment like a bank automated teller machine—connected to a reliable telecommunications infrastructure. If the latter is inadequate, then use of mobile or satellite communications may solve the problem in some instances.

Service production and delivery systems can be divided into "back office" and "front office," the latter being the portion of the service factory encountered by customers.[9] People-processing services necessarily involve a high degree of contact with service personnel and facilities; possession-processing and information-based services, by contrast, have the potential to be much lower contact in nature. Retail banking, for instance, can take place either through traditional branch banks or through such channels as mail, telephone, and Internet.

In this chapter and later ones, I will examine how globalization drivers and the use of global strategy might apply to various types of services, and what differences might exist relative to manufacturing businesses.

EFFECTS OF THE INTERNET ON INDUSTRY GLOBALIZATION DRIVERS

Globalization and the rise of the Internet are the two most powerful forces affecting business now—and probably will continue to be for at least the next decade. Much has been written separately on each, but we need to understand them *together,* not separately. Looking at them jointly is all the more important because the impact of the Internet is more multiplicative than additive (Exhibit 2-1). The Internet does not have

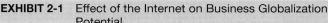

EXHIBIT 2-1   Effect of the Internet on Business Globalization Potential

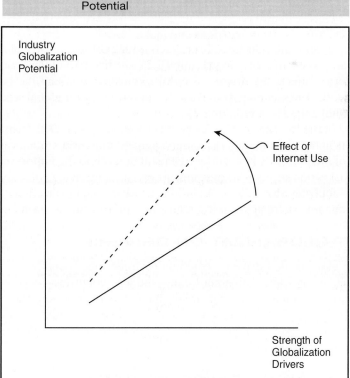

Source: George S. Yip, "Global Strategy in the Internet Era," *Business Strategy Review,* Vol. 11, No. 2, Winter 2000, pp. 1–14.

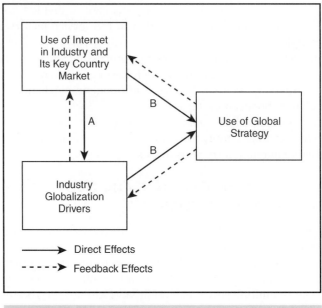

EXHIBIT 2-2   Framework for Global Strategy in Internet Era

Source: George S. Yip, "Global Strategy in the Internet Era," *Business Strategy Review,* Vol. 11, No. 2, Winter 2000, pp. 1–14.

equal effects on all industries: It interacts with existing industry globalization drivers and strategies in different ways (Exhibit 2-2). The first part of this article focuses on how the Internet affects the drivers of industry globalization and the barriers to it (A in Exhibit 2-2). The second part looks at the implications for global strategy and multinational companies (B in Exhibit 2-2).

Use of the Internet still varies greatly by country—in 2000, from nearly 50 percent of adults in the United States to under 5 percent in Russia, China, and India. So the location of an industry's key markets can still determine the importance of the Internet for globalization strategy in some industries. This underlying point needs to be borne in mind in applying what follows. As I discuss each set of globalization drivers below, I will also comment, where applicable, on how the Internet affects each individual driver.

MARKET GLOBALIZATION DRIVERS

Market globalization drivers—common customer needs and tastes, global customers, global channels, transferable marketing, and lead countries—depend on the nature of customer behavior and the structure of channels of distribution. These drivers affect the use of all five global strategy levers. As illustrated in Exhibit 2-3, different industries have different levels of market globalization drivers. *These comparative rankings are approximate only and will also change over time.*

COMMON CUSTOMER NEEDS AND TASTES

Common customer needs and tastes represent the extent to which customers in different countries want the same things in the product or service category that defines an in-

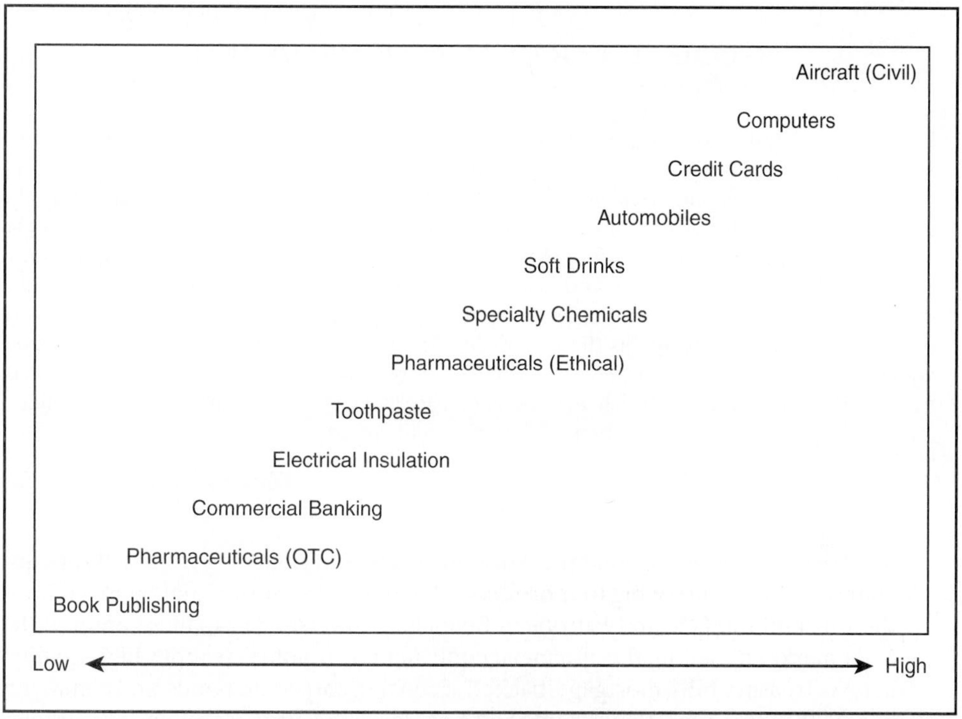

Aircraft (Civil)

Computers

Credit Cards

Automobiles

Soft Drinks

Specialty Chemicals

Pharmaceuticals (Ethical)

Toothpaste

Electrical Insulation

Commercial Banking

Pharmaceuticals (OTC)

Book Publishing

Low ◄─────────────────────────────► High

EXHIBIT 2-3 Strength of Market Globalization Drivers for Selected Industries

dustry. Many factors affect whether customer needs and tastes are similar in different countries. These factors include whether differences in economic development, climate, physical environment infrastructure, and culture affect needs in the particular product or service category, as well as whether the countries are at the same stage of the product life cycle.[10] Common customer needs particularly affect the opportunity to use the global strategy levers of global market participation, global products and services, and global competitive moves. Common needs make it easier to participate in major markets because a few product varieties can serve many markets. Thus, fewer different product offerings need to be developed and supported. Japanese companies have been particularly successful at exploiting common needs when they first entered world automotive markets. Toyota, Nissan, and Honda chose to focus on fundamental needs common to all countries—such as reliability and economy—rather than to focus on peripheral differences—such as styling. The underlying commonality of needs meant that their highly standardized global products were quite acceptable in most countries. Common needs also allow the sequenced invasion of markets with highly standardized products—again, a successful approach of many Japanese companies.

Common customer needs and tastes make entrants more dangerous by reducing the number of products or services that they need to develop for different countries. Success in one country with a global product can be used as a springboard for entering other countries. Thus, it is not surprising that Japanese entrants were most successful in the 1980s and 1990s in markets with fairly common customer needs—electronic and automotive products. The Japanese turned in the 1990s to financial services. The common

GLOBAL FOOD AND BEVERAGES

Even in food and beverages, where national taste seems dominant,[11] the speed of change of eating habits has been one of the most dramatic events of the postwar decades, spurred primarily by travel, tourism, and immigration. In only a few years, the Japanese were converted to eating donuts, gradually with more cinnamon, until they are now the same recipe as the American donut, but a little smaller to fit the Japanese hand.[12] The conservative British are increasingly abandoning their warm "pint of bitter" beer for cold American- and European-style lager. Heineken has successfully created a globally standardized beer that its fans buy all over the world. Americans now drink more and more French mineral water. According to executives in a leading multinational food and beverage concern, it seems that modern products without a tradition (or at least without a tradition in most countries) can most easily be globalized. Recent examples of such products include pizza and yogurt.

need of corporations around the world for sources of financing from debt or equity encouraged the Japanese big four brokers—Yamaichi, Nomura, Daiwa, and Nikko—to try their luck in the U.S. and European financial markets. The Japanese entered the New York market by selling the "financial equivalent of Toyotas" (simple, high-quality products)—Treasury bills, mortgage-backed securities, corporate bonds, and commercial paper. At the same time, they established a presence in European financial markets.[13] But the Japanese found much less success in financial services. In essence they lacked the specialized institutional and country knowledge needed in this highly regulated and relationship-based industry. Similarly, the Japanese have failed to make headway in industries with significant variations in customer needs and tastes, particularly consumer packaged goods. Here, the companies, such as Nestlé and Unilever, with a head start in deciphering local variations have maintained their dominance.[14]

Common needs and tastes across countries also make it more difficult for competitors to differentiate themselves from one another. Rivalry, therefore, becomes more severe. (It might be argued that globalization creates larger global segments that should have more room for competitors and, therefore, less rivalry. In practice, however, the lure of the large global market seems to raise the ambitions of competitors.) Consumer tastes in magazines are sufficiently common in Europe so that publishers can now sell pan-European offerings. Cultural differences do not seem great enough to prevent some magazines from crossing borders; consequently, publishing firms are making an effort to sell those magazines to all of Europe with only slight changes in content. The result is significant heightening of rivalry. In the mid-1980s, *Bella* was successfully launched as a European women's magazine, first in West Germany, then in Britain and Spain. Since then, *Elle* magazine has become a global women's fashion journal, publishing over 25 editions in more than 45 countries.

How common customer needs are across countries clearly varies greatly by industry and depends on such factors as the importance of national culture and tastes, income elasticity, and physical conditions that might affect the use of the product. For consumer businesses, the book publishing and magazine industries fall at the low end of the spectrum in commonality of needs, because of differences in both content and language, although both of these factors are changing rapidly. At the other end of the spectrum,

GLOBAL DIFFERENCES IN PHARMACEUTICAL PRODUCTS

Pharmaceutical products provide an interesting contrast between prescription (ethical) drugs and over-the-counter (proprietary) drugs. The types of prescription drugs used for a given ailment tend to be more similar across countries than the types of over-the-counter drugs. In the latter case national habits in treatment tend to create differences in what consumers buy for themselves. For example, executives in one major drug company consider that Americans focus on head pains while Japanese focus on stomach pains. The pharmaceutical industry also illustrates the critical difference between the *incidence* of a particular type of need and the *specific products* used to meet those needs. While the incidence of each disease varies greatly geographically, the products used to treat each disease are mostly identical.

travel-related industries, like airlines and traveler's checks, have needs that are inherently common across countries. Among consumer packaged goods, most food products tend to lie at the low end while household and personal care products are nearer the middle of the spectrum. For industrial businesses, commodities, such as many chemicals and other raw materials, tend toward very high commonality of needs. In contrast, more complex industrial products, such as computer equipment and process controls, range from moderate to highly common needs.

Customer needs may be more common than most executives think. *Managers, particularly those with single-country responsibilities, tend to focus on the differences between countries, because it is the differences that require effort in adaptation. But executives can find more commonality if they look for it.* This may also explain the varying strategies of companies. Some companies have looked for commonality and acted accordingly. Canon, for example, did this in developing a global photocopier that sacrificed the ability to copy certain sizes of Japanese paper.

Common Customer Needs and Tastes in Service Businesses

Service businesses usually involve the customer in production. But this effect reduces the degree to which many services can be standardized and still meet the needs of a broad cross section of customers around the world. In general the less the involvement, whether physical or psychological, the better the opportunity for a global approach. So we are more likely to see global standardization in fast food and airlines, where customer involvement is tightly controlled, than in medical care or education, where customer involvement is both stronger and more prolonged. Note that these observations apply to the broad "middle market" rather than to the relatively small market segment composed of affluent, highly educated, cosmopolitan customers.

Service staff form part of the service experience. This also limits the potential commonality of customer needs and tastes. Differences can arise even within the same industry. In banking the service provided by human tellers is far less standardized and standardizable than that provided by automated teller machines. Accounting services depend heavily on people. The higher status of accountants in Britain than in the United States means that British accountants provide more general business advice than do their American counterparts. And U.S.-style psychotherapy is unlikely to yield a global "McShrink" franchise.

Effect of the Internet on Common Customer Needs and Tastes

The Internet increases global commonality in customer needs and tastes. When customers in an industry have needs and tastes that are mostly common across countries, companies can make more use of global strategies, especially in offering globally standardized products and services. The Internet and the Web further expose customers to global offerings and other lifestyles. Individuals can now travel on the Web rather than physically but can have similar global exposure and global learning effects. So they are more likely to migrate to the highest or most popular global standard.

The Internet has two effects. First, it reinforces the appeal of those brands that are already globally recognized. Potential customers can get more information about these product offerings and have their desires further reinforced. At the same time, the Web creates more opportunities and churn in the next tier of contender brands. Relatively unknown brands will be able to rapidly build up word of mouth via the Internet and global presence via the Web. Superior design in Web sites can make up for currently low recognition. Both Schwab and Dell Computer massively shifted their marketing and ordering systems to the Web. The dramatic effects on their businesses are well recorded. Less obvious is that this shift helped propel both companies from the "possible" category of suppliers to the "must consider" category. Even if someone does not end up choosing Schwab or Dell, most potential customers now have to consider these two companies.

GLOBAL CUSTOMERS AND CHANNELS

Global customers buy on a centralized or coordinated basis for decentralized use, or at the least they select vendors centrally. As such, "global customers" can be distinguished from "international customers," "foreign customers," and "local customers," as shown in Exhibit 2-4. Global customers, compared with other types, have both more internationalized purchasing (in the sense of buying outside domestic markets) and more globalized purchasing (in the sense of global control by headquarters). A recent study found that multinational companies are rapidly increasing the globalization of their purchasing and are in turn demanding more in the way of global customer management from their vendors.[15]

There are two types of global customers—national and multinational. A *national* global customer searches the world for suppliers but uses the purchased product or service in one country. National defense agencies are a good example. A *multinational* global customer also searches the world for suppliers and uses the purchased product or service in many countries. Examples are the World Health Organization for medical products, and some automotive companies. The existence of global customers affects the opportunity or need for global market participation, global products and services, global activity location, and global marketing. Even if they do not purchase centrally, having global customers drives a business toward developing globally standardized products. Similarly, global customers can compare prices charged by the same supplier in different countries and tend to be unhappy with unexplainable discrepancies. Global customers usually occur in industrial categories, although in some consumer categories—such as cameras, watches, and luxury handbags—a significant portion of sales is accounted for by those buying while outside their home country.

The definition of a global customer or channel can be extended to "influencers" such as physicians who prescribe drugs, architects who specify building materials, and engi-

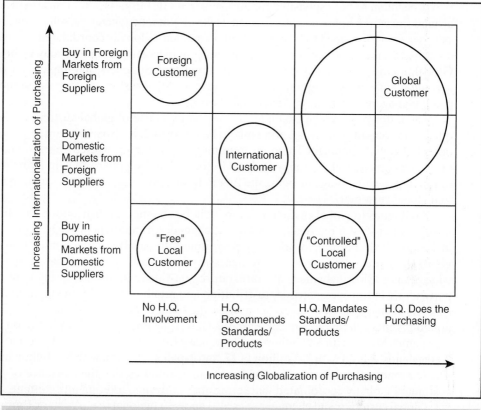

EXHIBIT 2-4   Types of Customers

neers and other technical experts who specify or recommend equipment and the like. Japanese trading companies, such as Mitsubishi and Mitsui, also act very much like global channels, although they typically make most of their "purchases" in one country—Japan.

To serve its global customers, the business needs to be present in all the customers' major markets. The U.S. advertising agency that used to have the Coca-Cola account (one of the largest in the world) was unable to serve Coca-Cola when it expanded to Brazil. So McCann-Erickson, another American but more global agency, took the account in Brazil. Then McCann used the Brazilian relationship to win the entire Coca-Cola account worldwide.[16] Chiat Day, famous for having created the world's greatest commercial ("Apple Macintosh 1984"), lost the Reebok (athletic shoes) account partly because it did not have an international network. In consequence, Chiat Day sold itself to a global agency, TBWA. In 1994, IBM replaced over 40 different advertising agencies that were serving it around the world and consolidated the company's entire $500 million account at one top 10 global agency, Ogilvy & Mather Worldwide. One reason for AT&T's push to expand globally is the fact that many of its customers are global and will use rivals like NEC, Siemens, or IBM for advanced voice and data networks if AT&T cannot meet their needs. Offering standardized products can also be a necessity for serving global customers. Increasingly, such global customers are requiring their suppliers to play the role of global coordination. General Electric has told many of its suppliers that it expects them to be responsible for ensuring that GE businesses get uniform products around the world. Some activities—such as development engineering, selling, and after-sales service—may need to be concentrated, or at least globally coordinated, in order to effectively serve global customers. Lastly, uniform marketing programs may be needed. Global pricing policies may be particularly important. Suppliers that implement global account management programs have to beware of global customers using the unified account management to extract lower global prices.

The latter provides an example of how the existence of global customers also requires the content of the marketing mix to be uniform. It is also important to recognize potential global customers. These are multinational customers who currently do not buy or coordinate centrally but may start to do so. A global supplier can gain a first mover or preemptive advantage by being the first to treat a potential global customer as an actual global customer.

Analogous to global customers, there may be channels of distribution that buy on a global or at least a regional basis. Global channels or middlemen are also important in exploiting differences in prices by performing the arbitrage function of transshipment. Their presence makes it more necessary for a business to rationalize its worldwide pricing. Global channels are rare, but regionwide ones are increasing in number, particularly in European grocery distribution and retailing. By 1998, the largest grocery retailers each operated in several countries: the United States' Wal-Mart with $137 billion in revenues in nine countries, France's Carrefour/Promodès with $56 billion in 26, Germany's Metro with $49 billion in 23, France's Intermarché with $37 billion in 7, the Netherlands' Ahold with $35 billion in 17, and Japan's 7-Eleven with $35 billion in 18.[17] The existence of global (or regionwide) channels requires, like the existence of global customers, globally coordinated marketing and uniform marketing mix content.

Global customer and channel issues also apply to regional (e.g., Asian or European) customers. Indeed, regional customers are probably growing at a faster rate than global customers, particularly in Europe.

The existence of global customers or channels cuts both ways for the threat of entry. On the one hand, it is much more difficult to displace an incumbent who is serving a customer in many countries. On the other hand, the essence of a global customer—centralized buying for multinational use—also makes a global account vulnerable to rapid total capture. A competitor may be able to capture a global account by selling to the head office only. Global or regional channels of distribution can also be exploited for rapid entry. Owing to the different regulatory, currency, and tax environments across Europe, many insurance companies have found the need to form alliances with foreign banks in order to enter new markets. By forming these alliances, insurers plan to take advantage of the banks' distribution networks (branches). Under a joint venture, Germany's Allianz sells life insurance policies through the branches of Spain's Banco Popular. In addition, Commercial Union, based in the United Kingdom, sells both life and nonlife insurance through Credito Italiano's branches in Italy.

The presence of global customers or channels increases rivalry among existing competitors. Global customers or channels become prizes to be fought over, and the fight is global in scope. As marketers aim to expand their brands to more countries, advertising agencies have been reorganizing in order to meet the demands of their global customers. In a preemptive move with its double-page advertisement in the *Wall Street Journal* and the *Financial Times* in 1984, Saatchi and Saatchi was the first agency to pub-

FLYING GLOBALLY

The international airline industry has a unique type of global customer. Most travelers, except the most patriotic, will consider all carriers that serve the route to be traveled and select on the basis of quality, reliability, frequent flyer programs, and other real and perceived attributes. At the same time, few travelers are free to start their travel in another country in order to find the best service (an exception would be Belgians who choose to fly KLM out of Amsterdam rather than a national carrier out of Brussels). On the other hand, even if airlines do not compete on points of origin and final destination, they certainly compete on intermediate destination. So British Airways and Lufthansa compete partly on the basis of the relative superiority of London and Frankfurt as airports through which to make connections in Europe.

licize its global capabilities. This move annoyed many rivals with more extensive global experience and customers. Some of these rivals then moved to enhance their own credentials. Both BBDO Worldwide and Lintas:Worldwide created European boards of directors; Ogilvy & Mather removed three subregional posts and appointed a European creative director and a new European chairman; DDB Needham Worldwide relocated its international headquarters to Paris from New York.

The reinsurance industry provides a more classic type of global customer. In the search for reinsurance, insurance companies, many of them multinational, scour the globe for the lowest premiums and best contracts. The high information content and relatively standardized nature of the product make it easy for reinsurance buyers to behave as global customers.[18]

Global Customers and Channels in Service Businesses

As large corporate customers become global, they often seek to standardize and simplify the array of services they consume. For instance, firms may seek to minimize the number of auditors they use around the world, using "Big Five" accounting firms that can apply a consistent worldwide approach (within the context of national rules within each country of operation). Corporate banking, insurance, business logistics, and management consulting are further examples. Individuals act as global customers when they purchase goods and services on their travels. The service characteristics of "a performance rather than an object" and "greater importance of the time factor" create special opportunities for travel-related services, a very large and growing segment that starts with transportation but extends to credit, communication, and emergency support.

Global customers for possession-processing services prefer common procedures and standards. For example, airlines absolutely depend on their aircraft being maintained in the same way everywhere and, increasingly, so do customers of factory and machinery maintenance services. Global customers for people-processing services may care particularly about ubiquity, especially when traveling. The New Zealander who breaks her leg in Pamplona needs medical treatment on the spot. Global customers for information-based services may have a more diffuse set of needs, but these certainly include comprehensiveness, accuracy, and accessibility. The American executive who has lost his traveler's checks in Shanghai needs reimbursement there, now, not back home in Indiana, later.

Effect of the Internet on Global Customers and Channels

Multinational companies increasingly act as global customers by globally coordinating or centralizing their purchases. But there are many obstacles, both external (finding and coordinating with vendors around the world) and internal (agreeing and coordinating requirements across international subsidiaries). The Internet and the Web make it easier to become global customers. Customers can search the Web for suppliers from anywhere in the world. Or they can go even further and place requests for proposals on their own Web sites and wait for vendors to bid. General Electric created The Trading Partner Network as an online auction site for customers and suppliers of nonproduction goods, such as office and computer supplies, and other nonproduction products and services that help to run day-to-day business operations.

The Web has accelerated the growth of regional and global channels of distribution, allowing traditional bricks-and-mortar channel firms to more easily complete their networks. And, of course, "clicks-and-limited-mortar" firms like Amazon.com jump straight into existence as global channels, although the real Amazon distribution system was Amazon + Ingram (the United States' largest book wholesaler, based in Seattle, since displaced by Amazon's own warehouse operations) + United Parcel Service in the United States and various other package deliverers elsewhere.

Lastly, the rise of Internet intermediaries (pure "click-and-mouse" firms with no physical assets) such as Autobytel.com and Carbusters.com creates a new dimension to longtime vendor-distributor relationships. In the automobile sector, carmakers have traditionally focused on mostly subnational, and occasionally national, area agreements. The new Internet channels bypass these relationships to seek out the best deals either on a national basis (as Autobytel does in the United States) or on a pan-European basis, as does the Carbusters.com partnership with *Which?* (Britain's consumer association). The immediate effect is that carmakers are rethinking their European pricing, having a degree of price convergence forced upon them.

TRANSFERABLE MARKETING

The nature of the buying decision may be such that marketing elements, like brand names and advertising, require little local adaptation; that is, brand names and advertising are readily transferable. Transferable marketing makes it easier to expand participation in markets: The business need not develop a new marketing approach. A worldwide business can also adapt its brand names and advertising campaigns to make them more transferable or, even better, design global ones to start with. Exxon chose its new name after an intensive worldwide search for a unique and easily pronounced name to replace Esso and a mixture of other brand names. The Exxon example also highlights the importance of trademark availability. Other companies owning the rights to the names desired hamper many companies in their efforts at consolidating around one global trademark or name. By definition, transferability enables the use of uniform marketing strategies. Offsetting risks include the blandness of uniformly acceptable brand names or advertising, and the vulnerability of relying on a single brand franchise.

The accepted wisdom in international marketing has long been that marketing approaches need to be tailored for each country. For example, advertising should be developed locally and designed to appeal to the local audience. But companies are finding ways to succeed with uniform or only slightly modified marketing.[19] Such transferable marketing greatly lengthens the reach and punch of global competitors.[20]

Marketing elements that are transferable across countries can both raise and reduce entry barriers. On the one hand, incumbent competitors can leverage global marketing to build high barriers in almost every market. Coca-Cola has created not just national but global barriers to entry with its global brand franchise. This franchise has been built in part through global advertising and packaging. On the other hand, potential entrants can use transferable marketing as a "gateway to entry."[21] Entrants can apply the advertising, packaging designs, and so on, that they have developed elsewhere. Transferable brand names and reputation need the additional factor of spillover media, foreign travel by potential customers, or other vehicles of communication before they can be used to reduce international entry barriers.

Transferable marketing adds a dimension to rivalry among existing competitors. Not only must rivals try to develop the best marketing programs in each country, but also they must compete in their ability to transfer successful programs from country to country. Companies without a transfer mechanism can find themselves out-marketed one country at a time by a rival that globally leverages a successful approach. In the toothpaste market, Colgate-Palmolive achieved global share leadership partly through its successful application of a global approach to branding, packaging, and advertising. In contrast, rivals like Unilever and Beecham lagged with different approaches in different countries.

Transferable Marketing for Service Businesses

Some kinds of marketing may make more use of local people for service than for manufacturing businesses, and thus be less globally transferable. For example, television commercials may feature service staff. For locally provided services, these would have to be depictions of local staff. So the executions would need to be different for each country, although the copy strategy and script may well be the same. In some cases, where the concept of the service has strong national traditions, even the strategy and script may have to differ. Interestingly, the need for adaptation depends on the extent to which the service proposition is itself globalized. A hotel chain that stresses its global uniformity, such as Holiday Inns, would use a more globally common advertising strategy. The target audience would also make a difference. Advertising to international travelers would be more common, while advertising a hotel's restaurants to local customers would be more local.

Effect of the Internet on Transferable Marketing

The Internet has two effects on the transferability of global marketing—enabling and demanding. In terms of *enabling* global marketing, Internet/Web-based marketing has inherent global reach. Further, users share a common style of interaction—they have been conditioned to interact with electronic communications in a certain way—browsing, searching, and impatient. Third, most users, by self-selection, have a working knowledge of English, itself the far dominant language of the Internet, even though more than half of the 280 million Internet users speak languages other than English.[22]

In terms of *demanding* global marketing, the Internet and the Web mandate that vendors use globally standard brand names. A simple example suffices to illustrate this new commandment. In an earlier era, Amazon.com would probably have been Amazon.com in Brazil only, but Mississippi.com in the United States, Thames.com in the United Kingdom, Rhine.com in Germany, and Yangtze.com in China. In the Internet era, the founder of Amazon.com chose the *world's* largest river as his company's global brand name. Similarly, other elements of the marketing mix, particularly price, need to be more uniform than in the pre-Internet era.

LEAD COUNTRIES

Innovation in products or processes may be concentrated in one or a few countries because of the presence of innovative competitors or demanding customers or both. In that case it becomes critical for global competitors to participate in these "lead countries" in order to be exposed to the sources of innovation. Customers may view market position in a lead country as a surrogate for overall quality. Companies frequently promote a product in one country as, for example, "the leading brand in the U.S.A."[23] Lead countries can be easily identified as those in which the most important product or process innovations occur.

In many industries, there are lead countries in which major global competitors are based and where the bulk of innovations occur. For example, Japan is a lead country for consumer electronics, Germany for industrial control equipment, and the United States for computer software and now the Internet. In such industries it is critical for all competitors with global ambitions to participate in the lead countries. In many industries the key lead countries are the United States, Japan, and major European countries like Germany or the United Kingdom. Other countries, of course, do take the lead in particular industries, such as Denmark for insulin and Italy for ceramic tiles.[24] Most American and European companies had until the 1990s a very small presence in Japan and worried that they were missing out on innovations in that country. In the 1990s American companies started to make the major commitments needed to set up R&D operations in Japan so as to be able to tap into the growing stream of Japanese innovations.

The existence of lead countries can increase the threat of entry. Potential entrants can readily identify the key innovations, even if they choose to enter other countries first. Furthermore, the lead countries become prized targets for entry. As Japan increasingly becomes in many industries an innovator rather than an imitator, American and European companies are increasingly recognizing the criticality of Japan as a lead country. There is certainly a gap to date as measured by the far higher ratio of patents filed in, say, the United States by Japanese companies relative to the number filed by American companies in Japan. Japan has even become a fashion lead country for the rest of Asia. In the foreseeable future, Russia, China, and India may become key lead countries in various technology sectors.

Rivalry is fiercer in lead countries as competitors recognize the strategic as well as financial importance of success there. In particular, companies need to recognize the value of investing to build a strong position in lead markets, particularly if those markets are the home of major global rivals.

Lead Countries in Service Businesses

Lead country effects apply equally for service businesses. Interestingly, the United States is far more dominant as a lead country for global service businesses than it is for manufacturing ones. In many categories of service businesses, the United States sets global trends and standards: in chain restaurants, hotels, entertainment theme parks, health care, delivery services, car rental, and so on. This may be because global service businesses depend less on technology or skilled labor, and more on having a strong business concept that is systematically applied globally.

Effect of the Internet on Lead Countries

The Internet has two effects on lead countries. First, it makes it easier for customers to identify lead countries and to monitor their offerings. The Web lets everyone visit Paris or Tokyo or Los Angeles. Consumers can rapidly identify the trends and fashions in lead countries and will become increasingly dissatisfied with inferior domestic offerings. The fall of the Berlin Wall cut demand for East German cars, such as the Trabant, from a 10-year backlog to zero. The Web brings down Berlin Walls all over the world.

COST GLOBALIZATION DRIVERS

Cost globalization drivers—global scale economies, steep experience effects, favorable logistics, differences in country costs, high product development costs, and fast-changing technology—depend on the economics of the business. These drivers particularly affect the use of the global activity location lever, as well as the global market participation and global product levers. Exhibit 2-5 ranks on cost globalization drivers, the same industries ranked on market globalization drivers in Exhibit 2-3. Notice some of the differences: Pharmaceuticals (ethical) rise to the top of the cost rankings while soft drinks fall to the bottom.

GLOBAL ECONOMIES OF SCALE AND SCOPE

Global scale economies or scope economies apply when single-country markets are not large enough to allow competitors to achieve optimum scale. Scale at a given location

EXHIBIT 2-5 Strength of Cost Globalization Drivers for Selected Industries

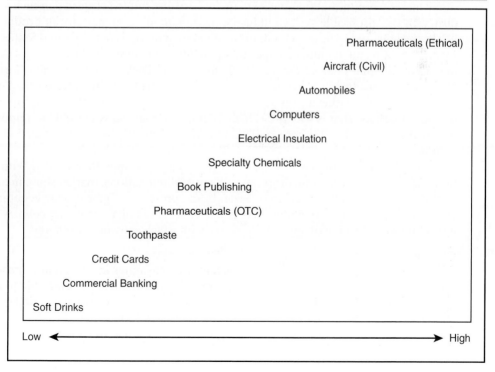

of an activity can then be increased through participation in multiple markets, combined with product standardization and/or concentration of selected value activities. But corresponding risks of increasing scale at one location include rigidity and vulnerability to disruption. There has been a shift in the economics of the electronics industry. As the cost of circuits has decreased, the cost advantage has gone to companies that can produce the lowest cost components. Size has become a major asset. Among others, Thomson, the French electronics maker, realized the need to have a worldwide presence in an industry characterized by economies of scale. Accordingly, Thomson instituted a major global expansion that included the acquisition of General Electric's RCA consumer electronics business.[25]

In many cases it seems to be *economies of scope* (the gains from spreading activities across multiple product lines or businesses) rather than economies of scale (the gains from increasing the volume of an activity) that push businesses to internationalize or to globalize. In consumer household products, such as detergent and toothpaste, economies of scale at the manufacturing level can typically be achieved by national plants in most but the smallest countries. In soft drinks, large cities in China can support several bottling plants. Yet these industries are dominated by a handful of multinational firms—Unilever, Procter & Gamble, Colgate-Palmolive, Coca-Cola, and Pepsico. It seems that the economies of scope involved in consumer research, product development, and the creation of marketing programs are a major source of the competitive advantage enjoyed by multinational companies in these industries.

Global scale economies reduce the threat of entry, particularly from potential entrants that are national companies. Where global scale economies apply, it will not be possible for an entrant to achieve competitive economic scale by entering a single national market. A non-multinational will find it very difficult to get started in such an industry. In the disposable syringe industry, the minimum economic size in production has been estimated to be 60 percent of the combined markets in the United States and Japan.[26] As a result, national competitors play little role in this industry that is dominated by multinational companies such as Becton Dickinson (U.S.) and Terumo (Japan). Conversely, where economies are not at a global scale, an entrant can start in a smaller country-market and gradually build the experience that will allow it to export to larger markets. That is why the U.S. market has become so vulnerable to imported personal computers and other products that can be effectively manufactured in low volumes.

Global scale economies also broaden the scope of competitive rivalry. With national scale economies, competitors have to worry about national market share in order to stay at the economically efficient scale. In the presence of global scale economies, competitors have to worry about their global share. Loss of share in any country will impact the cost position of any sister country with which activities are shared.

Global Scale Economies in Service Businesses

Certain service characteristics—lack of inventories, customer involvement in production, and people as part of the service experience—all work against being able to concentrate production to achieve scale. So service companies typically have to find global scale economies by standardizing production processes rather than through physical concentration, and in concentrating the upstream, rather than the downstream, stages of the value chain.

The effect of cost globalization drivers, like global scale economies, varies sharply according to the level of fixed costs required to enter an industry (although equipment leasing schemes, or awarding franchises to local investors, provide a way to minimize such entry barriers). So cost globalization drivers may be less favorable for services that are primarily people-based and face lesser scale economies and flatter experience curves. One common solution for the would-be global company is to substitute equipment for labor in order to achieve lower costs and better performance than local companies using traditional business systems, as has been done by McDonald's.

Effect of the Internet on Global Scale Economies

The Internet drives down global economies of scale and scope. The Web-induced transformation of businesses generally reduces minimum efficient scales. First, many physical activities are being replaced by Web-based virtual activities. Therefore, many scale and investment barriers to global spread are bypassed. For example, many already globalized companies are running down their international distribution systems, while newly internationalizing companies need to spend much less on international distribution. Second, value chains and business systems are being broken up or "deconstructed."[27] Inevitably, this means a consolidation of players and market share takes place at the deconstructed stages and therefore a larger scale. On the one hand this means that there is less pressure on the new entities to globalize. But on the other hand, these new entities have clearly focused business models and competitive advantages that are easily transferable and leverageable internationally.

This reduction in economies of scale and transaction costs will particularly help aggressive and well-managed smaller firms from emerging markets. For example, small firms in Asia will be able to combine to achieve global reach, reducing the customer proximity advantage of firms in developed economies.

STEEP EXPERIENCE CURVE

Even if scale and scope economies are exhausted, expanded market participation, product standardization, and activity concentration can accelerate the accumulation of learning and experience effects (learning effects apply to direct manufacturing while experience effects apply to the entire production process). The steeper the learning and experience slopes, the greater is the potential benefit. *Managers should beware, though, of the usual danger in pursuing experience curve strategies—overaggressive pricing that destroys not just the competition but the market also.* A steep experience curve has similar effects as global scale economies on the threat of entry and rivalry among competitors.

GLOBAL SOURCING EFFICIENCIES

The market for supplies may allow centralized purchasing to achieve savings in the cost of production inputs. Himont—at one time a joint venture between Hercules, Inc., of the United States and Montedison SpA of Italy—is the leader of the global polypropylene market. Central to Himont's strategy is global coordination among manufacturing facilities in the purchase of raw materials, particularly monomer, the key ingredient in polypropylene production. Rationalization of raw material orders significantly strengthens the venture's low-cost production advantage. Sourcing efficiencies have a similar effect as global scale economies on the threat of entry and rivalry among competitors.

Global Sourcing Efficiencies in Service Businesses

Many service businesses produce at the location of the customer and, hence, have multiple national sites. In many cases, satisfactory supplies can be sourced locally. But in many other cases, the need to maintain global standards will require global sourcing at higher cost. When McDonald's first went into Russia, the company imported some ingredients (potato chips) and set up special supply arrangements for others (beef). Professional service firms often face the need to fly in qualified staff from overseas.

Effect of the Internet on Global Sourcing Efficiencies

The Internet enhances global sourcing efficiencies. A primary Internet phenomenon has been the creation of global Web-based purchasing systems. Before the Web, globally centralized purchasing required complex, paper- and phone-based coordination of geographically dispersed subsidiaries and suppliers. Today, subsidiary requirements can be managed efficiently and democratically through intranets, and relationships coordinated using global extranets. For example, General Motors, Ford, and DaimlerChrysler have created the Automotive Exchange Network (ANX) to support automated interactions with their parts suppliers. ANX defines a set of technology and service-quality standards for exchanging critical transaction and planning documents over the Web.[28] European and Japanese automobile companies are developing similar systems. In electronics, Matsushita is building Web links among its 100 factories in Japan, and with 3,000 of its 7,000 suppliers.

FAVORABLE LOGISTICS

A favorable ratio of sales value to transportation cost enhances the ability to concentrate production. Other logistical factors include nonperishability, the absence of time urgency, and little need for location close to customer facilities. Low transportation costs allow concentration of production. Even the shape of the product can make a crucial difference. Cardboard tubes, such as those used as cores for textiles, are not economically shippable because the tubes are mostly air. In contrast, cardboard cones are transportable because they can be stacked, allowing many more units in the same space. In general, higher priced/higher quality products within any category face more favorable logistics. So French "vin de table" stays home while good Burgundies travel everywhere.

Favorable logistics increase the threat of entry. The low costs make it much easier for foreign entrants to enter markets, by exporting. Favorable logistics also increase rivalry among existing competitors by expanding the geographic scope of competition. Rivals can readily shift products from country to country, such that competition is between global production capabilities.

Favorable Logistics in Service Businesses

Low transportation costs allow concentration of production for physical goods. For services, "customer involvement in production" raises the logistical stakes in globalization. In most people-processing services, the need for convenience prevents concentration. But in some possession-processing services, customers are willing to transport their possessions to another location for better service. Thus, many airlines bring their aircraft to Singapore. Some people-processing services have achieved similar success in having customers come to them. London hospitals maintain a flourishing business among wealthy Middle Eastern patients, as do Miami hospitals for patients from Latin America.

VOLKSWAGEN'S RELOCATION
OF PRODUCTION

Under attack from lower priced cars, Volkswagen has been under pressure to reduce its costs. One of the primary ways it did this was by concentrating its production in various countries to take advantage of the differences in country costs. In Spain, hourly labor costs have been less than half that in Germany. To take advantage of this cost differential, the company moved production of Polos from Wolfsburg to Spain, freeing up the high-wage German labor to produce the higher priced Golf cars. Another example of this concentration occurred when Volkswagen shut down its New Stanton, Pennsylvania, plant that manufactured Golfs and Jettas. The lower end of the U.S. market was served instead by its low-wage facility in Brazil that produced the Fox. The higher end of the product line (Jetta and Golf) was exported from Europe. This concentration and coordination of production has enabled the company to make substantial cost savings.

Companies have to balance the trade-offs between logistics and appeal. Disney favored logistics over appeal in selecting northern France rather than southern Spain for the location of Euro Disney. More people can get more easily to the Euro Disney site outside Paris, but once there they often face cold weather and colder service. Service businesses can also create their own favorable logistics. Club Med organizes charter flights from urban centers to its off-the-beaten-path locations. Some airlines provide limousine ground transport to and from their first-class flights.

Lastly, logistics is seldom a barrier to globalization for information-based services. Using electronic channels to deliver such services allows providers to concentrate production in locations that have specific expertise and to offer cost savings or other meaningful advantages. For instance, banks in the Cayman Islands are not conveniently located from a purely geographic standpoint, but money can be shipped there electronically to take advantage of the tax benefits conferred by offshore status.

Effect of the Internet on Favorable Logistics

The Internet speeds up global logistics. The Web facilitates the operation of global production and supply networks. Boeing has created the Boeing Partners Network to connect with its 40,000 trading partners around the world. For example, 45 separate regulatory agencies in the United States, Canada, Japan, Russia, and Europe use the Boeing intranet to collaborate on its space station project. These networks can also be supported by third-party services, such as Information Resources Associates' Extranet Support Center.

DIFFERENCES IN COUNTRY COSTS

Differences in country costs can provide a strong spur to globalization. Factor costs generally vary across countries, and more so for particular industries. The availability of particular skills also varies. Concentration of activities in low-cost or high-skill countries can increase productivity and reduce costs. But managers need to anticipate the danger of training future offshore competitors.[29]

Large variations in costs among the countries that produce or might produce a particular product increase the threat of entry from foreign sources. Japan—and then the "four tigers" of South Korea, Taiwan, Hong Kong, and Singapore—has very successfully leveraged low factor costs in entering many international industries. Other Southeast Asian countries such as Thailand are making similar entries in high labor cost industries such as construction wallboard. Eastern European countries may be the next to exploit low-cost but high-skill labor in threatening entry. Having a low cost of goods sold, relative to the selling price, is often an industry's best protection from cheap imports. Thus, marketing-intensive consumer products businesses, such as disposable razors, are still the preserve of American and European producers.

Differences in country costs increase rivalry among existing competitors by creating differential sources of competitive advantage. Rivalry heightened between Japanese and European consumer electronics manufacturers when the Japanese discovered that it was cheaper to produce Europe-bound products in the United States than at home. Ricoh assembles photocopiers containing 90 percent Japanese parts in California and reexports them to Europe. Furthermore, Sony produces audiotapes and videotapes at an Alabama plant, and audio recorders at a Florida plant, and ships them to Europe for sale. Similarly, the United Kingdom has become the preferred European manufacturing site for many Japanese companies. As a result the United Kingdom government became embroiled in a dispute with other European Union governments on the extent of local content needed to qualify as "Made in Europe."

Exchange rates, and changes in them, provide a major source of the variation in costs between countries. But the effect of exchange rates works in one direction for the cost of local inputs, such as labor and some raw materials, and usually in the opposite direction for imported inputs and foreign services. So it is usually only labor-intensive industries, or those in which local materials and supplies are both important and plentiful, where exchange rates can have a major impact on relative country costs.

Differences in Country Costs in Service Businesses

Service businesses vary in their ability to exploit differences in country costs. People-processing businesses can do so the least as they usually need local operations wherever their customers are. Possession-processing businesses have more opportunities. Centralized processing facilities may have such low costs that they can afford to bring the possessions to the facility. For example, airplanes are now often serviced at specific hubs operated by third parties rather than the airlines owning the planes. Information-based services have the most opportunity as, in many cases, they can be based nearly anywhere, especially when linked in via the Internet.

Effect of the Internet on Differences in Country Costs

The Internet does not change relative country costs and skills, but it enables many activities to be shifted to lower cost countries. First, the Internet can be used as a means of efficient communication and coordination to make possible the "offshoring" of activities that would otherwise be too complex to manage. For example, some consulting firms have shifted document production to India, communicating via the Web and taking advantage of time-zone differences as well as lower costs. While U.S.- and Europe-based consultants sleep (when and if they ever sleep!), their documents and presentations are being produced for them. Second, the deconstruction of activities creates specialized Web-based functions such as customer service (particularly for information-rich services) that can easily be shifted to lower cost locales. The information database can remain in the home or other key country while being accessed by Internet from lower cost and perhaps less secure countries.

HIGH PRODUCT DEVELOPMENT COSTS

High product development costs relative to the size of national markets act as a driver to globalization. Philips, the Dutch multinational, estimated that technology developments in public telecommunications increased the cost of product development by enormous multiples. In the 1950s development costs for conventional electromechanical switching systems were about $10 million, and they had an expected life cycle of about 25 years. By the beginning of 1970 when the analog system was introduced, development costs had jumped to $200 million, while the life cycle fell to 12 to 15 years. In the 1980s, when the first digital systems were developed, costs had risen to $1 billion for a life expectancy of 8 to 12 years. Philips calculated that digital development expenses of $1 billion required roughly 8 percent share of the world market just to recover costs. The largest single market in Europe—Germany—could in total deliver less than that share.[30]

By 2000, developing a new pharmaceutical or agro-chemical product could cost $200 million or more, developing a new automobile platform could cost at least $1 billion, and developing the next generation of super-jumbo jets was projected to cost over $10 billion (for the Airbus A380). The A380 program is so large that Airbus needs alliances in Russia, China, and Japan, and substantial U.S. content.

Developing a few global or regional products rather than many national products can reduce high product development costs. But the process for designing global products must not be so cumbersome as to slow the entire process. The automobile industry is characterized by long product development periods and high product development costs. One reason for the high costs is duplication of effort across countries. In the 1990s, companies such as Ford consolidated design efforts, with different regions specializing in particular activities. High product development costs have a similar effect as global scale economies on the threat of entry and rivalry among competitors.

Effect of the Internet on Product Development Costs

The Internet reduces product development costs. Some aspects of the product, particularly supplementary ones such as service, can be shifted out of the physical product onto the Web. This allows the development of a simpler, global core product with lower development (and production) costs. In some cases, the customer can do the final customization online. Both Nike and IDwatch from IDtown (a Hong Kong firm) allow customers to design and order their own customized products, as does Dell Computer. Another cost reduction arises when companies use intranets to manage globally dispersed product development teams, thereby also enhancing effectiveness.

FAST-CHANGING TECHNOLOGY

Fast-changing technology, in products or processes, usually accompanies high product development costs, and in itself already increases industry globalization potential:

- The cost of embodying the technology changes typically drives companies to amortize that cost across as many markets as possible.

- Companies that pioneer a particular technology usually feel pressured to rapidly globalize that technology in order to exploit it before imitators do so. So both the cost and preemption reasons just cited spur companies to increase their global market participation.
- A company can better exploit and protect its new technologies by using globally integrated competitive moves that include a clear prioritization of when and where to use the technology against competitors.

Fast-Changing Technology in Service Businesses

For information-based services, the growing availability of broadband telecommunication channels, capable of moving vast amounts of data at great speed, is playing a major role in opening up new markets. But there may be no need to duplicate all informational elements in each new location. Significant economies may be gained by centralizing "information hubs" on a global basis, as FedEx does in Memphis. For all three types of services, the use of information technology may allow companies to benefit from favorable labor costs or exchange rates by consolidating operations of supplementary services (such as reservations) or back office functions (such as accounting) in just one or a few countries. While a globalization driver in its own right, information technology also interacts with all of the other drivers.

GOVERNMENT GLOBALIZATION DRIVERS

Government globalization drivers—favorable trade policies, compatible technical standards, common marketing regulations, government-owned competitors and customers, and host government concerns—depend on the rules set by national governments and affect use of all global strategy levers. Exhibit 2-6 ranks on government globalization drivers, the same industries ranked on market and cost globalization drivers in Exhibits 2-3 and 2-5. Again, notice some of the differences: Toothpaste rises to the top while electrical insulation falls near the bottom of the rankings.

FAVORABLE TRADE POLICIES

Host governments affect globalization potential in a number of major ways: import tariffs and quotas, nontariff barriers, export subsidies, local content requirements, currency and capital flow restrictions, ownership restrictions, and requirements on technology transfer.[31] Governments' exercise of these trade barriers makes it difficult for companies to use the global levers of global market participation, global products and services, global activity location, and global marketing and affects the need to use the lever of global competitive moves. Government policies greatly restrict global market participation in the media industries.

In many countries, foreign control of the media is restricted or prohibited. Some countries also impose other special restrictions. In Canada magazines must be printed in the country or else be charged a higher postal rate—in effect a local content requirement that restricts a company's choice on activity location.[32] The newsprint industry also faces unfavorable trade, probably because of its political salience as part of the natural resource sector. In the 1970s many national governments responded to the oil crisis and consequent business bankruptcies by intervening with subsidies, tax laws, cartels, and delays in scheduled tariff reductions and quota increases.[33] In the global recession of 2001,

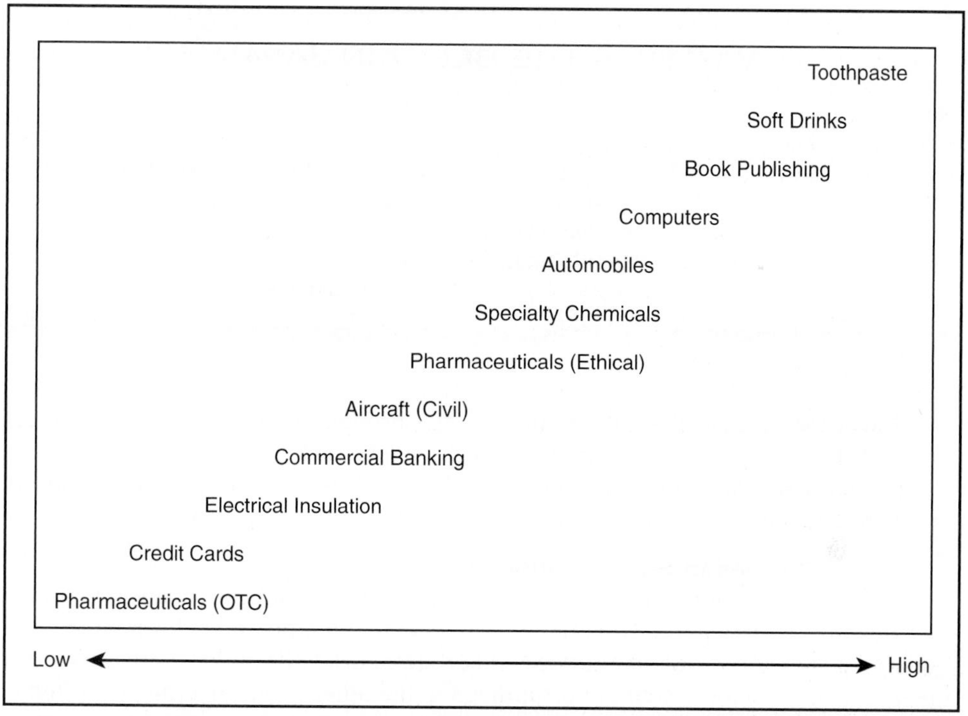

Toothpaste

Soft Drinks

Book Publishing

Computers

Automobiles

Specialty Chemicals

Pharmaceuticals (Ethical)

Aircraft (Civil)

Commercial Banking

Electrical Insulation

Credit Cards

Pharmaceuticals (OTC)

Low ⟵————————————————————————⟶ High

EXHIBIT 2-6 Strength of Government Globalization Drivers for Selected Industries

many national governments were struggling to find ways to support failing flagship companies, especially airlines.

National trade policies particularly constrain the extent to which companies can concentrate manufacturing activities. Aggressive U.S. government actions and threats on tariffs, quotas, and protectionist measures helped convince Japanese automobile manufacturers and other manufacturers to give up their concentration of manufacturing in Japan. Reluctantly, Japanese companies opened plants in the United States. Honda even made a public relations virtue out of necessity. It gave great publicity to the first shipment of an American-made Honda car to Japan.

The easing of government restrictions can set off a rush for expanded market participation. European Community regulations for banking and financial services were among those harmonized in 1992. The EC (now EU) decision to permit free flow of capital among its member countries in 1992 led to a jockeying for position among European financial institutions. Until then, the Deutsche Bank had only 15 offices outside Germany, but it has since established a major presence in the French markets. Deutsche Bank also moved into the Italian market by acquiring Bank of America's 100 branches there. Other financial organizations from different countries such as J. P. Morgan of the United States, Swiss Bank Corporation, and the S. G. Warburg Group in Britain increased their participation in major European markets through acquisitions.

Favorable trade policies increase rivalry among existing international competitors by making it easier for them to compete in each other's markets. The opening up of

WHERE'S THE BEEF? IN JAPAN

Favorable trade policies, by definition, increase the threat of foreign entry. Japan's agreement to eliminate the quota on American beef enabled many U.S. producers to enter the coveted Japanese market. U.S. trade representatives convinced Japan to replace the quota, which was equivalent to a tariff of 376 percent, with a tariff of 70 percent in 1989 and a tariff of 50 percent three years later. American beef may become as successful in Japan as American credit cards, which benefited from a similar removal of restrictions in the late 1970s.

European financial markets, created by the Europe 1992 changes, has made rivals of national European banks. Until the changes, banks such as Germany's Deutsche Bank, Britain's Barclays Bank, and France's Banque Nationale de Paris competed only in fringe activities. Now they increasingly recognize each other as major rivals.

Trade Policies in Service Businesses

For services, customer involvement in production may mitigate many government barriers to global strategy. Government drivers are often favorable for people-processing and possession-processing services that require a significant local presence, since they create local employment opportunities. On the other hand, governments often impose regulations to protect home carriers in the case of mobile services, such as passenger and freight transportation. For instance, restricting foreign airlines' landing rights or ability to pick up passengers at an intermediate stop ("third freedom" rights) provides a way to protect home-based airlines on international routes.

Nations may perceive both an economic and a cultural threat in unrestricted imports of information-based services through electronic channels. Government regulations range from controls on international banking to bans on private ownership of satellite dishes (as in countries such as China, Singapore, and Saudi Arabia). Some nations are now trying to manage citizen access to the World Wide Web.

For people-processing services, government barriers to global strategy include country differences in social policies (e.g., health) affecting labor costs, the role of women in frontline jobs, and the hours or days on which work can be performed. For possession-processing services, tax laws, environmental regulations, and technical standards may decrease/increase costs and encourage/discourage certain types of activity. For information-based services, special policies on education, censorship, public ownership of communications, and infrastructure quality may apply; technical standards may vary; and government policies may distort pricing.

Most global efforts at reducing trade barriers focused for many years on the movement of goods. But now bodies such as the World Trade Organization and the European Union are also freeing up services. The French insurer AXA's 1996 acquisition of rival UAP provides a good example of how governmental policies are helping to spur changes in the global insurance industry. The unification of Europe through the European Union propelled AXA to consolidate with another massive French insurance company to become the largest insurance company in the world. As a result of the unification, many tariffs and artificial price supports that protected the insurance industry in Europe were destructed. French insurance companies like AXA, therefore, were faced with increased competition from non-French insurance companies. In order to remain competitive in the global insurance industry, AXA chose to acquire its rival UAP.[34]

Effect of the Internet on Trade Policies

The Internet weakens many government barriers to globalization, often sidestepping trade policies. E-commerce reduces trade barriers in several ways, particularly in bypassing import duties and taxes. Most governments find it impossible to monitor or tax services delivered over the Internet, unless the government is actively engaged in monitoring and censoring Web traffic, as do a few authoritarian regimes. For products and services ordered over the Internet but delivered physically across borders, governments should, in theory, be able to catch these at the frontier. But in practice, most governments miss a significant portion of the increasing numbers of relatively low value items.

COMPATIBLE TECHNICAL STANDARDS

Differences in technical standards among countries affect the extent to which products can be standardized. Government restrictions in terms of technical standards can make or break efforts at product standardization. Often, standards are set with protectionism in mind.

Motorola's Struggle with Japanese Standards   Motorola, a leading American electronics manufacturer, found that many of its products were excluded from the Japanese market on the grounds that these products operated at a higher frequency than permitted in Japan. Motorola spent many years, with some notable successes, to get Japan to change its standards.

Over-the-counter pharmaceuticals, being sold directly to the public, face strict standards that vary from country to country. Maximum allowed dosage is perhaps the greatest source of incompatibility. In contrast, while still strict, governments are more liberal with prescription pharmaceuticals, so that standards are typically more compatible. At the other end of the scale, the airline industry has to have highly compatible technical standards in order to function at all. For example, all international airports have similar runway lengths to accommodate the largest passenger jets; and the universal language used around the world in cockpits and control towers is English.

Telecommunications have been regarded by governments as contributing to national security. So they have tended to rely on domestic suppliers. Consequently, the world faces a hodgepodge of standards in telecommunications. In Europe, Spain has a three-second busy tone while Denmark has a two-second one. German telephones operate on 60 volts while other European countries use 8 volts, and so on.[35]

Opening of Telecom Markets   The protection of national telecom markets is falling fast. In 1997, the World Trade Organization (WTO) brokered an agreement among 69 countries to open their telecom markets to competition, most by 1998.[36] In scope alone, the agreement was the most ambitious yet as it opened the three big telecom markets—America, the European Union, and Japan—to allow international and domestic competition by 1998. A total of 15 other countries would join them, and another 16 would open their markets over the next seven years (1997–2004). Most of the WTO signatories agreed, not because they abruptly saw the virtues of competition but in grudging recognition of the fact that developments in technology and business were making change inevitable.

Compatible technical standards can make it easier for new entrants to achieve the needed scale. With one product they can enter many markets at once. Lack of major differences in country technical standards greatly helped Japan's Canon enter the photocopier market in the early 1970s. Canon was able to design a single global product that needed only minor modifications for individual countries. Compatible technical standards also increase rivalry among existing competitors by making it easier for them to invade each other's market.

Effect of the Internet on Technical Standards

The Internet spurs global technical standards. The move to put standards on government Web sites and to allow public access is gradually increasing the transparency of the standard-setting process and should encourage the spread of global standards. For example, Japan is lobbying other G8 nations for unified global rules on e-commerce financial trading.

COMMON MARKETING REGULATIONS

The marketing environment of individual countries affects the extent to which uniform global marketing approaches can be used. Certain types of media may not be allowed or may have restrictions on their use. The United States is far more liberal than Europe in the kinds of advertising claims that can be made on television. The British television authorities even veto the depiction of socially undesirable behavior, such as scenes of children pestering their parents to buy a product. And, of course, the use of sex is different. At one extreme, France is far more liberal than the United States about sex in advertising. There can also be limitations on various promotional devices, such as lotteries. In the United States promotional competitions cannot require skill or special knowledge!

Common marketing regulations increase rivalry among existing international competitors by making it easier for them to invade each other's markets. British Airways has used a uniform global advertising campaign to help increase its market share in many countries around the world.

Effect of the Internet on Marketing Regulations

The Internet confronts diverse marketing regulations. Governments lag in their efforts to regulate marketing on the Internet. Differences in rules on Internet marketing can themselves pose a barrier to globalization. For example, the European Union is applying increasingly strict rules to prevent marketing e-mail from originating outside the EU. Many e-marketers are thus finding that, just like old economy producers, they need to set up operations inside the EU. Germany forbids all unsolicited marketing contact of consumers, including via e-mail. France forbids e-Bay and similar online auction services from allowing French users to access Web sites outside France itself.

The Internet also depends on national legal systems. Both overly weak and overly strong national legal systems deter international business. The critical issue for the Web revolves around the protection of free speech. Jurisdictions vary in the protection extended to content on Web sites, particularly regarding pornography and defamation. With pornography the problem lies with the huge variations in interpretation. What may be quite innocent in a liberal nation may be deemed criminal elsewhere. With defamation, some jurisdictions allow portal and Web operators the defense that they do not know what is mounted by content providers. Others do not. In response many service operators are shifting operations to host countries with more liberal rules.

CONSUMER E-COMMERCE: COUNTRY OF JURISDICTION

Web operators and e-businesses face the general problem that their inherent global reach exposes them to the laws, especially consumer protection laws, of all countries. The EU poses a special case of this general problem, with currently conflicting legislative proposals.[37] On the one hand, a proposed EU Directive would apply the internal market clause common in the EU. This would allow an e-operator to adhere only to the laws of its own country and rely on the EU principle of mutual recognition. On the other hand, a proposed "Brussels Regulation" would give the courts of a consumer's country of habitual residence jurisdiction over suppliers for goods and services, thus exposing e-operators to the varying laws of all 15 EU states. Companies can try to protect themselves with disclaimers such as "this site is not open to contractual offers by French consumers." But there is a large degree of legal uncertainty as to whether such a disclaimer would be valid. Adoption of the "operator country of jurisdiction" rule would favor smaller national companies (which lack the resources to understand and comply with the laws of 15 states). Adoption of the "consumer country of jurisdiction" rule would generally discourage e-commerce but also favor larger multinational companies, which can inherently cope much more easily with multiplicity.

GOVERNMENT-OWNED COMPETITORS

The presence of government-owned competitors can increase the globalization potential of an industry. Such competitors frequently enjoy subsidies as well as protected home markets and are often a major source of foreign exchange earnings. That combination both allows and spurs them to aggressively pursue foreign markets. In response other competitors need to have a global plan for fending off government-owned competitors.

The existence of government-owned competitors increases the threat of entry. Similarly, government-owned competitors increase rivalry because of their differing motivations from private competitors. According to a disgruntled American competitor, Spanish and Italian government-owned manufacturers of aluminum products typically act to depress prices in the European market.

GOVERNMENT-OWNED CUSTOMERS

In contrast to government-owned competitors, the presence of government-owned customers provides a barrier to globalization. Such customers usually favor national suppliers. The privatization of most European telecommunications companies spurred greater global competition in the equipment-supplying industry.

HOST GOVERNMENT CONCERNS

Lastly, in addition to the specific government drivers just discussed, firms pursuing a global strategy need to be aware of the concerns of host governments:

* Global businesses will quickly respond to shifts in the relative factor cost competitiveness of various manufacturing locations by relocating to different countries.

- Global integration gives multinational companies more opportunity to bias the financial results of subsidiaries to decrease total tax liability.
- Value-chain specialization within global businesses will keep key competencies outside their countries.
- The weakening of national decision centers under global strategy makes it more difficult for governments to deal with multinational companies.[38]

In addition, governments and companies usually have a desire for local reliance in major or strategic industries, for example, the textile industry in a number of Asian countries. So governments will seldom allow such major industries to depend for key inputs on supply from foreign countries, particularly distant ones.

COMPETITIVE GLOBALIZATION DRIVERS

Competitive globalization drivers—high exports and imports, competitors from different continents, interdependence of countries, and globalized competitors—raise the globalization potential of their industry and spur the need for a response on the global strategy levers. Exhibit 2-7 ranks on competitive globalization drivers, the same industries ranked on market, cost, and government drivers in Exhibits 2-3, 2-5, and 2-6. Civil aircraft and computers probably rank highest in competitive drivers while book publishing ranks lowest.

EXHIBIT 2-7   Strength of Competitive Globalization Drivers for Selected Industries

	Aircraft (Civil)
	Computers
	Automobiles
	Specialty Chemicals
	Pharmaceuticals (Ethical)
	Electrical Insulation
	Toothpaste
	Soft Drinks
	Commercial Banking
	Pharmaceuticals (OTC)
	Credit Cards
Book Publishing	

Low ◄─────────────────────────────────────► High

HIGH EXPORTS AND IMPORTS

The most basic competitive driver is the level of exports and imports of both final and intermediate products and services. The more trade there is between countries, the more competitors in different countries interact with each other. A global strategy is, therefore, more necessary. Furthermore, high levels of trade change the nature of competitive forces as discussed earlier on the threat of entry.

COMPETITORS FROM DIFFERENT CONTINENTS AND COUNTRIES

Another obvious driver of industry globalization potential is the extent to which major competitors come from different continents or countries. Because their differing backgrounds spur different objectives and approaches, global competition among rivals from different continents tends to be more severe.

INTERDEPENDENT COUNTRIES

A competitor may create competitive interdependence among countries by pursuing a global strategy. This effect arises from the sharing of activities. For example, a business may use a plant in Mexico to serve both the U.S. and Japanese markets. So market share gains in Japan will affect volume in the Mexican plant, which in turn will affect costs and ultimately the business's market share in the United States. Thus, with interdependent countries, a competitor's market share in one country contributes to its overall cost position and, therefore, its share position in another country. Such interdependence helps a company to subsidize attacks on competitors in different countries. But it also requires the company to jointly manage its competitive position in each country, rather than leave that task just to local management. Other competitors then need to respond via increased global market participation, global marketing, or globally integrated competitive strategy to avoid a downward spiral of sequentially weakened positions in individual countries.

Interdependence among countries makes entry more difficult. An incumbent competitor can be expected to retaliate more fiercely in order to protect its interdependent position. Protecting the share of a subsidiary becomes doubly important when that also means preserving the cost position of subsidiaries in other countries. Interdependence among countries also increases rivalry among existing international competitors. It requires competitors to worry about their market share in multiple countries simultaneously. In particular, they will be much more willing to give up profits in one country in order to protect their position in other dependent countries.

GLOBALIZED COMPETITORS

Competitors are globalized to the extent that they use the global strategy levers of global market participation, global products and services, global location of activities, global marketing, and global competitive moves. When a business's competitors use global strategy to exploit industry globalization potential, the business needs to match or pre-empt these competitors. These moves include expansion into or within major markets, being the first to introduce a standardized product, or being the first to use a uniform marketing program. Competitors pursuing a global strategy place pressure on the industry as a whole to globalize. For example, competitors that push globally standardized products or use globally uniform marketing will influence customers to find global products and marketing more acceptable.

UNILEVER'S FAILED BID FOR
RICHARDSON-VICKS

The need to preempt a global competitor can be the spur to increased market participation. In 1986 Unilever, the Anglo-Dutch consumer products company, sought to increase its participation in the American market by launching a hostile takeover bid for Richardson-Vicks, a U.S.-based multinational manufacturer of toiletry and health care products. Unilever's global archrival, Procter & Gamble, saw the threat to its home turf and outbid Unilever to capture Richardson-Vicks. With Richardson-Vicks' European system Procter was able to greatly strengthen its participation in Unilever's base markets in Europe. So Unilever's attempt to expand participation in a rival's home market backfired to allow the rival to expand participation in Unilever's home markets.

Globalized existing competitors reduce the threat of entry from new entrants: There are more likely to be powerful multinational incumbents defending each market. Incumbents with integrated global strategies can draw on their worldwide assets and resources to suppress potential national entrants. Major U.S. consumer goods companies have typically viewed Europe as a single, broad market and, consequently, deployed their assets across national boundaries. This globalized posture has made it more difficult for their European competitors to enter and compete in markets other than their home country. In contrast, until spurred by Europe 1992, European companies tended to focus their efforts in a single, national market. A 1988 study of 45 major European food companies found that half had a presence in only one or two countries.[39]

Globalized existing competitors also increase industry rivalry by increasing the geographic scope of competition. Competition between globally integrated competitors becomes battles between global systems, not just single-country one-on-one combat. In one household product category competitors began to pay more attention to each other once one company clearly became global and started to make major inroads into the other competitors' markets.

Citicorp's Moves in Asia   In the 1990s, Citicorp sought to strengthen its presence in Asia, a region where stiff competition already existed.[40] Chase Manhattan and J. P. Morgan, two other U.S.-based banks, and HSBC, a Hong Kong–based bank that already operated in 71 countries in the mid-1990s, were formidable Citicorp rivals in Asia.[41] Despite this stiff competition, Citicorp continued to generate impressive profits. Citicorp was able to build a successful franchise in Asia because Asians perceived the bank to be a sophisticated place to work and a harbor for serious money. Because of such an impressive image amongst Asians, Citicorp has been able to woo wealthy customers who demanded exceptional service.

TRANSFERABLE COMPETITIVE ADVANTAGE

Perhaps the ultimate globalization driver is the global transferability of competitive advantage. Some competitive advantages, such as technology-based ones, are easily transferable with little adaptation. In consequence, global companies engaged in global

GE'S GLOBAL MOVES IN MAJOR APPLIANCES

In the appliance industry, globalized competitors have greatly increased industry rivalry. The formation of strategic alliances between Whirlpool and Maytag in efforts to give them a global advantage provoked General Electric (GE) to alter its strategy and globalize its efforts as well. In the 1960s, GE had closed down its production operations in Italy to get out of the European appliance market altogether. By concentrating on the U.S. market, GE increased its market share to a comfortable 30 percent level.

But the globalization of its competitors exerted pressure on GE. In an effort to match its competitors' globalizing moves, GE decided to enhance its world market position before 1992, when the European Community would remove its remaining barriers to internal trade. In 1989, GE formed a joint venture with Britain's General Electric Company (GEC) whereby GE purchased 50 percent of GEC's European appliance business for $575 million.

competition populate such industries. Other advantages are much more locally rooted, especially advantages based on local knowledge or local relationships. Industries based on those advantages tend to be multilocal. The legal industry perhaps typifies the type of industry based on local knowledge (of laws) and local relationships (with mostly national or local clients). In consequence, there are few genuinely global law firms, although there are a number operating as global alliances.

COMPETITIVE GLOBALIZATION DRIVERS IN SERVICE BUSINESSES

Most competitive globalization drivers apply equally in service businesses. But at the same time, global competition seems to be seldom as fierce. Because most services cannot *yet* be centrally produced, these sectors lack the competitive disturbance of a rival operating globally from a low-cost/high-productivity base. So competition still tends to occur on a country-by-country basis where customers are located. In consequence the fiercest competition in services is often between firms from the same country: British Airways fights Virgin Atlantic, while allied with, rather than competing with, American Airlines; and Hertz versus Avis. But international competition in service businesses is starting to happen, especially as non-U.S. firms catch up with the lead of U.S. firms in many service sectors: Britain's WPP against U.S. advertising agencies, Europe's DHL versus the U.S.'s FedEx, Britain's BBC starting to challenge the U.S.'s CNN, and Hong Kong's HSBC going up against Citibank.

EFFECT OF THE INTERNET ON COMPETITIVE GLOBALIZATION DRIVERS

The Internet heightens the intensity of global competition in several ways. First, "Internet time" accelerates the needed speed of moves and countermoves. Second, the Web creates a public forum for signaling, making it easier for competitors to communicate with each other legally. Third, comparison of competitors becomes much easier for potential customers, especially in terms of price transparency—the Web allowing for both cross-competitor and cross-border comparisons. Fourth, the Web makes it easier for companies with a given

---

Market Globalization Drivers

The Internet
- Increases global commonality in customer needs and tastes
- Enables global customers
- Facilitates global channels
- Supports global marketing
- Highlights lead countries

Cost Globalization Drivers

The Internet
- Drives down global economies of scale and scope
- Enhances global sourcing efficiencies
- Speeds up global logistics
- Exploits differences in country costs
- Reduces product development costs

Government Globalization Drivers

The Internet
- Sidesteps trade barriers
- Spurs global technical standards
- Confronts diverse marketing regulations
- Depends on legal systems

Competitive Globalization Drivers

The Internet
- Accelerates needed speed of moves
- Creates public forum for signaling
- Makes competitor comparison easier
- Aids global transferability of competitive advantages
- Creates "born global" rivals

Source: George S. Yip, "Global Strategy in the Internet Era," *Business Strategy Review,* Vol. 11, No. 2, Winter 2000, pp. 1–14.

EXHIBIT 2-8   Internet Effects on Industry Globalization Drivers

competitive advantage to transfer and leverage that advantage globally in the ways already discussed (by reducing the amount of physical investments needed). Fifth, for existing industry leaders or incumbents, the Internet era has created the phenomenon of new "born global" Web-based rivals with global reach from the day they put up a Web site.

In this chapter we have discussed many effects of the Internet on all types of industry globalization drivers. Exhibit 2-8 summarizes these effects.

This chapter has described the external, industry-based globalization drivers that affect whether businesses should use globally integrated strategies. The next five chapters will address the use of each of the five major types of global strategy levers available to a business—global market participation, global products and services, global location of activities, global marketing, and global competitive moves.

GUIDELINES FOR DIAGNOSING INDUSTRY GLOBALIZATION POTENTIAL

Getting a good understanding of industry globalization potential is the starting point for developing an effective total global strategy.[42] In diagnosing this potential, managers should find the following guidelines useful:

- Do not assume that industries are either global or not global. Instead, nearly every industry has globalization potential in some aspects and not others.
- Different industry globalization drivers can operate in different directions, some favoring globalization and others making it difficult and inadvisable.
- Businesses can respond selectively to industry globalization drivers, by globalizing only those elements of strategy affected by favorable drivers.
- The level of globalization potential changes over time.
- Industry globalization drivers can work at a regional or continental scale as well as at a global scale.
- Industry competitors can themselves affect some globalization drivers. The competitors that stimulate these changes typically reap the major benefits.

Discussion and Research Questions

1. Select an industry and analyze its globalization drivers as they were five years ago, today, and what they are likely to be in five years' time.
2. Which aspects of this industry are most in favor of the use of global strategy? Which aspects are least in favor of its use?
3. What other drivers of globalization are not included in this chapter but should be?
4. How do industry globalization drivers affect companies' choice of global strategies?
5. What is different about globalization drivers for service industries?
6. How does the Internet affect industry globalization potential?

Notes

1. Comments on service businesses are adapted from Christopher H. Lovelock and George S. Yip, "Developing Global Strategies for Service Businesses," *California Management Review,* Vol. 37, No. 3, Winter 1996, pp. 64–86. Additional examples were developed by Christine Blanchet and Dominique Litmaath, both MBA students at the Anderson School at UCLA.

2. Comments in this chapter and elsewhere on the effects of the Internet are adapted from George S. Yip, "Global Strategy in the Internet Era," *Business Strategy Review,* Vol. 11, No. 2, Winter 2000, pp. 1–14.

3. Michael E. Porter, *Competitive Strategy: Techniques for Analyzing Industries and Competitors* (New York: The Free Press, 1980).

4. Ibid.

5. Michael E. Porter, *The Competitive Advantage of Nations* (New York: The Free Press, 1990).

6. Comments in this chapter and elsewhere about service businesses are drawn primarily from Christopher H. Lovelock and George S. Yip, "Developing Global Strategies for Service Businesses," *California Management Review,* Vol. 37, No. 3, Winter 1996, pp. 64–86.

7. Johny K. Johansson, "Japanese Service Industries and Their Overseas Potential,"

The Service Industries Journal, Vol. 10, No. 1, January 1990, pp. 85–109.

8. Christopher H. Lovelock, *Services Marketing,* 2nd ed. (Upper Saddle River, NJ: Prentice Hall, 1991); and Christopher H. Lovelock, *Product Plus: How Product + Service = Competitive Advantage* (New York: McGraw-Hill, 1994).

9. Richard B. Chase, "Where Does the Customer Fit in a Service Operation?" *Harvard Business Review,* November–December 1978, pp. 137–42.

10. See also Pradeep A. Rau and John F. Preble, "Standardization of Marketing Strategy by Multinationals," *International Marketing Review,* Autumn 1987, pp. 18–28.

11. The strength of national preference is illustrated by the French dictionary of food, which devoted many paragraphs to each of the many types of French cheese but had this entry only for cheddar: "a cheese much eaten by the English." Charles de Gaulle once complained that it was impossible to govern a country that had a thousand different cheeses. America, of course, has instead 31 flavors of ice cream (according to Baskin-Robbins at any rate).

12. David A. Stout, Head of Economics, Unilever PLC, "Competition in Foods on the World Stage," *Financial Times* Centenary Conference, London, England, February 8, 1988.

13. William Glasgall, "Japan on Wall Street," *Business Week,* September 7, 1987, pp. 82–90.

14. For a further analysis of Japanese global strategy, see George S. Yip, "Global Strategy as a Factor in Japanese Success," *The International Executive,* Vol. 38, No. 1, pp. 145–67, special issue on Japan, January/February 1996; and Yoko Ishikura and George S. Yip, "Chapter 2. Japan—Still Bubbling," in George S. Yip, *Asian Advantage: Key Strategies for Winning in the Asia-Pacific Region (Updated Edition—After the Crisis)* (Cambridge, MA: Perseus Publishing, 2000).

15. David B. Montgomery, and George S. Yip, "The Challenge of Global Customer Management," *Marketing Management,* October–December 2000.

16. David J. Collis, "Saatchi and Saatchi Company, PLC," Case No. 1-387-170 (Boston, MA: Harvard Business School, revised 4/88).

17. Data from McKinsey & Company study, "Managing International Retailers," London, 1999.

18. Takayuki Amano, Sheila Colgan, and Mika Palosuo, "Reinsurance Industry," unpublished study (Washington, DC: Georgetown Business School, 1989).

19. See John A. Quelch and Edward J. Hoff, "Customizing Global Marketing," *Harvard Business Review,* May–June 1986, pp. 59–68; and Dean M. Peebles, "Don't Write Off Global Advertising: A Commentary," *International Marketing Review,* Vol. 6, No. 1, 1989, pp. 73–78.

20. Gatignon and Abeele suggest that one test for the transferability of marketing is the extent to which sales response elasticities to marketing expenditures are the same across countries. Thus, if the response of sales to advertising expenditure is similar in two countries, that is a starting point for assuming that the content of the advertising may be transferable. See Hubert Gatignon and Piet Vanden Abeele, "Can You Standardize Marketing Programs Internationally? Cross-Country Determinants of Marketing Mix Effectiveness," Marketing Science Institute Mini-Conference on Global Marketing, Cambridge, MA, May 1990.

21. See George S. Yip, "Gateways to Entry," *Harvard Business Review,* September–October 1982, pp. 85–92.

22. Based on international polls and census information, Global Reach, a technology research firm in San Francisco, estimates that 128 million of the nearly 280 million people who use the Internet speak languages other than English. (David Kushner, *New York Times Service,* reported in "An Electronic Tower of Babel?" *International Herald Tribune,* April 24, 2000, p. 10.)

23. See Thomas Hout, Michael E. Porter, and Eileen Rudden, "How Global Companies Win Out," *Harvard Business Review,* September–October 1982, pp. 98–108; and Michael E. Porter, *The Competitive Advantage of Nations* (New York: The Free Press, 1990).

24. See Porter, *The Competitive Advantage of Nations,* who searched 10 countries, including smaller ones like Denmark and Switzerland, for industries in which these 10 countries led.

25. See also Janice McCormick and Nan Stone, "From National Champion to Global Competitor: An Interview with Thomson's Alain Gomez," *Harvard Business Review,* May–June 1990, pp. 127–35.

26. Marquise R. Cvar, "Case Studies in Global Competition: Patterns of Success and Failure," in *Competition in Global Industries,* Michael E. Porter, Ed. (Boston, MA: Harvard Business School Press, 1986), pp. 483–516.

27. See Philip Evans and Thomas S. Würster, *Blown to Bits: How the New Economics of Information Transforms Strategy* (Boston, MA: Harvard Business School Press, 1999).

28. J. E. Frook, "Automotive Extranet Lights Fire Globally," *Internet Week,* special volume, April 20, 1998, p. 1.

29. See Constantinos C. Markides and Norman Berg, "Manufacturing Offshore Is Bad Business," *Harvard Business Review,* September–October 1988, pp. 113–20.

30. Estimates provided by Gerrit Jeelof, vice-chairman, Board of Management, Philips N.V. See Gerrit Jeelof, "Global Strategies of Philips," *European Management Journal,* Vol. 7, No. 1, 1989, pp. 84–91.

31. See also Yves Doz, *Government Control and Multinational Management* (New York: Praeger, 1979); and —— , "Government Policies and Global Industries," in *Competition in Global Industries,* Michael E. Porter, Ed. (Boston, MA: Harvard Business School Press, 1986), pp. 225–66. In addition Spence cites three public sector activities that can protect domestic competitors: blocking access to the domestic market, providing subsidies, and creating spillovers in research and development. See A. Michael Spence, "Industrial Organization and Competitive Advantage in Multinational Industries," *American Economic Review,* Vol. 74, No. 2, May 1984, pp. 356–60.

32. Jane Ashton, William Kummel, Elizabeth Powell, and Mary Colman St. John, "The Magazine Publishing Industry: A Global Strategy Analysis," unpublished report (Washington, DC: Georgetown Business School, 1989).

33. Susan B. Berg, Richard B. Bruno, Michael J. Derr, R. Scott Handel, and Stephen B. Straske, "The Newsprint Industry: An Analysis of Globalization Potential," unpublished report (Washington, DC: Georgetown University, 1989).

34. Adapted from Joseph B. Treaster, "A Huge Insurance Merger: AXA and UAP in France," *The New York Times,* November 13, 1996, p. C2.

35. Stephen Bowen, senior vice president, Northern Telecom Limited (Canada).

36. Adapted from "Not Quite Magic," *The Economist,* February 22, 1997, pp. 67–73.

37. Lupton Alsop Dibb, "EU E-Commerce Policy," *DLA Upstream,* March 2000, pp. 2–7.

38. These four concerns are raised by Yves L. Doz, "Government Policies and Global Industries," in *Competition in Global Industries,* Michael E. Porter, Ed. (Boston: Harvard Business School Press, 1986). See also Yves L. Doz, *Government Control and Multinational Strategic Management* (New York: Praeger, 1979); and Dennis J. Encarnation and Louis T. Wells, Jr., "Competitive Strategies in Global Industries: A View from Host Governments," in Porter, *Competition in Global Industries.*

39. Study conducted by The MAC Group for *The Cost of Non-Europe,* Basic Findings, Vol. 12, Part B, Commission of the European Community, Brussels, 1988.

40. "The Top 500 World Banks," *Thomson Bank Directory,* June–November 1995.

41. Carol J. Loomis, "Citicorp: John Reed's Second Act," *Fortune,* Vol. 133, No. 8, April 29, 1996, pp. 88–98.

42. For an example of an analysis of the globalization potential of an industry, see George S. Yip and George A. Coundouriotis, "Diagnosing Industry Globalization Potential: The World Chocolate Confectionery Industry," *Planning Review,* January/February 1991, pp. 4–14.

3

BUILDING GLOBAL MARKET PARTICIPATION

—⫷⫸—

This chapter presents a new, global-strategy-oriented way of viewing market participation. Instead of selecting country-markets on the basis of stand-alone attractiveness, managers need to consider how participation in a particular country will contribute to globalization benefits and the global competitive position of the business.

Participating in markets outside the home country acts as a lever for both internationalization (the geographic expansion of activities) and globalization (the global integration of strategy). But in the internationalization mode managers select countries based on stand-alone attractiveness. In contrast, when used as a global strategy lever, market participation involves selecting countries on the basis of their potential contribution to globalization benefits and to the global competitive position of the business. The same considerations also apply to determining the level at which to participate—primarily the target market share—and the nature of participation—building a plant, setting up a joint venture, and so on. Managers may, of course, often make market selection decisions from a mixture of motives, and many multinational companies have grown that way.[1] The key is to recognize that there is a difference in the two motivations and in their potential consequences.

BASIS FOR GLOBAL EXPANSION

Chapter 2 discussed how industry globalization drivers decide the potential for companies in an industry to use global strategies. But the company itself and its characteristics also affect its potential for globalization. How does a company decide whether it even has a basis for global expansion? It is critical to have one or more of the following:

- A business model that is internationally transferable
- A strong basis of competitive advantage that can be leveraged internationally
- An economy where the company's industry is more developed than those in most other economies

TRANSFERABLE BUSINESS MODEL

Companies seeking to globalize need a globally transferable business model. Let's first distinguish between a *business model* and a *strategy*. A business model can be viewed as the way in which a company transforms inputs to add value for particular customer groups and includes the way in which it is managed. For example, McDonald's has a very clear business model: It takes relatively low-quality food ingredients, unskilled labor, retail locations, and buildings and—through a very rigorous, standardized process—transforms them into a particular kind of food service experience for mass market customers. A strategy can be better viewed as the way in which a company changes its business model. And global strategy can be thought of as the way in which

HEINEKEN'S FIRST INTERNATIONAL MARKETS

The internationalization history of Heineken, the Dutch brewer, provides a classic example of choices made on the basis of stand-alone attractiveness. Heineken's first international markets were Egypt, Ceylon, Singapore, Indonesia, the West Indies, and the Congo. What did these six countries have in common? Heineken chose the first five countries because they were either former Dutch colonies or on shipping routes to them. These factors made those markets very attractive to Heineken, even though each country had little effect on Heineken's global position. The last country on the list, the Congo, came about because a Belgian brewer, which also had business in the Congo, had been sold to a Belgian bank, which then asked Heineken to take care of the company.[2] Most other multinational companies can tell a similar story of one-by-one decisions based on country-by-country stand-alone attractiveness and happenstance. As the world's most global beer company (in terms of international revenues), Heineken now recognizes the global strategic importance of major markets like North America. The company has a major target of building up its business in the United States and Canada.

JAPANESE COMPANIES' EXPANSION PATHS

In contrast to Heineken's experience, the internationalization of Japanese companies provides many examples of a global strategy approach to market selection. One study found three typical paths of expansion, each exhibiting a clear global plan.[3] The most common was to move from Japan to developing countries to developed countries. This occurred in steel, automobiles, petrochemicals, consumer electronics, home appliances, watches, and cameras. In this path the Japanese companies built up experience and capacity in the smaller and easier developing countries. Typically, the United States was then the first developed country to be penetrated, because of its large size; its relative closeness to Japan; and the lower level of tariff, cultural, and language barriers than in Europe. The second expansion path—going straight to developed countries, particularly the United States—occurred in high-technology industries such as computers and semiconductors. In this expansion mode the Japanese also sometimes used countries similar to the United States as trial markets. Fujitsu used Australia this way in computers. A third expansion path was to start directly with developed countries. This happened with products for which the Japanese home market was still not developed or too small—videotape recorders, color televisions, and sewing machines.

a company adapts and globally expands its domestic business model to achieve a global business model.

At its simplest, the most globalizable business models are those that seek to impose the company's logic on the marketplace: The model requires customers to change their behavior rather than the company changing to meet customers' existing behavior. This sounds like the opposite of the marketing concept. But reflection will show that many

of the most successful new products and services have changed customer behavior—
Xerox copiers, Polaroid cameras, Sony Walkmans, Boeing 747, Apple Macintosh, and
McDonald's, as well as Internet services such as Amazon.com and Yahoo! This kind of
model finds international success easy because it minimizes the need to adapt to local
conditions and customers. In contrast, business models that depend on adaptation and
customization find globalization much more difficult.

Three examples from clothes retailing illustrate this point. Italy's Benetton has
been very successful in global expansion, while Britain's Marks and Spencer has not. In
2001, the Benetton Group operated in 120 countries, while Marks and Spencer was in
the process of closing most of its overseas ventures. Benetton's business model is to provide fashion clothing that has no distinct national characteristics and to promote it on
the basis that wearers become part of Benetton's global community, "The United
Colors of Benetton." In such a business model, finding and maintaining the right fashion edge is the difficult part, but globalizing it is easy. Benetton does little local adaptation, even though it allows local stores autonomy in what they order from the
company's fixed global ranges. Similarly, Spain's Zara clothing stores focus on a globally standardized range that imitates expensive designer labels. By 2001 Zara had expanded to 33 countries; and its parent company, Inditex, went public in the same year,
achieving a market capitalization of $10 billion. In contrast, Marks and Spencer's busi-
ness model has been to meet the distinct clothing (and grocery) needs of the middle
market of Britain. While quality and service are also essential parts of this model, it is
adaptation to the special needs of British customers that is the central part of the model.
Inherently such a model is far more difficult to export. The company tried and failed to
adapt this model to meet the special needs of French customers in France and other
countries. Its purchase of Brooks Brothers, an American company with a similar business model of local adaptation (albeit for a more upscale clientele), created no value as
Marks and Spencer could add nothing. Today, even its British business model is in serious trouble.

In contrast to Marks and Spencer, the U.S.'s Wal-Mart chain of discount stores continues to be hugely successful in its domestic market. But like Marks and Spencer, Wal-
Mart has found great difficulty in international expansion. For example, it took the
company a number of years to learn to adapt to the Argentine market. Why the difficulty? The problem lies in the broad scope of both Wal-Mart's and Marks and Spencer's
product ranges, inherent in being general merchandise stores. Niche retailers such as
Benetton, Zara, and IKEA need to make only minimal adaptations: Foreign customers
either like their focused offerings or they do not. Mass retailers need to adapt to *many*
aspects of the lives of their foreign customers, a far harder task.

LEVERAGEABLE COMPETITIVE ADVANTAGE

Firms usually need an initial competitive advantage that they can leverage into international markets. Recent research shows that for newly internationalizing firms, the initial competitive advantage is the single greatest determinant of international success,
outweighing the process used in internationalization.[4]

While there are many different bases of competitive advantage, companies may
find it useful to think about six categories of advantage: customer market, products and
services, business system or value chain, assets and resources, partners, and scale and

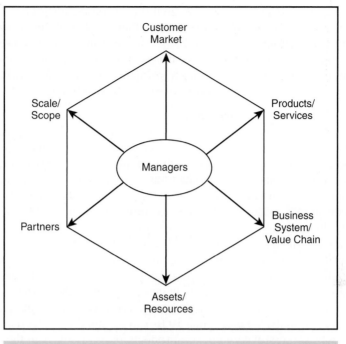

EXHIBIT 3-1 The Hexagon of Competitive Advantage

Source: George S. Yip, "Bases of Competitive Advantage," in Stuart Crainer and Des Dearlove, Eds., *Financial Times Handbook of Management,* 2nd ed. (London: Financial Times/Prentice Hall, 2001), pp. 253–263.

scope. Exhibit 3-1 depicts these categories around a hexagon, illustrating the idea that a company can start from any corner of the hexagon but needs eventually to add strength at every point.[5]

Customer Market Advantage

Being the first company to enter or create a new market, or the first to serve a group of customers, constitutes one of the most common early bases of competitive advantage. Initially, such a company has no competitors at all, which is the ultimate competitive advantage. When Xerox created the market for plain paper photocopiers, it totally dominated this new market, protected by its patents and unique products. Market dominance is a better way of viewing Xerox's competitive advantage at this stage rather than, say, product superiority. There simply were not any competitive products. Many new dot-coms also have this as their first basis of advantage (which also makes clear that once competition comes in, dot-coms need other bases of advantage).

It is also important to note that some successful companies never achieve an advantage in terms of market or customer dominance other than through other bases such as product superiority, which then yield preference by customers in market segments. A quintessential example is Singapore Airlines, which, starting from one of the smallest countries in the world (Singapore even today has a population of fewer than 3 million), has become one of the world's leading airlines and consistently one of the most profitable and most highly rated among business travelers. Lastly, owning a customer market can be a major basis of advantage even if the customers do not like the company. It has been estimated that in Britain the average bank account lasts longer than the average marriage. Do customers love their banks? No. But they stay with them through inertia. In contrast, some companies have such a good relationship with their customer base that the latter will buy almost anything from them—in the case of Britain's Virgin group, everything from air and train travel to music to investments.

Product and Service Advantage

Having a superior product or service is, of course, a very common basis of competitive advantage. Such superiority can range from minor items to very major ones. Toyota's innovation of a coffee cup holder in its automobile models represents perhaps one of the smallest yet most successful product-based advantages. This product feature, costing less than .01 percent of the total value of the car, gained Toyota many sales in the United States during the brief period before its competitors imitated this product innovation. At the other extreme, product superiority can be so great as to constitute a new category that in turn yields the additional basis of advantage of market dominance. Product superiority can also be built up slowly over time. Both Singapore Airlines and Toyota, starting from initial positions of product inferiority, continually improved their products until they achieved superiority in many aspects of their offerings. Only continuing product superiority has kept Apple Computer alive in its fight against the Microsoft standard, outnumbered more than 10 to 1 in installed base. At the same time, companies may be successful with inferior products, most famously in the case of Microsoft's DOS operating system.

We also have to be careful to understand the underlying reality of an apparent product-based source of competitive advantage. Often, this advantage springs from other bases in the hexagon. For example, the best-selling book *The Discipline of Market Leaders*[6] cites product superiority as a primary reason for Hertz's success in the automobile rental market, such as in its faster, more efficient express service (Gold Service in the United States). But why can Hertz offer a service superior to that of its competitors? Is it because Avis and National do not know how Hertz does it? No. There are no secrets in the car rental business. Nor is it because Avis and National do not have the desire to imitate Hertz. The real barrier to imitation lies in the sixth base of competitive advantage—scale. By virtue of being larger than its competitors, Hertz has more buses circling airports, larger facilities, better computer systems, more cars, and more staff. It is these scale-based advantages that yield the advantage of product superiority and not the other way around. So Hertz is not number one because it offers superior service. It is able to offer superior service because it is number one.[7]

Business System/Value-Chain Advantage

The value-adding chain, also known as the business system, comprises all the activities that a business conducts. A typical sequence begins with research and development, runs through production, and finishes with selling, marketing, distribution, and after-sales service. The value chain can provide advantage to a company, first, if the company is superior in one or more elements of the value chain. Many companies have built up superiority in particular elements over long periods of time: 3M's superior research and development capability, Procter & Gamble's marketing skills, Dell Computer's distribution system, Sony's innovative designs, Toyota's superiority in production operations, and companies such as American Express in customer service. An alternative or additional source of value-chain superiority is to coordinate the chain better than competitors.[8] The just-in-time movement can be interpreted as an effort at better coordination of the value chain. The enthusiasm for business process reengineering also qualifies as a way of obtaining competitive advantage through reconfiguration of the value chain. Southwest Airlines became the most profitable airline in the United States, partly through redesigning its value chain in order to speed up turnaround. This required the coordination of several elements of the business system: the passengers, the check-in process, the boarding process (boarding not by row numbers but by position in the row—window seats first, then center seats, then aisle seats), and in terms of operations and turnaround service of inbound and outbound flights. A number of Hong Kong hotel chains, such as The Peninsula and the Mandarin Oriental, are renowned for their impeccable service, the best in the world. But this service is merely the tip experienced by guests of an entire business system dedicated to supporting the point of customer interface. One way of viewing the efforts at achieving value-chain superiority is that they all have the same end objectives of delivering products and services better, faster, or cheaper.

Assets/Resources

Assets—tangible ones, which can range from factories to patents, and intangible ones, such as brand names and reputation—provide another powerful basis for competitive advantage. Perhaps the most interesting aspect of asset-based competitive advantage is that these assets have often been generated in much earlier periods. One of Coca-Cola's primary bases of competitive advantage is the fact that it has the best known brand name in the world (a fact confirmed in numerous surveys). Yet the power of this brand name has been built up over a period of 100 years through continual investment in advertising and other forms of promotion, as well as association with Coca-Cola's high-quality products. (But brands are a particularly tricky form of asset. For example, some analysts value Microsoft's brands at over $50 billion.[9] But people do not buy Microsoft products because of the brand. Without the patents and installed base, Microsoft's brands are worth almost nothing.) Another key basis of Coca-Cola's advantage is its asset of both its physical distribution system—comprising many company-owned bottling plants and trucks, warehouse, and other distribution facilities—as well as its less tangible network of franchised bottlers. This asset has also taken decades to build up. So a very high proportion of Coca-Cola's current competitive advantage is based on assets built up by previous generations of managers.

Sometimes an asset-based advantage can come from a complementary asset rather than one that is directly in the value chain of the company. Not least among Singapore Airlines' competitive advantages is the fact that its base, Singapore's Changi airport, is one of the world's finest. This airport is not directly owned by Singapore Airlines but by the government of Singapore, which is also the primary shareholder of Singapore Airlines. Most noteworthy is the fact that while Singapore is one of the world's smallest countries, with a physical area of only 250 square miles, its airport is among the most spacious in the world. The Singaporean government has chosen to make this investment.

For many natural resource companies, assets are often the sole basis of competitive advantage. This is the case for many state-owned energy companies, whose primary competitive advantage is the fact that they have assets in the ground—oil and gas reserves—that can be extracted at lower cost than those of rival countries. Generally, companies operating in the natural resource sector typically owe their competitive advantage to ownership or access to low-cost and/or high-quality sources of raw materials. As one executive from a major mining company put it, "Ownership of the ore in the ground is our only source of competitive advantage." Like any other basis of competitive advantage, assets and resources can be underutilized, perhaps more so. The dramatic improvement of Disney's fortunes from the late 1980s to the late 1990s, under Michael Eisner's stewardship, lay primarily in his ability to make much better use of Disney's underexploited assets of film properties, brand names, and characters.

Partner Advantage

Having the right partners can also provide a very powerful basis of competitive advantage. Microsoft's true initial basis of competitive advantage was its partnership with IBM. Rover was in serious difficulties until it acquired Honda as a new joint venture partner in the 1980s. Honda was able to help Rover so much that the British company became a valuable property and was able to sell itself to BMW, much to Honda's chagrin (but perhaps subsequent relief seeing that BMW turned out to be not such a successful partner). Many companies have gone on to surpass their partners. Microsoft's fortunes have certainly prospered much more than those of IBM. Numerous Asian manufacturers have begun as original equipment suppliers to American and European partners, only to overtake them later. The emphasis on strategic alliances illustrates the criticality of having the right partners. Indeed, Dow Corning, the U.S. chemicals producer, identifies its ability to create and manage alliances as one of its critical sources of competitive advantage.

Scale and Scope Advantage

Companies can also gain advantage from economies of scale or of scope, economies of scale being the reduction in unit cost with increased production volume, while economies of scope come from sharing costs across multiple products or lines of business. Market share usually drives these economies. Depending on the industry, economies of scale may flatten out at relatively small market shares. Such industries are fragmented ones in which no competitor can dominate the industry or gain a large share, such as many retailing sectors, apparel manufacturing, and the like. Economies of scale and scope, or even just sheer size, can yield many advantages, some of which may not be obvious to the companies themselves or their competitors. This chapter has already referenced the example of Hertz's express service. Other companies recognize that size is perhaps their main advantage. In early 2000, Barclays Bank began an advertising campaign in Britain to stress how "big" the company is, linking bigness to customer benefits such as being able to provide free Internet banking. By inference, Barclays was admitting that it could offer few other advantages.

Adding to Bases of Advantage

While it is important to be superior in some basis of advantage, the real power comes not from being good in one base but from putting together multiple bases of advantage. The truly successful companies are the ones that manage to build on their initial base of advantage, increasing the advantage in that base, while continually adding other bases of advantage.

Using Competitive Advantages to Globalize

Clearly, the more transferable advantages a company has, and the more dominant these advantages, the easier it is to globalize. Companies with highly dominant positions, such as Microsoft, can globalize very quickly indeed.[10]

HOW SINGAPORE AIRLINES FLEW TO THE TOP

Singapore Airlines provides an example of a company that started from one base of advantage and rapidly added others. Like many other companies from developing countries, Singapore Airlines' first source of competitive advantage was low labor costs, giving it an edge in the business system. So, initially, Singapore Airlines was able to offer cheaper flights. Another source of advantage was its ability to attain very high levels of service, partly due to cultural factors and partly due to management attention. So Singapore Airlines was rapidly able to add an advantage in the product/service corner of the hexagon. The Singapore government, which majority-owns Singapore Airlines, contributed significantly to building up a collateral asset, Changi airport, as an asset-based source of competitive advantage.

The company has consciously used its fleet of planes as a source of competitive advantage, constantly upgrading them, and proudly advertises that it has the world's youngest fleet of planes. The company has also assiduously built up a network of partners through alliances. These alliances improve the feed of passengers and also encourage passengers from Asia to use Singapore Airlines in order to make easier connections in the United States and in Europe. But despite all this success, Singapore Airlines is still a relatively small airline and does not much enjoy economies of scale and scope relative to its competitors.

Lastly, as discussed earlier, Singapore Airlines has never enjoyed an advantage in terms of dominance of a market or customer base, given how small its home country is. While the city of Singapore is geographically convenient as a hub for flights between Europe, North America, Southeast Asia, and Australasia, other nearby airports are similarly convenient—Kuala Lumpur, Jakarta, Bangkok. As these neighbors upgrade their airport facilities and the quality of service of their national carriers, Singapore Airlines will face increased competition. Singapore Airlines is also facing another source of competition. It has found that even Singaporeans are not particularly loyal to their national carrier when faced with the lure of frequent flyer miles from major American carriers. So, Singapore Airlines offered its own frequent flyer program by participating in a pan-Asian consortium, Passages.

BEING FROM A MORE DEVELOPED ECONOMY

In the case of global expansion, having an advantage need only be relative to each specific country entered. Hence, a firm with weak competitive advantages at home may still have a competitive advantage in foreign markets. This would be particularly the case for firms moving from more developed economies to less developed ones. This effect is illustrated by the "pyramid of international competitive advantage" in Exhibit 3-2. In this pyramid, firms selling "down" to less developed economies (which usually but not always have less demanding markets) find it relatively easy to have a competitive advantage in the entered market. Firms selling "sideways" to economies of similar development need to work a bit to create an advantage, perhaps through local adaptation. Lastly, firms selling "up" to more developed economies have to work really hard to establish a competitive advantage, perhaps through lower prices or by focusing on a market niche.[11]

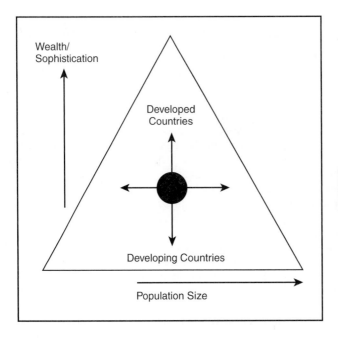

EXHIBIT 3-2 The Pyramid of International Competitive Advantage

Source: Stephen B. Tallman and George S. Yip, Chapter 12, "Strategy and the Multinational Enterprise," in Thomas Brewer and Alan M. Rugman, Eds., *The Oxford Handbook of International Business* (Oxford, England: Oxford University Press, 2001).

GLOBAL MARKET PARTICIPATION FOR SERVICE BUSINESSES

Global market participation can often be easier for service businesses:

- Being less visible, they usually provoke fewer trade and investment barriers (an interesting exception being that despite the North American Free Trade Agreement, Canada keeps out U.S. management consultants, to protect Canadian consultants? or Canadian clients?).
- Often having lower minimum efficient scale, service businesses can set up incrementally, incurring less risk, commitment, and competitive retaliation.
- But many regulated services, such as telecommunications and media, find foreign entry very hard (see discussion below on globally blocked industries).

Services that operate as part of a global network provide a special case in global market participation. For network firms—such as airlines, financial services, and logistics companies—highly specific geographic locations may be seen as essential. No financial service firm with global ambitions, for instance, can afford not to have a presence in New York, London, and Tokyo. Travel-related services benefit from wider global market participation: The service becomes more valuable to a customer. Thus, American Express traveler's checks and credit cards are useful precisely because they are widely accepted in most countries. Similarly, international airlines enhance their appeal as they fly to more destinations. (One exception is France's AOM, which advertises that it has daily flights to Tahiti and Nice but none to Detroit.)

ACCOR'S GLOBAL EXPANSION

Accor (the French-owned hotel company that operates under the Sofitel, Novotel, Mercure, Ibis, Motel 6, and Formula 1 hotel brands) has embarked on a series of acquisitions and pursued a number of management contracts in order to build a strong and balanced market presence as the premier low-budget hotel company in the world. In order to enter the United States, a large low-budget hotel market, Accor bought the Motel 6 chain in 1990. At the time of the acquisition, Motel 6 was one of the United States' largest low-budget hotels with over 500 motels in 42 states.[12] To build a market presence in Asia, one of the fastest growing areas of the world, Accor has either purchased hotels and/or signed management contracts in order to take control and change the names of already established hotels. In 1993, Accor purchased 40 percent of Quality Pacific, an Australian hotel chain, and, in the rest of the 1990s, aggressively pursued management contracts in order to establish the Novotel, Ibis, and Mercure names in Asia.[13] While gaining a strong foothold in the United States and Asia, Accor also continued to pursue strategic opportunities to expand its low-budget reach in Europe, its home market.

EFFECTS OF THE INTERNET ON GLOBAL MARKET PARTICIPATION

By substituting for or supplementing physical activities, the Internet makes it easier for companies to participate in foreign markets. The advent of global strategy meant that companies started to pull back from smaller or nonstrategic markets in order to reduce costs. The Internet makes it more economically feasible to once again serve these noncore markets. Ironically, the Internet is allowing companies to return to the multinational era when companies sought a presence in as many countries as possible. Today, companies can participate in core countries with physical presence supplemented by Web activities, while they can participate in noncore countries with a Web presence supplemented by some physical activities.

The instant global reach of the Internet also means that companies need to rethink their policies on new product rollouts. In the preglobal era, international rollouts took years, even decades, to reach most markets. In the global era, the inherent connectedness of markets meant that companies had to move much faster, entering all major and strategic markets as quickly as possible. For example, in the 1980s, General Electric recognized that it did not have the luxury of a gradual rollout of its new programmable controllers product line. Instead it rapidly entered the key markets of the United States, Germany, Japan, and the United Kingdom. By 1995, Microsoft had redefined the benchmark target for a global rollout by launching Windows 95 around the world in 24 hours.

In the Internet era, even 24 hours looks slow. Internet services have, by their nature, very strong network effects and related first mover advantages. Failure to rapidly extend into key markets can allow local rivals to take preemptive positions. Perhaps the most dramatic example of this effect is America On Line's slowness in international expansion. Its delay allowed internet service providers (ISPs) in other countries to build up locally dominant positions. AOL now trails Freeserve in the United Kingdom, UOL in Brazil, T-Online in Germany, and Tiscali in Italy. On the other hand, start-ups, in particular, need to understand the trade-offs involved in multicountry launches. One of the reasons for the dramatic failure in 2000 of boo.com, the U.K.-based fashion retailer, was its attempt to launch simultaneously in 18 countries, something that some of the largest e-business companies never attempted. Boo.com should have realized that, as a specialty retailer and not an ISP, preemption and first mover advantage were not nearly as important as developing a viable business in at least one country.

But the implication is not just a change in speed. With a Web site, a company reaches overseas customers from the start, *even if it is not ready to serve them.* Unsolicited foreign orders will start coming in. So companies will have to backfill quickly to provide support operations and services. Of course, a company can choose to not serve some or all foreign customers and post such notices prominently on their Web sites. But that creates negative messages on first contact. By the time the company is ready to serve those markets, it may have lost significant goodwill. Even those companies that intend to serve markets still have a lot to learn about the design of their Web sites. It can be as simple as getting their geography right. The Web site for one major Japanese electronics firm somehow fails to locate the United Kingdom within Europe nor offers the United Kingdom as a stand-alone choice (antagonizing both pro- and anti-European integrationists, as well as frustrating potential customers).

TYPES OF GLOBAL MARKET PARTICIPATION

The traditional view of being international tends to focus on the percentage of a business's revenues outside the home country and the number of countries in which the business participates. Corporate annual reports of both American and European companies almost invariably report these two statistics. But these two measures are of little use when we take a global strategy view of market participation. Knowing that a concern has 50 percent of its revenues outside the home market is meaningless without knowing the percentage of the worldwide market that is outside the home country. Similarly, being present in 10 countries that include the United States, Japan, and Germany is far more important, in most industries, than being present in 30 countries that exclude these three but include many small, less advanced countries.

To have a global level of market participation requires significant global market share, a reasonable balance between the business's geographic spread and the market's spread, and presence in globally strategic country-markets. Allianz Versicherungs AG, Europe's largest insurance group and headquartered in Germany, has a global strategy of gaining leading market positions in the United States, Europe, and Asia. Allianz built up a strong position in Europe primarily through acquisitions and pursued a similar acquisition strategy in the United States with its 1990 bid for Fireman's Fund, one of the largest insurance companies in the country.

GLOBAL MARKET SHARE

Achieving high market share in single-country markets has long been a key objective for most managers. The benefits include being able to exploit economies of scale, possessing greater bargaining power with suppliers and distribution channels, and enjoying more ready acceptance by customers. Some researchers have questioned these benefits.[20] But these benefits of high share seem even greater in highly global industries. That

HSBC'S GLOBAL EXPANSION

From the early 1980s, Hong Kong and Shanghai Bank (now HSBC and one of the largest banks in the world) embarked on a series of acquisitions and joint ventures to build a strong and balanced market participation in the key banking markets of the world.[14] To gain a dominant position in the European banking community, HSBC acquired Capel, a reputable research-based institutional brokerage house in London, in 1996 and Britain's Midland Bank in 1992.[15] With Capel under its belt, HSBC was able to take advantage of an extensive cross-selling network, and with Midland Bank, HSBC was able to gain a presence in Britain, an important European money center.[16]

HSBC also solidified its presence in the United States through acquisitions and joint ventures. In 1981, HSBC bought 51 percent of New York–based Marine Midland. This acquisition was HSBC's first significant move to expand outside of Asia to create a powerful international network. HSBC continues to build its presence in the United States. Its 1996 acquisition of J. P. Morgan's institutional U.S. dollar clearing business placed it among the top five dollar clearing organizations in New York.[17]

One of HSBC's strategies is to be the bank of choice for small Asian and Indian merchants engaged in import/export. The bank, therefore, has tried to build strong ties in the Asian and Indian small business communities in the United States and Asia. Marine Midland's acquisition of Bank of Chinatown enabled the bank to get numerous referrals of Asian customers who require trade services.[18] To gain a presence on the Pacific Coast — an area that has a much higher trade volume than the East Coast — HSBC created a joint venture with Wells Fargo Bank. Not only was HSBC able to gain access to a 2,100-branch network in 13 states, but it was also able to avoid the huge costs associated with establishing and/or even acquiring a West Coast banking franchise.[19]

is because the advantages of high market share can be leveraged across many countries and not just one. The advantages can be used again and again. A business that takes a global approach to manufacturing — by concentrating production in one or a few countries — in an industry where economies of scale are large can exploit the resultant low-cost advantage in country after country. That strategy worked for Japanese companies in industry after industry. Low share competitors may be able to resist in individual countries by developing specialized strategies, but that approach is unlikely to be available in the majority of countries.

GLOBAL BALANCE

High global market share is important but not sufficient for global market participation. A global business also needs to have its geographic distribution of revenues in reasonable balance with that of the worldwide market. That is, the business should usually not have most of its revenues concentrated in just a few countries, and its market share in each country should not be too different from its global market share. Global balance is important as a counterpoint to large market share, because the business usually needs to have significant presence in many countries in order to fully benefit from a global strategy. On a country-by-country basis, in some industries it may be better to have a large, significant share in some countries and a small share in others than to have a moderate share level everywhere.[21] But this effect may well be offset by the damaging effect of uneven market share on the ability to operate a global strategy.

An imbalanced level of market participation weakens the use of each of the other four global strategy levers. A business with revenues concentrated in a few businesses will find it difficult to develop global products that have wide appeal. Inevitably, the desires of the few dominant countries will take precedence. While this may be fine in the short term, such a situation makes it more difficult to expand geographically in the future. For the same reasons, and with the same consequences, such a business will find it difficult to develop global marketing programs. A concentrated business may also find it difficult to develop a globalized network of value-adding activities. Ideas for where to locate activities may be biased toward the needs of the dominant countries. In addition, there is usually a strong reluctance to move away from the status quo. Perhaps, most important, *a business with imbalanced market participation will find it difficult to make effective integrated competitive moves.* Because of its weakness in many markets, such a business will have fewer opportunities and leverage points for making preemptive and counterparry moves against competitors. Being aware of global balance can change the perception of competitive threats. A competitor with a large share but limited presence can be less of a threat than a competitor with a smaller share but broader market presence.

Most American companies probably have a significant imbalance with too great a proportion of revenues in the United States. Furthermore, in most industries the U.S. market is growing more slowly than the rest of the world, so that the imbalance will probably get worse.

PRESENCE IN GLOBALLY STRATEGIC MARKETS

Lastly, a large global market share and global balance need to be combined with presence in key or globally strategic country-markets. Perhaps the most important difference between market participation for the sake of internationalization and that for the sake of globalization is the role of *globally strategic countries.* Such countries are important beyond their stand-alone attractiveness. There are several ways in which a country can be globally strategic as a market:

- Large source of revenues or profits
- Home market of global customers
- Home market of global competitors
- Significant market of global competitors
- Major source of industry innovation

Large Source of Revenues or Profits

The size of a market is, of course, a major factor in country stand-alone attractiveness. Size is also important for global strategic reasons. The larger the market, the more it can contribute to a competitor's global scale economies. Success in a large market can, therefore, drive down worldwide costs for a competitor that shares costs across countries. Success in a large market can also provide funds to subsidize the business in other markets. Active subsidization across countries is a key feature of a global strategy. For these reasons it is critical to succeed in large markets and to deny success in such markets to global rivals. American and European companies suffer a common disadvantage in that Japan, the third major market after Western Europe and the United States, is so much more difficult for foreign competitors than are these other two markets.

THE LURE OF CHINA

From the 1980s, the opening up of China made it the largest source of *potential* future revenues. Most multinational companies have decided that China is too strategically important to ignore, even if it means many years of investment. For example, by 1996, Motorola had committed over $1 billion, Coca-Cola over $500 million, Ford over $250 million, and Rupert Murdoch's News Corporation changed many policies in order to gain favor with the Chinese government.

In most industries, Japanese competitors enjoy at home a well-protected major source of revenues and profits.[22] Conversely, the size of the U.S. market is rapidly turning from an advantage to a liability for American companies. When they had little global competition, American businesses could use their home scale advantage to muscle their way into overseas markets. But new, tough, and newly tough foreign competitors are irresistibly drawn to the U.S. market—still the largest single country-market in the world.

Markets that are large relative to their region can also be strategically important, particularly where it is impractical to ship between continents. For that reason, Brazil is commonly regarded in many industries as strategically important. That is despite the difficulties of doing business there. Brazil has had some of the highest trade barriers in the world, so that in most industries multinational companies have to set up local production rather than being able to import.

Home Market of Global Customers

Global competitors need a strong presence in the home market of global (and other major) customers. Relationships can be maintained best at the customer's home. The customer's foreign subsidiaries will also look askance at a supplier that does not have a major share of its home country business. Major customers are also the key source of ideas for innovation. So it is important to have a research and development presence in these customers' home markets. Having demanding customers can also be a key to global success.[23]

Home Market of Global Competitors

For many global competitors their home market represents a major source of revenues or profits, although the home market need not be the country in which the parent company has its head office.[24] A business needs a strong presence in these enemy home markets in order both to limit funds flow to its competitors and to act as a hostage for good behavior. One executive characterizes this motivation as an "in your face" strategy. Equally important, the business can learn firsthand how the competitor operates and more closely monitor developments. Being in the home market of major competitors greatly reduces the chance of being surprised. Kodak has now greatly strengthened its position in Japan, but at a far higher cost than if it had committed to Japan much earlier.

The air-conditioning industry provides an example of the dangers of ignoring the Japanese market. Major U.S. producers, who long dominated the world market, made much less of an effort in Japan, now the world's largest market for air conditioning (in revenues). Japanese manufacturers successfully applied a technology invented in the United States—the ductless split (which provides a smaller and quieter central air-conditioning

COMPETING IN JAPAN

In contrast to many other American (and European) companies, IBM's early and highly successful commitment to Japan has probably helped reduce the global threat it faces from Fujitsu and other Japanese computer manufacturers. Stunting the domestic growth of foreign competitors (as IBM did) is, of course, cheaper than fighting them after they have grown to global scale. Motorola has succeeded in this much tougher, latter task. In the early 1980s, Motorola found itself under attack in its home market by Japanese competitors in both its semiconductor and communication businesses. At the same time, Motorola faced seemingly insuperable barriers protecting its rivals' home markets. But undeterred, Motorola mounted a sustained effort to both defend its U.S. markets and invade markets in Japan. This effort included soliciting the threat of U.S. congressional action. Motorola's reward has been the gradual yielding of barriers in Japan and an increasing number of contracts won. In 1990 the Japanese Ministry of Post and Telecommunications even selected a Motorola design for a digital cellular telephone component as a national standard. Perhaps, more important, Motorola has been able to preserve its market leadership at home.[26] Citibank provides another example of an American firm that has undertaken the hard task of building a position in Japan. As part of this effort, Citibank has been willing to cut opportunistic deals with local partners such as the postal-savings system, installed an automated-teller network system, and leases space in Mitsubishi Bank offices. Furthermore, Citibank is making progress in part by offering services that are new to Japan but successful in the United States, such as telephone transfers and its CitiGold account for large depositors.

system than conventional methods)—and now seek international markets.[25] A stronger presence in Japan might have alerted American producers to the growing attraction of this technology rather than having to make up lost time now. Recognizing this failing, the U.S.'s Carrier Corporation, the original inventor of air-conditioning, formed an alliance in 1998 with Toshiba, a Japanese leader in this and related products.

Significant Market of Global Competitors
Participating in significant markets of global competitors brings benefits similar to those realized from participating in competitors' home markets. Sixt, a dominant car rental company in Germany, is seeking to expand into its rivals' major markets. But it faces formidable competitors—such as Hertz, Avis, and Europcar—that will protect their home markets and possibly retaliate in the German market.

Major Source of Industry Innovation
As discussed in Chapter 2, most industries have a few markets that act as "lead countries" in the sense of being the primary source of innovations. Very often, lead countries are also the home markets of global customers and global competitors. But identifying lead countries further helps the process of making correct decisions on market participation.

GLOBALLY UNIMPORTANT COUNTRIES

Just as less important markets need not be entered as part of a global strategy, the same markets, if already entered or entered for reasons of stand-alone attractiveness, can be left out of the global integration effort. So these countries need not be included when applying the other four global strategy levers of global products and services, global location of activities, global marketing, and global competitive moves, or they can be left to last in the globalization effort. In addition to the factors affecting global strategic importance, other factors should be considered in deciding whether a country should be integrated into the global strategy. These other factors include market size; competitive position; extent of ownership and control of the subsidiary; quality of the subsidiary's management; and the benefits, costs, and risks of change.[27]

BENEFITS OF GLOBAL MARKET PARTICIPATION

A global approach to market participation provides global benefits in each of the categories: cost reduction, improved quality, enhanced customer preference, and competitive leverage.

COST REDUCTION

Expanding market participation helps reduce costs by increasing volume for economies of scale. That benefit applies whether the expansion takes place for internationalization or for globalization reasons. But a global strategy approach to selecting the markets into which to expand, and in which to participate, can help make choices that have a more direct effect on the ability to achieve global scale economies.

IMPROVED QUALITY

Presence in lead countries, and exposure to their demanding customers and innovative competitors, can help a business improve the quality of its products. But a company reaps such benefits only if it is willing to learn from these countries. In general, Japanese companies have been much better at applying such lessons than American and European companies.

ENHANCED CUSTOMER PREFERENCE

As in the case of McCann-Erickson serving the Coca-Cola account, global market participation can enhance customer preference through global availability, global serviceability, and global recognition. The greater the percentage of purchases accounted for by global customers (whether organizations or consumers), the more benefits arise from global market participation. With the rise of global account management programs to serve global customers (discussed in Chapter 6), suppliers are finding it more necessary to participate in markets that are important to their global accounts. The supplier may not find a particular country profitable on a stand-alone basis but needs to be there to support the total global account.

COMPETITIVE LEVERAGE

A global strategy approach to market participation can increase competitive leverage in the various ways already described. In summary, these gains include the advantages of earlier entry into key markets, providing more sites for attack and counterattack, and creating hostages for good behavior. If choices need to be made among countries for participation, an important consideration is the choice among countries where global competitors are present and where they are not.

GOING NATIONAL BY GOING GLOBAL

Fosters Brewing provides a special case of using global market participation to strengthen a business's position in its home market. Fosters beer used to be a small regional brand in the state of Victoria in Australia. Fosters wanted to expand nationally but recognized that Australians were very loyal to their regional beers. So Fosters decided not to go head-to-head with its Australian competitors by directly challenging them in their home markets. Instead, Fosters hit on a global strategy of exploiting the *wanderlust* of young Australians. Fosters decided to seed its beer in those foreign locations where young Australian tourists congregated, such as Earl's Court in London. Thus, many young Australians acquired a taste for Fosters while overseas. When they returned home and wanted to celebrate their foreign memories, they would choose Fosters. This global market participation strategy greatly helped Fosters to become the leading brand in all of Australia.[28]

A global presence also helps guard against complacency and gives the ability to retaliate against competitors in their home markets, as mentioned in Chapter 1. For example, the strength of the Kellogg Company in global markets for ready-to-eat cereals has been a major reason why large foreign competitors such as Nestlé have a limited presence in the U.S. cereal market.[29] Indeed, Kellogg's archrival, General Mills, has had to resort to establishing a partnership (Cereal Partners Worldwide) in Europe with Nestlé, which will manufacture and market General Mills' products.[30]

DRAWBACKS OF GLOBAL MARKET PARTICIPATION

A global approach to market participation also has the clear drawback of an earlier or greater commitment to a market than warranted on its own merits. In addition, the more the business is managed on a globally integrated basis across many geographic markets, the more coordination costs will be incurred. The cost of coordinating across countries depends in part on the differences and barriers between the countries. Using Profit Impact of Market Strategy (PIMS) data, this author found that continental-scale businesses in Europe performed financially worse than national-scale businesses in the period 1972 to 1987, that is, before the 1992 creation of the single European market would reduce barriers. This study also found that, in the United States by contrast, where barriers and differences between regions are much less than in Europe, continental-scale businesses performed better than regional-scale businesses. Other drawbacks arise from the crossing of national frontiers and the loss of customer focus.[31]

COORDINATION COSTS

Expansion in geographic scope across national boundaries is particularly likely to increase coordination costs. The simple need to set up separate legal entities much of the time provides one major source of additional complexity. Furthermore, the legal entity usually requires some management structure to be responsible for it. Thus, a multicountry business will typically require more layers of management than a national business covering the same geographic size of territory. Other sources of increased coordination cost include international differences in technical standards, language, culture, and operating practices.[32]

CROSSING NATIONAL FRONTIERS

A business that operates across national frontiers incurs trade barrier costs, transportation costs, and inventory costs. Tariff and nontariff trade barriers hurt performance by reducing sales and increasing costs. Transportation is slower and more costly because of border checks. Also, the combination of trade barriers and transportation difficulties may require a multicountry business to maintain more inventory relative to sales than a single-country business.

LOSING CUSTOMER FOCUS

Multicountry businesses are also less likely to be able to customize for buyer needs than single-country businesses. A multicountry business may have to offer many more product versions or else provide lesser customer satisfaction than single-country competitors. Offering more products incurs more cost, while providing less customer satisfaction hurts sales.

GLOBALLY BLOCKED INDUSTRIES

In some industries, government barriers prevent direct participation in foreign markets. In particular, regulated industries allow only limited internationalization, such as in sensitive industries like defense, where home governments discourage the overseas relocation of critical activities; or in industries where the minimum efficient scale of operations, particularly production, is so great that concentration is best. Typical companies and industries are British Aerospace and Northrop Grumman in their defense-related businesses, British Telecom and other national telecom service operators, most airline companies, most utility operators, most law firms, and many media companies.

For internationally blocked industries, there are three main paths for global expansion. First, they can make acquisitions of foreign participants in the same industry, if allowed. But there are severe restrictions in many industries on foreign ownership—including airlines, defense, and media. Rupert Murdoch had to become a U.S. citizen in order to be able to buy U.S. radio and television companies. Second, they can form international strategic alliances. British Airways continues to seek to build a transatlantic alliance that can operate as seamlessly as will be allowed by national regulators. Its global One World alliance (co-led with American Airlines), the Star Alliance (spearheaded by the U.S. United Airlines), and the pan-European Qualiflyer alliance[33] all seek to achieve in alliance mode what their members are not allowed to do as national air carriers. Third, companies in blocked industries can hire out their expertise to foreign partners or customers, or globalize in unrestricted activities. For example, Singapore Airlines has many training and support contracts with other carriers and also operates globally some specialized airline-related businesses, such as catering. Thames Water, one of the United Kingdom's largest utility companies, is taking both the acquisition and technology transfer modes in its globalization efforts.

AT&T'S EFFORTS IN ITALY

Entering a blocked market requires great patience and effort, as illustrated by AT&T's strategies for breaking into Italy's telecommunications market.[34] Since entry into Italy in 1987, AT&T has used five strategies:

1. Identified its competitive advantages and selected specific areas in which to compete.

2. Tried to thoroughly understand the local market.

3. Actively encouraged rapid telecom liberalization through direct dialogues with the Italian government.

4. Cooperated and collaborated with the national operator on a wide range of activities, as the liberalization process began to take hold.

5. Forged a local partnership to complete full-scale entry into the market.

AT&T's competitive advantages were obvious: They were able to combine the technological muscle of AT&T Labs with an exceptional branded image and an unsurpassed worldwide network that reaches more than 280 countries and territories. In Italy, the company conducted an intensive market research program to segment the market and assess their telecommunications needs. This fact-gathering phase enabled AT&T to establish contact with the future participants in Italian telecommunications, companies that would soon be its competitors—or potential partners. Whatever the outcome of AT&T's hunt for the optimal partner, the company's global presence and worldwide reputation make it an extremely attractive ally.

THE SPECIAL CASE OF JOINT VENTURES

International joint ventures represent a special case in market participation.[36] They provide a rapid way of expanding the geographic scope of a business. Managers need to beware, however, of thinking that setting up a joint venture in a country means that market is covered and can be counted as part of a business's global presence. Whether joint ventures represent genuine market participation depends on how the venture is set up and on how the partners behave. Strategic success in global joint ventures may depend more on how partners behave than on how the venture is set up.[37] Let's look at one situation. An American multinational company, "AMSUPP," had very strong market positions in an industrial supplies business in all major countries except Japan. There they had set up a joint venture with the leading Japanese company in the industry, "NIPPONSUPP." The venture gave AMSUPP a 45 percent ownership in return for technology transfer as well as capital investment. In discussing global coverage and global market share, the AMSUPP managers included Japan in their calculations. With Japan, AMSUPP's global market participation looked very complete. Japan's inclusion was particularly important because, using the criteria discussed earlier in this chapter, the AMSUPP managers identified Japan as the most globally strategic country, even more than the United States. Unfortunately, the way in which the venture was set up and the way in which the AMSUPP managers operated really negated the possibility of genuine participation by AMSUPP.

First, AMSUPP owned a share only of the manufacturing subsidiary of NIPPON-SUPP and not a share of the parent company, which was responsible for marketing and sales. AMSUPP, therefore, had no legal right of access to NIPPONSUPP's markets and

ARTHUR ANDERSEN BECOMES A GLOBAL LAW FIRM

As discussed in Chapter 2, law firms face many barriers to globalization. But as law and accounting increasingly intersect, Andersen is using network alliances to create one of the largest law firms in the world.[35] Andersen has created a network of law firms consisting of more than 800 lawyers in 30 countries. As clients become more global, the percentage of accounting billings drops relative to tax and legal services, and cross-border deals increase. So Andersen perceives the need for lawyers to be included in their list of services that can be offered. Since most countries bar nonlawyers from having equity interests in law firms, Andersen signs up law firms as independent affiliates. The law firms that join the network pay for some of the costs of Andersen's extensive worldwide communication system, and in return they receive legal work through Andersen as well as access to Andersen's communication system. This is considered a win-win system, with law firms getting more work and Andersen increasing its worldwide service capabilities.

customers. Second, while NIPPONSUPP had sent marketing representatives to the United States to learn from AMSUPP about the American market, AMSUPP had not done the same in Japan. Many American companies have found that in joint ventures with Japanese companies, the latter have gained far more access to their American partners' knowledge than have the former to their Japanese partners' knowledge. In effect, AMSUPP did not participate in the Japanese market in any strategic sense: They had merely a financial investment and not a very profitable one either. When the AMSUPP managers understood their problem and tried to change it, they found that they were in the proverbial position of riding a tiger: They could not get off for risk of being eaten. In this case, if AMSUPP ended the joint venture, they would lose all their business in Japan. Worse, they had created the tiger themselves by setting up NIPPONSUPP with the best technology. That, combined with NIPPONSUPP's manufacturing skills, resulted in NIPPONSUPP's products being of higher quality than those manufactured by AMSUPP. AMSUPP now had to maintain the relationship in order to prevent NIPPONSUPP from becoming a fearsome global competitor. So, joint ventures and alliances help much more in strengthening the core strategy and the internationalization strategy than the globalization strategy.

DIFFERING STRATEGIC ROLES FOR EACH COUNTRY

A global strategy approach to market participation also means that different countries should have different roles within the total business. The collection of country-businesses should be viewed as a strategic portfolio rather than as a passive one. The Boston Consulting Group (BCG) popularized the use of cross-subsidization of businesses within a corporate portfolio. The same approach can be applied to countries in global strategy. Typically, the home country needs to subsidize markets that are newer to the business. That contrasts with what has been a common mindset in companies dominated by the home business. Such companies often treat international markets opportunistically as ways to balance capacity utilization.

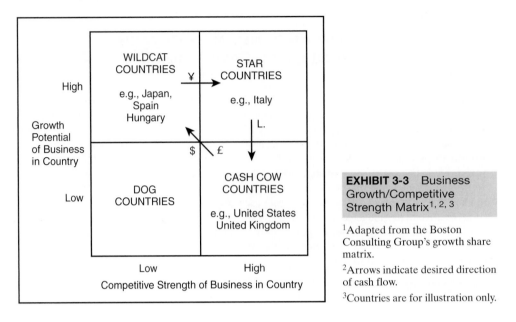

EXHIBIT 3-3   Business Growth/Competitive Strength Matrix[1,2,3]

[1]Adapted from the Boston Consulting Group's growth share matrix.

[2]Arrows indicate desired direction of cash flow.

[3]Countries are for illustration only.

BUSINESS GROWTH/COMPETITIVE STRENGTH MATRIX

A comprehensive way of allocating country roles is to use an adaptation of the BCG matrix.[38] In Exhibit 3-3, the horizontal axis uses competitive strength (which includes market share) instead of BCG's relative market share (and is reversed in direction from the BCG matrix), and the vertical axis uses growth potential of the business instead of BCG's industry growth rate. In this business-growth/competitive-strength matrix "cash cow" countries provide funds for investment in "wildcat" countries that may become future "star" countries. For a typical U.S.-based business, the cash cow countries might include the United States and the United Kingdom; the star countries might include Italy; and the wildcat countries might include Japan, Spain, and Hungary.

GLOBAL STRATEGIC IMPORTANCE/COMPETITIVE STRENGTH MATRIX

Another important way of allocating roles to countries is to take a competitive approach based on the global strategic importance of each country. The country strategic importance/competitive strength matrix in Exhibit 3-4 keeps the same horizontal dimension as Exhibit 3-3 but uses as the vertical axis the global strategic importance of each country. Countries in each cell of the matrix have a different competitive prescription. *Maintaining* and *enhancing* the business's position in countries that are of high global strategic importance, and where the business is strong (upper right cell), must be viewed as a very high priority. It may also be important to *preempt* possible competitive threats. For a typical U.S.-based business, countries in this cell might include the United States and Germany. The top left cell, where countries have high global strategic importance but the business has a weak competitive position, presents a *danger* area that managers need to *fix*. For many, perhaps most, American (and European) businesses today, Japan and China loom large in this cell. As the arrow in-

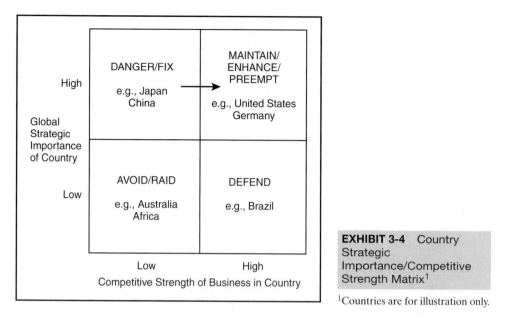

EXHIBIT 3-4   Country Strategic Importance/Competitive Strength Matrix[1]

[1]Countries are for illustration only.

dicates, the business should seek to move itself in Japan or China to the upper right cell. The lower right cell represents countries with low global strategic importance but where the business has high competitive strength. The business should *defend* its position in these countries, but not at exorbitant cost. For a typical American business, many Latin American countries might today be in this cell. Lastly, the lower left cell indicates countries that have low global strategic importance and where the business has low competitive strength. These countries should probably be treated opportunistically. Managers should *avoid* them or *raid* them for short-term profits. For many American businesses, countries like Australia might fall in this cell.[39]

IMPLEMENTATION ISSUES

In using both matrices shown, attention should be paid to likely changes over time as country-markets evolve. Users may also want to use refinements such as placing businesses in positions that straddle two cells or designating likely or planned directions of movement. Another very important consideration is the organizational and political aspects of designating portfolio roles to countries. The corporate portfolio approach came to some grief in the 1980s because of both conceptual flaws and the demotivating effects it had on managers responsible for businesses dubbed as dogs or cash cows.[40] The issue of motivation is part of the larger topic of global organization and management that will be covered in Chapter 8.

INDUSTRIES THAT NEED MULTIMARKET PARTICIPATION

Industry globalization drivers affect the importance in each industry of participating in multiple markets and of defining the market globally. Are there particular industries where companies have chosen multiple- rather than single-market participation? Various studies have identified the industries dominated by multinational rather than national companies. But the fact that industries have multinational companies does not mean that the industries are inherently global. They could just as easily be inherently multilocal.

Some of the industries most dominated by multinational companies have been very multilocal. For example, most consumer packaged goods industries—detergents, toiletries, many food categories—are dominated by multinationals—Unilever, Procter & Gamble, Nestlé, and so on. But in these industries the primary strategy has been to transfer the multinational's expertise—in product development, quality manufacturing, and marketing—but then to manage each country on a more or less stand-alone basis. But, as cited elsewhere in this book, even in these industries companies are beginning to take a more global approach.

GUIDELINES FOR BUILDING GLOBAL MARKET PARTICIPATION

Participating in the right countries and at the right level provides the foundation on which a successful total global strategy needs to be built. The following guidelines summarize the global, rather than multilocal, approach to building market participation:

- Managers need to select countries for entry and investment on the basis of global strategic importance as well as of stand-alone attractiveness.
- The most strategic countries can often be the most expensive ones in which to build up a significant market presence.
- Managers should particularly worry about the home countries of major global competitors or *potential* global competitors.
- Managers need to evaluate multiple, sometimes conflicting, criteria in identifying globally strategic markets. So selecting the markets in which to participate is somewhat more complicated than using a simple rule of thumb like "be in the 'triad' markets of the United States, Europe, and Japan."
- Different countries can play different strategic roles as part of the total global strategy.
- Alliances and joint ventures can provide a quicker and easier way to build global market participation, but also weaken the potential for a fully integrated global strategy.

Discussion and Research Questions

1. What are the most important countries in which a global business should participate today, and why? What will this list of countries look like in 10 years' time?
2. How should a company select countries for market participation?
3. Compare and contrast the "multilocal" and "global" approaches to market participation.
4. What priorities should be assigned by a multinational computer company to North America, Latin America, Western Europe, Eastern Europe, the Middle East, Japan, East Asia, and other regions? How would your answer differ for other types of companies? How would your answer differ based on the home country of the company in question?
5. What is different about global market participation for service businesses?
6. How can companies use the Internet to participate in overseas markets?

Notes

1. The literature on foreign direct investment (FDI) provides extensive treatment of companies' motivations for internationalization. See, for example, Peter J. Buckley and Mark Casson, *The Future of the Multinational Enterprise,* (New York: Holmes and Meier Publishers, 1976), Alan M. Rugman, *International Diversification and the Multinational Enterprise* (Lexington, MA: Lexington Books, D. C. Heath, 1979); Peter J. Buckley, *The Theory of the Multinational Enterprise* (Uppsala, Sweden: Acta Universitatis Upsaliensis, *Studia Oeconomiae Negotiorum* 26, Uppsala, Sweden, 1987); and John H. Dunning, "The Eclectic Paradigm of International Production: A Restatement and Some Possible Extensions," *Journal of International Business Studies,* Spring 1988.

2. This history was provided by G. Van Schaik, vice chairman and executive board director, Heineken N.V., at the Annual Conference of the Strategic Management Society in Amsterdam on October 19, 1988. Mr. Van Schaik went on to say that if Heineken were going international for the first time today, it would choose some very different markets.

3. This paragraph is based on Philip Kotler, Liam Fahey, and S. Jatusripitak, *The New Competition* (Upper Saddle River, NJ: Prentice-Hall, 1985), p. 174.

4. George S. Yip, Javier B. Gomez, and Joseph Monti, "Role of the Internationalization Process in the Performance of Newly Internationalizing Firms," *Journal of International Marketing,* Vol. 8, No. 3, 2000, pp. 10–35.

5. This section is based on George S. Yip, "Bases of Competitive Advantage," in *Financial Times Handbook of Management,* 2nd ed., Stuart Crainer and Des Dearlove, Eds. (London: Financial Times/Prentice Hall, 2001), pp. 253–63.

6. Michael Treacy and Frederick Wiersema, *The Discipline of Market Leaders* (Reading, MA: Addison-Wesley, 1995).

7. Hertz is now only the second largest car rental company in the United States, behind Enterprise rent-a-car, but it is still the largest for business and vacation rentals, as Enterprise focuses on accident replacement rentals.

8. See Michael E. Porter, *Competitive Advantage* (New York: The Free Press, 1985); and Michael E. Porter, "What Is Strategy?" *Harvard Business Review,* November–December 1996.

9. Study by Interbrand, Newell and Sorrell, London, 1999.

10. For a discussion of how newer companies are globalizing quickly, see Harry Korine, "Fresenius AG: High Speed Globalization," *Business Strategy Review,* Vol. 11, No. 2, Summer 2000, pp. 47–57.

11. See also Stephen B. Tallman and George S. Yip, Chapter 12, "Strategy and the Multinational Enterprise," in *Oxford Handbook of International Business,* Thomas Brewer and Alan M. Rugman, Eds., (Oxford, England: Oxford University Press. 2001.)

12. Adapted from "France: Accor—Rooms for Further Expansion," *Euromoney Corporate Finance,* November 19, 1990.

13. Adapted from "Going for the Middle; A Global Name Targets Asia's Middle-Class Travelers," *Asiaweek,* February 2, 1996, p. 42.

14. "The Top 500 World Banks," *Thomson Bank Directory,* June–November 1995.

15. Adapted from Martin Van der Weyer, "Hong Kong Officer Corps Builds a Global Empire," *Euromoney,* April 1993, p. 52.

16. Adapted from William Purves, "Turbulent Times for Banks," *Asian Business,* Vol. 29, No. 2, February 1993, p. 38.

17. Adapted from "HSBC's Dollar Clearing Boost," *Banker,* Vol. 146, No. 847, September 1996, p. 8.

18. Adapted from James L. Strodes, "Hong Kong and Shanghai Bank Goes Bicoastal," *World Trade,* Vol. 9, No. 9, September 1996, p. 38.

19. Adapted from Daniel S. Levine, "Wells, HSBC Hope for Right Combination in Left Coast," *World Trade,* Vol. 9, No. 9, September 1996, p. 40.

20. There is significant controversy in the academic literature about the direction of causation between market share and profitability, and some even question whether there is a positive association. The key literature on

this topic includes Robert D. Buzzell, Bradley T. Gale, and R. G. M. Sultan, "Market Share—A Key to Profitability," *Harvard Business Review*, January–February 1975, pp. 97–106; Richard P. Rumelt and Robin Wensley, "In Search of the Market Share Effect," *Proceedings, Academy of Management Annual Meeting*, pp. 2–6, 1981; Robert Jacobson and David A. Aaker, "Is Market Share All That It's Cracked Up to Be?" *Journal of Marketing*, Vol. 49, No. 4, Fall 1985, pp. 11–22; John E. Prescott, A. K. Kohli, and N. Venkatraman, "The Market Share—Profitability Relationship: An Empirical Assessment of Major Assertions and Contradictions," *Strategic Management Journal*, Vol. 7, 1986, pp. 377–94; Robert D. Buzzell and Bradley T. Gale, *The PIMS Principles: Linking Strategy to Performance* (New York: Free Press, 1987); and Robert Jacobson, "Distinguishing Among Competing Theories of the Market Share Effect," *Journal of Marketing*, Vol. 52, No. 4, October 1988, pp. 68–80.

21. See, for example, Porter's ideas about the disadvantages of being "stuck in the middle": Michael E. Porter, *Competitive Strategy: Techniques for Analyzing Industries and Competitors* (New York: The Free Press, 1980).

22. Yoffie and Milner argue that, contrary to classical trade theory, preserving access to large markets can justify government intervention in trade, when competitors practice protectionism in industries characterized by large economies of scale, steep learning curves, or sizable R&D requirements. See David B. Yoffie and Helen V. Milner, "An Alternative to Free Trade or Protectionism: Why Corporations Seek Strategic Trade Policy," *California Management Review*, Summer 1989, pp. 111–31.

23. See Michael E. Porter, *The Competitive Advantage of Nations* (New York: The Free Press, 1990).

24. Ibid.

25. Todd Vogel and Chris Perry, "How Japan Is Beating the Others Cold," *Business Week*, September 3, 1990, p. 79.

26. See David B. Yoffie and John Coleman, "Motorola and Japan," Case No. 9-388-056 (Boston: Harvard Business School, 1988).

27. See also Pradeep A. Rau and John F. Preble, "Standardization of Marketing Strategy by Multinationals," *International Marketing Review*, Autumn 1987, pp. 18–28.

28. See also Geoff Lewis, "Carlton & United Breweries," in *Cases in Australian Management*, Geoff Lewis and Peter Fitzroy, Eds. (Sydney, Australia: Prentice Hall, 1991).

29. Kasra Ferdows et al., *The Internationalization of U.S. Manufacturing: Causes and Consequences* (Washington, DC: National Academy Press, 1990), p. 13.

30. This partnership was announced in 1991.

31. See George S. Yip, "A Performance Comparison of Continental and National Businesses in Europe," *International Marketing Review*, Vol. 8, No. 2, 1991, pp. 31–39.

32. Hofstede's classic study has highlighted the major differences in culture within one multinational corporation. See Geert Hofstede, *Culture's Consequences: International Differences in Work Related Values* (Beverly Hills, CA.: Sage Publications, 1984).

33. Qualiflyer includes Swissair, Austrian Airlines, Sabena, Air Portugal, Turkish Airlines, AOM, Crossair, Lauda-air, and Tyrolean.

34. This section is based on "Playing to Win in a Monopoly Market: AT&T Italia," *Hemispheres*, August 1997, pp. 35–38.

35. Adapted from "Global Lawyers," *Forbes*, November 3, 1997, pp. 340–44.

36. Joint ventures are a very large topic in their own right. See, among others, Larry G. Franko, *Joint Venture Survival in Multinational Corporations* (New York: Praeger, 1971); Kathryn R. Harrigan, *Strategies for Joint Ventures* (Lexington, MA: Lexington Books, 1985); ——, *Managing for Joint Venture Success* (Lexington, MA: Lexington Books, 1986); and Joseph L. Badaracco, *The Knowledge Link* (Boston: Harvard Business School Press, 1991). See also Michael E. Porter and

Mark Fuller, "Coalitions and Global Strategy" and Pankaj Ghemawat, Michael E. Porter, and Richard E. Rawlinson, "Patterns of International Coalition Activity" in *Competition in Global Industries,* Michael E. Porter, Ed. (Boston: Harvard Business School Press, 1986). See also Michael Y. Yoshino and U. Srinivasa Rangan, *Strategic Alliances: An Entrepreneurial Approach to Globalization* (Boston: Harvard Business School Press, 1995); Paul Beamish and Peter Killing, Eds., *Cooperative Strategies* (Lanham, MD: Lexington Books 1997).

37. See Gary Hamel, Yves L. Doz, and C. K. Prahalad, "Collaborate with Your Competitors and Win," *Harvard Business Review,* January–February 1989, pp. 133–39.

38. See also Jean-Claude Larréché, "The International Product-Market Portfolio," in *Readings in Marketing Strategy,* Jean-Claude Larréché and Edward E. Strong, Eds. (Palo Alto, CA.: The Scientific Press, 1980).

39. A key challenge for governments in such countries is to increase the global strategic importance of their markets.

40. See Philippe Haspeslagh, "Portfolio Planning: Uses and Limits," *Harvard Business Review,* January–February 1982, pp. 58–73; and Richard G. Hamermesh, *Making Strategy Work: How Senior Managers Produce Results* (New York: John Wiley & Sons, 1986).

4
DESIGNING GLOBAL PRODUCTS AND SERVICES

—◈◈◈—

Using global products and services constitutes the second global strategy lever. Globally standardized products or "global products" are, perhaps, the one feature most commonly identified with global strategy. But *the idea of a fully standardized global product that is identical all over the world is a near myth that has caused great confusion.* Such products are very rare and hard to attain, like an "edible Walkman"—the dream of multinational food companies.[1] Standardization occurs, of course, along a continuum. The benefits of global products (or services) can be achieved by standardizing the core product or large parts of it, while customizing peripheral or other parts of the product (Exhibit 4-1). For example, most of Sony's consumer electronic products are primarily standardized except for the parts that meet national electrical standards.

The passenger automobile industry provides an excellent example of the wide range of global standardization, both between companies and between model lines within a company. At one end, both Mercedes and Honda, for example, sell products that are highly standardized globally. At the other end, General Motors has had little in common between its North American and European product offerings, although that is now changing. Furthermore, all of the automotive manufacturers are striving to increase their level of standardization. Ford does this in part by assigning responsibility to different parts of the company in developing major portions of a new car for world markets. Mazda, in Japan, of which Ford owns 34 percent, has the main responsibility for small cars, Ford in Europe for medium-sized cars, and Ford in North America for larger cars.

In passenger automobiles product standardization comes primarily in the "platform" (the chassis and related parts) and to a lesser extent the engine. Developing the

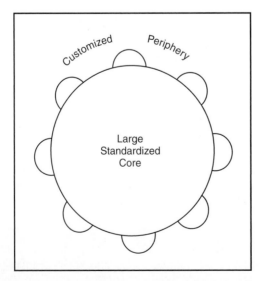

Customized   Periphery

Large
Standardized
Core

EXHIBIT 4-1   The Ideal
Global Product

HONDA'S ADJUSTABLE-WIDTH PLATFORM

To solve the car platform problem, Honda developed in the late 1990s the world's first adjustable-width automobile platform.[2] The platform, developed over a three-year period by Honda's engineers, allowed three distinct Accords that cost 20 percent less to bring to market than the single Accord developed in 1994. Honda's strategy in developing this global platform differed from the larger automakers that budget much higher R&D expenditures. Honda executives challenged its engineers to come up with different designs for each region while working on a very small budget. A single frame was the only solution, and engineers developed a way to vary the platform's width by using adjustable brackets. The brackets allowed Honda to cheaply and easily push the car's wheels together or apart. The innovations have allowed Honda to inexpensively and without difficulty customize and design products for each region around the world. In Europe, the Accord has a short, narrow body geared to handle tiny streets; in the United States, the body was stretched to allow for a roomier interior that caters to the family mid-sized market. This flexibility might give the Honda Accord the distinction of being the first truly global car, defined as the single car that can satisfy the masses worldwide.

platform can account for 30 percent of the total development cost of a new vehicle. So automobile companies hardly ever design different platforms for different countries but may use different bodies on standardized platforms. For example, the Toyota Camry in the United States appears to be a somewhat different car from the Toyota Carina in the United Kingdom, but both use the same platform and engine family.

Faster new product development methods coupled with flexible manufacturing have also allowed manufacturers to develop and produce many more models than before, making it more possible to customize for local markets while enjoying global scale economies. So, for example, Toyota, which used to field fewer passenger car models than its American rivals, by 1990 offered more models than Ford (59 versus 49). But Toyota developed and made these 59 models from just 22 basic designs. So the company still benefits from focus on a relatively small number of core products. Improvement in design and development methods, particularly in the use of overlapping rather than consecutive stages of development, has allowed Toyota and other Japanese manufacturers to drastically shorten the time from drawing board to market.[3] Flexible manufacturing, including the use of just-in-time inventory management, has then allowed Toyota to efficiently produce the large number of models put out by the development process. In summary, Toyota now seems to be able to benefit from both the global benefits of product and production focus and the local benefits of product proliferation.

Some Japanese companies were particularly successful in the 1980s and 1990s at getting countries to accept their standardized version of the product. This was a case of necessity because, when they first entered international markets, Japanese companies simply could not afford to offer different models to each country, or even a broad product line within the same country. Where they succeeded was in identifying those core product features that customers truly wanted and then providing that basic product at a price low enough and at a quality high enough that customers would give up the frills. American manufacturers' position of being able to afford many versions of a product

VOLKSWAGEN'S OVERCUSTOMIZATION

Volkswagen's experience as the first foreign manufacturer to locate in the United States provides a poignant story of the risks of not standardizing enough, that is, customizing *too much* for local tastes. Volkswagen had set a target of increasing its U.S. market share from 2 to 5 percent by targeting the 60 percent of buyers who normally considered domestic models only. So Volkswagen adapted its products to American tastes by softening the suspension and the seats, placing carpeting instead of map pockets on the insides of the doors, and color coordinating the interiors to liven up the standard gray Volkswagen interiors. The result was disastrous. Subsequent market research showed that instead of attracting domestic-loyalists, the changes merely drove away import-loyalists! Volkswagen has taken this lesson very much to heart and today insists on retaining the special German and Volkswagen characteristics whenever localization to suit different market conditions is undertaken.

FIAT'S THIRD-WORLD GLOBAL CAR

Fiat used its Brazilian market as a base for designing a global car, the Palio, for poorer countries.[4] From its design to its manufacturing, the Palio was different from Fiat's European cars. Utilizing an experienced staff who understood the necessary adaptations to meet the demands of Brazilian roads and tastes, Fiat produced a car tailored to local tastes. For example, the Palio is bigger and stronger than its European counterpart. These features attracted consumers by handling better on the rough interior roads in Brazil and by serving as the sole family car for many Brazilian buyers. Now Fiat is seeking to extend the Palio to other third-world markets, such as India and China.

turned out to be an Achilles' heel. This was particularly the case in automobiles, where domestic manufacturers were wedded to the multioption approach and most of the options were superficial to the basic function of an automobile. Furthermore, American automobile manufacturers made no attempt until very recently to market the same product around the world. They had trained the U.S. consumer to want a product that was very different from what the rest of the world could afford.

Ford's Global Focus. Launched in 1999, Ford's subcompact model, the Focus, constitutes perhaps the first truly global car from an American automobile company. Focus is the first vehicle to be built under the "Ford 2000" global development strategy. The program is designed to produce vehicles with a streamlined development and production process, less duplication, and considerable cost reductions. The all-new platform developed for the Focus will also be the basis for a number of future products that will be sold in more than 60 countries worldwide. The Focus is sometimes described as the Model T for the twenty-first century, and it has received wide acclaim in both North America and Europe.

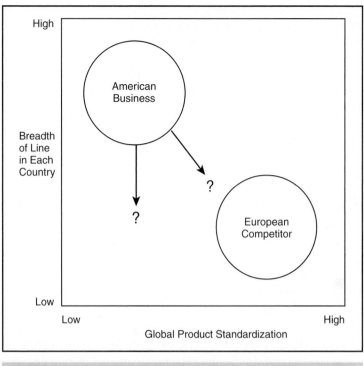

EXHIBIT 4-2   Options in Global Product Line Strategy

Steelcase's Global Office Furniture. Steelcase, a major U.S. manufacturer of office furniture, offers its mostly standardized Ellipse "desking system" in the United States, Germany, and France in spite of very different customer preferences in each country. For the U.S. market, Steelcase makes the colors more subtle, the wires and cables reachable from the user side of the desk, and changes top sizes to reflect U.S. norms. Herman Miller, another U.S. furniture manufacturer, sells its Newhouse desk system on five continents. The only modification that Herman Miller makes in this line is to use lower heights for Japan.

Globalizing Pop Records. Recording companies sell records, discs, and tapes that are essentially standardized globally. But they have also learned to make small local adaptations. For a "pop" record that is marketed in several countries, a company may sometimes get the recording artist(s) to add a single line in the local language. This single line then allows local audiences to relate better to a song that is otherwise foreign. "Shout lines" for dancing in clubs are particularly suitable for such local translation.

Businesses can standardize the worldwide *mix* of products as well as the *content* of a product. A globally standardized product mix means that the business sells the same range or list of models around the world. In contrast, global content standardization involves the extent to which individual product items or models are the same around the world. For example, candy companies like M&M Mars try to sell pretty much the same range of products around the world, even though the products themselves vary in content to allow for differences in tastes.

It can be helpful to map mix standardization against content standardization for the business and its competitors. Exhibit 4-2 illustrates a situation in an American chemical additives business. The business had long pursued a product line strategy of customizing to meet differing customers' needs. The result was a very broad product line, most of which was offered in every country. Furthermore, there was little standardization within each product line, so that the business maintained an inventory of many thousands of individual items. In contrast, its leading competitor, a European firm that was just as profitable, sold a much narrower product line that was also much more standardized across countries. Presenting the information in the manner of Exhibit 4-2 helped raise two questions. First, did the competitor's approach suggest that customer needs were as different as this business's executives assumed? Second, did this business's product line strategy incur unnecessary costs?

BENEFITS OF GLOBAL PRODUCTS AND SERVICES

This author has identified four categories of benefits from globalization: cost reduction, improved quality, enhanced customer preference, and competitive leverage. Each of these benefits applies to global product or service standardization.

COST REDUCTION

Reducing costs is probably the most common motivation in standardizing products. These cost savings include development, purchasing, production, and inventory costs. Thus, as described in Chapter 2, high product development costs act as a globalization driver of product standardization. The higher the development cost relative to expected revenues, the more need there is to develop a few global or regional products rather than many national products. It is important to distinguish between technical and market development costs. Technical, rather than market, development costs act as a driver for product standardization. For example, in the pharmaceutical industry, ethical (prescription) drugs require many years and great expense in technical development, perhaps $200 million for a major new drug. Consequently, pharmaceutical companies try to develop as few national variants as possible: Drugs like Smith Kline's Tagamet and Hoffman La Roche's Valium are essentially the same worldwide. In contrast, proprietary (nonprescription or over-the-counter) drugs cost relatively little in technical development but a great deal in market development. Since national regulations for nonprescription drugs vary a great deal from country to country (more so than for prescription drugs), and developing variants is relatively cheap, companies are happy to market many national versions of over-the-counter drugs. The expensive market development costs are mostly incurred locally and, therefore, cannot be much reduced by globalization.

Savings on purchasing, production, and inventory accrue when standardization reduces the number of products and increases the volume per product. Black & Decker was particularly successful in reducing its number of products. Before Nolan Archibald became CEO of Black & Decker in 1985, the company was "a confederation of nearly sovereign fiefdoms," where British, French, and German country managers developed and sold their own products in their own countries. For example, the company made over 100 different motors worldwide. Not surprisingly, Black & Decker had tremendous overhead that was not offset by any efficiencies or economies of scale. When Archibald came on board, he instituted the development of standardized products that

WHIRLPOOL'S PLATFORM FOR GROWTH

To bring product design in home appliances into line with the automotive industry's concept of a "world car," Whirlpool, the producer of major appliances, implemented in the late 1990s a plan to globalize the development of new products.[5] The plan mobilized more than 2,000 engineers to collectively develop new products on common platforms, analogous to those for cars. Although Whirlpool recognizes that it must respect local needs of the consumer, the company asserts that the basic product technology is the same around the world. Therefore, it believes that the product can be split up into two parts: the parts that the consumer sees that are built onto the platform, and the common parts and subsystems that make up the platform. The company seeks to reduce the number of platforms worldwide from 135 to 65. Dishwasher platforms that vary significantly across continents will be cut from six to three by 2002. Refrigerators, also a difficult product to standardize globally, will have almost 50 percent fewer platforms by the early 2000s (from 48 to 25). In addition, Whirlpool is looking to reduce its $200 million annual development costs by 10 percent, increase productivity of design teams by 30 percent, and reduce purchasing costs by $180 million due to global sourcing efforts.

could be sold around the globe. By 1989, Black & Decker made only 20 different motors and was planning to reduce that number to five. Philips, the Dutch multinational company, also drastically reduced its product lines, such as in television receivers, in the late 1980s.[6]

Product standardization also multiplies the gains from concentrating production to exploit economies of scale. As will be discussed in the next chapter, activity concentration can reduce costs even without product standardization, but with it the potential savings become far greater.

IMPROVED QUALITY

Less obvious than cost reduction, but potentially as important, product standardization can also improve the quality of the products themselves. Reducing the worldwide number of products, through standardization, allows financial and management resources to be focused on the smaller number of products. Braun—the German manufacturer of shavers, coffee makers, and other consumer durable goods, and now a subsidiary of Gillette—maintains a very high reputation partly by restricting the number of products it offers. This parsimony applies across countries as well as across the product line. Braun does little tailoring for national tastes but single-mindedly maintains its distinctive, global design style.

ENHANCED CUSTOMER PREFERENCE

Although product standardization can reduce customer preference by failing to tailor for national needs, in many situations standardization can actually increase preference. For consumer products and services that are bought while abroad as well as in the consumer's home country, the availability of the same product or service can frequently be a plus that reinforces preference. Frequently consumed products like soft drinks, fast food, cigarettes, and candy lend themselves most to this effect. Not surprisingly, Coca-Cola, McDonald's, Philip Morris, and Nestlé derive much of their revenues from globally standardized products. In contrast, products that are seldom purchased while abroad, like detergent or floor wax, do not gain preference from global standardization. Similarly, travel-related consumer services, from credit cards and traveler's checks to airlines and automobile rental, all need to be as standardized as possible. Some companies like American Express do an excellent job, while others are surprisingly lax. Automobile rental companies such as Hertz and Avis have failed to standardize the way in which they classify their types of vehicles and do not even provide a guide to comparing American and European classifications. Because few American travelers are familiar with individual European models, they sometimes wind up renting cars in Europe too small for their families and baggage. Europeans have the opposite problem. They can find themselves trying to drive an "intermediate" in North America that is larger than most passenger cars on European roads.

Global standardization also enhances consumer preference when being global is an essential part of the category's or brand's appeal. Thus, part of Benetton's appeal to teenagers is the implication that wearing its (globally standardized) clothes somehow contributes to world unity; part of Louis Vuitton's appeal is that wealthy and discerning buyers around the world have the same taste in luggage and accessories. Furthermore, when users of Benetton or Vuitton products travel, the items bring global recognition of the travelers' affinity, taste, or wealth. So LVMH, the parent company of Louis Vuitton and other luxury brands, adapts its product ranges very little around the world: Its luggage, watches, and champagnes are globally the same. Even its DFS duty-free chain retained the same approach and merchandise mix as it expanded from Asia to the United States.

Industrial or commercial products and services sold to multinational customers can also gain increased preference from standardization. The more the customers themselves have a global strategy, the more need they have to purchase globally standardized products and services. Some executives worry that standardizing products will make it easier for competitors to steal business with imitative products. But this risk can be greatly reduced by continuing to differentiate *among* multinational customers while standardizing *within* a given multinational customer.

COMPETITIVE LEVERAGE

Globally standardized products can increase competitive leverage by providing low-cost products that can be the basis for invading markets. When they first entered international markets, most Japanese companies lacked the resources to develop and support different products for different countries. Turning this weakness into a strength, they focused on a small number of globally standardized products that initially via low cost, then via superior quality, allowed them to conquer market after market. In contrast, Western companies that are market share followers tend to defend against larger competitors by offering locally customized products. The Japanese experience suggests that smaller competitors may have greater need for standardized products.

DRAWBACKS OF GLOBAL PRODUCTS AND SERVICES

The most important drawback of global product standardization is that some aspects of national needs may have to be sacrificed. As a result, customer preference in some countries may be less than for a product customized for the local market. Stories abound of companies that have made mistakes by not customizing for local needs, such as American appliances that are too large for Japanese kitchens or Japanese calculator pads too small for American fingers. The key is to find a balance between the benefits and drawbacks of standardization. Furthermore, the benefits can be increased and the drawbacks reduced by designing global products from scratch. These global products (or services) should seek to satisfy the most important common needs of the most important markets.

Canon's product strategy when it first entered the photocopier business in the early 1970s provides one of the most powerful examples of sacrificing the ability to meet local needs. Canon chose to design from scratch a global product. In doing so, Canon realized that it could not keep the feature of being able to copy all sizes of Japanese paper if the product cost was to meet its target. Canon willingly gave up the ability to meet all the needs in its *domestic* market in order to maximize its prospects in the *global* market.[7] Few companies would find it easy to make such a decision.

GLOBAL STANDARDIZATION IN SERVICE BUSINESSES

One of the greatest dilemmas in global strategy for manufacturing businesses is the need to balance global standardization with local customization. Designing, then manufacturing, a global product with a degree of local customization requires major trade-offs. In contrast, the nature of service delivery—at the point of consumption in many cases—makes both standardization and customization equally feasible. Local elements (e.g., mariachi bands in Mexico) can be easily added to a global formula (Club Med vacations); using local nationals as service providers may overcome the foreignness of a standardized service (e.g., use of local cabin crews by international airlines). The practice of augmenting a core service with many supplementary elements makes it relatively easy to provide a globally standardized core service augmented (and differentiated) by nationally customized supplementary service elements. This tends to be easier than for manufacturing businesses.

So services can be particularly easy to both globalize and localize. In perhaps the most extreme example, McDonald's opened restaurants in India that, in deference to Hindu reverence for cows, do not serve hamburgers at all. Were McDonald's a goods-based business, that could be equivalent to selling a car without an engine. But as a service-based business, the other core and supplementary elements can make up for the lack of beef. McDonald's also adds items, such as Veggie Burgers, to menus to meet local tastes. In Britain, McDonald's includes both tea and coffee in its menus; while in France and Germany, it also serves beer. Interestingly, these local variations are in the food itself, the product element, rather than in the service elements. In services, McDonald's allows little variation in its core formula of restaurant design, service approach, and key menu items. In opening its Moscow restaurants, McDonald's made great efforts to maintain its standard formula, right down to the smiles of the servers.

Hewlett-Packard is a global leader in computer-based customer support services. It maintains a globally standardized set of services that range from site design to systems integration and remote diagnostics. This global standardization includes seamless service at any hour of the day or night from anywhere in the world.

Professional service firms vary in their ability to provide a globally standardized service. Some firms, such as those in the accounting industry, face significant international differences in technical standards, making uniformity more difficult. But it is also a matter of strategy. Andersen Consulting (now Accenture) chose to lead in offering globally standardized services. Its competitors had to play catch-up. Similarly, advertising agencies face international differences in culture and consumer behavior, but some have chosen to overcome these differences.

Given that people are part of the production system, some service businesses have to work quite hard at global standardization. To implement its ambition of becoming the world's premier global consumer bank, Citibank is investing heavily in technology to ensure that the 65,000 Citibank personnel worldwide, many speaking different languages, deliver the same experience. The global standard also applies to the "model" branch, by 1997 in place in over half of its 1,100 plus branches around the world. While fast-food chains commonly standardize formats, banks have typically been given the latitude to choose their own layout at the local level. Citibank, however, intends to give customers the same retail services and experiences everywhere.

EFFECT OF THE INTERNET ON GLOBAL PRODUCTS AND SERVICES

The Internet enhances the ability to both globalize and localize. Web sites lend themselves marvelously to being both global and local at the same time. A global portal can offer the user a large number of regionally or nationally tailored sites. As old-economy companies increase the Web-based component of their offerings, they can exploit this duality of the Web. New-economy companies that sell primarily over the Internet have to race to increase the number of their national Web sites. As of early 2000, fewer than one-third of major online companies had localized Web sites for their international customers.[8] Even Amazon.com still offered only two non-U.S. Web sites, for Britain and Germany. On the other hand, *Elle,* the leading women's fashion magazine, had 12 national Web sites covering five continents.

Companies also need to think about global commonality and recognizability across their various national sites. Amazon.com does a minimal job, with common blue horizontal bars. MTV does not even try. Its U.S. and U.K. sites currently have no elements in common. In contrast, Yahoo! has nearly identical home pages for its 24 national Web sites. Another issue is whether companies wish to make cross-country web-hopping easier or more difficult—easier if users can transfer to other countries' sites without reverting back to the global home page.

The ability to customize the Web site for individual regular users raises issues of global product and service design. The vendor can in principle totally vary the national mixes offered to the individual customer, and the latter is freed from the tyranny of location. For example, an American customer need no longer be offered just American styles and sizes by a clothing company, but whatever national preferences he or she has expressed through clicking and purchasing behavior, or by stated preferences. At the same time, firms must consider the supply chain issues of offering everyone, everything, everywhere. Citibank, as yet the only retail bank with a significant global presence, lets its customers do business with the bank "any way, any time, any where."

Lastly, where the service is delivered over the Web, companies may increasingly seek to design standard offerings that have maximum global appeal. Perhaps the ultimate example was the launch on April 19, 2000, of the world's first virtual broadcaster, Ananova. This product of the British national news agency, the Press Association, was designed as a simulated female "cybercaster" with broad global appeal (with a mid-Atlantic accent and vague ethnic origin), out-globaling the real-life newscaster Christiane Amanpour of CNN fame. But Ananova and Amanpour make an interesting contrast. The former is global by virtue of being from nowhere, while the latter is global in combining three very specific but contrasting origins: Iranian, British, and American. Companies, too, can choose to position their products as "global from nowhere" or "global from somewhere."

WHEN TO USE GLOBAL PRODUCTS AND SERVICES

As with the other global strategy levers, the condition of industry globalization affects the use of global products and services.

MARKET GLOBALIZATION DRIVERS FOR GLOBAL PRODUCTS

Among market globalization drivers, the extent of *common customer needs* and of the importance of *global customers* provides the main stimulus to using globally standardized products and services.

Common Customer Needs

The extent to which customers in different countries have the same needs and tastes in a given product or service category provides the primary determinant of how much to standardize. In the pharmaceutical industry fundamental customer needs are highly common as disease and ailments strike all of humanity and in mostly similar ways. Many afflictions are universal: from the common cold to heart disease. There are some geographic differences, with tropical diseases being the largest group of location-specific afflictions. Similarly, national diets and lifestyle affect the relative incidence of different diseases, such as the well-known high incidence of heart disease in Western countries arising from high-fat diets and the high incidence of hypertension in Asian countries arising from high-salt diets. But, like other differences in national habits, these dietary differences and their related health consequences are declining. Ice cream is becoming increasingly popular in Japan while Oriental food is joining the menu of American fast food. So overall, needs are highly common. But even if the *incidence* of a particular disease varies, its treatment is usually the same. So multinational drug companies are able to market nearly identical products around the world, and successes in one country can rapidly become global successes.

At the same time, national practices differ somewhat in how ailments are treated. Some countries are more eager users of surgery, some rely more on medicines prescribed by doctors, and others depend on over-the-counter remedies suggested by pharmacists. In particular, the preferred form of the medicine varies greatly. For example, in Britain many people prefer to take aspirin in powder form dissolved in water instead of the tablet or capsule form popular in the United States. People in some countries like to take medicine via suppositories. Preference for folk remedies over manufactured medicines also varies. The return-to-nature trend has created the new category of "phaetopharmaceuticals," which are made from natural, nonchemical ingredients. These new medicines have captured a very large share of the market in Germany. Even diagnosis can be affected by national culture: Americans tend to focus on head pains while Japanese tend to focus on stomach pains. National difference in treatment tends to be much greater for over-the-counter drugs, which consumers select for themselves, than for prescription drugs, which are chosen by doctors.

Computer products also have high levels of global standardization. While local business practices and government regulation may affect the content, format, and frequency of, for example, accounting reports, the need for hardware is not fundamentally affected by these variations. So in the computer industry, companies usually find it easier to globally standardize hardware than software. But various cultural factors affect both hardware and software: Computing is particularly affected by language differences. For example, Japanese *kanji* characters require two bytes to store, in contrast to one byte for Western alphabetical characters. One computer company accommodated these differences by designing a global product from the start, with broad capabilities. Also, in Japan, dedicated word processors (capable of handling Japanese characters) are far more common than in Western Europe and the United States, where dedicated word processing machines have dwindled as a product segment. The need to translate software and documentation for the various European and Asian markets also poses a barrier to the easy dissemination of application software. In health care software systems, the key distinction between countries in the commonality of software needs turns on whether medicine is socialized.

In textbook publishing, the potential for global products is limited by the desire of teachers to use books that reflect the national perspective on history, sociology, psychology, and other subjects. Other than primary sources and some scholarly books, college textbooks in the social sciences and humanities remain largely domestic in origin. Textbooks at the precollege level are even more restricted to national markets. One significant exception to the lack of global textbooks is English as a second language (ESL) instruction, where standardized texts abound. Even so, the world market has long been divided between instruction in American English and British English, with textbook sales following the relative influence of the two countries. For example, American English is taught in Japan, but British English is taught in Malaysia. In some countries, such as Brazil, there is competition between the two forms of English.

Global Customers

Global customers often demand global products and services. So the incidence of global customers has a major effect on the need and potential for product standardization. In the computer industry, customers who globally coordinate their purchases are becoming an increasingly important driver. As customers become more sophisticated computer system buyers, and as they become globalized themselves, they are also becoming more willing to look beyond a single vendor. Their purchasing criteria have changed from focusing on the security provided by a single vendor to maximizing system performance at minimal cost. Further, as companies adopt "open systems" architectures, they frequently do so with the realization that their corporate information systems need to be coordinated on a global scale. But as yet, only perhaps 10 to 15 percent of buyers act as global customers. A larger number of buyers (perhaps 20 to 25 percent) look regionally.[9] But because of their investment in proprietary systems, many buyers are reluctant to consider new suppliers. Even multinational firms may choose to replicate their headquarters' computer system in their foreign affiliates instead of adopting a newer global hardware standard because the costs of transferring software, writing new programs, and training staff on new systems can be prohibitive.

A Stanford–UCLA study in 1997 of 165 multinational companies found that while the average revenues from all international customers were 46 percent, those from multinational customers were 26 percent, and those from globally coordinated multinational customers were only 13 percent.[10] So although revenues from all international customers were 46 percent (fairly typical of a Fortune 500 type of firm population), only 13 percent of revenues were from truly global customers. While 13 percent may seem low, these revenues usually come from the most prestigious and most sophisticated customers. Few multinational suppliers can afford to underserve such customers. Furthermore, this percentage will increase, as other evidence shows. The study also found that demand for all aspects of global account management increased dramatically from 1992 to 1997. Suppliers' use of all aspects of global account management in 1997 was at the moderate level, somewhat below the levels of customer demand in 1997. But suppliers expected to greatly increase their use of all aspects, with scores in the five-figure range in five years' time (by 2002).

In the process control industry, many multinational customers now demand globally standardized products. For example, Royal Dutch Shell, a major customer, might order 16 identical units for its different plants around the world because it wants each plant to be a mirror image of the others.

Most consumer packaged goods industries have few global customers, but the chocolate industry provides an interesting exception. The chocolate industry has global customers in one special sense. Many consumers buy chocolate as a gift to others (or for themselves) while traveling abroad. The ease of customizing chocolate to incorporate local specialties also encourages purchases by travelers (chocolate with macadamia nuts in Hawaii or with kiwi fruit in New Zealand). Such purchases abroad expose consumers to different types of chocolate around the world, helping to establish global standards in perceived quality and perhaps taste also. So companies can benefit by maintaining similar brand images, packaging, and quality standards for their chocolates around the world. The impact of global customers is even greater for more frequently purchased consumer packaged goods items like soft drinks and cigarettes.

COST GLOBALIZATION DRIVERS FOR GLOBAL PRODUCTS

Among cost globalization drivers *global scale economies, high product development costs* and *fast-changing technology* have the most effect on the need for global products and services.

Global Scale Economies

Global-level scale economies in the production process encourage businesses to centralize production. Typically, the technological imperatives that yield global scale production economies also yield important production economies in product rationalization. Thus the gains from centralized production can usually be multiplied when combined with a focused, global product line. Both Black & Decker in small appliances and Becton Dickinson in disposable syringes have greatly benefited from using global product ranges with limited items.

High Product Development Costs/Fast-Changing Technology

High product development costs provide a major motivation for using globally standardized products and services. This motivation is particularly important in industries with rapidly changing technology, such as electronics, or risky development efforts, such as pharmaceuticals. As technology becomes more important in more and more industries, companies in even the food industry are finding that it no longer pays to develop national products. In the coffee industry, for example, the cost of developing new forms of soluble coffee is so great now that companies work on developing new forms (e.g., freeze dried) for global markets only, even though they may adapt blends (e.g., types of coffee beans used) for individual markets.

GOVERNMENT GLOBALIZATION DRIVERS FOR GLOBAL PRODUCTS

Among government globalization drivers *favorable trade policies* and *compatible technical standards* have the greatest effect on the potential for global products and services.

Favorable Trade Policies

Trade barriers, particularly nontariff ones such as quotas and local content rules, can greatly restrict a company's ability to produce and market a globally standardized product line. In products where the source of raw materials is critical, or the production process is difficult to reproduce in some countries, trade restrictions can prevent the use of global products.

Compatible Technical Standards

Differences in technical standards and related rules directly affect the extent to which products can be globally standardized. Fortunately, differing national standards are converging in many industries toward common global standards. The increasing convergence of standards in telecommunications is making it easier to design global products in that industry. For example, instead of designing products for just the North American market, as it used to do, Northern Telecom, the Canadian telecommunications company, now designs global products for all of its markets, making only minor software modifications.

COMPETITIVE GLOBALIZATION DRIVERS FOR GLOBAL PRODUCTS

Lastly, having *globalized competitors* who themselves use globally standardized products or services can provide a powerful spur to developing global products of one's own. It is Japanese companies who have tended to lead in this strategy, forcing their rivals to play catch-up in designing global products, for example, American and European manufacturers in both automobiles and consumer electronics.

GLOBAL STANDARDIZATION IN FINANCIAL SERVICES

Despite regulatory barriers, many companies in financial service industries manage a surprisingly high degree of global standardization. Although differences in financial products exist, many are becoming increasingly standardized.[11] Barclays, a leading British bank, aims to ensure through its global customer information system that its multinational corporate customers can have access to a uniform range of products at a uniform level of service in a familiar Barclays environment. Because credit cards have become standardized, Citicorp introduced its bank cards into Europe with little modification. American Express is, perhaps, the master of offering a standardized global product in financial services. French banks have introduced standard leasing arrangements with particular success in Spain and Portugal. Letters of credit have been standardized to the extent that they are almost exclusively written in English to facilitate international transactions and to ensure consistency of contract language. Some products, however, are difficult to standardize because of long-standing differences in national practices. In the United States, the 30-year mortgage is standard, while in Europe the 10-year mortgage is more common. Despite these differences, many financial product modifications are not too costly, so that national differences can often be accommodated. The potential for further global standardization seems high as regulatory changes continue to further standardize banking practices and foster greater international competition.

DEVELOPING GLOBAL PRODUCTS AND SERVICES

There are two primary ways to develop global products and services. The first, and preferred, method is to develop products and services with the global market in mind, as Canon did for its first photocopier. This approach has the obvious advantage of taking into consideration the needs of major markets right at the start, rather than having to retrofit a product developed for one national market. *Managers should start by identifying globally strategic markets and then understanding the needs of those markets. Perhaps most important, managers should search for commonalities rather than for differences.* Such an approach should allow managers to design the largest possible standardized core, while allowing for necessary customization at the same time.[12]

The second, less desirable but more common, approach is to adapt existing products or services. In adapting from an existing mix of national products, managers need to start by understanding the causes of the national variants. Have these variants arisen from a deliberate response to real differences in needs and tastes? Or are they accidents of independent development? Very often the answer is much more accident than deliberation. Many businesses wind up with product lines that are much less standardized than they could be, simply by not having a global perspective, so that countries make decisions independently of each other.

A European manufacturer of semidurable consumer products found itself with half the countries in the world selling products in one set of colors and the other half in another set. These were not major color differences, but differences, for example, in the shade of blue. This situation arose because most of the world was supplied out of two manufacturing plants, one in the United Kingdom and one in Germany, and the two general managers in these two countries made decisions independently. When first asked to explain the difference, the executives in this business tried to justify their decisions on the basis of differences

USG'S SUCCESSFUL EUROPEAN PRODUCT STANDARDIZATION

The experience of USG Interiors, a subsidiary of USG Corporation (formerly U.S. Gypsum), with acoustic ceiling tiles in Europe provides a useful example of why and how one company pushed for product standardization.[13] While limited to Europe, the same principles apply in a global program. In 1986, USG had acquired a German-based manufacturer of building products, DONN, which was the dominant supplier of ceiling suspension products in the commercial construction market in Europe. The four DONN companies — in Germany, France, the United Kingdom, and Scandinavia — operated very independently, and the localized approach seemed to be one of DONN's greatest strengths. The acquisition by USG brought a new name, USG Interiors Europe, and a whole new product line — the APCO line of acoustic ceiling tile, manufactured by USG in the United States — that seemed a natural fit with the DONN suspension product. USG Interiors Europe decided to introduce APCO as a standardized pan-European product that had minor modifications from the North American product and did not take DONN's old multilocal approach of allowing each country to develop its own products and programs.

Europe 1992 provided the impetus for this change in approach. The European interior building industry had been very fragmented for many years, as the different national, and even local, requirements made it very difficult to ship and install materials across boundaries. Consequently, many small manufacturing and installation companies existed, and most of them operated within a limited geographic range only. But with Europe 1992, regulations, style, norms, and quality standards would be harmonized within the different countries in Europe. USG Interiors predicted that business

opportunities would increase, and the industry would consolidate into fewer but larger manufacturing companies producing very similar products for all EC markets at lower costs.

The second reason for standardization was that all manufacturing of the new line would be done in the United States. Given that Europe would use different sizes from the United States and would require short production runs, it was imperative for the U.S. factory that Europe standardize on one product line and not require many different, national lines. Even so, it was the first time that the U.S. operations would have to deal with packaging restrictions, stock quantities in non-U.S. sizes, as well as different colors and formulas for what appeared on the surface to be the same product. The U.S. workers would also have to deal with the aesthetic requirements of a European-based community that was decidedly different from North America. European standards for color and tolerances on sizes and texture were more stringent than those in the U.S. market.

USG's approach to anticipating the 1992 changes involved taking the most strict national standards and making them their overall European standards. USG also used a team approach to specify the product requirements and marketing needs and to develop an integrated approach to launching into the different markets. Most important, this integrated approach was sensitive not to upset the local marketing practices already established and that had proved so effective historically in each of their four European companies. The new product line was introduced from late 1987 through 1989. USG judged the new pan-European approach to be highly successful: By late 1989, revenues and profits had tripled from those in 1983.

in consumer preference. But when pushed, the executives admitted that the differences did not arise from perceived consumer differences but from the independent decision-making process. In contrast, the business's major competitor had great success with a highly standardized product line, confirming that customer preferences were not that different.

GUIDELINES FOR DESIGNING GLOBAL PRODUCTS AND SERVICES

Successfully designing global products and services requires managers to make tough trade-offs between global and local demands. Several guidelines apply, including the following:

- Globally standardized products and services can bring the benefits of not just cost savings, but also those of improved quality and customer preference.
- The best global products are usually those that are designed as such from the start rather than being adapted from national products later.
- Designers of global products and services should try to maximize the size of the common global core while also providing for local tailoring around the core.
- In investigating customer needs around the world, managers should look for similarities as well as for differences.

Discussion and Research Questions

1. What is the difference between a local product and a global product?
2. Identify a global product or service. Describe what is standardized about it and what is localized.
3. Which of the following products and services are more globally standardized and why?
   Apple Mac computers
   Sony Walkman
   American Express Gold Card
   Disney theme parks
   Mercedes automobiles
   Nestlé coffee
4. How should a company go about developing a global product?
5. Select one product or service and discuss which aspects of it are global and which local, and why.
6. Which service elements are more easy to standardize globally?
7. How does the Internet affect product standardization and localization?

Notes

1. This term was coined by David Stout, head of Economics, Unilever PLC.
2. Adapted from "Can Honda Build a World Car?" *Business Week,* September 8, 1997, pp. 100–8.
3. See George Stalk, Jr., and Thomas M. Hout, *Competing Against Time* (New York: Free Press, 1990).
4. Adapted from "A Car Is Born," *The Economist,* September 13, 1997, pp. 68–9.
5. Adapted from "Whirlpool's Platform for Growth," *Financial Times,* March 26, 1998, p. 8.
6. Francis J. Aguilar and Michael Y. Yoshino, "The Philips Group: 1987," Case No. 9-388-050 (Boston, MA: Harvard Business School).
7. See also Michael E. Porter, "Changing Patterns of International Competition," *California Management Review,* Vol. 28, No. 2, Winter 1986, pp. 33–34.
8. David Kushner, "An Electronic Tower of Babel?" *International Herald Tribune,* April 24, 2000, p. 6.
9. These estimates of global customers and global channels were made by senior executives in a major computer manufacturer.

10. David B. Montgomery and George S. Yip, "The Challenge of Global Customer Management," *Marketing Management,* Vol. 9, No. 4, Winter 2000, pp. 22–9.

11. This paragraph is based on Julie Carson, Sanjay Dube, Shyh-jaw Chien, Eric Crabtree, and Mitsuhisa Ashida, "Worldwide Commercial Banking in the Late 1980s," unpublished report (Washington, DC: Georgetown Business School, 1989).

12. See also Ilkka A. Ronkainen, "Product-Development Processes in the Multinational Firm," *International Marketing Review,* Winter 1983, pp. 57–65. For a comprehensive description on how to develop multinational product policy, see, for example, William H. Davidson, *Global Strategic Management* (New York: John Wiley & Sons, 1982).

13. This example is based on a presentation by Dietmar Neupert, managing director, USG Interiors, Inc. (Germany), at the Planning Forum Conference on Europe 1992, in Boston, on October 16, 1989.

5
LOCATING GLOBAL ACTIVITIES

The global location of activities represents the third global strategy lever. Where to locate a business's activities and how to coordinate them constitute critical choices in global strategy.[1] Every functional or value-adding activity, from research to manufacturing to customer service, is a candidate for globalization. Traditionally, multinational companies have faced two choices in activity location. On the one hand, they can duplicate an activity in multiple foreign locations. The classic multinational strategy has been to reproduce activities in many countries, particularly the production function by setting up factories and other manufacturing assets. On the other hand, multinational companies can keep activities concentrated in the home country. Exhibit 5-1 summarizes some key choices in terms of location and coordination.

The classic *export-based strategy* has been to locate as much of the value chain as possible back home, while locating overseas only downstream activities—such as selling, distribution, and service—that have to be performed close to the end customer. This was the typical strategy of Japanese and Korean companies in the 1970s and 1980s, before they began to move production overseas. Not much coordination is needed as there are few assets overseas and little international variation in product offerings.

As discussed in earlier chapters, there is also a *multilocal strategy* in which activities are geographically dispersed and only loosely coordinated. Dispersed activities combined

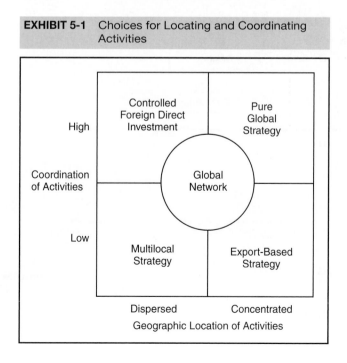

EXHIBIT 5-1   Choices for Locating and Coordinating Activities

with high coordination can be viewed as *controlled foreign direct investment*. This is a form of global strategy and is often a transition phase from multilocal strategy. For example, many older European multinational companies found themselves in the 1980s and 1990s with activities that were too dispersed for the new economics in a globalizing world. An initial response was to increase coordination as a precursor to reducing the number of locations for activities.

A *pure global strategy* also concentrates activities, but in contrast to an export-based strategy, these activities are not all concentrated in the home country but in one or a few best different countries for each different activity. For example, such a strategy might locate research in the United Kingdom, development in Germany, raw material processing in Mexico, subassembly in the United States, final assembly in Ireland, and so on. Exhibit 5-2 shows an extreme case of a global value chain in which every activity occurs in one different country only. In reality most companies would, and should, provide for some duplication of most activities. Such duplication provides security against supply disruptions and provides some flexibility in the system. Another way of viewing the global approach to activity location is the following. Global activity location means deploying one integrated, but globally dispersed, value chain or network that serves the entire worldwide business, rather than separate country value chains or one home-based value chain.

Increasingly, multinational companies are trying to head toward the center position in Exhibit 5-2, that of the *global network*.[2] Here there is more dispersion and perhaps

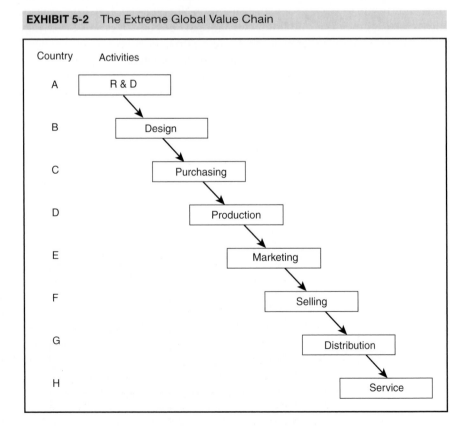

EXHIBIT 5-2   The Extreme Global Value Chain

Country Activities

A   R & D

B   Design

C   Purchasing

D   Production

E   Marketing

F   Selling

G   Distribution

H   Service

less coordination than in a pure global strategy. No part of the organization, whether headquarters or subsidiary, is self-sufficient. Instead, all work together in a network. The global network is made possible as technical developments in the transfer of data and falling transportation costs make it less and less necessary to co-locate functions.[3] It is now viable to integrate operations on a global basis and put parts of the value chain in different parts of the world. Nippon-Denso, a Japanese producer of air conditioners and other automobile parts, operates an Asia-Pacific network in which starters, alternators, and wiper motors are made in Thailand; engine control units (ECUs), alternating current amplifiers, and relay arms in Malaysia; compressors and spark plugs in Indonesia; meters in the Philippines; and evaporators and condensers in Australia.[4]

Most leading American, European, and Japanese companies (e.g., Toyota and Sony) are now converging on the global network model, albeit from different starting points—many Japanese companies from pure global strategy, many older European companies (e.g., Philips and Unilever) from multilocal strategy, and many American companies (e.g., Coca-Cola and General Electric) from controlled foreign direct investment. The Internet and the Web have consolidated the global network as the dominant model of multinational companies for the foreseeable future. This model seeks to reduce duplication of activities. The Web, through both intranets and extranets, offers the potential to complete this process of de-duplication. This model is, therefore, also ideal for Internet-based new-economy companies, many of which are "born global."

Perhaps the most important consideration in a global strategy approach to activity location is to take a "zero-based" view and to ask what would be the optimal pattern and location of each activity if the company could start from scratch. Hardly any company is likely to be able to conclude that its current pattern of location is optimal. Because globalization conditions have changed and continue to do so, and because of a lack of global thinking in the past, many, perhaps most, companies find themselves saddled with activity networks unsuited to the globalization potential of the industries in which they operate. Companies in Europe in the 1980s provided the most extreme example. With the coming single European market many companies there found themselves with factories 50 kilometers apart on either side of a frontier that would no longer exist. The 1990s saw major restructuring and concentration of production and other activities in Europe, and this process continues in the 2000s. Clearly, changing the location of activities, particularly of major fixed assets like factories, is expensive and, in many cases, not justified. But global managers need to operate with an understanding of where their activities ought to be located even if they cannot easily move them there. Such knowledge is essential in planning investments to upgrade or expand existing facilities and to create new ones.

EFFECT OF THE INTERNET ON GLOBAL ACTIVITY LOCATION

The Internet helps to solve the longtime dilemma facing multinational companies— how much of their value chain to re-create overseas? In earlier eras of poor transportation and communications, the solution generally required the foreign location of a lot of expensive assets and activities. In the global era, beginning in the 1980s, many companies found that they could reduce duplication by operating *physical* networks with specialized nodes. As an *electronic* network, the Web reinforces this process of consolidation. Smart companies are shifting the burden of proof in two ways. First, they ask which activities have to be conducted physically rather than on the Web. Second, they ask which activities have to be physically duplicated in more than one country (the one country not necessarily being the home country either).

Many downstream and support activities lend themselves well to Web-based replacement for local physical presence. Globalizing R&D has been a key aim of many companies, but this has often meant centralizing at one location to achieve the required scale. The Web now enables virtual R&D teams that concentrate and pool expertise and resources from separate locations, so that firms can tap into local expertise and still achieve global scale. The Web can also be used to coordinate globally dispersed productions. The General Motors intranet, Socrates, helps coordinate 100,000 workers spread across 125 countries. In global distribution, third-party providers such as DHL are using the Web to improve their services. DHL is piloting a Web system to let shippers determine duties and tariffs before their products cross international borders. Maersk Logistics, based in Denmark, markets a Web-based supply chain system in 55 countries. Many companies now handle much of their global after-sales service through their Web sites. Cisco, for example, provides 80 percent of its service over the Web.

ROLE OF NATIONAL FACTORS

Many factors affect the choice of location for activities. Global managers need to distinguish between traditional country considerations and global strategic importance, among other considerations.

TRADITIONAL COUNTRY CONSIDERATIONS

Traditional international economic theory has stressed the importance of "comparative advantage" in addressing where multinational companies should locate their activities.[5] In particular, they should locate in countries where the costs of raw materials, labor, and other production inputs ("factor costs") are lowest for a given level of productivity. But production cost is only one consideration. Furthermore, production costs themselves are subject to broader influences such as tax benefits and other forms of aid that may be provided by national and other country authorities. Japanese automobile manufacturers seemed particularly astute in garnering the maximum governmental benefits from their production location decisions. In placing their American production plants in the 1980s, not only did they extract many concessions from states eager for their patronage, but Honda, Nissan, and Toyota each located in a different state (Ohio, Tennessee, Kentucky, respectively), perhaps to maximize their political lobbying effectiveness by each having two senators to represent their concerns. Interestingly, in the 1990s, two German car firms located new factories in yet two other states: BMW in South Carolina and Mercedes in Alabama.

Other considerations include broader issues of productivity and quality, convenience for shipping to other countries, reliability of the workforce, the cost of capital, the economic infrastructure, and the extent of political risk. Some developing countries with low costs and high productivity may seem ideal, but they may need to be avoided because of their high level of political risk. While the risk of outright expropriation has declined, the risk of government interference as well as political and economic disruptions continues. For example, many Western companies manufacturing in China and other countries have suffered from sudden clampdowns on foreign exchange that they needed to purchase raw materials, equipment, and supplies. Multinational companies also need to worry about the social and ethical standards of suppliers from developing countries, especially if they are not themselves controlling the factories. In the 1990s, Nike, Wal-Mart, and many others were hit by protests and negative publicity about the practices of their third-world suppliers.[6] Another type of issue concerns the so-called country-of-origin effect, in which customers give preference to goods produced in certain countries or that they believe to come from those countries.[7]

The country-of-origin effect in the U.S. automobile market partly explains why the Toyota Corolla, a nearly identical car to General Motors' Geo Prizm, and produced on the same assembly line in the United States, commanded a 10 percent or so price premium in the market. (The next chapter, on global marketing, will also address this effect.) All of these considerations in the location of activities, including from where to source production inputs, should be familiar to multinational companies in developing their internationalization strategy. So in keeping with the focus of this book on globalization rather than internationalization, this author assumes a basic understanding of these issues and addresses them only in terms of how they affect globalization strategy.[8]

GLOBALLY STRATEGIC COUNTRIES FOR ACTIVITY LOCATION

Just as countries can be globally strategic from the viewpoint of market participation, they can be globally strategic in terms of activity location, for some of the same, but also some different, reasons. Two activities, R&D and production, particularly need to be located in globally strategic countries.

For R&D Location

For R&D, globally strategic countries have the following characteristics:

- Major source of industry innovation
- Presence of highly skilled and/or low-cost R&D workers
- Highly demanding customers

As in the case of market participation, the R&D activity benefits from location in countries that are major sources of industry innovation. R&D workers in those countries can gain direct access to the many sources of the innovations being created—via face-to-face contacts with university researchers, participation in conferences, quicker access to publications, competition in the job market, and so on. Monitoring from a distance cannot achieve the full benefits possible through physical location. For example, many scientific journals in Japan are published only in Japanese and circulate little outside the country. While the countries making the major innovations in an industry also tend to have the most skilled R&D workers, other countries can also be important sources of highly skilled or low-cost staff. Several Asian countries have demonstrated this capability.

With the opening up of Eastern Europe, similar opportunities are emerging. The countries of the former Soviet Union, for example, have very well-trained scientists who may have much to contribute to commercial R&D efforts. Because of continuing turbulence in Russia, many multinational companies are choosing to hire away Russian scientists and technologists rather than setting up R&D facilities there.

Lastly, locating R&D in countries with highly demanding customers helps the R&D staff there to better understand the nature of their needs. Furthermore, the same tactic

INDIA'S EMERGING ROLE IN GLOBAL R&D

India is emerging also as a major R&D sourcing center.[9] Companies such as Abbott Laboratories, Acer Computer, Akzo, Du Pont, Eli Lilly, FMC, General Electric, Haldar Topsoe, Hewlett-Packard, Hughes, Lummus, Motorola, Nova Nordisk, Smith Kline Beecham, Telstra, and Unilever have R&D alliances with government-run laboratories under the Council for Scientific and Industrial Research or with private companies. Companies with local R&D can implement product adaptations more quickly than those companies exporting from other markets. Motorola set up a corporate research center in Bangalore to develop software for all Motorola companies worldwide. Where Motorola finds sufficient market demand, it commits complete manufacturing operations. For example, while semiconductors continue to be imported, pagers for the Indian market are manufactured locally. Furthermore, Motorola created an R&D center for pagers in Bangalore that will develop pagers capable of transmitting Hindi and Gujarati messages. Even Chinese companies are setting up R&D in India. In 2001, China's Huawei Technologies Limited, a major telecom company, chose Bangalore for its largest software development center outside China.

might bring benefits even for the home market. American automobile manufacturers, facing severe attacks from Japanese and European competitors, have made some efforts at designing cars with a European or Japanese feel (e.g., General Motors' Chevrolet Celebrity "Eurosport" model and the Ford Taurus). If they seriously want to do this, they might consider moving their design staff to Europe or Japan, or using their European divisions to design some of the models for their American market.

For Manufacturing Location

For manufacturing, globally strategic countries are those that offer an attractive investment climate as well as factors and conditions on which to build comparative and strategic advantage. Companies choosing to make investments in manufacturing facilities, as opposed to sourcing from outside suppliers, need to consider a long list of factors affecting the investment climate. This list includes the level of political stability, government policies toward foreign investment, trade policies, tax policies, legal factors, the macroeconomic environment, and policies on international payments. These considerations are the usual ones that have to be dealt with when a company internationalizes through foreign direct investment.[10] The additional factors that produce comparative and strategic advantage—and, therefore, render a country globally strategic for manufacturing—include the following:

- Favorable factor conditions
- Close location to major markets
- Favorable country-of-origin effect
- Manufacturing presence of global competitors

Favorable factor conditions—such as low-cost raw materials or labor, or highly skilled or productive labor—form the traditional basis for comparative advantage of one country relative to others.[11] Similarly, location close to major markets can be viewed as a type of factor advantage that lowers transportation cost or speeds up response time, thus providing both comparative and strategic advantage.[12] Countries that lead in innovation, that produce high-quality products, or that have highly demanding customers often enjoy a positive country-of-origin effect, though typically only within specific product categories. Lastly, the manufacturing presence of other global competitors can create a positive spiral of rivalry and imitation that continually upgrades the level of manufacturing capability for all competitors in the country.[13] So a global strategy for activity location can also be viewed as a means to get access to resources on which to build both comparative and strategic advantage.

ROLE OF EXCHANGE RATES

Currency exchange rates have a direct effect on relative country costs and, therefore, on the competitive positions of companies. In the construction equipment business Caterpillar Tractor depended heavily on U.S.-based production, while its Japanese rival, Komatsu, manufactured mainly in Japan. In 1979 Caterpillar was the low-cost producer, but by 1985 most of its product lines were priced over 40 percent above Komatsu's. One reason was that the U.S. dollar had increased by 50 percent over the yen and most key European currencies. This price difference greatly helped Komatsu to penetrate many of Caterpillar's traditional markets.[14] In response and as an operating hedge against currency fluctuations, the company moved much of its manufacturing overseas during the 1990s. By 1998, approximately half of Caterpillar's plants were overseas.

Companies that shift to lower cost countries for offshore production are taking a bet, in part, that these low costs will not be eroded by currency changes. The European introduction of the euro currency in 1999 and its nearly immediate drastic fall in value (by about 25 percent against the U.S. dollar as of mid-2001), and Britain's retention of its pound sterling, caused great problems for exporters who had located in Britain while it was relatively low cost compared to Continental Europe. In 2001, foreign investors, such as Japanese and German automobile companies, were threatening to move production out unless Britain rapidly joined the single European currency.

Perhaps most important, *companies need to recognize the strategic as well as financial risk posed by currency changes.* Traditional definitions of currency exposure concentrate mainly on foreign currency flows that relate to the company's own operations. This internal focus ignores the fact that an unfavorable currency movement may not just be unfavorable; it could be favorable to the competition. But exchange rate changes can also favor a company in the short term and hurt it in the long term. In the late 1980s depreciation of the U.S. dollar relative to the Japanese yen improved the competitive position of American companies relative to their Japanese rivals. But the higher value of the yen also allowed Japanese companies to make many bargain acquisitions that would enhance their long-run competitive capabilities. So exchange rate changes can act as catalysts in the restructuring of companies and industries.[15]

But forecasting long-term exchange rates is generally acknowledged to be very difficult. About the only consensus is that the currencies of countries with high or fast-growing productivity tend to appreciate relative to currencies in countries with low or slow-growing productivity rates. Even so, differences in productivity did not account for the down-up-down, doubling, and halving path of the U.S. dollar against the Japanese yen, Deutsche mark, and other major currencies in the 1970s and 1980s. Nor were many experts able to predict this path. Currency volatility continued in the 1990s, spurred in part by financial crises in Latin America, Russia, and Asia. One view is that companies should locate production in countries with low productivity, with the expectation that the currency will stay weak. Furthermore, these companies can increase their advantage by increasing their productivity in the country faster than the country's overall rate of productivity growth.

Another view takes into account "parity purchasing power" exchange rates that adjust for differences between countries in the prices of similar goods and services. So a country with a high relative nominal (official) exchange rate but high relative prices also has a lower parity purchasing power exchange rate. Some studies provide evidence that nominal exchange rates tend to move toward their parity purchasing power exchange over time.[16] Thus the latter rate can be used to forecast the movement of the official exchange rate. Perhaps the best that can be said is that companies looking for exchange rates that will stay weak should locate operations in countries with weak economies. Even then, it is only the nominal exchange rate that might weaken, and real exchange rates might still go up with wage and other factor price increases. Offsetting that exchange rate benefit is, of course, all the other disadvantages in terms of infrastructure and productivity inherent in weak economies. On the other hand, if a company wishes to locate in strong, or at least, developed economies, it should probably not make its choice among such countries on the basis of expected currency movements. Any likely differences in nominal exchange rates are likely to be offset by movements toward the parity purchasing power exchange rate. To maintain its comparative advantage over foreign competitors, a producer also needs to increase its productivity, *relative* to that of the country in which the production activity is located, *faster* than its competitor does in its country. Otherwise, the firm will find its productivity gains more than offset by increases in the currency exchange rate where it is located. So it is dangerous to invest in locating activities in a country with one strong sector, unless the activity is in that sector. For example, because of the effect of oil exports on strengthening Norway's exchange rate, other industries there have had great difficulty in being competitive internationally.[17]

So given the difficulty of forecasting exchange rates, global managers can choose among alternative ways of handling the uncertainty. They can speculate, hedge, or be flexible.[18] *Speculation* involves committing to one or a small number of countries as production sites. This approach, of course, runs the risk of betting the wrong way. *Hedging* means spreading out production and other activities so that losses from exchange rate rises in one country can be offset by gains from exchange rate declines in other countries. But diversifying the manufacturing base around the world may be insufficient. Managers also need to consider what competitors are doing. So a global strategy needs to consider strategic foreign exchange exposure as well as operating exposure, and strategic flexibility as well as operating flexibility. A strategy of *being flexible* means investing in excess capacity in several locations and then shifting production with exchange rate shifts. This last option provides the best chance of reducing strategic risk as well as reducing operating risk. In particular, a really cautious strategic approach to being flexible would be to manufacture in some of the same locations as major global competitors. That way, the competitor would stand less chance of gaining an advantage from movements in exchange rates.

AVON PRODUCTS' STRATEGIES FOR THE ASIAN FINANCIAL CRISIS

During the Asian financial crisis of the late 1990s, Avon Products reduced its vulnerability to currency volatility in the region by using operational and financial hedging as part of its global strategy.[19] Although Avon suffered some losses due to currency devaluation in Asia, it managed to maintain profits due to its global risk management strategy. To minimize currency risk, Avon bought raw materials and produced almost all its products in local markets where its products were sold. This "operational hedge" reduced risk, as local operations did not have to be concerned about paying high dollar denominated import costs due to a local currency devaluation. In addition, borrowing from local banks for operational purposes prevented Avon from having to pay back dollar denominated loans in devalued currencies. Avon also bought financial contracts once devaluation spread to other Asian countries.

STRATEGIC ADVANTAGE VERSUS COMPARATIVE ADVANTAGE

The previous discussion of exchange rates highlights the difference between strategic advantage and comparative advantage. In global competition, companies need to exploit both. *Strategic* advantage springs from the core business strategy, as discussed in Chapter 1. This advantage can be spread and applied around the world without depending on country-based sources of *comparative* advantage such as low labor costs or superior technological infrastructure. Apple Computer's strategic advantage came primarily from its pioneering position in the personal computer business, its unique user-friendly designs, and the strong name recognition and loyalty that it quickly built. But as both domestic and international competitors encroached on Apple's turf, the company had to add comparative advantage also by shifting some of its production activities offshore in order to reduce costs. So, today, Apple's remaining competitive advantage depends on a combination of strategic and comparative advantage.

Federal Express, now FedEx, developed a core business strategy for the document and package delivery market that gave it significant strategic advantage in its home country, the United States. The company then sought to expand its business globally. A key issue was whether its core strategy could provide the same extent of strategic advantage abroad. But it came up against entrenched competitors: DHL in Europe and, to a lesser extent, Australia's TNT in Asia-Pacific. FedEx's home-based strategic advantages were insufficient to overcome the local first mover advantages of these foreign rivals. And as a service business based in many countries, FedEx could not exploit comparative advantage either. So FedEx has been significantly less successful outside its home market. In contrast, Japanese automobile manufacturers, such as Toyota, in the 1980s successfully added quality-based and design-based strategic advantages to the cost-based comparative advantage with which they entered international markets in the 1960s. *The best global strategies combine strategic and comparative advantage to yield global competitive advantage.*[20]

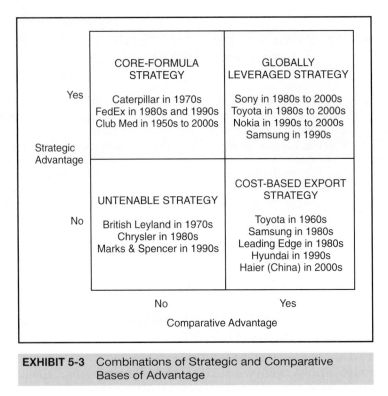

	No	**Yes**
Yes	CORE-FORMULA STRATEGY Caterpillar in 1970s FedEx in 1980s and 1990s Club Med in 1950s to 2000s	GLOBALLY LEVERAGED STRATEGY Sony in 1980s to 2000s Toyota in 1980s to 2000s Nokia in 1990s to 2000s Samsung in 1990s
No	UNTENABLE STRATEGY British Leyland in 1970s Chrysler in 1980s Marks & Spencer in 1990s	COST-BASED EXPORT STRATEGY Toyota in 1960s Samsung in 1980s Leading Edge in 1980s Hyundai in 1990s Haier (China) in 2000s

Strategic Advantage (left axis); Comparative Advantage (bottom axis)

EXHIBIT 5-3   Combinations of Strategic and Comparative Bases of Advantage

Exhibit 5-3 illustrates some possible combinations of strategic and comparative advantage. Companies with only strategic advantage have a *core-formula strategy* (upper left cell), as Caterpillar, the construction equipment manufacturer, had in the 1970s and FedEx in the 1980s and 1990s. Similarly, Club Med's all-in vacation resorts continue to benefit from the company's highly successful core formula, although the latter has gradually changed as the client base has aged. Companies with only comparative advantage tend to have to compete on the basis of low cost as many Japanese companies did in the 1960s, many Korean companies did in the 1980s, and many Chinese companies (such as Haier in air conditioners) in the 1990s and 2000s, in a *cost-based export strategy* (lower right cell). Some Korean concerns like Samsung's microwave oven business were able to move beyond low-cost–based comparative advantage to add quality-based strategic advantage. Others, like Leading Edge in microcomputers, succeeded for a while on the basis of comparative advantage but lost their position when they could not develop high enough quality to achieve strategic advantage. Still other Korean concerns, such as Hyundai's passenger automobile business, are at the cusp of transition. Companies with both sources of advantage have a *globally leveraged strategy* (upper right cell), as Sony has had for a long time and that Toyota achieved in the 1980s. Companies with neither source of advantage have an *untenable strategy* (lower left cell) and will fail to hold their position, as happened to British Leyland and Harley-Davidson in the 1970s, Chrysler in the 1980s, and Marks and Spencer in the 1990s.

The sources of strategic and comparative advantage also change over time. They change for external reasons, such as differing productivity growth rates among nations

CHANGING LOCATION IN THE CERAMICS INDUSTRY

The ceramics industry provides an example of how the ideal country for activity location changed over time with changing sources of strategic advantage.[21] In the 1960s and 1970s, the central driving factor for strategic advantage was the conversion of a craft skill into high-volume industrial production. This conversion required highly skilled workers found best in Germany. So a German firm, Villeroy and Boch, pioneered and led the shift. In the 1980s, the basis of strategic advantage shifted to design, continuous process operation, and the new single-firing technology. These advantages were both developed by Italian firms and most readily available in Italy where there were many designers, a low cost of capital, and less skilled but lower cost labor than in Germany.[22] In the 1990s having strong logistic systems and presence in key markets were added to the sources of comparative advantage. Firms gained advantage by locating in Milan and Paris for design, in Italy and Portugal for low-cost labor, and in Germany and the United States for exposure to the customers in these very large and demanding markets.

and the advent of new technologies, and for competitor-driven reasons, such as one competitor committing to exploit an emerging technology, as Hattori-Seiko did to the quartz technology for watches in the 1970s. Similarly, Japanese competitors' commitment in the 1980s to multipurpose, rather than specialized single-purpose, industrial robots dramatically enhanced their strategic advantage relative to American competitors. In the 1990s, investment in flexible manufacturing provided one of the most important sources of strategic advantage. In the 2000s, the Internet and the Web are providing some of the greatest sources of competitive advantage, which can in turn be leveraged globally. Both Dell Computer and Schwab (in investment brokerage) transformed their existing business models using the Internet, while newcomers, such as Britain's easyGroup (owner of easyJet and easyRentacar), use the Internet as the starting points and bases of their business models.

BENEFITS OF GLOBAL LOCATION OF ACTIVITIES

A global strategy for activity location can achieve each of the major globalization benefits of cost reduction, improved quality, enhanced customer preference, and increased competitive leverage.

COST REDUCTION

Multinational companies, whether using multilocal or global strategies, need to minimize the tariffs, taxes, and transportation costs they pay. In addition, compared with a multilocal approach, a global approach to activity location can reduce costs in further ways. It can *reduce duplication of activities* by eliminating and consolidating identical activities from many country locations into one or two globally centralized locations. In 1973, Unilever had 13 factories for soap production in Europe. As part of its globalization and Europeanization drive, Unilever had reduced these to three factories and one finishing plant by 1989. Similarly, N.V. Philips closed 80 factories in the 1970s to consolidate and to reduce duplication. In the 1980s Philips changed the role of the remaining factories from local production operations to "international production centers" that provided large-volume production for world markets.[23] Lastly, although a global approach to activity location means fewer locations than under a multilocal strategy, it may involve more locations and duplication than under a pure export approach.

A global approach to activity location can help exploit *economies of scale* by pooling production or other value-adding activities. For each activity, there can be an overall effect for the industry as a whole. The global benefits of manufacturing concentration are generally greater in the commercial aircraft business than in the apparel business—because the minimum efficient production scale requires a much higher share of the global market in aircraft than it does in apparel. But the specific effect for individual firms depends on the actual production technology used by the firm and by the market position of the firm. So firms that use a lower scale technology face fewer potential benefits from global concentration unless they change their technology approach also. Similarly, firms with a large share of large national markets will, other things being equal, gain less from global concentration than firms with small market shares, because these larger firms may already be able to achieve the minimum efficient scale. Smaller firms usually face a tough choice. They can try to overcome their size disadvantage by concentrating more than their larger competitors, but they run the risk of being swamped if these competitors adopt the same strategy. Or the smaller firms can stay with multiple, low-scale, national activities that depend on differentiation, quality, service, and other non-cost-based sources of strategic advantage. In industries where price is the primary customer concern, such strategies restrict the user to a small portion of the market. Furthermore, even in industries where product features and quality are also important, a cost advantage can be converted into not just lower prices but greater investment in improving product features and quality.

In the commodity chip market, economies of scale and learning/experience effects result in lower cost for high-volume plants. These drivers resulted in huge factories in Japan belonging to companies such as NEC, Fujitsu, and Hitachi. The output of these factories was much more than any one market could absorb, both allowing and requiring the Japanese companies to make large volume sales in the United States. In the United States, on the other hand, companies such as Texas Instruments and Micron Technology (of Boise, Idaho) had smaller plants and higher costs, putting them at a cost disadvantage. The consolidation of production by the Japanese chip makers and the global strategy that they have followed were two of the factors responsible for their greater competitiveness in the global commodity chip market. This greater competitiveness is illustrated by the growth of their world market share in all memory products from 25 percent in 1980 to 64 percent in 1986 (before declining in the face of new Korean competition).[24] In the 1990s, U.S. chipmakers recaptured the lead, with 45 percent global market share by 1996, in large part due to Intel's dominance of the PC market and subsequent economies of scale, as well as technological leadership.

The global concentration of activities can exploit *economies of scope* (which apply to the gains from spreading activities across multiple product lines or businesses) as well as economies of scale. The same kind of issues apply, with the complicating need to coordinate across different product lines and businesses. These complications include the possibility that one link in the value-added chain should be global for one business but local for another business and will be further addressed later in this chapter.

Exploiting flexibility can be another way in which a global approach to activity location can reduce costs and applies primarily to production and sourcing activities.

GLOBAL MANUFACTURING OF DISPOSABLE SYRINGES

Becton Dickinson's global manufacturing strategy in disposable syringes combined all three elements of global cost reduction: reducing duplication, exploiting economies of scale, and exploiting flexibility. The significant economies of scale and experience effects in the disposable syringe business encouraged Becton Dickinson to build a global manufacturing network that concentrated production primarily in the United States, Ireland, Mexico, and Brazil. Each production facility served multiple markets. For instance, in the early 1980s, 50 percent of the U.S. production, 90 percent of the Irish production, and 70 percent of the Mexican and Brazilian production was shipped to other markets. This concentration and coordination of production was made possible by the company's use of highly standardized global products and standardized production processes. In addition to reducing duplication and increasing economies of scale, this global product and manufacturing strategy gave Becton Dickinson the flexibility to take advantage of exchange rate fluctuations. For example, when the Mexican peso plummeted in value, Becton shifted much of the production in Mexico to serve overseas markets. Sourcing out of Mexico then gave Becton Dickinson a cost advantage vis-à-vis its competitors who were locked into producing in higher cost countries.[25]

Partial concentration allows flexibility in regard to changes in exchange rates and in bargaining with suppliers, labor unions, and host governments. The requirement for achieving this benefit lies not so much in the existence of multiple locations, which a multilocal strategy would have, and even more so, but in the capability to switch activities between locations. Such a capability has to exist in the configuration of physical assets, in the product policy, and in the management structure, policies, and processes of a company. First, flexibility in production requires investment in excess capacity that can produce to meet the needs of multiple countries. But such investment may be too costly in some industries and companies. Second, such production flexibility is greatly enhanced by the use of global products—products with a high degree of cross-country standardization. (The specific strategy of "flexible manufacturing" will be discussed shortly.) Third, the management system must allow production to be switched between countries without penalizing the individual managers and units giving up that production. Often, these management issues pose the greatest barrier to global flexibility. Chapter 8 will devote itself to the role of management and organization in global strategy. Putting these three requirements together—excess capacity, global products, and a global management system—can create a global network that allows a business to profit from the uncertainty of the world market.[26]

IMPROVED QUALITY

A global approach to activity location can improve product and program quality by focusing on a smaller number of products and programs than under a multilocal strategy. This quality-enhancing focus can occur in a number of elements in the value-added chain, particularly for R&D and production activities. Concentration of the R&D function allows a company to devote greater resources to the projects undertaken. At the

DEVELOPING SOFTWARE IN INDIA

In the late 1980s Texas Instruments set up a software design subsidiary in Bangalore, India, in order to access the low-cost but highly skilled technical workers available there. This subsidiary communicated with Texas Instruments' R&D center in the United States via satellite each day, thus operating very much as part of a global network. This location strategy, and resulting benefit of high-quality design work at low cost, is made possible by the strength of the industry globalization driver, differences in country costs. In the 1990s and early 2000s, many more companies followed TI's example as India developed as a major R&D sourcing center. Matsushita is developing an R&D base in India, not only to adapt existing products but also to develop new products from scratch. Its South Asia regional office in New Delhi will play a key role in the activities of Matsushita.[27]

same time, a concentrated R&D function can also be the center of a global network that taps into selected skills and knowledge in particular countries.

Concentration of the production function allows investment in better facilities and equipment than can be afforded under a multilocal strategy. These superior assets can then produce higher quality as well as lower cost products. *Studies increasingly show that low cost and high quality are not alternative, but complementary, strategies.*[28] In highly globalized industries, having both low cost and high quality is particularly important because buyers have more choice in where they buy and have access to the best products or services offered in the world. In addition, competitors will be able to pursue low-cost strategies through global centralization and standardization. Concentration of the production function should also allow more consistent quality control.

Lastly, taking the zero-based approach inherent in a global approach to activity location may open up unlikely and fascinating possibilities. Many U.S. banks now fly batches of checks and other financial instruments to be processed in the Far East in order to benefit from the higher quality standards there as well as lower costs and higher productivity. One American banker, who uses Asian financial processing, commented that "for Asian checkers, it's a matter of pride. They feel a deep sense of personal embarrassment if they make a mistake that results in a loss to the bank. This results in very high standards of accuracy."[29] McKinsey & Company centralized all production of PowerPoint presentations in one of its offices in India and takes advantage of time-zone differences as well as lower cost and higher accuracy. The British Post Office routes to India photo images of envelopes that cannot be read by machines. There, human readers retype the addresses and route them back electronically.

ENHANCED CUSTOMER PREFERENCE

Globalized activity location has only an indirect effect on customer preference, via possible improvements in product design and quality. Other global strategy levers—global market participation, global products, and global marketing—have more direct effects. On the other hand, globalized activity locations that are too far from customers can cause problems. Obviously, activities that are time- or service-sensitive or that require a great deal of customer interaction need to be located close to customers. But the Internet and other forms of communication are making it easier to achieve both global activity concentration and effective customer interaction.

INCREASED COMPETITIVE LEVERAGE

A global strategy for activity location can increase competitive leverage by bringing the resources of the worldwide network to bear on the competitive situation in individual countries. Under a multilocal strategy in which products are supplied by local manufacturing facilities, each subsidiary's competitive position—as based on its cost and quality position—depends on that subsidiary's own market share and revenues. So a subsidiary that loses market share under competitive attack also loses the operating scale needed to maintain the very cost and quality advantages needed to defend its market position. This was the losing position in which Philips, with its highly independent subsidiaries relying on local production, found itself in country after country, facing the Japanese electronics onslaught in the 1970s and early 1980s. In contrast, under a global strategy, each subsidiary's cost and quality position depends much more on the global market position of the worldwide business. So loss of local market share has little effect on cost and quality. In other words, *a global strategy for activity location can greatly reduce the dependence of each subsidiary's competitive position on local conditions.*

Such independence from local conditions also applies under an export strategy for activity location. But, as discussed in relation to exchange rates, a global approach with a network of locations provides more flexibility relative to exchange rate and other changes. So, again, a global approach can provide more leverage against competitors.

DRAWBACKS OF GLOBAL LOCATION OF ACTIVITIES

A global strategy for activity location also has drawbacks. Exhibit 1-5 in Chapter 1 summarized the major potential problems in such a strategy. These possible drawbacks include *lessened responsiveness to customers, increased currency risk, increased risk of creating competitors,* and *difficulties in managing the value-added chain.*

LESSENED RESPONSIVENESS TO CUSTOMERS

In comparison with a multilocal strategy in which most activities are located in the same countries as customer-markets, a global strategy of partial concentration of activities distances many of these activities from customers. The same applies even more so, of course, to an export-based strategy of total concentration. Obvious drawbacks include increased inventory costs, transportation expenses, and tariffs. These additional costs need to be less than the cost savings discussed earlier.

INCREASED CURRENCY RISK

Performing value-adding activities in countries where the company obtains little revenue means incurring costs in currencies different from that of revenues. As discussed earlier, this currency risk needs to be managed in a number of possible ways. Such management can verge on speculation, and companies need to beware of playing the foreign exchange markets for the sake of trading gains alone.

INCREASED RISK OF CREATING COMPETITORS

One approach to building a global manufacturing network is to use "offshore manufacturing" in which the home country-market is supplied from production facilities located elsewhere. This strategy is, of course, a special case of the more general one of global activity location. But offshore manufacturing has received the most attention and criticism, particularly in regard to the danger of "hollowing out" the corporation as more and more parts of the value-added chain are moved offshore.[30] Offshore manufacturing is particularly risky when the suppliers are collaborators rather than fully owned subsidiaries. Numerous offshore suppliers have learned the business of their customers sufficiently well to develop into full-fledged competitors.[31] Even the use of fully owned subsidiaries runs the risk of creating new competitors if local managers spin off on their own.

DIFFICULTIES IN MANAGING VALUE CHAIN

A global network of activities, in which interdependent elements of the value-added chain are spread across different countries, is inherently difficult to manage. In contrast, the centralized network of an export-based strategy or the mostly independent value-added chains of a multilocal strategy pose much less of a management task. If managed badly, a global network can be both less efficient and more costly.

GLOBAL ACTIVITY LOCATION FOR SERVICE BUSINESSES

It is difficult to speak broadly about product-service differences in activity location. But it is somewhat easier when we focus on the next level of distinction: among people-processing, possession-processing, and information-based services (as elaborated in Chapter 1).

PEOPLE-PROCESSING ACTIVITIES

In most cases, people-processing businesses have to locate the processing activity where customers live, work, or shop. This means that typical people-processing services—such as airline, hotel, restaurant, and car rental—need to maintain facilities around the world. In a few cases, specialized services, such as high-quality or advanced medical services, may be able to attract customers to travel to them. For example, some top hospitals in the United States and Britain are able to attract patients from Latin America and the Middle East.

POSSESSION-PROCESSING ACTIVITIES

Location needs for possession-processing activities depend on the ratio of service value to transportation cost. For example, it is increasingly more cost-effective to fly airplanes to a few specialized service centers rather than maintain service centers all over the world. Companies, such as Singapore Airlines, now do major business in servicing other airlines' planes at their domestic hubs. In contrast, the servicing of passenger automobiles continues to be a highly local, subnational industry.

INFORMATION-BASED ACTIVITIES

By their "virtual" nature, most information-based services should find it the easiest to locate globally. In many cases, such as pure information services, no local physical presence may be needed at all. In other cases, information services that also have a physical component (e.g., the provision of currency or traveler's checks) or require specialized delivery equipment (e.g., pay-per-view entertainment) will need some local physical presence, provided by the company itself or by local partners.

FUTURE LOCATIONS OF SERVICE FACILITIES[32]

In the future, we shall see a greater distinction between services that require an on-site "factory" in each country and those that require only a delivery system. By definition, all people-processing services that do not require customers to travel outside their home country for service delivery will require on-site operations in each country. The same will be true of any possession-processing service that cannot readily transport the object in question to another location for servicing. In these instances, managers may find that the best way to achieve global consistency in the core product is to create easily replicable service concepts, backed by clear standards, that allow for either franchises or country managers to clone the original core product in a new setting.

Information-based services offer management greater flexibility to split the back office and front office, with opportunities to centralize the former on a global or regional basis. Production can thus take place in one location (or just a few), yielding economies of scale and access to global expertise, while delivery remains local. Banking, insurance, and other financial service products lend themselves well to delivery through electronic channels. Many forms of news, information, and entertainment can also be delivered worldwide through public or private networks. Key issues in globalization include the constraints imposed by language, culture, and government regulations.

GLOBAL LOCATION OF SERVICE VALUE CHAIN[33]

Different service elements can be sourced from different locations. The physical supplies needed for certain types of service delivery (such as food for hotels, fuel for transport vehicles, or spare parts for repair jobs) are often shipped from one country for consumption in another. The same is sometimes true for imported labor. But some companies, like McDonald's, are choosing to build up a network of local suppliers and to train host country nationals for local jobs as quickly as possible.[34]

As noted earlier, information-based services can be produced in one part of the world and delivered through electronic channels for consumption elsewhere. Indeed, information technology is emerging as a key globalization driver for such services. In mutual funds, for instance, offerings are now being pieced together from elements created in many different countries. Unlike physical goods, the logistics of service "assembly" and delivery tend to be much simpler once the necessary infrastructure and network are in place. Further, a majority of supplementary services (such as billing, payment, consultation, and advice) are information-dependent and can potentially be delivered from remote locations. In theory, a global company could centralize its billing on a global basis, using postal or telecommunication distribution channels to deliver the bills to customers, suitably converted to the relevant currency.

Similarly, information, consultation, order-taking/reservations, and many aspects of problem solving and payment could all be handled through telecommunications channels, ranging from voice telephone to the Web. So long as service personnel speaking the appropriate languages are available, many such service elements could be delivered from almost anywhere. Recent patterns of immigration in a country may create a comparative advantage in multilingual capabilities. By contrast, hospitality and safekeeping will always have to be provided locally, because they are responsive to the physical presence of customers and their possessions.

Like manufacturers, service firms should be looking for opportunities to exploit differences in national comparative advantages as they seek to build more efficient value chains. Significant economies may be gained by centralizing "information hubs" on a global basis, as FedEx does in Memphis. Through outsourcing, firms can also reduce the need for large fixed-cost investments. Taking advantage of favorable labor costs and exchange rates, a growing number of service-based businesses have identified key back-office activities that can be conducted more cheaply but without loss of quality in a different country from where their customers are located. This is happening with front-office elements, too, as companies build global reservation and customer service systems that are networked around the world.

LOCATING INDIVIDUAL ACTIVITIES

Thinking in terms of a global value-added chain makes it clear that a global strategy can be applied to different links of the chain. Some elements of the chain can be geographically concentrated while others are duplicated and dispersed. So how should each element of the value-added chain be located in a global strategy? The next sections discuss how to configure the elements whose location is most affected by globalization drivers.

GLOBAL FINANCING

This book concerns global strategy at the business rather than the corporate level. So issues like financing, a corporate function, are not really within the scope of this work. But one issue worth highlighting is how the financing task should differ between companies pursuing multilocal strategies and those pursuing global strategies. In particular, the finance function for global strategy needs to match *global* competitors' costs of capital, not just those of competitors in each national market.[35] Such matching requires in the first place that the company have a good understanding of global competitors' true cost of capital. That task is not so easy, as witness the debate in the 1980s and 1990s on whether or not Japanese firms had, on average, a lower cost of capital than Western companies.[36]

Companies that aspire to be global in operations are finding that they must also be global in their approach to financing.[37] High domestic costs and international competition are forcing many companies to borrow at the lowest cost of capital. Therefore they must tap global equity markets, which are increasingly interconnected and open to international firms. Global financing, however, has led to increased complexity of financing. Financial derivatives, hedging, and the volatility of many financial markets are among those risks that create tension between headquarters and their subsidiaries. As a result, global firms have tended to centralize these financing responsibilities, ensuring control over such risky endeavors as hedging. Japan's Sony has gone one step further. In 2001, it became the world's first large multinational company to move its treasury and foreign currency operations to a different country from that of its headquarters. Sony planned to move this operation to London, in the hope of saving six or seven billion yen a year in commission payments to market intermediaries.

LOCATING R&D OVERSEAS

Canon conducts R&D activities in eight facilities in five countries, Motorola has 14 facilities in seven countries, and Bristol-Myers Squibb has 12 facilities in six countries.[38] Microsoft has invested in an R&D center in Cambridge, England, in order to tap into the expertise of Cambridge University, Cambridge's Science Park, and the area's phenomenon of "Silicon Fen." In a classic example of locating in a lead country to tap into its R&D resources, Japanese computer and electronics companies have opened laboratories to do basic research in the United States, partly it seems in order to lure the most creative American computer scientists to work for them. Japanese companies are also increasingly buying into already developed technology through acquisition of foreign companies.[39]

Overall, a global approach to financial management "requires creating and sustaining financial management platforms and practices that minimize the firm's real after-tax cost of capital, diversify capital sources, minimize financial risks, and realize savings through globalization."[40] Issues to do with the management, rather than the location, of global financing will be discussed in Chapter 8.

GLOBAL RESEARCH AND DEVELOPMENT

In parallel with the notion of global products, the essence of a global strategy for R&D is that it be conducted to serve the entire global market rather than individual countries. Most multinational companies have historically run their R&D operation to stress serving either the home market or individual foreign markets, rather than the global market as a whole.[41] Global excellence in R&D means being able to access new knowledge and capabilities anywhere in the world and being able to develop globally appealing products and services that can be produced on a globally competitive basis.

In terms of accessing knowledge, multinational companies historically have concentrated their R&D activities in their home countries, thereby greatly reducing their ability to access overseas knowledge and innovation. This mattered less when the creation of new knowledge was the near monopoly of North America, Western Europe, and Japan (Kenichi Ohmae's triad economies),[42] also the home bases of most multinationals. But the exponential rise in technology and knowledge creation has created a global diaspora of expertise. Global companies now need to access knowledge and development capabilities not just in triad nations but also in emerging economies such as China, India, and Russia. Several routes exist: physically setting up R&D overseas but keeping these units plugged into the global network, by electronic means constantly and in-person sometimes; hiring scientists and technologists from overseas; or frequent visits to and other contacts with countries that are sources of innovation.

The location and management of the R&D activity can have a major effect on how well it serves such a global function. Many executives consider that the output of R&D activity serves end markets best when the activity is also located in those markets.[43] But a global strategy for R&D needs to balance this need with several others:

- Global R&D needs to tap into sources of knowledge and information wherever they might be located on the globe.
- Global R&D needs to transmit that knowledge back to the central R&D management wherever that might be.
- The central management function needs to ensure that this knowledge is used as appropriate.
- There has to be a process for allocating priorities on a global basis of strategic need rather than of proximity. Otherwise, the R&D staff are likely to favor the projects of the managers they see regularly rather than those of distant foreigners.
- The global R&D activity has to be able to develop global products with the capability for customization for major markets.

All of these tasks have to be performed while balancing the need to achieve critical mass and economies of scale, which varies by industry. Analysis of the industry's globalization drivers helps determine how best to locate and manage the R&D activity to meet these needs.

To meet the above needs, multinational companies have developed multiple approaches to R&D configuration:[44]

- *Home base model*—one country location for all technology development
- *Multiple home bases*—one country location for each technology or business, but not always the same country
- *Worldwide lead center*—one center in a dispersed network identified as the core location for specific business technology and responsible for managing dispersed technology management units worldwide
- *Regional bases*—one center in each region
- *Regional technology headquarters*—one regional center designated as the lead center for the region, managing a regionally dispersed network of centers and coordinating with other regional headquarters
- *Hetararchy*—lead centers chosen on a project-by-project basis.

Effects of Market Globalization Drivers on Global R&D

A number of market globalization drivers affect where R&D should be located and how it should be managed. *Common customer needs* make it less necessary to locate R&D in multiple countries, so favoring concentration to achieve scale benefits. The presence of *global customers* encourages companies to place some of their R&D activities close to their most important global customers. The existence of important *lead countries* strongly encourages companies to locate at least some of their R&D activities in those countries. As a minimum, companies should locate in lead countries a scanning function to gather information on developments. A recurring theme found in the research conducted for this book was the need for American companies to locate some R&D activity in Japan. Many of these companies face strong Japanese global competitors and are also very weak in the Japanese market. R&D presence in Japan would help them to better understand the sources of their Japanese competitors' technical capabilities, as well as to improve their ability to serve the Japanese market, and perhaps global markets also.

One American company, W. R. Grace, a large, diversified manufacturer of chemical and other products, had made the move to conduct R&D in Japan. Believing that the

MOTOROLA'S R&D IN SINGAPORE

Motorola takes advantage of Singapore's lower costs, yet high-quality R&D technologists, to operate a major R&D facility there.[45] The company's Innovation Center conducts product and technology research as well as design and marketing for the Paging Products Group in the region and beyond. The design center has been responsible for several innovations conceived and produced in Singapore, including the first credit card–sized pager. In addition, Singapore operations serve as the regional R&D center for paging products. This center has successfully introduced a number of products designed for the region, but which have subsequently been adopted globally.

United States, Europe, and Japan were the leaders in technological innovation in the chemicals industry, the company opened a research center in Japan. Grace already had R&D facilities in the United States and Europe but felt the need to complete the triad by establishing a presence in Japan. Grace executives believe that this development will enable them to stay on top of, and potentially have access to, Japanese developments. Grace made contacts with researchers in Japan's universities and governments and also hired Japanese scientists.

Third-world countries can also be lead markets for R&D. Astra Zeneca, the second largest pharmaceutical company in the world, operates an R&D center in Bangalore, India, to research tropical diseases.

Effects of Cost Globalization Drivers on Global R&D
Cost is easily the most important globalization driver in affecting the location of R&D activities. R&D activity seems, in most industries, to need a large amount of expensive equipment and many scientists to work in close collaboration to achieve any significant results. So companies have traditionally favored concentrating the activity. In addition, the high cost of R&D makes the international duplication of facilities very difficult. Increasingly, however, the need to locate R&D in globally strategic countries and the spreading availability of R&D skills are encouraging companies to spread their R&D efforts and to find creative ways to maintain a globally integrated network of R&D workers, as mentioned earlier in the case of Texas Instruments' operation in India. Computer and communications technology is also making it more possible to have geographically dispersed R&D. As part of its computer utilization program, Dow Chemical's R&D activities in its U.S. and Europe centers are integrated through use of software and hardware programs shared throughout the Dow global network.

Effects of Government Globalization Drivers on Global R&D
While government trade policies—through tariffs, quotas, and local content rules—may force multinational companies to manufacture locally, government regulation can have a less direct effect on R&D. Companies may sometimes find it necessary to locate in particular countries in order to better understand the technical specifications and regulations. For example, the drug approval process is so complex that having a local R&D presence can help companies deal with the process more successfully. Governments are

also eager for technology transfer into their countries. So a local R&D facility that operates as part of a global network can be used to enhance relations and bargaining power with host governments.

Effects of Competitive Globalization Drivers on Global R&D

As with other global strategy levers, companies need to be concerned if their competitors pursue a globally more astute strategy for R&D. In particular, companies that conduct their R&D primarily at home may well need to reciprocate when foreign competitors set up R&D on their territory. Lastly, companies may find acquisitions of competitors particularly helpful in strengthening their global R&D, both as a way of obtaining technical expertise and as a way of enhancing the scale of R&D operations.

GLOBAL PURCHASING AND SOURCING

Using a global strategy for purchasing is the mirror image of catering to global customers. A globally centralized and integrated approach to purchasing can ensure that the business has access to the best possible materials and components as well as the best possible prices. Whether to incur the costs and additional management requirements of global purchasing depends on the specific potential benefits. For example, Singer Furniture found its own offshore sourcing to be inefficient and unable to exploit the potential for sourcing economies. So it contracted with another company, IMX, to be its exclusive agent for overseas purchasing. IMX uses its own global network to find low-cost sourcing opportunities that lower purchasing and shipping costs of Singer goods. In addition, Singer benefits from the increased purchasing clout and economies of scale from sharing this activity with another company.

The automotive industry has probably gone the furthest in the use of global sourcing. For example, the European Ford Escort, which was designed to be a world car and wound up as a pan-European model, sources components from 15 different countries: the United Kingdom and Germany, where it is final-assembled, as well as Norway, Sweden, Denmark, Belgium, the Netherlands, France, Austria, Switzerland, Italy, Spain, the United States, Canada, and Japan.[46] Jose Ignacio Lopez led global cost-cutting efforts in procurement at General Motors and then at Volkswagen. Breaking from traditional relationships, Lopez put suppliers through rigorous rounds of bidding, demanding increased supplier efficiencies and lower prices. The Internet has further accelerated the trend to global procurement. The three major U.S. automobile companies have combined to create a joint purchasing Web site, ANX, where potential suppliers can access these companies' requirements. Other industries are beginning to develop similar shared procurement Web sites.

Global sourcing has also been enabled by the emergence of global air cargo companies that provide end-to-end logistics services and delivery anywhere in the world within 48 hours. After constructing global networks in the 1990s, the four major companies (DHL, FedEx, UPS, and TNT) now operate in more than 200 countries.[47]

GLOBAL PRODUCTION

Production and manufacturing cover a large number of activities, including the development of product and process technology, the building of production capacity and plant facilities, maintaining the manufacturing information system, managing materials and inbound and outbound logistics, maintaining quality and reliability standards, planning production, and managing the actual production operations. Typically, most of these activities need to be performed in close proximity to each other, so that location decisions tend to cover these activities as a package. Nevertheless, to the extent that a particular activity can be separated from the others, the location strategy for it can be different.

Global sourcing and production have to reconcile several conflicting objectives: cost, productivity, quality, reliability, protection of expertise, and trade barriers. So there is seldom a single sourcing and production configuration that can maximize all of these objectives, but they can be optimized. In 2001, hourly labor costs ranged from over U.S.$25 an hour in Germany to under 25 cents in Indonesia, or a ratio of more than 100 to 1. With such large differences, even companies in non-labor-intensive industries need to seriously think about where to locate activities. Furthermore, companies should not be put off by the low *average* productivity in low-cost economies. These figures include all the unmodernized, often state-owned, companies. The whole point is to achieve higher levels of productivity by making investments and transferring technology and expertise. Motorola, the proselytizer of "six-sigma" quality, excels at operating world-class manufacturing in developing countries.

There are many arguments for and against foreign manufacturing, some of which were covered in the discussion of offshore manufacturing. Reasons for foreign manufacturing include enhancing customer relations outside the home country; getting closer to markets; gaining access to local, immobile factors of production and technological resources; reducing transportation costs; avoiding tariff and nontariff barriers; satisfying some demands of and gaining benefits from local governments; hedging against country-specific risks and preempting competition.[48] This author assumes that the reader already understands these issues or can learn about them elsewhere[49] and concentrates instead on the issue of how to configure a global manufacturing network in the sense defined earlier.

Cost globalization drivers constitute the key reason for using global manufacturing, with government drivers also important, and market and competitive drivers less so.

Effects of Cost Drivers on Global Production

Probably the most important cost driver for global manufacturing is the nature of *scale economies*. As discussed earlier, globally centralized manufacturing is favored to the extent that the minimum efficient scale is greater than the volume the firm can sell in individual national markets. Playing catch-up to its global rivals, General Motors began in 1998 to consolidate its North American and international operations. Steep *learning and experience effects* also favor global manufacturing in order to move down the curve faster. So it is no coincidence that competitors in the semiconductor industry, well known for its steep experience effects, primarily use globally centralized manufacturing.

Having *favorable logistics* is also a critical requirement for global manufacturing to work. Shipping costs must not be so great as to offset the cost savings from centralization. But creativity can sometimes be applied to reduce transportation barriers. An American manufacturer of medical sterilization equipment manufactured in its local markets because the product, with its large sterilization chamber, was too bulky to be shipped economically. But this manufacturing strategy left the company operating below full capacity in each of its minimum efficient scale plants. Eventually the company hit on the solution of centralizing in the United States manufacture of the sterilizing controls, which constituted the more valuable part of the product, shipping

CENTRALIZING CALL CENTERS

Service businesses can also benefit from globally centralized production. Call centers have become a very important service activity for both product and service businesses. Many companies economize here by creating "shared services" that service multiple countries while providing the necessary localization. Alamo Rent-A-Car has a center in Brighton, England, serving the United Kingdom, Germany, Spain, and Italy. The center takes 4,500 calls a day with 90 lines, 100 agents, and customer-controlled call routing to match the language. Delta Airlines has a center in London that consolidates reservation offices in 12 cities in Europe. It has 200 agents and 11 European languages. IBM has a pan-European call center in Greenock, Scotland; Adobe Systems has one in Edinburgh. In Germany, Land's End has a center in Mettlach, and Hewlett-Packard has one in Amsterdam.

Centralizing call centers also depends on cheaper international telephone calls, such that the expense of calling overseas is outweighed by savings on cheaper labor costs, or perhaps by workers who have the longitudinal advantage of being awake at different times.[50] Call centers have created a new and often international service industry. Firms have taken to commissioning outside specialists to speak to customers for them, rather than investing in equipment and a multitude of customer service representatives themselves. Outsourcing of this sort has created jobs in remote places. Ireland's well-educated inhabitants have accents that please many other English speakers. The country provides relatively cheap labor for many European call centers. Internet help sections are the newest manifestation of geographic shifting of service centers. For example, America Online provides much of its live, online help from the Philippines. Its center there employs 900 young Filipinos, who, working on computers in three 8-hour shifts, handle about 90 percent of the 600,000 online billing and technical questions that AOL receives each month.[51]

Beyond call centers and help desks, many multinational companies now run all kinds of backroom operations in the Philippines: Andersen for custom software, Barnes and Noble for inventory management and online purchases, Bechtel for engineering design, Caltex for finance and accounting support, Citibank for systems development and support, Procter & Gamble for accounting services, Fluor Daniel for regional design work, Alitalia for global accounting, and Mitsubishi for engineering design.[52]

these high-value controls, using local suppliers to provide the low-value sterilizing chambers, and then conducting final assembly in the local countries. Similarly, Gettinger, a subsidiary of Electrolux, the Swedish appliance manufacturer, set up in several countries local manufacturing of the bulky appliance shells. Some products, however, such as explosive chemicals, face other, more difficult, logistical barriers.

Differences in country costs also favor the use of global manufacturing by making it worthwhile to locate in specific countries. Particularly when looking to exploit low labor costs companies need to consider what percentage of total costs (both purchases and value added) is accounted for by labor costs and the differences in labor productivity between countries. Differences in tax rates also provide another source of differences in country costs. Using a global manufacturing network, rather than duplicated multilocal facilities or a single exporting facility, offers two ways to reduce taxes. First, the selective location of manufacturing facilities, inherent in global strategy, allows the company to pick countries with low (either official or negotiated) tax rates. Second, the transshipment of raw materials, and intermediate and final products, within a global manufacturing network provides opportunities to set transfer prices and subsidiary re-mittances so as to minimize total tax liability.

Some researchers argue that in most manufacturing industries, labor costs have been outweighed by market access, quality control, timely delivery, and responsiveness to customers as determinants of global competitiveness. Therefore, global site selections might hinge on the cooperation, flexibility, and trainability of the labor force rather than on its cost.[53]

Effects of Government Drivers on Global Production

Whether an industry has *favorable trade policies* greatly affects the potential for global manufacturing. In essence, greater protectionism reduces the ability to operate with a global manufacturing network.[54] Ironically, while mature industries with their more sta-ble product and process designs suit themselves to global manufacturing, protectionism is often more prevalent in such industries also, both because local production has had time to spread and because jobs lost to imports cannot be readily re-created. Many trade barriers are now falling, which is one of the major drivers spurring companies to investigate global manufacturing. The global network can also be used to circumvent or reduce the impact of trade barriers such as through the judicious use of local content. By assembling and conducting some manufacturing operations in Britain, Japanese au-tomobile manufacturers were able to get their vehicles certified as European origin even though a very high percentage of the content is originally imported from Japan. The Goodyear Tire Company wanted to strengthen its production base in the global tire industry by setting up a manufacturing subsidiary in Korea. But Goodyear faced stiff government regulations against its move. Only by agreeing to become an exporting plant was Goodyear able to win government approval for the ownership that the com-pany wanted. Similarly, China, India, and many other countries often require high per-centages of local manufacturing.

Compatible technical standards also make it easier to use global manufacturing, by reducing the need for running different product lines. So the task of a centralized man-ufacturing plant is simplified.

Effects of Market Drivers on Global Production

Product designs that are changing rapidly to meet changing market needs tend to re-quire a close linkage between marketers, designers, and manufacturing. So the stable product designs that dominate in the mature stage of the product life cycle should make it easier to use global manufacturing, provided that *common customer needs* across countries also apply. Furthermore, the cost savings from global manufacturing are most needed in mature industries where customers use precise, hard criteria based on prod-uct price performance relationships in their purchasing decisions.[55] It is probably no co-incidence that maturity in the U.S. and European automobile and consumer electronics markets has coincided with dominance by Japanese manufacturers using globally cen-tralized manufacturing.

An additional market driver affecting global manufacturing is the country-of-origin effect discussed earlier. A dilemma that companies face in locating production facilities is that many low-cost countries do not have a high reputation for quality. One solution may be to use quality control managers from countries that have high reputations for quality, such as Germany or Japan, and to ensure that potential customers know about this fact. There is the apocryphal story that in the 1950s a town in Japan changed its name to Usa in order to be able to label products manufactured there as "Made in USA." In another example of how the preferred countries of origin have changed over time, nineteenth-century German toolmakers used to imitate the Sheffield (England) trademark. To minimize the negative connotations of manufacturing in a country with a poor image, Façonnable, a French clothing producer, sells garments with labels that say "Designed in France, Made in China."

Effects of Competitive Drivers on Global Production

As with the use of the other global strategy levers, global manufacturing may be mandated by competitive actions. If the industry has characteristics favoring global manufacturing, competitors that move first will gain scale, experience, or other advantages that can keep them ahead of slower movers. So in such industries firms need to match or preempt their *competitors' use of global manufacturing.*

Additional Factors

Each factory can also have a different role in a global network. That role then affects the degree of integration needed as well as the sophistication and content of the support activities that should be located at the factory.[56] These roles include getting access to low-cost production factors, using local technological resources, and gaining proximity to local markets. Furthermore, for each of those roles, a factory can play more passive or active roles within the global network. Integration of the different factories within a global network is becoming increasingly important. In a multicountry study of international manufacturing, managers at several U.S. multinational corporations reported that their primary challenge in coming years is integrating their existing global operations to perform as a single system rather than as islands of manufacturing and technological capabilities.[57]

In addition, some specific characteristics of a company's manufacturing process may make it easier to shift from a situation of duplicated independent plants to one of an interdependent global network. One characteristic is that the plants should have manufacturing processes that are more or less similar. A second characteristic is that the pattern of material flows between plants and warehouses should be relatively simple. A third characteristic is that manufacturing configurations should be relatively simple.[58]

Role of Flexible Manufacturing and Production

As mentioned in the last chapter, the advent of computer-based "flexible manufacturing" (using computer-aided manufacturing—the CAM in CAD/CAM) redefined the notion of globally standardized products.[59] Flexible manufacturing is an important option that needs to be factored into global manufacturing strategy.[60] In particular, the use of flexible manufacturing interacts with both the use of globally standardized products and the use of geographically concentrated manufacturing.

In terms of market globalization drivers, the presence of *common customer needs* favors product standardization and the subsequent manufacturing concentration to produce those products. But flexible manufacturing allows more scope for producing customized variants of a core global product. So even in industries where customer needs are not that common, a business with a flexible manufacturing capability can design a standardized global core that it then customizes, in a centralized manufacturing facility, for different national or regional markets. Markets at an earlier stage of the product life cycle face greater variety in product design, which would usually prevent the use of globally standardized products. But, again, a flexible manufacturing capability may allow earlier use of standardized core global products and concentrated manufacturing. In terms of cost globalization drivers, high *economies of scale* favor concentrated manufacturing but have conflicting effects on the need to use flexible manufacturing. On the one hand, companies will not be able to support many minimum efficient scale plants, so having the flexibility to produce many different products in each plant will be an advantage. On the other hand, by their nature, flexible manufacturing techniques tend to reduce the gains from large-scale production.

Some experts believe that flexible manufacturing can be used to increase product variety without increasing costs.[61] But some increase in cost seems typically necessary. For example, the National Bicycle Industrial Company, a subsidiary of Matsushita, the Japanese electronics concern, has a factory that makes customized models, under the Panasonic brand, to individual order. With 20 employees and a computer capable of design work, its small factory can produce over 11 million variations on nearly 20 models in about 200 color patterns and almost any size. Customers are fitted as for a made-to-measure suit before any production begins. The finished bicycles sell for $500 to $3,000 compared with $250 to $500 for standard bicycles. But it might be argued that these customized bicycles are based on a standardized core set of parts and designs. Furthermore, the large price differential over the mass production models limits the share of the market that can be obtained by the customized products.

Managing Interdependence Between Businesses

Although not a central theme of this book, interdependence among different businesses within a company has implications for activity location. Many companies share activities across different businesses, and such sharing often takes place in several countries. For example, in many paper-based companies, different businesses share upstream pulp-processing facilities. Or different businesses in a company may share a distribution system or sales force as in many consumer packaged goods companies. In these cases, problems arise when one business requires a more globalized strategy in a shared activity than does another business. Two businesses in the same company may share two activities in their value-added chains, such as purchasing and manufacturing. But one business should have a primarily global strategy while the other business should not. So the first business should ideally have globally centralized manufacturing of standardized global products, while the second business needs locally adapted products and could use local manufacturing also. But the economics are such that both businesses' production costs are lower when they share centralized manufacturing facilities. So a possible compromise solution would be to allocate one corner of the factory to work on customizing products for the second business. In addition, any extra costs that the second business incurs because of having to accommodate the first business's need for centralized production, such as for transportation of finished goods, should be ameliorated by giving some break in the transfer price to local subsidiaries.

GLOBAL DISTRIBUTION AND LOGISTICS

Global logistics embody the challenge for global companies to be able to deliver their intermediate and final products anywhere in the world in a cost-effective and timely manner. The solution can seldom be one single distribution hub, but again a network of hubs, exemplified by the systems of the global delivery companies, such as FedEx, DHL, and UPS. Another issue is whether to use a globally common distribution system or a differentiated one. Coca-Cola has achieved great success by replacing local distribution systems with its effective and efficient standardized distribution methods.[62] In Japan, it achieved a 70 percent market share in its category by displacing the country's traditional seven-layer distribution system.

Most of the issues in the location of distribution activities relate to classic marketing and internationalization concerns. Logistical factors become doubly important in an international context. But globalization drivers can also change how these factors apply. In particular, changes in government globalization drivers can redefine the optimal configuration of a global distribution system. The advent of the single European market provided the most dramatic application of this effect. The removal of border controls allowed distribution managers to redraw the maps that show time from their distribution centers to various delivery points. Maps that had been contorted by the time taken for trucks to pass frontier controls now show smooth concentric circles instead. As a result, distribution centers have been consolidated and centralized, as with manufacturing sites. Intel reduced shipping costs by at least 7 percent by consolidating its worldwide freight expenditures with four transportation firms. As a result, from its 14 manufacturing sites around the world, Intel improved on-time delivery performance into the high 90th percentile and significantly improved the level of service that Intel is able to provide its customers.

Benetton's Global Distribution Strategy. Creative thinking along the global value-added chain can produce highly effective global distribution. Benetton provides one of the best examples of a global distribution strategy. From a single computerized warehouse in Treviso, Italy, Benetton ships its products all over the world directly to the independent, but contractually tied, retail stores that sell its clothing. This distribution centralization is made possible, in part, by Benetton's use of just-in-time ordering. Benetton makes no garment until it is ordered by one of its stores. So an innovative approach in its order-taking and manufacturing value-added activities allows global strategic advantage to be attained via the distribution element of the value chain.

GLOBAL SERVICE

The last activity in the value chain, customer service, usually, by its nature, has to be performed locally. Even so, some aspects such as information and communication systems can be centralized. Furthermore, providing a uniform standard of service provides assurance to global customers—whether organizations or individuals. At the same time, differences in both culture and custom particularly affect what customers may expect in different countries. On weekends in Japan medical equipment company sales representatives wash the cars of the doctors that they call on! These representatives will even collect their customers' children from school.

Global success in service now requires the availability of consistent, effective, timely, and convenient customer service around the world on demand. Customers today require service anytime, anywhere. As the world's leading global retail bank Citibank goes a bit further. Its global motto is that customers can do business with it "anytime, anywhere, anyway." Citibank invested hugely in the 1990s in both physical infrastructure, such as branches and ATMs, and computer and communication systems to make real its boast.

Success also requires building close customer relationships through customer service and knowledge sharing. Hewlett-Packard is a global leader in computer-based customer support services for its customers. It maintains a globally standardized set of services that range from site design to systems integration to remote diagnostics. This global standardization includes seamless service at any hour of the day or night from anywhere in the world.[63] To provide this, H-P maintains a global chain of 30 customer response centers, integrated into a global network. Diners' Club uses information technology to provide global services to customers as a means to maintain a competitive edge in the credit card industry. To satisfy the needs of its corporate customers, Diners' Club created Global Vision, a software program that tracks transactions and account balances, and reports multiple currencies and summarizes them into a master currency. Global Vision, therefore, enables customers around the world to see their transactions in local and foreign currencies.[64]

Global companies also need to be sensitive to cross-cultural customer service issues. Infowavz, an Indian company that provides outsourced customer support services primarily over the Internet, gives American names to its Mumbai-based staff and trains them in colloquial American English. Other global service operations provide pop-up menus with weather and local news items, such as sports results, so that service staff can make small talk with callers.

GUIDELINES FOR LOCATING GLOBAL ACTIVITIES

An effective global network can locate activities to achieve the benefits of cost reduction, increased competitive leverage, and so on. At the same time this network must be able to serve the key needs of local markets around the world. The following guidelines summarize the key issues on this topic:

- In locating global activities, managers should free up their thinking by starting with the "zero-based" assumption that their business has no activities located anywhere in the world. Then ask what the ideal pattern of location would be. Only then should managers bring back into consideration the reality of where the business's activities are actually located now, and what it would cost (in the broadest sense) to relocate activities.
- Different activities have differing needs for global centralization, local dispersion, or some combination in between.
- The ideal pattern of location changes with circumstances and the evolution of the business.
- The best pattern of location usually allows for some duplication in order to provide flexibility and safeguards against disruption.
- Coordination of geographically dispersed activities can substitute in some cases for global centralization.
- Managers should consider both strategic advantage and comparative (country-based) advantage in locating activities to maximize competitive advantage.
- Some activities, particularly research and development, need to have presence in globally strategic countries.

Discussion and Research Questions

1. What is the difference between a multilocal and a global approach to locating value-adding activities?
2. What is the difference between strategic and comparative bases of advantage?
3. Select one company or business and trace how it has developed its strategic and comparative bases of advantage over time.
4. What parts of its value chain should an American manufacturer of automobiles consider relocating, and where, in the light of the North American Free Trade Agreement? Would your answer be different for a major insurance company?
5. Select one company or business and describe how the location of its value-adding activities has shifted over time.
6. How does the Internet affect the global location of activities?
7. Which aspects of service businesses are most suited to global centralization?

Notes

1. Michael Porter calls these choices configuration (location) and coordination, and he provides a four-cell typology of types of international strategy: high foreign investment with extensive coordination, country-centered strategy, export-based strategy, and purest global strategy. While these types provide helpful summaries, this author's approach views location and coordination choices as providing a continuum rather than discrete choices. Furthermore, the location and coordination of activities constitute only one each of the five global strategy dimensions and the four organization dimensions. See Michael E. Porter, "Competition in Global Industries: A Conceptual Framework," *Competition in Global Industries,* Michael Porter, Ed. (Boston: Harvard Business School Press, 1986); and Porter, "Changing Patterns of International Competition," *California Management Review,* Vol. 28, No. 2, Winter 1986, pp. 9–40. For an in-depth discussion of the role of value-adding activities in competitive strategy, see Michael E. Porter, *Competitive Advantage* (New York: The Free Press, 1985).

2. Both Prahalad and Doz (1987) and Bartlett and Ghoshal (1989) advocate the use of a global network in which subsidiaries and the center specialize in different activities. See C. K. Prahalad and Yves L. Doz, *The Multinational Mission: Balancing Local Demands and Global Vision* (New York:

The Free Press, 1987); and Christopher A. Bartlett and Sumantra Ghoshal, *Managing Across Borders: The Transnational Solution* (Boston: Harvard Business School Press, 1989). See also Nitin Nohria, Sumantra Ghoshal (contributor), and Cedric Crocker (editor), *The Differentiated Network: Organizing Multinational Corporations for Value Creation* (San Francisco: Jossey-Bass Business and Management Series, 1997).

3. Thomas C. Lawton, "Exploding the Value Chain," research presentation at Judge Institute of Management Studies, University of Cambridge, February 3, 2000.

4. See Mari Kondo and George S. Yip, Chapter 16, "Regional Groupings — ASEAN, AFTA, APEC, Etc.," in George S. Yip, *Asian Advantage* (Reading, MA: Addison-Wesley, 1998); and *Asian Advantage: Updated — After the Crisis* (Cambridge, MA: Perseus Books, 2000).

5. See, for example, Rudiger Dornbush, Stanley Fisher, and Paul A. Samuelson, "Comparative Advantage, Trade and Payments in a Ricardian Model with a Continuum of Goods," *American Economic Review,* Vol. 67, December 1977, pp. 823–39.

6. For a discussion of the ethical issues in manufacturing in poor countries, see Christopher Avery, *Business and Human Rights in a Time of Change* (London: Amnesty International Publications, 2000).

7. There is extensive literature on the country-of-origin effect. See, for example, Johny K.

Johansson, "Determinants and Effects of 'Made in' Labels," *International Marketing Review,* Vol. 6, No. 1, Spring 1989, pp. 47–58.

8. For a guide to these fundamental issues in internationalization see, for example, Michael R. Czinkota, Ilkka A. Ronkainen, and Michael Moffett, *International Business,* update 2000 (Harcourt, 2000); and Beamish, Morrison, Rosenzweig, and Inkpen, *International Management: Text and Cases,* 4th ed. (New York: Irwin McGraw-Hill, 2000).

9. This section is based on K. Ramachandran and George S. Yip, "India—Giving Multinationals a Chance," in George S. Yip, *Asian Advantage: Key Strategies for Winning in the Asia-Pacific Region (Updated Edition—After the Crisis)* (Cambridge, MA: Perseus Publishing, 2000), p. 274.

10. There are many sources of advice on evaluating foreign direct investment. See, for example, Franklin R. Root, *Entry Strategies for International Markets* (San Francisco: Jossey Bass, 1994), Chapter 5, on which this list is based. Root also characterizes four kinds of risk in foreign direct investment—general instability risk, ownership (expropriation) risk, operations risk, and transfer risk. See also Stephen J. Kobrin, *Managing Political Risk Assessment* (Berkeley: University of California Press, 1982).

11. But Porter has challenged this traditional notion by espousing a concept of the competitive advantage of nations that includes factor conditions, demand conditions, related and supporting industries, and firm strategy, structure, and rivalry. See Michael E. Porter, *The Competitive Advantage of Nations* (New York: The Free Press, 1990).

12. Some strategists now argue that time is a critical source of competitive advantage. See George Stalk, Jr., and Thomas M. Hout, *Competing Against Time* (New York: The Free Press, 1990).

13. See Porter's discussion of the role of firm strategy, structure, and rivalry in spurring performance improvement in Michael E. Porter, *The Competitive Advantage of Nations* (New York: The Free Press, 1990).

14. This analysis is based on Abraham M. George and C. William Schroth, "Managing

Foreign Exchange for Competitive Advantage," *Sloan Management Review,* Winter 1991, pp. 105–16.

15. See also W. Carl Kester and Timothy A. Luehrman, "Are We Feeling More Competitive Yet? The Exchange Rate Gambit?" *Sloan Management Review,* Winter 1989, pp. 19–28.

16. See Donald R. Lessard, "Finance and Global Competition: Exploiting Financial Scope and Coping with Volatile Exchange Rates," in *Competition in Global Industries,* Michael E. Porter, Ed. (Boston: Harvard Business School Press, 1986).

17. See Marcus C. Bogue III and Elwood S. Buffa, *Corporate Strategic Analysis* (New York: The Free Press, 1986), pp. 69–74 and 93.

18. These three options are suggested by Bruce Kogut, "Designing Global Strategies: Profiting from Operational Flexibility," *Sloan Management Review,* Fall 1985, pp. 27–38.

19. Adapted from "Avon Struggles to Cope with Fallout from Asia's Financial Crisis," *Dow Jones Online News,* December 26, 1997.

20. See also Bruce Kogut, "Designing Global Strategies: Comparative and Competitive Value-Added Chains," *Sloan Management Review,* Summer 1985, pp. 27–38.

21. This example is developed from a presentation by Dr. Burkhard Wittek, "Competitive Market Strategy for the Global Business," The Boston Consulting Group, Munich, at the Strategic Management Society's 8th Annual Conference in Amsterdam, October 1988.

22. See also Porter, *The Competitive Advantage of Nations,* pp. 210–24.

23. Gerrit Jeelof, "Global Strategies of Philips," *European Management Journal,* Vol. 7, No. 1, 1989, pp. 84–91.

24. Dataquest, reported in Clyde V. Prestowitz, Jr., *Trading Places* (New York: Basic Books, 1988), pp. 144–5; and also from a private communication with a (U.S.) Semiconductor Association spokesman, March 8, 1991.

25. This example is adapted from Marquise R. Cvar, "Case Studies in Global Competition: Patterns of Success and Failure," in *Competition in Global Industries,* Porter, pp. 483–516.

26. See Kogut, "Designing Global Strategies: Profiting from Operational Flexibility."

27. K. Ramachandran and George S. Yip, "It's Time to Globalise Now," *General Management Review (Economic Times, India)*, Vol. 2, No. 1, 2000, pp. 40–7.

28. The need to choose between low-cost and differentiation strategies, suggested by Michael E. Porter, *Competitive Strategy: Techniques for Analyzing Industries and Competitors* (New York: The Free Press, 1980), has been challenged in a number of studies. See, for example, Roderick E. White, "Generic Business Strategies, Organizational Context and Performance: An Empirical Investigation," *Strategic Management Journal*, Vol. 7, 1986, pp. 217–31.

29. From a 1989 study conducted by Hamilton Consultants, Cambridge, Massachusetts.

30. See, for example, Constantinos C. Markides and Norman Berg, "Manufacturing Offshore Is Bad Business," *Harvard Business Review*, September–October 1988, pp. 113–20.

31. Markides and Berg, "Manufacturing Offshore Is Bad Business," cite Hitachi, which made microprocessors for Motorola, introducing its own 32-bit microprocessor; Toshiba, which acted as a supplier of copying machines to 3M, now promoting its own brand name; and Daewoo, while still a subcontractor to U.S. companies, now selling its own personal computer. See also Anthony Leung and George S. Yip, "Enter the Global Original Equipment Manufacturer: A New Type of Multinational Company," Working Paper, London Business School, October 31, 2000.

32. This section is drawn from Christopher H. Lovelock and George S. Yip, "Developing Global Strategies for Service Businesses," *California Management Review*, Vol. 38, No. 2, Winter 1996, pp. 65–86.

33. This section is drawn from Lovelock and Yip, "Developing Global Strategies for Service Businesses."

34. Andrew Server, "McDonald's Conquers the World," *Fortune*, 1994.

35. See Donald R. Lessard, "Finance and Global Competition: Exploiting Financial Scope and Coping with Volatile Exchange Rates," in *Competition in Global Industries*, Michael E. Porter, Ed. Boston: (Harvard Business School Press, 1986).

36. See George N. Hatsopoulos, "High Cost of Capital: Handicap of American Industry," report sponsored by the American Business Conference and Thermo-Electron Corporation, April 1983; and Carliss Y. Baldwin, "The Capital Factor: Competing for Capital in a Global Environment," in *Competition in Global Industries*, Michael E. Porter, Ed. (Boston: Harvard Business School Press, 1986).

37. "A Global Approach to Financing," *The Financial Post*, November 11, 1997.

38. Walter Kuemmerle, "Building Effective R&D Capabilities Abroad," *Harvard Business Review*, March–April 1997.

39. *Business Week* cites Hitachi Koki Co. and Nissei Sangyo Co.'s acquisition of Dataproducts Corp. (computer printers), Chugai Pharmaceutical's acquisition of Gen-Probe (biotechnology), Fujisawa Pharmaceutical's acquisition of Lyphomed (drugs), NKK's acquisition of Silicon Graphics (3-D workstations), and Nikko's acquisition of Electro-Scan (electron microscope). "A Shopping Spree in the U.S.," Special Issue on "Innovation: The Global Race," June 15, 1990, pp. 86–7.

40. Deloitte & Touche, *Leaders in Innovative Globalization Program*, report, London, 1998.

41. Jack N. Behrman and William A. Fischer, "Transnational Corporations: Market Orientations and R&D Abroad," *Columbia Journal of World Business*, Fall 1980, pp. 55–60.

42. Kenichi Ohmae, *Triad Power: The Coming Shape of Global Competition* (New York: Free Press, 1985).

43. Ronstadt and Kramer, "Getting the Most Out of Innovation Abroad."

44. D. Eleanor Westney, "Research on the Global Management of Technology Development," *Business Review*, Vol. 46, No. 1, August 1998, pp. 1–21.

45. Kulwant Singh, Joseph Putti, and George S. Yip, "Singapore—Regional Hub," in George S. Yip, *Asian Advantage: Key Strategies for Winning in the Asia-Pacific Region (Updated Edition—After the Crisis)* (Cambridge, MA: Perseus Publishing, 2000), Chapter 7, pp. 155–79.

46. See Peter Dicken, *Global Shift: Industrial Change in a Turbulent World* (London: Harper and Row, 1986), p. 304.

47. Lawton, "Exploding the Value Chain."

48. See M. Therese Flaherty "Coordinating International Manufacturing and Technology" in Porter, *Competition in Global Industries;* and Kasra Ferdows, "Mapping International Factory Networks," in *Managing International Manufacturing,* Kasra Ferdows, Ed. (Amsterdam: Elsevier, North Holland, 1989).

49. See, for example, William H. Davidson, *Global Strategic Management* (New York: John Wiley & Sons, 1982), Chapter 5; and Wickham Skinner, *Manufacturing: The Formidable Weapon* (New York: Wiley, 1985).

50. "Please Hold," *The Economist,* February 22, 1997, p. 68.

51. Thomas L. Friedmann, "For a Lesson on Globalization, Ask AOL's Filipino Help Staff," *International Herald Tribune,* September 30–October 1, 2000.

52. Hugh Williamson, "Philippines Casts Support Services Net to Entice More International Clients," *Financial Times,* December 1, 2000, p. 36.

53. See Kasra Ferdows et al., *The Internationalization of U.S. Manufacturing: Causes and Consequences* (Washington, DC: National Academy Press, 1990), pp. 23–4.

54. National trade policies are, of course, an enormous topic. For guidance see, for example, Raymond Vernon and Louis T. Wells Jr., *Manager in the International Economy* (Upper Saddle River, NJ: Prentice-Hall, 1986); and Michael R. Czinkota, Ilkka A. Ronkainen, and Michael Moffett, *International Business,* update 2000 (New York: Harcourt 2000).

55. Yves L. Doz, "Managing Manufacturing Rationalization Within Multinational Companies," *Columbia Journal of World Business,* Fall 1978, pp. 82–94.

56. This section is based on Ferdows, "Mapping International Networks."

57. Kasra Ferdows et al., *The Internationalization of U.S. Manufacturing: Causes and Consequences* (Washington DC: National Academy Press, 1990), p. 30.

58. Flaherty, "Coordinating International Manufacturing and Technology."

59. A survey study found flexibility to be an important concern of Japanese manufacturers. See Arnoud de Meyer, Jinichiro Nakane, Jeffrey Miller, and Kasra Ferdows, "Flexibility: The Next Competitive Battle – The Manufacturing Futures Survey," *Strategic Management Journal,* Vol. 10, 1989, pp. 135–44.

60. For reviews of flexible manufacturing, see Joel D. Goldhar and Mariann Jelinek, "Computer Integrated Flexible Manufacturing: Organizational, Economic, and Strategic Implications," *Interfaces,* Vol. 15, May–June 1985, pp. 94–105; and Ramachandran Jaikumar, "Postindustrial Manufacturing," *Harvard Business Review,* November–December 1986, pp. 69–76.

61. James C. Abegglen and George Stalk, Jr., *Kaisha: The Japanese Corporation* (New York: Basic Books, 1985), pp. 89–90.

62. Kenichi Ohmae, *The Evolving Global Economy: Making Sense of the New World Order* (Boston: Harvard Business School Press, 1995).

63. Lovelock and Yip, "Developing Global Strategies for Service Businesses."

64. Stanley B. Lemons, "Diners Club International's Global Marketing Strategy," The Anderson School at UCLA, June 6, 1996.

6

CREATING GLOBAL MARKETING

〜✦〜

Global marketing constitutes the fourth global strategy lever that companies can use to globalize their strategy. A worldwide business uses global marketing when it takes the same or similar approach or content for one or more elements of the marketing mix, that is, the same or similar brand names, advertising, and so on, in different countries. Multinational companies increasingly use global marketing and have been highly successful—Nestlé with its common brand name applied to many products in all countries, Citibank with its global advertising themes, Hewlett-Packard with its global account management programs, and Xerox with its global leasing policies. But *global marketing is not about standardizing the marketing process.* Standardizing the way in which country subsidiaries analyze markets and develop marketing plans is merely good multinational practice—a way of transferring skills and setting high standards for the marketing function.[1]

Global marketing and selling means striving for the appropriate balance of global uniformity and local adaptation in all elements of the marketing mix, but with a probable bias in favor of uniformity unless a good case can be made for local exceptions. This means casting aside the previous conventional wisdom that companies should globally standardize the marketing process but not the marketing content. Global excellence in marketing now means looking for uniformity. For example, Unilever has recognized that marketing too many different brands around the world hampers it. In 1999 it began an initiative to reduce its number of brands from over 1,600 to about 400 and to emphasize a dozen or so global brands. Diageo's United Distillers Vintners unit now focuses on nine "global power brands." Research on global marketing shows that different elements of the mix need to have different degrees of global uniformity, with brand names and packaging needing the most uniformity; pricing, advertising, and distribution moderate uniformity; and selling and promotion the least.[2] Germany's Beiersdorf, the produce and marketer of the Nivea brand, provides an excellent example of global marketing that maintains tight and effective worldwide consistency. But companies can go too far. In the late 1990s British Airways made an attempt to further reposition itself as a global rather than just a British airline by replacing the national flag on the tails of its planes with art designs from around the world. Domestic opposition mounted, and the designs were dubbed "global graffiti." British Airways ended this experiment after just a few years.

Every element of the marketing mix—product design, product and brand positioning, brand name, packaging, pricing, advertising strategy, advertising execution, promotion, and distribution—is a candidate for globalization. As with other global strategy levers, the use of global marketing can be flexible. A business can make some elements of the marketing mix more global and others less so. Within each element, some parts can be globally uniform and others not. For example, a "global" pack design may have a common logo and illustration in all countries, but a different background color in

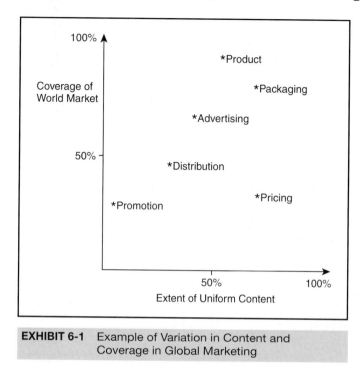

EXHIBIT 6-1   Example of Variation in Content and
Coverage in Global Marketing

some countries. So both marketing as a whole and each individual marketing element can be global to a greater or lesser extent in its *content*.[3]

Global marketing can also vary in its geographic *coverage*. Few global marketing programs can realistically apply to all of the worldwide market. A marketing element can be global without being 100 percent uniform in content or coverage. Exhibit 6-1 illustrates a possibly typical pattern. In this hypothetical example, packaging is highly uniform in both content and coverage, pricing is highly uniform in a small number of countries, while the global promotion program has a great deal of local variation and is applied to a small number of countries only. The benefits of global marketing (and other global strategy levers) can be realized without total uniformity. A mostly uniform marketing approach that covers the major markets accounting for, say, 80 percent of revenues may be more than adequate. Indeed, there are probably diminishing returns to extreme uniformity as illustrated in Exhibit 6-2. The net benefits can rapidly decline if global marketing (and other global) programs are pushed to extremes of uniformity. The key in global strategy is to find the best balance between local adaptation and global standardization. *So global marketing is not a blind adherence to standardization of all marketing elements for its own sake, but a different, global approach to developing marketing strategy and programs that blends flexibility with uniformity.*

BENEFITS OF GLOBAL MARKETING

The conventional wisdom in international marketing has been that multinational companies should standardize marketing process rather than marketing content.[4] But worldwide businesses can use globally standardized marketing content to great effect. Like the

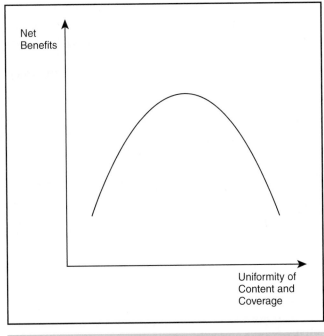

EXHIBIT 6-2 Net Benefits Versus Degree of Uniformity

other global strategy levers, global marketing can achieve one or more of four major categories of potential globalization benefits: cost reduction, improved quality of products and programs, enhanced customer preference, and increased competitive leverage.

COST REDUCTION

In global marketing *cost reduction* arises from savings in both workforce and materials. Personnel outlays can be reduced when multiple national marketing functions are consolidated. In addition, personnel outlays are reduced when the use of global marketing eliminates duplication of activities so that national managers do not waste time reinventing each other's wheels. Materials costs are saved in producing global advertisements and commercials (which can represent up to 10 percent or more of the total advertising budget) and producing promotional materials and packaging print. (Savings from standardized packaging go well beyond the marketing sphere into that of inventory costs. Each packaging variant creates an additional stockkeeping unit. With typical inventory carrying costs at 20 percent of sales, any reduction in inventory can have dramatic effects on the profit margin.) As global and regional media—such as satellite television, multicountry programs, and international journals—increase in scope, global marketing can achieve additional cost savings by mounting multicountry campaigns through these vehicles. For example, EC Television, a subsidiary of the Interpublic Group (one of the largest multinational advertising agency concerns), created a pan-European soap opera, action-adventure series, and variety show. The rise of CNN, MTV, Asia's Star TV, and others as global or regional television networks has greatly increased the opportunities for global advertising.

Cost savings can also translate into improved program effectiveness by allowing more money and resources to be put into a smaller number of programs. More lavish advertising executions can be afforded for a single global campaign than for multiple national ones. British Airways was able to afford very spectacular, and expensive, special effects for its highly memorable "Manhattan Landing" global television commercial (in which Manhattan skyscrapers were shown landing on an English village).

ENHANCED CUSTOMER PREFERENCE

Global marketing helps build global recognition that can *enhance customer preference* through reinforcement. For many products and services, their buyers, whether consumers or members of organizations, travel, get transferred, or become exposed to multicountry media. So, a uniform marketing message—whether communicated through the brand name, packaging, or advertising—reinforces their awareness, knowledge, and attitudes of the product or service. Anyone who has seen a billboard for a global product in a remote part of the world (such as a Coca-Cola advertisement at the Great Wall of China) will know the feeling of reinforcement such an experience provides. Many global consulting firms choose airports as their locale for global advertising messages.

IMPROVED PROGRAM EFFECTIVENESS

Much of the previous debate on global marketing has identified cost savings and increased recognition as the primary benefits and reduced program effectiveness as a major drawback. But a strong case can be made that *improved program effectiveness is often the greatest benefit of global marketing. Good ideas in marketing are scarce.* So a globalization program that overcomes local objections to allow the geographic spread of a good marketing idea can often raise the average effectiveness of programs around the world. Of course, objections are not couched as "not-invented-here" (often the real problem) but as "you-don't-understand-we-are-different" (the most common argument). In addition, globalization of some elements of the marketing mix, for example, the positioning strategy, would free up national managers' time to improve other elements, such as trade relations.

Exhibit 6-3 illustrates how global marketing can improve program effectiveness. Left on their own to develop, say, an advertising campaign, the businesses in different countries will achieve different levels of program effectiveness. So, as in Exhibit 6-3, there will be a wide range of effectiveness. But a global program can raise the average level of effectiveness. The two dashed lines in the exhibit show that the key in global marketing is to select a program that is *more* effective than the average of all the countries rather than to select one that is on average less effective. Exhibit 6-3 also shows that some loss in effectiveness is incurred even in the case of the successful global program—in countries G and H. In that case, why not let G and H opt out of the global program? First, the countries that will produce the better programs may not be known before the event, but only after letting each country duplicate the development effort. Second, allowing some countries to opt out may reduce the willingness of the others to use the global program.

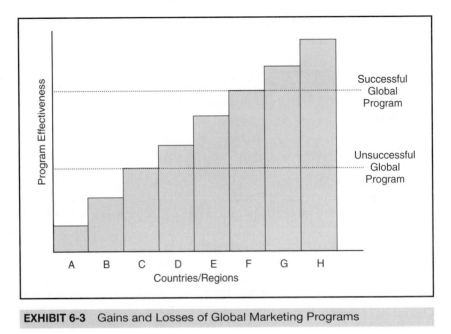

EXHIBIT 6-3 Gains and Losses of Global Marketing Programs

INCREASED COMPETITIVE LEVERAGE

Global marketing can *increase competitive leverage* in two ways. By focusing resources into a smaller number of programs, global marketing can magnify the competitive power of marketing efforts. While larger competitors may have the resources to develop different high-quality programs for each country, a smaller competitor may not. Using global marketing then allows the smaller competitor to lessen its disadvantage. But perhaps the most important competitive benefit is that global marketing can get the entire organization behind one idea. Avis rental car created a global advertising and promotion campaign ("We're number two. We try harder.") that communicated in single-minded fashion not only to customers but to employees as well. As a result the entire organization pulled together to deliver on the global promise, not just in marketing but also in all other activities.

DRAWBACKS OF GLOBAL MARKETING

As with the other global strategy levers, global marketing can seem to run against the conventional wisdom of tailoring for local markets. The annals of international marketing overflow with horror stories arising from insufficient adaptation. For example, Pepsi-Cola once translated its advertising slogan "Come alive with the Pepsi generation" into Chinese for the Taiwan market. The selling pitch became "Pepsi brings your ancestors back to life"! But amusing though such stories may be, they are mistakes of *international* marketing rather than of *global* marketing. These mistakes occur through poor or inadequate adaptation *after* a marketing program has been created for one country. But global marketing is not about forcing a domestic program onto the international subsidiaries. Instead, a global marketing program should be designed from the start with the needs of major target countries in mind. This last approach has its own dangers. In particular, programs designed for the global market run the risk of overaveraging or aiming for the lowest common denominator.[5] In addition, potential users of global marketing need to review the specific industry globalization drivers applying to their industry.

WHEN TO USE GLOBAL MARKETING

Industry globalization potential affects when to use global marketing. Market globalization drivers, not surprisingly, provide the strongest impetus for global marketing, while cost, government, and competitive globalization each have some effect also.

MARKET GLOBALIZATION DRIVERS FOR GLOBAL MARKETING

All of the individual market globalization drivers have major effects on the potential for using global marketing.

Common Customer Needs

The more common customer needs are across countries, the more opportunity there is for marketing to customers in the same way around the world. The same types of appeals and promises can be made. Some marketing-related determinants of common customer needs include the similarity of the stage of market development and market segmentation and the role of psychological appeals.

Global Customers and Channels

The presence of global customers requires a globally coordinated marketing effort, so that the business makes either the same claims, promises, or terms of trade around the world or knows when and why these differ. A recent study found that global customers particularly want global consistency in service quality and performance, global contracts, uniform terms of trade, and global pricing.[6]

Transferable Marketing

When marketing is globally transferable, it allows the use of the same marketing approaches and content around the world. A key determinant of marketing transferability is the extent to which usage of the product or service is rooted in national traditions. So, for example, the marketing of household cleaning products is rooted in traditional concepts of the role of homemaking. As these roles (or the concept of these roles) mostly differ from country to country, there is little transferability of those marketing elements, such as advertising, that depend most on these roles. In essence, there is not yet a concept of the "global homemaker"—almost a contradiction in terms. In contrast, products and services with little national culture attached to them tend to allow transferable marketing. Most industrial products and services fall in this category, as do many newer consumer products and services, such as fast food and credit cards.

COST GLOBALIZATION DRIVERS FOR GLOBAL MARKETING

The more expensive it is to develop marketing programs and to produce them, the greater the incentive to use global marketing that avoids national duplication. The cost of marketing programs and production (e.g., television commercials) is probably a function both of individual company approaches and of the industry as a whole—as lavish productions by one competitor spur others to match them. Not surprisingly, it is some of the most expensive to produce advertising that gets used globally—like Coca-Cola's mountaintop commercial of the 1970s, British Airways' "Manhattan Landing" in the 1980s, and Citibank's global branding commercials in the 1990s.

GOVERNMENT GLOBALIZATION DRIVERS FOR GLOBAL MARKETING

Whether governments set *common marketing regulations* in this industry significantly affects the use of global marketing. Each element of the marketing mix can be subject to special regulation by a government in an important market. Advertising content is probably the most heavily and differently regulated marketing element. For example, comparative advertising is not allowed in several European countries.

COMPETITIVE GLOBALIZATION DRIVERS FOR GLOBAL MARKETING

As with each of the other global strategy levers, it can be important to match or pre-empt competitors in their use of global marketing. Being the first to use global branding is probably one of the most effective ways to get a first mover marketing advantage relative to competitors. Perrier's partial rebound in global markets, after its contamination problem in 1990, was due in large part to the preeminent position it occupied as the first global mineral water brand. Andersen Consulting's aggressive use of globally standardized and ubiquitous advertising helped cement its claim to be the world's leading systems integration consulting firm. In its new guise as Accenture, the firm continues this competitive strategy.

HOW TO USE GLOBAL MARKETING

Having reviewed when to use global marketing, this next section discusses how to use global marketing for each element of the marketing mix. Each of the individual marketing elements has special considerations in globalization. These can be summarized as shown on the next page:

We have already discussed global products in Chapter 4 and global distribution in Chapter 5. But each of the other marketing elements needs attention. *Also, both the global marketing of service businesses and the effects of the Internet on global marketing are so intertwined with issues affecting individual elements of the marketing mix that we will discuss them under each element below.*

GLOBAL POSITIONING

Positioning is the act of designing the company's product and marketing mix to fit a given place in the customer's mind, usually with regard to competitive offerings.[7] A common global positioning can both strengthen the effectiveness of marketing programs and increase competitive leverage. It can strengthen program effectiveness by providing a positioning that is tried and tested in many countries and that provides the basis for commonality in other marketing elements. A common global positioning can increase competitive leverage by putting all of the resources of the business behind developing assets and qualities (such as superior reliability in the case of Volkswagen or Toyota cars or easy replacement in the case of American Express traveler's checks or credit cards) to support that positioning. The head of global marketing in a major household products business considers brand positioning, rather than the brand name itself, to be the most

Marketing Element	Major Considerations in Globalization
Products	Commonality of customer needs and usage and of national technical standards
Positioning	Similarity of business's competitive position, purchase motivation (e.g., psychological appeals, ego involvement), and use/consumption patterns
Brand name	Global acceptance/prestige of home country of brand name; importance of having a name that means something; ease of pronunciation
Packaging design	Amount of information that needs to be communicated; similarity of distribution conditions (e.g., importance of display appeal); need for differentiation from local competitors; similarity of usage patterns and measurement systems; acceptability of multilanguage labeling
Absolute pricing	Similarity of market price levels, laws, role of price, business's delivered cost position
Relative pricing	Similarity of business's competitive position, delivered costs, and market objectives
Advertising strategy	Similarity of business's competitive position and market objectives, stage of product life cycle, and buying motivation
Advertising execution	Universality of images, situations, and characters to be used; global recognizability of personalities; need for differentiation from local competitors
Advertising media	Availability of desired media; lack of restrictions on use
Sales promotion	Lack of legal and customary restrictions; similarity of incentive effect
Selling approach	Similarity of channel structure and customer buying methods and behavior
Sales personnel	Importance of technical expertise; acceptability of foreigners
Distribution	Similarity of distribution structure and business's relationship with channels
Customer service	Similarity of customer need and support infrastructure (e.g., toll-free phone service)

important marketing element to be globalized. If a global brand positioning succeeded in several countries, then managers in other countries would "stop monkeying around" with the formula. In addition, more effort could be devoted to implementation. On the other hand, differences in the business's competitive position, purchase motivation (e.g., psychological appeals, ego involvement), and use/consumption patterns may argue for differing positions. For example, Volvo is positioned as a fairly unsophisticated automotive brand with high market share in Sweden, but it is positioned further upscale elsewhere in Europe. Many other automobile manufacturers, however, do position their marques, particularly luxury ones, the same way globally.

Companies that use a common positioning often find that they can make a large part of the marketing mix globally uniform. For example, M&M Mars was so confident of the similarities between the European and U.S. markets that it introduced two of its European brands, Bounty and Balisto, into the United States without any prior test marketing, based on the European positioning. The company used the same packaging for the two brands, and advertising for the brands was similar. Packaging across markets was for the most part standardized. The company's slogan "melts in your mouth, not in your hands" is also used successfully across markets. The company used the same slogan to introduce M&M candies in Mexico.

Global Positioning on the Internet

In many ways, a company's Web sites constitute its positioning in cyberspace. For example, is the Web site cluttered and busy or is it cool and sophisticated? Is it the same around the world or is it very different? Does it use just one language or many?

Language on the Net. The choice of languages makes a very powerful positioning statement. Staying with just the home country language sends a strong message, probably an unfavorable one. International marketers, pre-Internet, generally translated to the local language, unless there were special reasons, such as favorable country-of-origin effects, to use a foreign language. On the Internet, the ubiquity of English allows many English-language companies to build up significant international business with English-only Web sites. For example, Amazon.com stayed English-only for the first three years of its life, until it added a German Web site in 1998. But sooner rather than later, e-marketers will have to build fully fluent foreign language Web sites, not necessarily for their biggest foreign markets but for the biggest foreign markets for whom the e-marketer's home language is not accessible for a large proportion of the target audience.

The advent of Web translation software for both Web creators and Web users will reduce the problems of language.[8] But companies probably want to control the translation rather than rely on third-party software translating for their users. Automatic translations will not be able to avoid the translation mistakes common in international marketing and in machine translators.

The Country-of-Origin Issue

A critical issue in global positioning is the country of origin that the company wants to adopt.[9] Following the concept of lead countries (discussed in Chapter 2), a company may want to position itself or its products or brands as coming from a country other than the home base. And increasingly, some companies find it hard to identify a single home base anyway (e.g., ABB, DaimlerChrysler, and other products of multicountry mergers). Britain has a commercial image that greatly lags reality. Consequently, many British companies have tried to hide their British origins, particularly by dropping the "British" in their names and switching to initials that start with "B" (from British Airways to BA, from British Petroleum to BP, from British Oxygen to BOC, etc.). Perhaps, the Italian clothing company Benetton has gone the furthest in positioning itself as global without a distinct national origin. Its theme of "The United Colors of Benetton" and its supporting advertising say to its customers that wearing Benetton clothes makes them a part of a global culture. This is in distinct contrast to the many American consumer companies that trade on promoting Americana.

Backlash Against Globalization

Being too strongly positioned as a global company, especially for consumer products and services, now invites attention from antiglobalization protesters and rioters. It is no coincidence that McDonald's has become the favorite target of antiglobal violence. Similarly, by positioning itself as the global car for conspicuous consumption, BMW's cars also attract more than their share of street attacks. Critics of global capitalism have also targeted other companies such as Nike, Shell, Wal-Mart, and Microsoft.[10]

GLOBAL BRAND NAMES

Using a globally uniform brand name provides the easiest way of building global recognition.[11] Around 1990 M&M Mars changed the name of its Marathon product, in the United Kingdom and other countries, to Snickers, an American name. In the United Kingdom, M&M Mars went so far as to run a television commercial (featuring a frustrated Australian tourist) that explained the name change in terms of preventing confusion for traveling consumers. Furthermore, the possibility of combination names such as a globally standard umbrella name combined with a local product name provides flexibility. The Eveready Battery Company, a division of Ralston-Purina, consolidated its various national brand names—such as Ucar, Wonder, and Mazda—into one global name, Energizer, for its premium batteries. This move was partly necessitated by the fact that its major competitor, Duracell, already operated with one global brand. Whirlpool has created a three-tier branding structure to accommodate its various acquisitions in Europe.[12] The three brands are Bauknecht, featuring premium German engineering at the top; Whirlpool in the middle market; and Ignis at the budget level. In this process, Whirlpool also gradually dropped the Philips brand name that it acquired in Europe.

Volkswagen's Name Adaptations.   Volkswagen has a model name series that denotes winds—Golf (Gulf wind), Scirocco (the hot wind from North Africa), and Passat (trade wind)—but made a highly successfully switch of the Golf to Rabbit for the U.S. market, which made for a much better fit with the youthful segment that was the target in the United States. Similarly, in the 1980s Volkswagen renamed its Santana line as Quantum for the American market, perhaps to avoid connotations of the General Santa Anna who captured the Alamo. But Volkswagen tries to mostly use the same model names around the world, because it views the car-buying public as very mobile.

The desirability of a global brand name depends in part on the global acceptance or prestige of the home country of the brand name, the importance of having a name that means something, and the ease of pronunciation. Its tongue-twisting name (for Japanese) caused Baskin-Robbins to use in Japan the name "31 Ice Cream" in English with the same logo that it uses in the United States, the "31" referring to the number of flavors sold. Brand names that mean something may need to be translated in order to perform the positioning task for which they were designed. Thus, Unilever's Close Up toothpaste became for some years Très Près (Very Close) in France but retained its positioning (promotion of social confidence). Having established the brand in France, Unilever was later able to switch back to close up in its drive for global branding. In some cases companies adopt a foreign brand name that would never be used in its home country, witness the Nissan Cedric, which is sold in Japan, but certainly not in the United Kingdom or the United States.

In many product and service categories the preeminence of producers from particular countries encourages customers to prefer brand names indicating origin from that country. With the rise in prestige of Japanese products, companies like Toyota moved in the 1980s to model names with Japanese rather than American connotations—like Celica, Corolla, and Camry. In the 1990s, Nokia, the Finnish mobile phone company, was initially happy to be mistaken for Japanese. Having achieved preeminence in its category, Nokia now boasts in the 2000s of its Finnish origins.

Many companies have overcome company or brand names not designed for easy worldwide pronunciation (e.g., Nestlé, being pronounced "NES-sull" by many in Britain), but few have designed a global brand name from scratch. An exception was Unilever's Omo brand of detergent, which was designed to be easily pronounced in any language. But Unilever never backed this up with global positioning. So Omo continues to be among the world's least consistent global brands.

Datsun's Switch to Nissan.   Perhaps the biggest mistake in failing to use a global brand name comes, interestingly, from a Japanese company—Nissan. When Nissan first exported its automobiles, it used the name Datsun. After many years of establishing the name in the United States and elsewhere outside Japan, Nissan dropped the Datsun name in the early 1980s and went to the company name.[13] The goal of the worldwide name change, as stated by the Nissan Management Council, was to create a unified international image for the company. Before the change, Nissan had been the largest Japanese automobile importer into the United States. Ever since the change it has lagged both Toyota and Honda in share of the U.S. market. While a string of relatively weak Nissan products bears the brunt of the blame, the name change must also have played a major role in the decline.

Companies, particularly in Europe, are now adapting their names to globalize them. The second-largest dairy cooperative in Europe, Mejeriselskabet Denmark, changed its name in the late 1980s to MD Foods and its packaging colors from red and white (as in the Danish flag) to green and yellow. The change was intended to underscore the international reach of its business and the fact that it sells much more than just dairy products. This changed image also helped make MD Foods much more attractive to job applicants. With a change in name and image came a change in organization design to coordinate production and marketing. Multiple subsidiaries in other countries were combined as a result. Interestingly, in another case, it was the marketers of an American product with purely domestic ambitions that created the fictitious, Scandinavian-sounding name Häagen-Dazs.

While many companies use global brand names, few seem to have achieved the status of wide recognition as global brands. A 1990 study found only 19 truly global brands in the sense of high worldwide awareness and esteem. These brands were ranked as shown on the following page.

Value of Global Brands
In recent years companies have begun to put financial values on their brands. Not surprisingly, the most valuable brands in the world are those that cross borders, even if they are not fully global. For example, the brand, Coca-Cola, has been valued at over $80 billion, and another 60 brands at a minimum of $1 billion each.[15]

Global Branding for Service Businesses
Because of their greater global variability in makeup and quality, service businesses need stronger global brands. Such brands will reinforce customer expectations and experiences and, just as important, act as a motivator for employees. The minimum wage worker for McDonald's or FedEx in some developing country knows that he or she is expected to live up to the global standards represented by the brand.

THE WORLD'S MOST GLOBAL BRANDS

1. Coca-Cola
2. Sony
3. Mercedes-Benz
4. Kodak
5. Disney
6. Nestlé
7. Toyota
8. McDonald's
9. IBM
10. Pepsi-Cola
11. Rolls-Royce
12. Honda
13. Panasonic
14. Levi's
15. Kleenex
16. Ford
17. Volkswagen
18. Kellogg's
19. Porsche

(This study seemed biased against some very well known brands that may not have high esteem, for example, Marlboro, or that are more visual than verbal, for example, the Shell logo.)[14] This study surveyed consumers only. More specialized buyer groups would doubtless have identified other global brands that were relevant to them.

Most recently, a 2001 study by Young and Rubicam measured brand strength defined as a combination of growth potential and favorable perception. The agency questioned over 45,000 adults and teenagers in 19 countries. The top 10 brands were:

1. Coca-Cola
2. Disney
3. Nike
4. BMW
5. Porsche
6. Mercedes-Benz
7. Adidas
8. Rolls-Royce
9. Calvin Klein
10. Rolex

Global Brand Names on the Internet

The Internet mandates globally uniform brand names, at least at the umbrella level (e.g., FedEx) and perhaps even at the sub-brand or product level (e.g., FedEx International Priority). Although local customers may stay mostly within national sites, it is very easy to stray. Becoming an international customer requires a few clicks, not a cross-border journey. So companies, will find it increasingly difficult to maintain national variations in brand and sub-brand names. FedEx used to keep different brand names in different countries. But now, it uses all globally common names.

The Internet also makes it easier to build global branding and recognition, particularly for Web names with the right connotations. Chinadotcom was a tiny Hong Kong company that jumped to almost instant global recognition by virtue of its site name, china.com. The brand recognition led to a highly successful initial stock offering, building a market capitalization of $3 billion by January 2000, which in turn fueled a long string of acquisitions and partnership deals.

Requirements to Be a Global Brand

In summary, a global brand needs several features:

- A broad geographic reach, that is, availability on most continents and in most countries
- A mostly uniform image and positioning worldwide
- Perception by consumers as global

Making the Change

Because of history many companies, particularly in packaged goods, find themselves stuck with a wide variety of brand and product names that have little justification in real differences between countries. The brand management system encourages innovation, so that left to their own devices, national brand managers are liable to convert a "Boggo" brand into Bloggo, Bloxxo, and Bingo, making it far more difficult to use global packaging and advertising. A vice president of global marketing in a large American multinational consumer packaged goods business viewed ease of internal communication as an additional benefit of global brands. This company has a category of "federal charter brand" that is designated to be controlled by the center, with power as the absolute court of last resort. Only very large and important brands are accorded this status.

In implementing a change to global branding, managers need to consider:

- Market issues—what will happen to customer and trade loyalty, sales, and market share?
- Disposal issues—can regional or local brands be disposed of at a reasonable price and in a way that does not create future competitive problems?
- Internal barriers—are there internal constituencies that will block or hinder this move?

GLOBAL PACKAGING

The ability to use global packaging depends on several factors:

- Amount of information that needs to be communicated; the similarity of distribution conditions (e.g., importance of display appeal)
- Need for differentiation from local competitors
- Similarity of usage patterns and measurement systems
- Acceptability of multilanguage labeling

The high proportion of camera film bought by travelers makes it imperative to use globally recognizable packaging, as Eastman Kodak has done so well with its ubiquitous bright yellow boxes and stylized "K" logo. Fuji Photo Film has copied this approach with its distinctive green boxes. Gillette has achieved highly uniform packaging for its shaving products by substituting visual graphics for most of the wording that would otherwise be there. Furthermore, Gillette's use of consistent color, logo, and graphics provides a powerful umbrella image that makes it easy to introduce changes and new products with minimal disruption.

In the 1980s, 3M discovered that its segmented approach to the markets for magnetic tape products was inefficient. Because there were similar features in all markets,

3M decided to introduce a new global brand identity and packaging for the magnetic products line, developing a global marketing strategy. The new identity was designed to be used uniformly for all of the division's products in all markets and all countries. 3M developed a global advertising program that emphasized the logo and took advantage of the global transferability of the packaging. The new global marketing program boosted volume and market share, and the uniform packaging and design reduced the cost of marketing. In addition, the uniform marketing package exposure achieved quick customer recognition of 3M products.

Many companies have allowed unnecessary differences in their packaging. In the late 1980s a major New Zealand–based forest products company updated its corporate logo—a lion's head—that was printed on all its packaging, but in North America only! So customers, many of whom were global, saw a modern lion in North America and a traditional one elsewhere. Other companies simply fail to identify their products consistently. The management of a major manufacturer of textile tubes belatedly realized that many of its products lacked any corporate identification at all. The company had to make rapid efforts to correct that lapse. Many Japanese companies, particularly newly internationalizing ones, converted their corporate logos from the Japanese *kanji* characters to more globally recognizable versions. Fuji Bank, for example, now uses a stylized image of Mount Fuji for its logo and spells out its name in English.

But many customers seem to dislike packaging that signals foreign origin. Even multilanguage labeling has its potential pitfalls— companies selling in a particular country need to avoid adding the languages of those other countries that might trigger prejudice or connotations of poor quality—"If this is used in Country X then it can't be very good." In contrast, Zara, the highly successful Spanish fashion retailer, takes multicountry labeling to extremes. Each item of clothing in its stores carries price labels that show up to a dozen national flags and prices in national currencies. The one label may show prices in U.S. dollars, British pounds, French francs, German marks, and so on. (Zara's labels will be simplified after the introduction of euro notes and coins in 2002.)

Differences in national culture have a surprising effect on labeling. In Germany and Japan, customers expect products to perform to high standards but do not expect performance beyond the stated level. So if a product is labeled as being able to bear, 1,000 kilograms, it will do that and no more. In America standards can be lower, but customers also expect a lot more leeway in performance beyond standards.[16] So in the United States, labeling needs to allow for overloading or overdosage or else expect a lot of complaints and lawsuits. In Germany and Japan, the same policy would mean understating what the product can do, thus putting it at a competitive disadvantage.

Global Packaging on the Internet

While physical packages do not travel through the Internet, pictures of them are often displayed on Web sites. Companies need to think out a deliberate policy as to whether they wish to facilitate or discourage cross-border recognition or comparison. The knee-jerk reaction may be that we do not want our customers comparing prices and items across our different national Web sites. But then customers may migrate to competitors' sites that make comparison easy. In 1980, some strategists advised companies to keep their customers as ignorant as possible.[17] In 2000, it is both insulting and futile to try to keep Net-savvy customers ignorant. The competition is not down the street or in the next town or country, but a few clicks away.

GLOBAL PRICING

Global pricing can bring the benefits of consistency with global customers and distribution channels and the avoidance of "gray market" parallel importation or "transshipment."[18] Multinational companies often find themselves charging the same price to global customers without good justification. An international vice president of sales and distribution found that his company sometimes quoted the same customer different prices and availability in different countries, while finding it very difficult to explain why.

Charging the same absolute price can be very difficult because of inherent international differences in market price levels, laws, and the role of price, as well as differences in the business's market position and delivered costs. The creation of the single European market is rapidly eliminating any government sources of price differences, such as tariffs and taxes, within the European Union, as well as encouraging buyers to cross borders. So companies in the EU need to rapidly rationalize the wide price differences that many now have. To start with, headquarters managers need to know the prices in different countries. But surprisingly few companies have sufficient information about their worldwide pricing to make decisions on global strategy.

Another way to have global pricing is to charge the same prices *relative* to competitors in each market. Using uniform relative pricing helps provide a consistent positioning in the market. Its viability depends on the similarity of the business's competitive position, delivered costs, and market objectives. Most commonly, it seems to be luxury products that manage to have pricing consistency, probably because being expensive is an essential part of what they offer.

Global Pricing for Service Businesses

Manufacturing businesses increasingly need to charge globally uniform prices to provide consistency with global customers and distribution channels and to avoid "gray market" parallel importation or "transshipment." In contrast, the lack of inventories in many service businesses means that such firms need worry less about using global pricing. It is relatively difficult to buy a service in one country and to resell it in another.

McDonald's prices certainly vary, so much so that *The Economist* magazine uses a "McDonald's Big Mac Price Index" to compare the cost of living in major business cities around the world. In the case of multinational customers as opposed to individuals, however, even service businesses need to avoid charging different prices in different countries to the same customer without good justification. DHL, the express delivery company, manages to maintain significant disparities across regions, but only where the company faces little competition, such as in many African markets.

Global Pricing on the Internet

The Internet provides a major driver for global pricing in two ways. The Internet makes it far easier for potential customers to check prices for the same product or service in different countries. Price-oriented search engines also facilitate this process. So multinational companies now have to work even harder at justifying cross-border price differences. Knowing that customers will compare across a supplier's national Web sites, suppliers should provide explicit explanations on their Web sites for price differences. For example, an American supplier's Japanese Web site, which shows a higher price for Japan, might state that X amount of the price is for freight, customs charges, and the like, from the United States.

GLOBAL ADVERTISING

Global advertising has received more attention and publicity than any other aspect of global marketing, probably because of its visibility. Essentially, global advertising can be used at three levels:

- *Same copy strategy*—the brand is positioned in the same way making the same claims. Colgate toothpaste has long used the globally common claim of protection against cavities. Using a common copy strategy depends on worldwide similarity of the business's competitive position and market objectives and similarity of the stage of market development and buying motivations.
- *Same script*—the advertising uses the same script in different countries, while the actual execution is different. Using a common script depends on the universality of the images chosen and of the situations and characters to be used, and also the need for differentiation from local competitors. Coca-Cola has often taken this second approach of a common script, as in its famous "little-boy-gives-Coke-to-sports-hero" campaign. In America, the hero was Mean Joe Green of the Pittsburgh Steelers football team; in Latin America, Diego Maradona, the Argentine soccer superstar; and in Thailand, a local soccer star named Niwat. Rarely can the same personality be used, although IBM did this with its Charlie Chaplin campaign.
- *Identical advertisement*—where each country uses the same commercial or advertisement with only the voices or text translated. Coca-Cola used this approach very successfully in its Italian hilltop chorale commercial in which youngsters from around the world stood together singing that they wanted to give the world a Coke.

As already mentioned, Saatchi & Saatchi's "Manhattan Landing" commercial for British Airways is probably the most famous piece of global advertising. But Benetton, the highly successful Italian clothing manufacturer, has probably produced the most courageous examples. Benetton has run a globally uniform "Colors of Benetton" advertising campaign that features interracial harmony as a central theme. Some of its global images backfired in the United States when American audiences saw racist stereotypes rather than harmonious integration (a black wrist and a white wrist handcuffed together and a white baby feeding at a black breast). Levi Strauss has used a mixture of all three levels of advertising uniformity. Its advertising strategy used a common positioning stressing the all-American heritage of its jeans. An Indonesian television commercial showed teenagers in Levis cruising around Dubuque, Iowa, in 1960s convertibles. In Japan, Levi's used James Dean, the 1950s American film star, as the centerpiece in virtually all their advertising. Some of Levi's advertising execution was uniform too: In most advertisements for Levi's 501 button-fly jeans the dialogue was in English.

Ironically, the one type of advertising that cannot be used worldwide is one that stresses the country of origin. By definition, such a claim usually has little benefit at home, unless the company is making patriotic as opposed to benefit claims. For example, Volkswagen greatly boosted its advertising awareness in the U.S. market with its *Fahrvergnügen* (joy of driving) campaign that directly played on the image of German cars as having superior handling and drivability. Neither the claim nor the attention-grabbing German-language headline would have worked at home. Audi followed suit with its advertising slogan of *Forsprung dürch Technik*. Similarly, British Airways' long-time use in U.S. advertising of an actor embodying the stereotypical Englishman would have done nothing for British audiences. BA's later global advertising evolved to avoid British references. One commercial featured different nationalities of people meeting each other, brought together by BA. Another featured a group of hundreds of people of all ethnicities, forming one face that then morphed into a picture of Earth from space—about as global as one can get in the use of people in advertising.

Being able to use the same advertising media worldwide depends on the availability of the desired media, and on the lack of restrictions on the content of the advertising. The existence of national media with global reach forces advertisers to be consistent. In many industrial and scientific fields, journals published in one country have very wide circulation. A manufacturer of chemical and process equipment advertises in industry journals that have worldwide circulation and had to stop its European subsidiaries from running in these journals advertisements that differed from the global positioning.

Taking a totally uniform advertising approach can limit competitive flexibility. So some companies increasingly use two campaigns—a globally uniform one setting out the main theme, and local campaigns for tactical purposes—while using local campaigns to address particular local communication needs.

Global Advertising for Service Businesses

Global advertising works equally for goods-based and service-based businesses. Whether to use it depends on such industry globalization drivers as common customer needs and the salience of global customers or global channels. Travel-related services can obviously benefit from global advertising, although the communications task may vary by country. A solution is the dual campaign, one for global themes and one for local messages. For many years, British Airways (BA) has used a succession of dramatic global advertising campaigns to establish its position as "The World's Favorite Airline" (backed up by significant improvements in service quality since privatization). At the same time, British Airways provides a smaller budget for local campaigns that focus on schedules, prices, and promotion of special tour packages. Singapore Airlines has achieved significant advertising impact with its temporally and globally consistent theme of the "Singapore Girl," a highly successful way of personalizing and differentiating a commodity service.

While most services are not physically packaged, staff uniforms and the layout and decor of facilities can be considered part of the package. Global consistency can bring significant benefits. Singapore Airlines has maintained the same uniform for its stewardesses for over 35 years. The *sarong kebaya,* designed by Paris couturier Pierre Balmain, makes the Singapore Airlines stewardess globally recognizable, unlike those of most other airlines. And like McDonald's, Citibank designs its new retail branches to look and operate in the same way around the world.

Global Advertising on the Internet

Companies that sell over the Internet (e.g., book and travel sellers) and those that only present or advertise themselves on it (e.g., automakers) face different international challenges, while those who do both (e.g., airlines) face both challenges. The global advertising challenge for e-sellers is to either find e-copy (graphics, words, and click structure) that is equally compelling for all target nationalities and countries or else find simple ways to customize. For example, Amazon.com simply changes the books featured on its home page in each country site. In addition, a side bar on the home pages lists the top 100 books sold on that country's Amazon site—a very simple and automatic method of local customization.

The global advertising challenge for e-advertisers is to find ways to convert their traditional media copy to accessible and relevant e-copy. Some companies offer the ability to download TV commercials or magazine stills, but only for those used in the country of the Web site address. Would globally minded users also want to access advertising from other countries without having to separately enter each country's Web site for the company?

Translation and National Style on the Internet.   Internet advertising obviously needs to be in a language understood by the recipient. But translation may not be enough. Like traditional advertising, Internet ads may need to be adapted for national styles. Pioneering Web users and e-business customers to date have tended to be younger (the generation that grew up with personal computers), and for these "Netizens" an Internet style has overridden national styles. A 1999 study comparing Korean and American Web advertising found differences only in the informativeness of advertising messages, not in creative strategy or technological level.[19] But as e-commerce reaches into older and more traditional segments of populations, national culture and style will become more important. Two issues seem prominent: the degree of busyness and clutter, and the degree of formality in addressing users.

Much has been debated about the pros and cons of global advertising in traditional media. The Internet provides a uniquely global medium that marketers may well wish to use to try out global advertising. They can still run national advertising in traditional media.

GLOBAL SALES PROMOTION

The tactical and short-term nature of sales promotion makes it probably the least likely candidate for globalization. Globalizing promotion probably makes sense on an opportunistic basis only—encouraging other countries to adopt a campaign or device successful elsewhere. Even then, barriers may arise from legal and customary restrictions and differences in how buyers react to promotional incentives. Countries vary particularly in the kinds of promotion they allow. In Europe, Great Britain, Ireland, Spain, Portugal, and Greece permit virtually every type of promotion; while Germany, Norway, and Switzerland forbid or restrict most types.

Trade shows provide an important exception to the desirability of globalizing promotions. In many industries they act as major communication and selling opportunities. More relevant to global strategy, they are often frequented by global customers. So it becomes important for a company to coordinate its trade show efforts around the world. Sharing trade show materials like booths and exhibits can save money.

The extent to which headquarters should be involved in local promotion strategies depends in part on whether local, regional, or global brands are involved.[20] For a global brand the center should define an overall promotional strategy that has guidelines for the relative emphasis on sales promotion versus media activity, for the relative weight of consumer and trade promotions, and for the role of price deals versus value-added offers. This central coordination will then help protect the integrity of the brand across national markets, particularly important in the case of promotion, which can easily destroy a brand franchise if misused. For global brands, the center should also encourage the cross-fertilization of promotional ideas and facilitate information transfer, particularly about successes and failures in promotional activities. For regional brands, the objectives can be more modest. The target should be brand harmonization rather than standardization, and the center's optimum role may be to encourage cross-fertilization of ideas. Lastly, for local brands, the center's task should be that of information transfer only. But effective transfer will help ensure that local managers benefit from the broader collective wisdom of the worldwide business.

Global Promotion and Selling on the Internet

International promotion and selling generally need the most local adaptation as they usually take place in the country, involve dealing with local buyers, and make country-specific offers. Increasingly, multinational companies treat these more tactical or below-the-line marketing activities more locally and treat the more strategic or above-the-line activities, such as positioning and advertising, more globally. The same holds true on the Internet. E-marketers can use the old above- and below-the line distinction literally on the Internet. The upper (higher) pages, or even the upper parts of pages, can be used for more global, strategic presentations and messages; while the lower (deeper) pages and parts can be used for more local, tactical messages. The tree structure of the Web lends itself perfectly to such an approach. For example, British Airways has a common first page for both the United Kingdom and the United States, while later pages offer specific and different promotions for the two countries.

GLOBAL SELLING

Global selling can involve using a uniform selling approach, global account or customer management, or a centralized sales force. Using a *uniform selling approach* can bring the usual multinational benefits of ensuring best practice and high standards of behavior. Doing so depends on the similarity of channel structure and customer buying methods and behavior. Successful selling approaches can often be easily globalized, as IBM did with its highly trained sales personnel and systematic methods, and as Avon Products did with its use of part-timers calling on friends and neighbors. A uniform selling approach can be useful in industries where global customers or global channels are important.

Using Global Account Management Can Provide a Highly Effective Way of Serving Global Customers.   Global account managers can perform similar functions to those of national account managers, and companies need to be concerned with analogous issues, including how to select global accounts; how to manage them; how to develop, manage, and evaluate global account managers; how to organize a structure for global account management; and where to locate global account management in the organization.[21]

Global account managers have to deal with customer demands such as for:[22]

- A single point of contact
- Global coordination of resources for serving customers
- Globally uniform prices
- Globally uniform terms of trade
- Global standardization of products and services
- Global consistency in service quality and performance
- Service in markets in which the supplier has no operations

In response to such demands, suppliers are implementing global customer management programs that include:

- Global account managers and support staff
- Global revenue and profit measures
- Global reporting processes
- Global customer information systems
- Global personnel evaluation
- Global incentives and compensation
- Global customer councils or panels

While national account managers typically control their accounts, the geographic scope of global account management makes such control much more difficult and perhaps politically hazardous. A global account manager can probably be more effective by merely coordinating the selling efforts of national sales forces and acting as the one interface with the customer at its head office. So in almost all cases the global account manager should be located in the home country of the global customer.

One manager may be able to wear two hats—as a national sales executive and as a global account manager. The global account manager position is particularly vulnerable to turf battles and jealousy: National sales managers tend to resent interference with their local customers. If one manager becomes the global account manager, he or she may get little cooperation. But if several national sales managers are assigned global account responsibilities, then they all have to cooperate with each other. Global account management certainly brings the benefit of speaking to a customer with one voice and avoiding having subsidiaries compete with one another for a customer's business. But companies also need to recognize the risks involved in global account management. Customers may use the centralized contact to demand that the lowest national price become the global price (or, more generally, that the most favorable national terms of trade become the global terms). An effective global account manager will have good justification of international differences in prices and terms. In particular, this manager needs to know *all* the prices and terms being offered by his or her company in different countries.

Many multinational companies are adopting global account management or global customer management programs. These include technology companies such as ABB, IBM, Hewlett-Packard, and Xerox; banks such as Bank of America, Citibank, HSBC, and Standard Chartered; most major advertising agencies; and many consumer companies for dealing with their retail customers. The trend in the advertising business toward global account management was perhaps the major factor behind the top 10 international agency networks increasing their share of global advertising in the 1990s. Most dramatic of all, in 1994 IBM's new CEO, Louis Gerstner, initiated the firing of over 40 different agencies around the world and consolidated the company's entire $400 to $500 million account at one top 10 global agency, Ogilvy & Mather Worldwide.

Another way of globalizing selling is to use a *centralized sales force,* probably based at a number of regional head offices, rather than one global head office, because of the extensive travel required. In addition to the logistical issues, companies using global or regional selling need to worry about customer acceptance of foreign sales representatives. Sales specialists with technical expertise are usually quite acceptable, in contrast to foreign regular sales representatives responsible for the ongoing customer relationship. Customers would be much more willing to accept foreigners in the latter role.

MARLBORO'S AVOIDANCE OF TOO MUCH NATIONAL RESEARCH

This potential danger of excessive research is illustrated dramatically by the experience of Marlboro cigarette's world-famous cowboy advertising campaign—probably one of the most widely recognized icons in the history of advertising. A senior executive at Philip Morris, the marketer of Marlboro, has commented that too much national research would have prevented the cowboy campaign from being adopted globally. National market research would probably have identified a boxer as the best symbol in Britain, a bullfighter in Spain, a cyclist in France, and a sumo wrestler in Japan. The power of the common global identity would then have never been achieved.

WHERE TO USE GLOBAL MARKETING

A global marketing program need not be applied to every country. In general, a company can derive greater benefits by applying global marketing to larger countries, because all categories of benefits—cost reduction, improved program effectiveness, enhanced customer preference, and increased competitive leverage—will be larger. On the other hand, larger markets tend to be more demanding of local adaptation than smaller ones. Customers in smaller countries are more used to products and programs not being adapted for them and are typically subject to more cultural influence from larger neighbors. In contrast, customers in larger countries are somewhat spoiled by the importance of their market. Canadian customers are probably more willing to accept foreign products and programs than American customers, Dutch customers more than German ones, Belgians more than the French, and Koreans more than the Japanese. So companies face a trade-off in terms of whether to globalize in larger or in smaller markets. One way to solve this dilemma is to design core global products and programs more for the needs of larger countries than of smaller ones.

CONDUCTING GLOBAL MARKET RESEARCH

Global marketing presents a special difficulty in market research. Good marketing practice requires that most new marketing programs undergo some research to test their likely effectiveness. The potential pitfalls of translation (in its widest sense—linguistic, cultural, institutional, and so on) in international marketing make research doubly important. But global marketing also carries great dangers of doing too much research or doing the wrong kind of research.[23] In particular, testing a global program head-to-head against a best local program may result in the local programs winning many of the contests. But such market research cannot examine the strategic benefits of a unified global approach.

In essence, if there are good strategic reasons for global marketing, market research should be used to discover how to make a global program work better (and to avoid pitfalls in linguistic and cultural translation) rather than to pit it against each possible local program. If such head-to-head tests are conducted, the companywide benefits of global marketing mean that the global program need not achieve parity with the local alternatives in order to justify adoption. So executives might set some achievement benchmark, such as the global program achieving 90 percent as much favorable purchase intention as the local program, in countries accounting for 80 percent of worldwide volume.

Using global marketing also allows managers to compare market research results from different countries. Provided the global marketing programs have a large enough common core, findings in one country can usefully be studied in other countries. Similarly, global market research can be used in experiments to find the best core global programs. Conducting global market research has become more feasible as suppliers of marketing information like A. C. Nielsen and newer vendors themselves globalize. Nielsen now offers a global information service that provides headquarters executives in multinational companies with a cross-country summary of the detailed data supplied to national subsidiaries. Another supplier, International Ratings Services, has begun to offer a subscription service that tracks the performance of specific U. S. television shows overseas. The service translates and standardizes ratings from over 20 countries and is aimed at movie studios and independent producers selling television shows abroad.

COLLECTING GLOBAL MARKETING INFORMATION

Collecting marketing information from most of the countries in which the business participates and might participate is essential for the ability to create global marketing programs. Such information is not the monthly sales and activity tracking data that the national companies collect for operating purposes. Instead this global marketing information should be strategically oriented and needs to be collected periodically only, probably once a year. The country subsidiaries should be asked to provide information on the business and the largest local competitors as well as all global competitors designated by headquarters management. These designated competitors should include all key actual and potential global competitors. All countries should report on these competitors, however small the latter may be locally. Without such a directive, a complete worldwide picture of such global competitors would not be built up. A 5 percent market share in a single country for a local or regional competitor is typically trivial but may mean much more for a global competitor. For example, the global competitor may be in the process of creating a base for further expansion into that or neighboring markets. Similarly, tracking worldwide share changes over time for these global competitors will help identify the direction of their efforts, and possible threats and opportunities. The information reported from each country for the business and its competitors should include:

- Market share
- Products and sizes offered
- Brand names
- New product introductions
- Prices
- Advertising and promotion expenditures
- Advertising positioning and claims
- Product quality
- Customer satisfaction
- Distribution methods and penetration
- Delivered costs
- Estimated profitability

ORGANIZING FOR GLOBAL MARKETING

Global marketing raises some special issues for organization and management. In addition to global account managers, the other key organization element that can help implement global marketing is the use of global product or brand managers. Beginning in the 1980s Unilever, L'Oreal (the French cosmetics company), and Beiersdorf (a major German manufacturer of household products) all added European brand managers responsible for coordinating the strategy of brand groups that cut across countries. Many other companies have since added similar roles. At the same time, national marketing managers need to participate in the process of developing global marketing.[24]

Advertising agencies can play a helpful role in helping companies implement global marketing. Most companies seem to use too many advertising agencies around the world to allow for easy coordination of global advertising. As part of its globalization drive, Black & Decker consolidated its worldwide advertising in 1986. From the previous 20 or more advertising agencies around the world, Black & Decker selected two principal agencies to coordinate worldwide advertising. (Packaging and distribution were also harmonized around the world. B&D has similarly styled multilingual packages available at retail outlets.)[25] Saatchi and Saatchi played a major role in helping British Airways' corporate management convince its country subsidiaries to adopt the Manhattan Landing commercial, often reluctantly. The results seemed worthwhile. Tracking studies showed increases in unaided awareness and recall of British Airways in almost all of the 20 countries using the campaign, especially in the United States.[26] Clearly, only the larger agencies with wide global networks can perform such a function. But potential clients of such agencies need to look a bit closer to see how well the global network is integrated.

In addition to experience with global accounts, factors affecting an agency's global integration capability include the following:

- A network grown internally over time rather than put together from acquisition
- Fully owned subsidiaries rather than affiliates
- Frequent exchange of managers and staff between country subsidiaries

A rule of thumb that can help encourage the adoption of global marketing is to charge subsidiaries extra for products and programs that need to be different from the global standard or that require more than some minimum level of adaptation. When asked to pay a premium, national managers often realize that perhaps they do not need that "essential" local version after all.

A GLOBAL CONSUMER MARKETING SUCCESS STORY

The Kuschelweich/Robijn/Bamseline/Cajoline/Coccolino/Mimosin/Yumos/Snuggle/Fofo/Fafa/Pomi/Baubau/Huggie Brand

Unilever's creation of a new worldwide fabric softener product provides an illuminating example of the flexible and successful use of global marketing.[27] Perhaps the most interesting aspect of this strategy is its use of globally standardized positioning, global advertising, and many other globally standardized marketing elements, but a different brand name in each country. In the early 1970s, Unilever trailed Procter & Gamble in the fabric conditioner category in most countries. In 1970, Sunlicht, Unilever's German household products subsidiary, introduced a new product that was targeted at the economy end of the fabric softener market. To offset the negative quality implications of its claims of economy, Sunlicht devised two elements to connote softness—the key benefit desired by users. These two elements were the name "Kuschelweich," which means enfolded in softness in German, and a picture of a teddy bear on the bottle. The bear was just a symbol of softness and had no active role in the advertising. Sunlicht's success with the new product encouraged Unilever in France to introduce a similar product. But the French company changed the name to Cajoline, which has connotations of softness in French, and adapted the advertising by bringing the teddy bear on the bottle to life in a television commercial, so that it became a more active symbol of quality and softness. Success in France then led to adoption by many other countries. In each case the local Unilever subsidiary kept the positioning of economy and softness, changed the brand name to something indicating softness in the local language, but used virtually the same advertising with little change except for redubbing the voiceover. In Taiwan and Korea a scientific-style magnified closeup of fabric strands was added in the commercials to appeal to the desire of customers in those countries for scientific proof. The bottle was kept virtually identical in all countries, except for a few in which the base color was changed to provide more contrast with local competition.

By 1990 Unilever marketed the teddy bear brand as Kuschelweich in Germany, Robijn in Belgium and the Netherlands, Bamseline in Denmark, Cajoline in France, Coccolino in Italy, Mimosin in Spain, Yumos in Turkey, Snuggle in the United States, Fofo in Brazil, Fafa in Japan, Pomi in South Korea, Baubau in Taiwan, and Huggie in Australia. But in every country, the same teddy bear provided the brand identity and positioning. Only in the United Kingdom where there was already a strong Unilever brand, Comfort, was the new product not launched. Unilever considers the product a great success. Its worldwide introduction has boosted Unilever's share of the category to the number one rank in many countries and second in many others.

Lintas:Worldwide, one of the major advertising agencies used worldwide by Unilever, played a key role in developing and adapting this global marketing effort. Lintas helped develop the positioning and advertising strategy as well as creating the actual advertising. Lintas set up a European account team coordinated through its Paris office and its international head office in London. Eventually creative work was also performed in New York, Tokyo, and Sydney. Unilever's use of Lintas for the product in almost all countries (except in South Korea, where a local agency accepted guidance from Lintas) made it much more possible to maintain and improve on the common marketing program. Lintas's coordination also saved a great deal of money in advertising production costs. Most of the television commercials in different countries used a large amount of common footage—helped greatly by the absence of human characters in the advertising.

This story has several lessons:

- Global companies need to seize on a big marketing idea—in this case, using a teddy bear to symbolize softness and to build brand identity in fabric care—and promote its widespread adoption.
- Such global marketing can be highly flexible. Only the marketing elements that can benefit from standardization should be standardized, and local adaptations to a core strategy can, and should, be allowed.
- Industry globalization drivers help to identify which elements should be standardized and which not. In particular, the fact that consumers do not buy fabric

softener when away from home negated any need for a common name. So the company standardized the meaning of the brand name rather than the name itself.

- A highly successful program was developed by a number of countries building on each other's efforts.
- Encouragement from head office, the involvement of some lead countries, and the participation of a global advertising agency all contributed to the rapid and successful worldwide adoption of the program.

A GLOBAL BUSINESS-TO-BUSINESS MARKETING SUCCESS STORY

Hewlett-Packard's Use of Global Account Management

Hewlett-Packard's use of global account management illustrates successful use of global marketing in the business-to-business environment.[28]

GLOBALIZATION DRIVERS AFFECTING THE COMPUTER SYSTEMS INDUSTRY

In the late 1980s and early 1990s, marketing within the computer systems industry was evolving toward a more customer-focused approach. First, in a strengthening of the *global customers* driver, customers' demands for more consistent worldwide service and support as well as increased standardization drove hardware producers into complex and occasionally secret alliances.

Second, *fast-changing technology* caused the old mode of centralized mainframes with massive headquarters support teams to rapidly evolve to the new mode of decentralized, networked computer systems linking divisions around the world. With this evolution, vendors are required to be more than just suppliers. Multinational customers demand that vendors be strategic partners who demonstrate an understanding of specific international business needs and deploy these solutions on a global basis without compromising customer satisfaction.

Third, another aspect of fast-changing technology and also reflecting the globalization driver of *high product development costs,* time to market and continuous innovation played a critical role in the computer systems industry. In 1993, more than half of HP's revenues stemmed from products less than two years old. Rapid technological changes, such as improvements in computing power combined with a continuous decline in the cost of memory, force firms to reevaluate their relationships with customers and suppliers as well as their practices regarding the use of strategic alliances.

Fourth, alternative channels of distribution—such as dealers, two-tier suppliers, systems integrators, or resellers—were prevalent throughout the computer systems industry and continue to grow. In 1980, approximately 80 percent of HP's customers purchased their computer equipment directly from HP. Today, dealer outlets represent all but a few percentage points of desktop sales. HP needed to identify a strategy to capture these alternative channels, many of them *global channels* or *regional channels,* and to maximize the opportunities they present.

Fifth, HP faced difficulties in building a *global organization.* It needed to develop a global program that promoted synergy and coordination across all three major field operations: the Americas, Asia Pacific, and Europe. Within HP's national sales program coordination barriers existed across geographic regions, posing a major constraint in providing consistent service and developing new business. HP's performance measurement system was based on product quotas per region, and no incentives existed for managers to pursue or coordinate business outside their regions (i.e., on a global basis). In one instance, this lack of coordination led to HP's Australian subsidiary inadvertently establishing a new worldwide low price for a major customer. The Australian account manager had given a special discount without realizing that this would trigger a clause in HP's worldwide contract with the account.

HP's ORGANIZATIONAL RESPONSE

In 1991, HP implemented a global account management pilot program for its largest division, the Computer Systems Organization (CSO). The program, initiated for six accounts, was extremely well received by customers, has since grown to over 30 accounts, and is currently being diffused across other product divisions within HP. The company's focus was to provide direct customer support for key global accounts and, in doing so, has changed all four aspects of its organization: *structure, management processes, people,* and *culture.* The main components of HP's global account management program involve coordination along global lines—balancing geographic, product, and customer strategies; refining the worldwide sales organization structure to match multinational customer requirements; empowering and rewarding global account managers; capturing alternative channels and opportunities; measuring and tracking all performance variables on a global basis; restructuring the headquarters account program; formalizing an account assigned executive program; and selecting the right global accounts.[29]

COORDINATING ON GLOBAL LINES: BALANCING GEOGRAPHIC, PRODUCT, AND CUSTOMER FOCUS

To address the demand for more consistent worldwide service and support, the program established a global distribution channel by introducing the global account manager (GAM). GAMs are located near the customer headquarters, are responsible for and directly manage HP's relationship with the global account, and serve as the focal channel of distribution for the global account. GAMs' responsibilities involve (1) worldwide customer sales, support, and satisfaction; (2) ensuring that HP is perceived as one company at all customer locations; (3) working with HP's senior management to ensure HP is organized and resourced to service opportunities identified in the global account; and (4) establishing a close working rapport with the senior corporate executives assigned to support the account.

HP also defined a new organizational structure for the program based on a dual reporting system. GAMs report to the country/region and industry manager and to a field operations global accounts sales manager who is responsible for all global accounts business within a particular field operation. The global accounts sales manager for the field operation reports to the field operations manager and to the head of the global accounts program. The global account headquarters staff report directly to the GAM, while district sales managers and sales representatives dual report to the GAM and the local area sales manager. The dual reporting structure is critical to the overall program success, reinforces geographic responsibilities for the sales force, and empowers the GAM to make decisions independent of geography and to manage his or her sales team to satisfy customer needs.

GAMs are evaluated on the worldwide performance of the global account, while country managers are evaluated on the worldwide performance of global accounts headquartered in their country and overall country performance. This approach provides incentives to country managers to coordinate and cooperate with the GAMs.

EMPOWERING GLOBAL ACCOUNT MANAGERS

To empower managers and ensure the appropriate vision, GAMs are responsible for the growth and health of the entire account including all sales and expense metrics. GAMs set revenue and cost targets that are reviewed at annual quota setting meetings. Once the targets are agreed upon, individual account targets are established such that the collective sum of these targets supports the total program objectives. This flexibility allows success in one global account to directly support another and is essential to program effectiveness.

MEASURING PERFORMANCE

An essential element of HP's program involves measuring performance on a global account basis rather than a product or geographic basis. The GAM program defines a worldwide measurement system aimed at understanding the full costs associated with implementing the global account program for any major account and providing a tracking mechanism for global account performance. Two metrics form the basis for the measurement system: (1) the selling cost envelope (SCE) and (2) the account specific field selling cost model (FSC). The SCE measures all selling costs associated with obtaining a list order. The FSC involves identifying all costs associated with worldwide implementation of the global account sales team and supporting programs. GAMs are responsible for identifying the FSC and the SCE.

The FSC and SCE estimations enable HP to determine if an account merits the use of a full-time or half-time GAM. In addition, GAMs are responsible for identifying the level of support needed for an account, such as the appropriate sales staff level including whether the account affords a full-time or half-time headquarters account manager (HAM). The intent is to institute a program that allows global account sales quotas and expense targets to be compiled by country, and held separately within that country, so that quotas or expenses are less likely to move in or out of the global accounts channel to other channels. The program also establishes clear cost and revenue objectives for the global accounts channel. The metric system defined as part of the GAM program assists HP in measuring performance by account rather than by product or region.

SETTING QUOTAS

GAMs are also responsible for setting an overall sales objective for the upcoming year through detailed analyses of account quota by country and, in turn, country quota by product line. In order to ensure that the process provides a profitable investment for HP, GAMs are required to meet a specific objective that tracks worldwide FSCs and discount expenses. In addition, global account quotas and the nonglobal account quotas are combined to form the country and industry quotas. Country and industry managers maintain the global quotas and funding separate from their other accounts.

RESTRUCTURING HEADQUARTERS ACTIVITIES

The global program also redefined HP's headquarters account management program. The mission of this latter, preexisting program and its headquarters account managers (HAMs) is to "champion the critical needs and significant opportunities of the global account within HP headquarters and to establish HP as a strategic vendor of Cooperative Computing Systems through long-term sales growth and customer satisfaction."[30] HAMs dual report to the GAM and the CSO product division headquarters and assume global responsibility and ownership. HAMs are also responsible for global account development, issue resolution and customer satisfaction, strategic deal ownership and management, and sales and marketing goal congruence. The HAMs provide a focused channel for product divisions, a strategic partner for account assigned executives, and are advocates for the customer at HP headquarters as well as the main representatives for the global account manager.

To support the program, HP enlisted the aid of high-level executives, including the CEO, as account assigned executives (AAEs). The purpose of the AAE program is to define and encourage the active involvement of key HP executives in current or target major accounts that are considered crucial to HP's long-term success. Customers have come to appreciate the establishment of a focal point at HP headquarters (the HAM) to represent their interests, as well as the connection to upper management through the AAE program.

EFFECTS ON STRATEGY

HP's global account management program resulted in more use of each global strategy lever. First, HP moved to more *globally uniform marketing,* particularly for pricing and other terms of sale. Second, the program involved a more consistent offering such that clients received *globally standardized products and services.* Third, selecting the right global accounts involved better use of *global market (and industry) participation.* Global accounts are selected based on specific industries where HP has the potential to be the most successful over the long term. Critical dimensions of account selection involve the analysis of several parameters including long-range projections of industry segment performance, evolving business conditions and needs within those segments, and HP's ability to deliver solutions for those business problems. Global accounts must also have a serious open systems client/server commitment to HP, demands consistent with worldwide sales and support programs, annual HP computer sales plus service revenue greater than $10 million, significant computer sales across two or three field operations, and be in a globally strategic industry segment. In addition, the account should provide HP with an opportunity to develop a defensible position as a strategic supplier.

Fourth, the program integrates a product focus with a customer focus and facilitates consistent sales and support across regions and countries, in effect changing HP's *location of value-adding activities.* In addition, the restructuring of the worldwide sales force eliminates coordination barriers that existed across geographic regions. By focusing on the global channel, the program assists HP in capturing all order activity including indirect sales (through value-added resellers). HP positions the global channel to operate more efficiently than other channels due to the benefits of global sales leverage and economies of scale.

Fifth, the GAM program differentiates HP from its main competitors—IBM, Sun, and Digital—improving its *global competitive position*. Resultant competitive benefits include providing one face to the customer, sharing of best practices with the customer as well as across accounts, improving alternative channels development, empowering the GAMs and HAMs to pursue business development opportunities that would otherwise have been missed, encouraging coordination and value-added activity across geographies, and establishing a global position in the marketplace.

IMPROVING FINANCIAL PERFORMANCE

The program and resultant changes in strategy have had significant performance effects. In 1993 and 1994, the global account program was HP's fastest growing channel. The CSO's net revenue growth exceeded 20 percent over the first phase of the program. The sales cost envelope significantly decreased from a range of 47 to 50 percent to a range of 38 to 41 percent. Overall, senior management and HP's customers believe the program is extremely effective, and HP is challenged with determining how large the program should grow.

EVOLUTION OF HP's GAM PROGRAM

HP's global account management program began with 26 accounts in 1993 and was so popular that by 1996 it had expanded to 250 accounts. A change of management led in 1997 to refocusing on a smaller group of 95 most important accounts. A new CEO, Carly Fiorina, took the program one step further in 1999, taking out the most important 100 or so accounts and managing each as a separate business, each with its own P&L statement. These accounts enjoyed dramatic revenue and profit growth.

GUIDELINES FOR CREATING GLOBAL MARKETING

In many ways marketing is the most difficult strategic element to globalize. Differences between countries are often greatest in the customer attitudes and behavior that marketers try to influence. Furthermore, many of the benefits of global marketing can be subtler than for the other elements of global strategy. At the same time, using global marketing can integrate the worldwide efforts of an organization in a more visible and powerful way than any other. The following key guidelines should be considered:

- Marketing can be, and sometimes should be, uniform in its content as well as its process.
- Each element of the marketing mix has its own unique opportunities and limitations in global uniformity.
- Managers should seek to push the limits of their imagination in devising global marketing programs. They should not be constrained by conventional wisdom about national preferences and prejudices.
- Testing global marketing programs against national alternatives requires care to avoid both underestimating and overestimating nationalistic reactions.
- National marketing managers need to remember that they have been trained to look for local differences. Creating successful global marketing requires a reorientation to look for similarities.

Discussion and Research Questions

1. What is the difference between a multilocal and a global approach to marketing?
2. Select a company or business and describe which aspects of its marketing mix are local, and which global.
3. How should a company go about developing a global segmentation strategy?
4. Which elements of the marketing mix are the easiest to make global, and which are the hardest?
5. When should a company use a global brand name and when should it use different local names?
6. Identify a global advertising campaign not described in this chapter. What makes this campaign effective, and why?
7. What are the benefits and drawbacks of global account management?
8. What is different about global marketing for service businesses?
9. How can global marketers make effective use of the Internet and the Web?

Notes

1. Some researchers have focused on a standardized marketing process as the key attribute of global marketing. See discussion by Pradeep A. Rau and John F. Preble, "Standardization of Marketing Strategy by Multinationals," *International Marketing Review,* Autumn 1987, pp. 18–28.
2. George S. Yip, "Patterns and Determinants of Global Marketing," *Journal of Marketing Management,* Vol. 13, 1997, pp. 153–64.
3. Keegan (1989) identified five combinations of product and promotion adaptation— straight extension, communication adaptation, product adaptation, dual adaptation, and product invention—but there are many more combinations possible when each element of the marketing mix is considered. See Warren J. Keegan, *Multinational Marketing Management,* 4th ed. (Upper Saddle River, N.J.: Prentice Hall, 1989), pp. 378–81.
4. See Ralph Z. Sorenson and Ulrich E. Wiechmann, "How Multinationals View Marketing Standardization," *Harvard Business Review,* May–June 1975, pp. 38–45; and Pradeep A. Rau and John F. Preble, "Standardization of Marketing Strategy by Multinationals," *International Marketing Review,* Autumn 1987, pp. 18–28.
5. For further discussion of the barriers to global marketing, see Robert D. Buzzell, "Can You Standardize Multinational Marketing?" *Harvard Business Review,* November– December 1968, pp. 102–13; Susan P. Douglas

and Yoram Wind, "The Myth of Globalization," *Columbia Journal of World Business,* Vol. 22, No. 4, Winter 1987, pp. 19–29; and Kamran Kashani, "Beware the Pitfalls of Global Marketing," *Harvard Business Review,* September–October 1989, pp. 91–8. See also Subhash C. Jain, "Standardization of International Marketing Strategy: Some Research Hypotheses," *Journal of Marketing,* Vol. 53, January 1989, pp. 70–9, for a review of some of the conceptual research issues in global marketing, and Susan P. Douglas and C. Samuel Craig, "Evolution of Global Marketing Strategy: Scale, Scope and Synergy," *Columbia Journal of World Business,* Fall 1989, pp. 47–57, for a review of the evolution of global marketing strategy.
6. David B. Montgomery and George S. Yip, "The Challenge of Global Customer Management," *Marketing Management,* Vol. 9, No. 4, Winter 2000, pp. 22–9.
7. Philip Kotler, *Marketing Management,* 5th ed. (Upper Saddle River, NJ: Prentice-Hall, 1984), p. 272.
8. Various programs are being developed, including those from Everymail.com, Slangsoft.com, and Worldpoint.com.
9. There is an extensive literature on country-of-origin effects. See, for example, Johny K. Johansson, "Determinants and Effects of the Use of 'Made in' Labels," *International Marketing Review,* Vol. 6, No. 1, 1989, pp. 47–58.

10. See Naomi Klein, *No Logo* (London: Flamingo, 2001).

11. D. A. Aaker and Joachimsthaler, "The Lure of Global Branding," *Harvard Business Review,* November–December 1999, pp. 137–44.

12. John A. Quelch, "Global Brands: Taking Stock," *Business Strategy Review,* Vol. 10, No. 1, 1999, pp. 1–14.

13. In mid-1981, Nissan announced it would gradually phase out the Datsun brand in favor of the Nissan name worldwide. In the United States, the first model to bear the transition name (Datsun by Nissan) was the 1981 Maxima 810 (also the first export model to have a partly nonnumeric name). In 1982, the Nissan Stanza was introduced, and by 1985 all U.S. models and all U.S. dealers bore the Nissan name exclusively.

14. Landor Associates, an image consulting concern based in San Francisco, conducted this study. Landor questioned 5,000 consumers in the United States, 3,000 in eight European countries, and 1,000 in Japan about 800 trademarks. See "Coke's Kudos," *The Economist,* September 15, 1990, p. 88; and "More Brand Names Gain Recognition Around the World," *Wall Street Journal,* September 13, 1990. See also Landor Associates, "The World's Most Powerful Brands" (San Francisco, 1990).

15. Valuations by Interbrand, London. But their methodology probably greatly overstates the value of many brands, especially of technology companies, such as Microsoft.

16. Michael Czinkota and Ilkka Ronkainen, *International Marketing,* 2nd ed. (Chicago: Dryden Press, 1990), p. 270.

17. Michael E. Porter, *Competitive Strategy: Techniques for Analyzing Industries and Competitors* (New York: The Free Press, 1980).

18. Gray market activity refers to the legal importation of genuine goods into a country by intermediaries other than the authorized distributors. See S. Tamer and J. Sikora, "How Multinationals Can Cope with Gray Market Imports," Working Paper No. 87–109 (Cambridge, MA: Marketing Science Institute, 1987).

19. Kyu-Won, Chang-Hoan Cho, and John D. Leckenby, "A Comparative Analysis of Korean and U.S. Web Advertising," paper presented to 1999 Annual Conference American Academy of Advertising, Albuquerque, New Mexico (uts.cc.utexas.edu/~kwoh/3A/99AAA.html)

20. This paragraph is based on Kamran Kashani and John A. Quelch, "Can Sales Promotion Go Global?" *Business Horizons,* Vol. 33, No. 3, May–June 1990, pp. 37–43.

21. This list is adapted from Kotler's (*Marketing Management,* p. 683) discussion of national account management.

22. Montgomery and Yip, *The Challenge of Global Customer Management.*

23. For a discussion of the problems in translating market survey instruments, and a guide to conducting international market research, see Susan P. Douglas and C. Samuel Craig, *International Marketing Research* (Upper Saddle River, NJ: Prentice-Hall, 1983), pp. 186–90.

24. Solberg 2000, "Standardisation or Adaptation of the International Marketing Mix: The Role of the Local Subsidiary/Representative," *Journal of International Marketing,* Vol. 8, No. 1, pp. 78–98.

25. Laurence J. Farley, "Going Global: Choices and Challenges," *Journal of Business Strategy,* Vol. 1, Winter 1986, pp. 67–70.

26. See John A. Quelch. "British Airways: Teaching Note," No. 5-587-016 (Boston: Harvard Business School, 1987).

27. I thank Michael Bowman of Lintas: Worldwide for making the details of the Unilever teddy bear brand history available to me.

28. This example on Hewlett-Packard is drawn from George S. Yip and Tammy L. Madsen, "Global Account Management: The New Frontier in Relationship Marketing," *International Marketing Review,* Vol. 13, No. 3, pp. 24–42, special issue on Global Marketing Implementation, 1996.

29. Greg Mirhan, "Advantage: Hewlett-Packard," *Global Executive,* March/April 1993, pp. 10–13.

30. Ibid.

MAKING GLOBAL COMPETITIVE MOVES

~~~

Making globally integrated competitive moves constitutes the fifth and last set of global strategy levers that a company can use to globalize strategy. In many ways it is the most difficult of the five levers to use, because its consequences are less directly visible than globally standardized products or globally uniform advertising. At the same time, not making globally integrated competitive moves can undermine the competitive advantages built up in individual countries and weaken a business's worldwide position, as happened to Kodak.

KEY FEATURES OF GLOBAL COMPETITIVE MOVES

The Kodak–Fuji story illustrates how the last (and most often forgotten) global strategy lever, globally integrated competitive moves, can be highly effective. A global strategy approach to competitive moves means integrating competitive moves across countries rather than making moves one country at a time. Integrated competitive moves also affect all of the other global strategy levers of global market participation, global products, global activity location, and global marketing, typically needing to be used in conjunction with one or more of the other global strategy levers.

Global competitive moves have several aspects:

- Cross-subsidization of countries within the same business
- Use of counterparries
- Globally coordinated sequence of moves
- Targeting of actual and potential global competitors
- Developing plans for each major country-competitor combination
- Preemptive use of global strategy

These types of moves can be described as follows:

Type of Move	Definition
Cross-country subsidization	Using profits from one country in which a business participates to subsidize competitive actions in another country
Counterparry	Defending against a competitive attack in one country by countering in another country
Globally coordinated sequence of moves	Simultaneous or planned sequence in which competitive moves are made in different countries in the same business
Targeting of global competitors	Identifying actual and potential global competitors and selecting an overall posture—attack, avoidance, cooperation, or acquisition—for each
Developing country-competitor plans	Analyzing strengths and weaknesses, opportunities and threats for each global competitor in each major country, and developing a competitive plan of action for each country-competitor combination
Preemptive use of global strategy	Being the first competitor to make use of a particular element of global strategy—global market participation, global products, global activity location, and global marketing

KODAK'S MISTAKES AND RECOVERY
IN JAPAN

In the 1980s, Eastman Kodak lost share in the U.S. and European markets for photographic film that it had long dominated.[1] These losses resulted from a fierce global onslaught by a newly internationalized competitor, Japan's Fuji Photo Film. Kodak's response, which included drastic attempts to cut costs and prices, cost it dearly in margins and profitability. Kodak had seemed impregnable with a strong basis for competitive advantage—its high-quality, worldwide name recognition, and distribution system—and had also globalized this strategy successfully. Kodak had widespread global market participation, a globally standardized product line, an efficient and concentrated activity chain, and memorable global marketing, including its highly distinctive and recognizable global packaging. But Kodak's global strategy had a number of potentially serious flaws. First, although its global market participation was widespread, it had neglected a globally strategic country, Japan, which was the home of a strong potential global competitor and the market for some of the world's most demanding customers. In this omission, *Kodak was making the same mistake that many other Western companies had done—avoiding Japan as unattractive on a stand-alone basis, while not seeing its global strategic importance.* So Kodak made little investment in Japan and relied on a Japanese trading company to act as its local distributor. As part of this neglect, Kodak did not adapt its core strategy sufficiently to meet Japanese needs—such as printing Japanese on its packaging (not until 1984) or offering the right kind of products. This ignoring of the Japanese market allowed Fuji to grow little challenged until it was powerful enough to take on Kodak outside Japan.

By the early 1980s, Fuji held 70 percent of a very large Japanese market, while Kodak held only a few percentage points. Then Kodak made a second mistake, in terms of the globally integrated competitive moves lever. Kodak defended against Fuji's challenge in the same countries in which it was attacked. With its larger sales base, any price cuts and special promotions that Kodak made wound up hurting itself more than Fuji. Eventually, around 1984,

Kodak realized that it needed to use the fifth global strategy lever—the counterparry—as part of globally integrated competitive moves in conjunction with the first global strategy lever—increasing market participation in Japan. Kodak decided to counterattack its rival's home market by investing an estimated $500 million to revamp its distribution system (taking control by setting up a joint venture with its distributor), taking equity stakes in its suppliers, and investing heavily in promotion. This counterstrategy worked, squeezing Fuji's domestic margins, forcing it to recall some of its best executives from abroad, and generally weakening its global competitive capabilities. By 1990, Kodak had multiplied its share of the Japanese amateur photographer market to 15 percent *and* had started to turn back a severe global challenge.

FUJI'S ATTACK IN THE UNITED STATES

While Kodak was distracted in Japan, Fuji steadily built up its market share in Kodak's U.S. home market, reaching the 20-percent level by the late 1990s, and a global share of nearly 40 percent.[2] Fuji's main goal since it first entered the American market was to increase market share by getting its film onto as many American retail shelves as possible. Its strategy encompassed many factors. Fuji kept its wholesale prices 15 percent lower than those of Kodak, which allowed for higher retail margins. In addition, the company invested heavily in local manufacturing and employees, spending over $1 billion on factories and hiring 8,000 American employees. Furthermore, the company managed to capitalize on marketing mistakes made by Kodak. Many analysts criticized Kodak for taking American loyalty for granted. Fuji capitalized as a result. For example, because Kodak refused to pay $1 million to be the official film of the 1984 Olympics, Fuji was able to embrace the sponsorship. It managed to spend an additional $7 million to promote its brand, particularly by using the Fuji blimp to fly over events. Fuji claimed that its efforts resulted in 70,000 new stores selling its film.

CROSS-SUBSIDIZATION OF COUNTRIES

Being willing and able to subsidize across countries within the same business is perhaps the key requirement of a global strategy. As described in the previous four chapters, the overall use of global strategy levers such as global products and global marketing can provide a worldwide platform of competitive advantage. But this advantage cannot be fully exploited unless global resources can be selectively focused on points of competitive pressure or opportunity. In other words, the worldwide business needs to practice cross-country subsidization. This cross-subsidization should not apply to the same countries all of the time but to different countries as needed.[3] Global managers should view portfolio roles as long-term postures that may be modified to meet short-term competitive pressures and opportunities. A country designated for a maintenance role may need temporary extra spending, subsidized by the rest of the world, to fend off a competitive thrust.

COUNTERPARRY

The counterparry represents a special case of cross-subsidization in which an attack by a competitor in one country is countered by a response in another.[4] Such a counterparry has the intention of retaliating where the competitor can be hurt most. In practice, the effectiveness of the counterparry depends both on cooperation among countries in the business using it and on the competitor receiving and understanding the signal.[5] The counterparry is most easily understood when two home countries are involved—a business attacked in its home country retaliates in the home country of the attacker. So Kodak's response in Japan provided a classic example of a counterparry involving two home countries. To make a counterparry effective, a business typically needs to have a large enough presence in key countries, particularly the home countries of global competitors, to provide a base for counterattack.

GLOBALLY COORDINATED SEQUENCE OF MOVES

Globally integrated competitive strategy also requires that competitive moves such as price changes and the introduction of new products or programs be coordinated across countries in their timing. That does not necessarily mean that they take place at the same time, only that there be a planned sequence to the moves. Why does this matter? First, competitive moves use resources and also usually spur competitor responses that may require even more resources in counterresponse. So the timing of competitive moves in each country needs to be planned to make best use of available resources.

A business with a global strategy would usually find it difficult to sustain a price war in the United States, Germany, and Japan simultaneously, especially if the contest is with different competitors in each country. Second, *a major benefit of global strategy is being able to apply experience from one country to another.*[6] *The experience gained and transferred is most useful when the right countries make the first moves.* For example, entering markets in the right sequence can enhance the competitive advantages that build up with experience. Making a move on a tough market before the business is ready for it can damage long-term global prospects and not just performance in the specific market entered. Japanese companies were particularly successful in sequencing perhaps this very important type of competitive move—market entry.

TARGETING OF GLOBAL COMPETITORS

Actual and potential global competitors need to be identified and a worldwide competitive strategy developed for each one. A global competitor has significant market share on two or more continents and uses some elements of global strategy. So a potential global competitor for a business can be either a multinational company already competing in some of the same markets as the business that does not now use a global strategy but may do so; or a multinational that already uses a global strategy but is not yet competing in the same markets as the business. *Targeting one competitor in many countries is likely to bring greater long-term gains than targeting several competitors in a few countries each, because opposition should be weaker in the former case.* But a multilocal approach to competitive strategy typically results in the latter pattern, because each local management selects its most troublesome local competitor. Similarly, the most dangerous global competitors may not receive the highest priority unless a global view is taken of them. For example, a competitor with a strong number two position in many markets may be globally more dangerous than other competitors with leading positions in a few markets only.

The strengths and weaknesses of each targeted competitor need to be analyzed. In addition, their current and potential use of global strategy needs to be evaluated. An overall posture needs to be decided on for each competitor. Key choices include the following:

- Attack
- Avoid direct competition
- Cooperate
- Acquire

In *attacking a global competitor,* the business must develop a global plan rather than leave local management to develop separate plans. At the same time, local management must be involved in the formulation of the plans. Key decisions include which product lines and customers of the competitor to target, and the selection and timing of countries for offensive moves. While a simultaneous attack on many fronts has more chance of overwhelming a competitor, it also makes it more likely that the competitor will recognize the severity of the threat and retaliate correspondingly. Instead, a sequential, but coordinated, plan of attack may lull the competitor into a pattern of country-by-country surrenders, none crucial in itself, but accumulating to an irreversible loss of position.

Avoiding direct competition with a global competitor can require as much planning and forethought as attack. Retreating into multilocal protected niches offers the simplest way to avoid confrontation with global competitors. But such a strategy depends on the long-term sustainability of the conditions, external or internal to the business, that allow protection from global competition. Furthermore, under this approach, headquarters management can do little to help the local businesses as they develop their own niches. A globally coordinated approach to avoiding competition may hold better hope of sustainability. To take such an approach requires predicting the likely expansion paths of global competitors in terms of products, customers, and geographic markets. It also requires prediction of how competitors will develop their sources of competitive advantage, such as in proprietary technology. Then the business needs to decide on which of these competitor expansion paths it can afford to get out of the way, and on which of these paths it has to dig in. For example, the business may be able to identify product lines, customers, and geographic markets that are less crucial than others, and be prepared to give ground there in order to better defend the remaining higher priority products, customers, and markets. Unfortunately, the track record of selective retreat has not been stellar in the face of determined global competitors. Both American and British motorcycle manufacturers retreated to larger engine models in the face of Japanese competition, only to find each engine size not defensible after all.

Cooperating with competitors via international joint ventures and alliances became highly popular in the 1980s and 1990s. Several authors have provided very thorough frameworks for joint venture strategies, so none will be offered here.[7] The global strategies of Northwest Airlines (U.S.-based) and KLM (Netherlands-based) depend greatly on their alliance, widely regarded as the most successful in the airline industry. These two mid-sized competitors survive against global giants by operating a tighter alliance than can be done by their larger rivals. Similarly, Columbia Business School and London Business School, both top ten global players but lacking the size and resources of their largest rivals, have formed an alliance to offer a combined dual executive M.B.A. degree.

A few aspects of joint ventures that are crucial in globally integrated strategy need to be highlighted here. All joint ventures need to achieve some match between what each partner has to offer and what each partner will give up. In the specific context of global strategy, as opposed to corporate and competitive strategy in general, a key decision is the choice of geographic markets that will be made part of the joint venture. A joint venture can provide both defensive capabilities and offensive opportunities in the markets covered. But, at the same time, a joint venture can limit growth potential and, as argued in Chapter 3, reduces the degree to which the business is able to operate a truly integrated global strategy.

A worldwide business that operates as a self-contained globally integrated system rather than relying on joint venture partners will find it much easier to achieve the coordination and agreement needed to make a sequence of globally integrated competitive moves. In contrast, an open system that has outside organizations as partners will be much more difficult to manage for global strategy, particularly for this last lever. Making globally integrated competitive moves typically requires self-sacrifice and cross-subsidization by geographic entities. That is difficult enough to achieve among fully owned subsidiaries. With external partners, it becomes nearly impossible. Lastly, there is the argument that joint ventures serve as a crutch that discourages companies from developing their own capabilities.[8]

Acquiring competitors is the most effective means of eliminating competition. In the global context, acquisition can bring the added benefit of filling out geographic coverage. So in selecting acquisition candidates, managers should apply a global strategic perspective of seeking those companies that can strengthen the business's position in key countries, as well as the other usual acquisition criteria. Other things being equal, acquirers should be willing to pay a higher premium for acquisitions that improve their geographic balance, improve their position in key countries, or strengthen other aspects of their global strategy.

DEVELOPING COUNTRY-COMPETITOR PLANS

The targets for individual global competitors can be further developed into plans for individual country-competitor combinations. To make these plans, it is first necessary to understand the strategic position of each global competitor in each country. To do so requires conducting the usual type of analysis of strengths, weaknesses, opportunities,

ENLISTING GOVERNMENT HELP IN GLOBAL COMPETITIVE MOVES

Getting the help of the home government can often be essential in global competitive moves. Airbus has been able to grow to equal Boeing in size only because of the massive support from several European governments. Airbus justifies this support by claiming that Boeing's commercial operations benefit from U.S. government support of its military programs.

Toys R Us was able to break into the Japanese market only because it enlisted U.S. lobbying pressure to get the Japanese government to change the rule that allowed local stores in Japan to veto the opening of new stores in their neighborhood.

But even government support does not always work. In 1997, the World Trade Organization rejected claims by the United States and Kodak that the company had been shut out of the Japanese market through a combination of government and private blocking actions.[9] The WTO ruled in favor of Japan, insisting on the need for ironclad proof linking government policies to Kodak's problems. Although documents showed that the government tailored its policies to block Kodak, the WTO absolved the Japanese of all wrongdoing.

and threats. Exhibit 7-1 provides an illustrative example of the summary output of such an analysis.

Following this analysis of country-competitor strategic positions, plans can then be developed for each country-competitor combination. In particular a target needs to be set for each combination. These overall targets can include several possibilities, for example,

- Attack
- Defend
- Avoid direct competition
- Stay out
- Preempt
- Cooperate
- Acquire

Exhibit 7-2 provides an illustrative example of a set of targets for one business. Presenting all country-competitor combinations together helps make it clear whether or not the business is being too ambitious. Exhibit 7-2 shows that the business has targeted one competitor, Westminster PLC, for all-out attack throughout the globe. For another competitor, Tokugawa K.K., the strategy is to hold defensively in all parts of the globe. Lastly, there is a selective strategy for Copeland, Inc., and Schumann AG that varies by region.

PREEMPTIVE USE OF GLOBAL STRATEGY

Great advantages accrue for the first company in an industry that uses a global strategy. For global market participation, the first company to build a network of strong positions in all of the globally strategic countries gains a preemptive advantage, as

EXHIBIT 7-1 Strategies for Country-Competitor Combinations: Illustrative Example

Competitor	Region			
	N. America	*S. America*	*Europe*	*Far East*
Copeland, Inc.	Defend	Opportunistic attack	Avoid direct competition	All-out attack
Westminster PLC	All-out attack	All-out attack	All-out attack	All-out attack
Schumann AG	Opportunistic attack	Defend	Avoid direct competition	Preempt entry
Tokugawa K.K.	Defend	Defend	Defend	Defend

EXHIBIT 7-2 Situation Analysis for Country-Competitor Combinations: Illustrative Example

Competitor	Region			
	N. America	*S. America*	*Europe*	*Far East*
Copeland, Inc.	Market leader	Weak products and distribution, slipping share	Increasing share, strong product line	Recent entrant, trying to build position
Westminster PLC	Market follower	Overpriced products	Market leader in some countries, but slipping share	Share is holding steady but not reinvesting much
Schumann AG	Market follower, some weak product lines	Market leader, building position further	Market leader in some countries, gaining share in others	Not yet present
Tokugawa K.K.	Small share but growing fast	Strong number two in market	Strong number two in most countries, share growing fast	Market leader with strong product lines and customer relationships

well as boosting scale advantage. For global products, the first company to introduce a globally standardized product can reap the advantage of setting industry standards and customer expectations and preferences. For activity location, the first company to build a global network of optimally concentrated and located activities reaps early cost and quality advantages that competitors should find difficult to match. For global marketing, the first company to promote global brands and global advertising can build image and preference leads that are difficult to dislodge.

GLOBAL COMPETITIVE MOVES FOR SERVICE BUSINESSES

Service businesses need to make globally integrated competitive moves as much as product-based businesses. But the key feature of such moves, cross-country coordination, can be both easier and more difficult. Coordination can be easier for those service businesses that reproduce a strong core formula around the word. In such businesses,

JAPANESE STRATEGY IN VCRs

In the videocassette recorder industry, Japanese manufacturers such as Sony and Matsushita combined rapid coverage of all key markets, with offering the first global products, and an efficient production network based in the Far East, to secure adequate volume and a strong competitive position, including in the U.S. market. American competitors such as RCA, Zenith, or General Electric never had a chance to put up a fight, let alone take the battle to Japan. By the time these companies had set up their activity network with production and component purchasing in the Far East, the Japanese products were established and competing no longer on price but on recognized quality.[10]

NOKIA FINISHES FIRST

Finland's initially tiny Nokia was able to overtake the U.S. giant Motorola in mobile telephone sets for several reasons, some related to global strategy and some not. Most important, in terms of global strategy, Nokia was able to benefit from the fact that Europe used a digital GSM technology that could be used in every European country and in much of Africa, Asia, and the Americas. In contrast, Motorola was the leader in the older analog technology phones and, most importantly, that worked only in the Americas. With this advantage, Nokia was quick to expand all over the world, while Motorola was slow to switch from analog to digital. Nokia was then able to leverage its global advantages to successfully invade the U.S. market.

corporate headquarters plays a continuing role in monitoring the strategies of overseas units. Examples include chain restaurants and hotels. But the prevalence of franchising in services, and its concomitant dispersion of ownership, makes global coordination much harder. Until they changed their international ownership structures, the major accounting firms, for example, operated on global basis mostly as quasi-franchises, with little sharing of ownership or profits across countries. Arthur Andersen pioneered the global consolidation of ownership, allowing the firm to be the first in the industry to develop global competitive strategies. Coordination may also be less necessary where both production and consumption occur locally, and central support plays a minor role. In contrast, manufacturing companies with factories serving multiple country markets find it essential to coordinate their different country strategies.

EFFECT OF THE INTERNET ON GLOBAL COMPETITIVE MOVES

The Internet clearly creates new forms of competition and among previously separated players. Focusing on just the global aspects, the Internet creates global competitive spaces so that there is both cross-border and cross-format competition. Amazon.com's U.S. Web site has become a powerful competitor for bookstores on the other side of the world.

Several of the largest automobile producers are developing a business-to-business Web site that will stimulate competition among far-flung suppliers. General Motors, Ford, DaimlerChrysler, Nissan, and Renault have created Covisnt to work with about 35 leading suppliers to the automotive industry. Before the Web, local suppliers enjoyed some advantages of proximity over distant rivals. Now they compete on virtually equal footing. The upshot of all this is that multinational companies need to plan their global moves much more effectively. Issues include the following:

- Using the Web to monitor competitors more closely
- Responding more quickly via Web offerings
- Using deep linking, metatags, and other techniques to hijack potential customers from competitors' Web sites
- Choosing the right mix of competitive and cooperative behavior with rivals and other partners
- Establishing global standards to limit or preempt competition

BENEFITS AND DRAWBACKS

The key benefit of globally integrated competitive moves lies in magnifying the resources available in any single country for competitive actions by leveraging the global resources of a business. So head office managers can design competitive strategies that involve the power of multiple moves, while local managers can call on help beyond that available in just their own countries. In addition, taking a globally integrated approach to competitive moves simply provides more options in attack and defense. Such an approach also helps managers to see country linkages so that they recognize the competitive interdependence of countries. That way the business can avoid the piecemeal, country-by-country conquest that has been the fate of many industries. Furthermore, managers taking a globally integrated approach to competitive moves are more likely to spot the preemptive actions that need to be taken—such as Becton Dickinson's moves to block Japanese expansion in Southeast Asia in the disposable syringe market.

On the other hand, integrating competitive moves can have drawbacks also. It can mean sacrificing revenues, profits, or competitive position in individual countries, particularly likely when the subsidiary in one country is asked to attack a global competitor in order to send a signal or to divert that competitor's resources from another country. The manager of the sacrificing subsidiary may be reluctant to perform such a selfless role. Overcoming such reluctance requires a performance evaluation and reward management system that encourages rather than discourages global cooperation.

CHOOSING THE SPEED OF GLOBALIZATION

As part of their global competitive moves, companies can choose whether to try to speed up or slow down the pace of globalization. In some industries and product categories, a diversified multinational company may be already well entrenched in multiple local markets with locally tailored offerings. In those industries, the company may want to avoid moves to greater global standardization as that would reduce its existing localization advantages and make it easier for new competitors to enter with global offerings. On the other hand, where a company is late or behind multilocal competitors, its best strategy would be to speed up globalization by playing a standardization game.

For example, Unilever enjoys a dominant multilocal position around the world in many food and other consumer product categories. In these categories Unilever tries to hold on to its advantages of local differentiation. On the other hand, because the company was late into the ice cream category, it chose a global approach as a way of challenging already established rivals. Obviously, the prospects for such moves depend on industry globalization drivers, but most industries offer some scope for strategic choice.

Some companies may have little choice. Many of the younger, technology-based companies do not have a long history of local adaptation. For them, the only game is to be as global as possible. Even a company with a moderately long history, such as Hewlett-Packard, needs to play a global and not a multilocal game. At the extreme, Microsoft is so young as a multinational that it does not even try to play a multilocal game. Perhaps the most distinctive aspect of Microsoft's international approach is that *it seeks to adapt the world to its global strategy rather than the other way around.*

Successful global companies transfer their competitive advantages quickly and effectively around the world. Global transfer of critical capabilities and advantages is probably the single biggest factor in the success of overseas subsidiaries and hence the overall global strategy.[11]

GUIDELINES FOR MAKING GLOBAL COMPETITIVE MOVES

Perhaps the ultimate test of a total global strategy is whether a worldwide business can make globally integrated competitive moves. Some guidelines help managers to perform this difficult task:

- Global competitive moves require coordination and agreement among national managers. In some cases it also requires national sacrifices for the sake of the worldwide business.
- Not making global competitive moves can be particularly damaging in the long term for a business's worldwide competitive position.
- It is critical for senior management to design and implement a system to both recognize the need for globally integrated competitive moves and achieve cooperation among different countries.

Discussion and Research Questions

1. What is the difference between a multilocal and a global approach to making competitive moves?
2. Describe a competitive action or series of actions by a company that you think particularly exemplify a global competitive move.
3. What should be the response of a company when a foreign competitor is dumping in that company's home market? Would your answer differ if the foreign competitor were (a) an exporter producing only in its home country or (b) a multinational company with production and sales around the world? Would your answer differ by the nationality of the foreign competitor?
4. What organizational mechanisms are needed to allow a company to make effective global competitive moves?
5. What is different about global competitive moves for service businesses?
6. How does the Internet affect global competitive moves?

Notes

1. This example draws on "The Revenge of Big Yellow," *The Economist,* November 10, 1990; and "Kodak Chief Is Trying, for the Fourth Time, to Trim Firm's Costs," *Wall Street Journal,* September 19, 1990, pp. A1, A18.
2. "Fuji Builds a Brand as Kodak Fumes," *The New York Times,* December 12, 1997, p. 15.
3. It is in the area of cross-subsidization, and also coordinated moves, that global strategy comes closest to military strategy. In the latter arena, concentration of forces at selected points to outnumber the enemy is perhaps the key maxim (or "get there fastest with the mostest," as one American general once said). For a more general discussion of analogies between business and military strategy, see Philip Kotler and Ravi Singh, "Marketing Warfare in the 1980s," *Journal of Business Strategy,* Vol. 1, No. 3, Winter 1981.
4. See Michael E. Porter, "Changing Patterns of International Competition," *California Management Review,* Vol. 28, No. 2, Winter 1986, pp. 9–40.
5. See Michael E. Porter, *Competitive Strategy: Techniques for Analyzing Industries and Competitors* (New York: Free Press, 1980), Chapter 4, and A. Michael Spence, "Entry, Capacity, Investment and Oligopolistic Pricing," *Bell Journal of Economics,* Vol. 8, Autumn 1977, pp. 534–44, on the role of signaling in competitive strategy.
6. Sumantra Ghoshal, "Global Strategy: An Organizing Framework," *Strategic Management Journal,* Vol. 8, No. 5, September–October 1987, pp. 425–40, char-acterizes the ability to learn and adapt as one of the three key objectives in global strategy, the other two being achieving efficiency and managing risk. See also Christopher A. Bartlett and Sumantra Ghoshal, *Managing Across Borders: The Transnational Solution* (Boston: Harvard Business School Press, 1989), on how to organize for global learning.
7. See the works cited in Note 36 in Chapter 3. See also Michael Y. Yoshino and U. Srinivasa Rangan, *Strategic Alliances: An Entrepreneurial Approach to Globalization* (Boston: Harvard Business School Press, 1995); and Paul Beamish and Peter Killing, Eds., *Cooperative Strategies* (Lanham, MD: Lexington Books 1997). See also the "coopetition" concepts in Adam M. Brandenburger and Barry J. Nalebuff, *Coopetition* (New York: Currency Doubleday, 1996).
8. As argued by Michael E. Porter, *The Competitive Advantage of Nations* (New York: The Free Press, 1990).
9. "The WTO Gets It Wrong," *The New York Times,* December 6, 1997, p. 8.
10. This example is adapted from Herbert Henzler and Wilhelm Rall, "Facing Up to the Globalization Challenge," *The McKinsey Quarterly,* Winter 1986, pp. 52–68.
11. Henry P. Conn, and George S. Yip, "Global Transfer of Critical Capabilities," *Business Horizons,* Vol. 40, No. 1, January–February 1997, pp. 22–31.

BUILDING THE GLOBAL ORGANIZATION

O rganization factors form the third corner of the globalization triangle, along with industry globalization drivers and global strategy levers. They affect what the nature of global strategy should be as well as the effectiveness of its implementation. Here we focus on how the nature of the organization—its structure, management processes, people, and culture—affects the use of global strategy levers and the ability to implement global strategy. The chapter describes these organization factors in depth and discusses how to build a global organization.[1] Key issues in global organization include how to achieve balance between autonomy and integration. Subsidiaries need autonomy in order to adapt to their local environment. But the business as a whole needs integration to implement global strategy.[2] Global organizations need to achieve both integration and autonomy while fostering the increasingly important tasks of learning and knowledge transfer.[3] Being able to transfer knowledge from one country to another provides a key source of advantage for multinational companies.[4]

Many companies today are struggling to achieve a globally integrated organization that retains the capability for local flexibility and responsiveness. Virtually no company has achieved a totally satisfactory solution, but a few have created highly successful elements in the global organization and management puzzle. Black & Decker has already been described in earlier chapters. Another company that seems to have developed effective global solutions is ICI in the United Kingdom, once one of the world's largest chemical companies. In the 1980s, ICI's management began the process of replacing its U.K. divisions and overseas national companies with global business units. These units have responsibility for overall global strategy, R&D, and resource allocation. While ICI still uses a matrix structure that has product, geographic, and functional dimensions, it is now the product dimension that takes the lead. About half of ICI's activities are now organized into globally integrated "international businesses" that have clear global strategies. The remaining businesses are more localized within Europe while also exporting to the rest of the world.

Organization provides the vehicle by which strategy can be formulated and implemented. The nature of the organization also affects the kind of strategy that can be developed. This is particularly true of global strategy. An organization of highly autonomous national business units, in which the managers from different countries seldom meet, with little transfer of personnel or information between countries, and with a nationalistic culture, is scarcely likely to be able to formulate a global strategy in the first place, let alone implement it. Such an organization may well believe that it does not need a global strategy—because it is not exposed to the information that might show otherwise.

Building the kind of company capable of formulating and implementing total global strategy is not easy. The task is achievable if managers break it down into digestible pieces and if they relate changes in organization to the specific changes needed

in global strategy. A workable approach to global organization has two key requirements. First, it is no use announcing that the company needs a "global organization"
without specifying the details of that organization. So managers need to view a global
organization as comprising several factors and several elements within each factor. The
second key requirement is to recognize that specific elements of global organization affect the ability to use specific elements of global strategy. For example, having a separate international division (an element of organization structure) makes it very difficult
to design global products. So managers need to take an *elemental* approach to designing
the global organization. The advantage of this elemental approach is that managers can
make small changes that can build up over time[5] and can change one aspect of organization when blocked in another. Reorganizing the structure can be politically difficult,
while less drastic changes in management process may meet less resistance. Changes in
some elements can reduce the barriers to more major changes.

Four factors and their individual elements determine the crucial organization
forces that affect a company's ability to formulate and implement global strategy:

- *Organization structure* comprises the reporting relationships in a business—the
  "boxes and lines."
- *Management processes* comprise the activities such as planning and budgeting that
  make the business run.
- *People* comprise the human resources of the worldwide business and include both
  managers and all other employees.
- *Culture* comprises the values and rules that guide behavior in a corporation.

Each of these factors directly affects the others and the use of global strategy. Each
operates powerfully in different ways. A common mistake, in implementing *any* strategy, is to ignore one or more of them, particularly the less tangible ones such as culture.
A blockage in even one dimension of organization can severely cramp the ability to
think and behave globally. Exhibit 8-1 lists the key factors and their key elements.

Each organization factor and its elements have distinct effects on the use of each
of the five global strategy levers. For example, having centralized global authority allows a more global approach to market participation—by allowing countries to be chosen more on the basis of global strategic importance and less on the basis of which
regional manager has more political power. Centralized global authority also helps the
development of global products, helps make global choices on the location of activities,
and makes it easier to develop global marketing and to make global competitive moves.

The organization and management requirements of a global business can also be
contrasted with those of a multilocal or export-based business. For these different businesses, each organization factor needs to stress different features. A *global* business
needs some form of centralized global authority. But a *multilocal* business does better
with dispersed national authority that allows each country to make its own decisions in
adapting to local conditions. Lastly, an *export-based* business also needs centralized authority but one that takes the viewpoint of the home country business rather than that
of the entire worldwide business. Exhibit 8-2 summarizes the desired organization features for each type of geographic strategy.

But, as in global strategy levers, companies need not adopt every global organization approach. Managers should select those global organization elements that seem
the most helpful in achieving their global strategy objectives. Furthermore, as change is

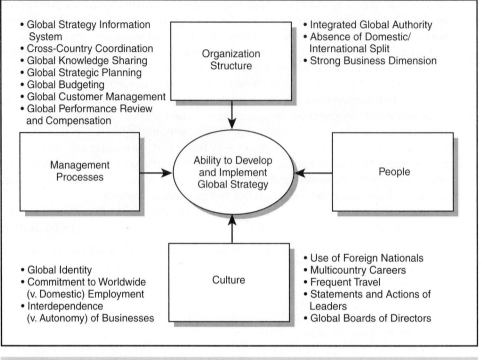

EXHIBIT 8-1 Elements of Global Organization

Source: Adapted from Yip, Loewe, and Yoshino (1988).

usually necessary, managers should select those changes that they think their organization is capable of making. And, if the company cannot make the needed organization changes, it should not even try to have a global strategy.

ORGANIZATION STRUCTURE

The first organization factor, organization structure, has the most obvious and direct, although not necessarily the most important, effect on global strategy.[6] Changes in organization structure (and, therefore, lines of reporting) send the clearest signals, which can be good or bad. So such changes need to be used with caution. In some cases, changes in other, less direct, aspects of organization, such as management processes, may need to be made first to pave the way for changes in structure.

INTEGRATION OF GLOBAL AUTHORITY

One of the most effective ways to develop and implement a global strategy is to integrate or centralize authority so that all units of the same business around the world report to a common *global sector head*. Surprisingly few companies do this. Instead, they are tied for historical reasons to a strong country-based organization structure where the main line of authority runs by country rather than by business. In some businesses, however, particularly vertically integrated ones in raw-material processing industries

EXHIBIT 8-2   Desired Organization Features for Types of Geographic Strategies

Geographic Scope	Organization Structure	Management Processes	People	Culture
Global	Centralized global authority	Extensive coordination processes	Multicountry careers	Global identity
	No domestic-international split	Global sharing of technology	Foreign nationals in home and third countries	Interdependence
	Strong geographic dimension relative to business and function	Global strategy information system	Extensive travel	
		Global strategic planning, budgets, performance review, and compensation		
Multilocal	Dispersed national authority	Transfer of technology from headquarters out	Professional expatriates	Multinational identity
	No domestic-international split	National information systems	Nationals run local businesses	Autonomy
	Strong geographic dimension relative to business and function	National strategic planning, budgets, performance review, and compensation	Limited travel	
Export-Based	Centralized home country control	Direction not coordination	Home country nationals run local marketing subsidiaries	Home country culture
	Separate domestic and international divisions	One-way information flow to headquarters		
	May have strong functional dimension	No technology transfer Focus on sales targets		

such as chemicals or pulp and paper, it can be very difficult to carve out stand-alone lines of business in each country. Each factory, for example, may serve several businesses both inside and outside the country in which the factory is located. In such cases an alternative structural solution is to appoint *global business directors* who operate in matrix fashion across the functional and geographic organizations.

The roles and responsibilities for such global business directors can include the following:

• Taking profit accountability for individual lines of business
• Coordinating all functions affecting these lines
• Developing a strategic plan and financial budgets in cooperation with the functions and regions

DEVELOPMENT OF FORD'S EUROPEAN AND GLOBAL ORGANIZATIONS

Although on a continental rather than global scale, Ford of Europe, created in 1967, provides an excellent example of how organization changes facilitated strategy changes.[7] Ford of Europe was created to coordinate the company's activities in the region and to break down the barriers dividing Ford's country-based operations. The effects of this reorganization were far reaching over the next two decades. For example, the German divisions built special strengths in manufacturing while the British division excelled in product development and general enterprise management. Together they created cars for all of Europe (and eventually the world) and saved the rest of the company financially during the difficult 1979–1984 period. The change in organization culture that followed the creation of Ford of Europe helped to make Ford one of the most global automobile companies. Ford executives also believe that Ford's leading-edge aerodynamic designs, cost-cutting programs, and the emphasis on quality all grew out of the new ways of working. The different country operations not only canceled out each other's weaknesses but set a higher base level for the quality of all operations. Good ideas and solutions to problems were sought throughout the company and flowed rapidly through the entire organization. The strengths of the European operation (exemplified in the Taurus and other European-styled cars) are now being imported to the United States. Another benefit of creating a central organization is that Ford of Europe became much more attentive to what the Japanese were doing well and was able to act on that knowledge to keep pace.

In the 1990s, Ford sought to apply on a global scale the lessons it learned from Europeanization, particularly in order to compete against the global strategies of its Japanese rivals.[8] In 1994, Ford underwent a management restructuring, eliminating its regional companies to turn itself into a global company that makes global cars, in an effort that its then CEO, Alex Trotman, dubbed the "Ford 2000 Program." The goal of the restructuring was to leverage any economies of scale achieved to offset the company's engineering and development costs without angering the heads of Ford's national companies. Selling this idea to these "barons" and the rest of the workforce was Ford's biggest hurdle. By 1995, approximately 25,000 managers had moved to new jobs or reported to new bosses. The consolidated European and American division was renamed Ford Automotive Operations with four vice presidents running the company's global operations: new product development, marketing and sales, manufacturing, and purchasing. The new global structure was expected to produce $3 billion in annual savings through lower product engineering and development costs by implementing "best practices" and streamlining Ford's suppliers. The new structure was also aimed at improving communications throughout the organization by empowering employees to make quicker decisions.

- Working with the functions and regions to implement the strategic plan
- Contributing to the design, creation, and maintenance of global strategy, marketing, and financial information systems
- Contributing to performance evaluations for functional and regional managers
- Traveling frequently

Another way of centralizing global authority is to have *global heads of individual functions* or value-adding activities. These heads can have either direct line authority over the function or a staff-like coordination responsibility. Functional heads can be very effective. The corporate head of global marketing in a major American household products company viewed his role as partly to explain why ideas had failed in other countries. He would often say to a national manager: "You know more about your country than I do. I know more about the rest of the world. This strategy you propose has been tried in eight other countries. It failed in seven and here is why. Now let's examine your idea." But having real power can also be elusive. Companies sometimes delude themselves that they have created global authority by giving responsibility for global integration to an executive. The head of business planning in a large American computer equipment business commented that while his business had one global product head "on paper," the latter had no real control and, therefore, little effect on global strategy.

ABSENCE OF DOMESTIC–INTERNATIONAL SPLIT

A common structural barrier to global strategy is the presence of an organization split between a domestic and an international division.[9] Typically, the international division oversees a group of highly autonomous country subsidiaries, each of which manages several distinct businesses. A global strategy for any one of these businesses can then be fully coordinated only at the level of the CEO's office. Until the 1990s, this split was very common among U.S. firms, partly for historical reasons and partly because of the enormous size of the U.S. market. Ironically, some European multinationals with small domestic markets have separated out not their home market but the U.S. market. As a result they find it difficult to get their U.S. subsidiaries to cooperate in the development and implementation of global strategy. In one major European company, the heads of worldwide business sectors had to go "cap-in-hand to New York" to solicit support for their worldwide strategies. This company has now strengthened the business sectors' direct authority over American operations.

Many American companies have separate international divisions and domestic divisions. There is a trend toward disbanding international divisions. A major financial service company has shifted to three regions for the whole world. Its business head viewed this eliminating of the U.S. divisions, and consequent breaking down of regional barriers, as one of the company's greatest successes in globalizing strategy. The benefits included better allocation of resources and the recognition that business lost in one country need not necessarily be replaced in the same country, but can be recouped elsewhere. The head of international sales and distribution for a leading U.S. industrial controls business views its domestic–international split as the biggest obstacle to global strategy. The head of another business complains that its heavily regional organization discourages global strategy by restricting the flow of information and technology. The head of marketing in the international division of a food and beverages business commented that the original advantage of having a separate international division was in building up a power base. But now, with a global brand fighting a global competitor, the business needs to use its U.S. profits to subsidize international efforts, and the current structure does not allow that.

BUSINESS DIMENSION STRONGER THAN GEOGRAPHIC DIMENSION

Issues of central control affect the global strategy capability of a worldwide business. But most worldwide businesses are part of multinational companies that operate multiple

COCA-COLA'S REORGANIZATION

In the mid-1990s, Coca-Cola eliminated the concept of "domestic" and "international" divisions and instead organized six international units that form the company's global geographic regions.[10] The move was the first for any major U.S. consumer products company. A benefit of the change was that it suggested equality at an international level, where each international business unit reported directly to the president. At the shareholder level, the move also sent a message to investors: Rather than invest in an international portfolio in order to diversify risk, they could invest in the global operations of Coca-Cola.

businesses. The need to manage across both countries and businesses adds to the complexity of the challenge. Most multinational companies have evolved a matrix form of organization structure that combines business and geographic as well as functional dimensions.[11] In the 1990s, this matrix form has evolved to a global network, sometimes called the "transnational" company.[12]

Unilever has long operated with a matrix system. Its global integration has been provided by a team of "coordinators" at the head office responsible for business sectors such as detergents and foods (the latter coordination being split at one time into Foods I, Foods II, and Foods III). These coordination executives have mostly held senior country and regional general management positions. Its archrival, Procter & Gamble, was slow to take a similar approach. In the 1980s P&G adopted a matrix type of structure, first in Europe and then worldwide. A brand manager now reported both to his or her country manager and to a category manager. This change helped the company react more quickly to global competition.[13] At the same time some observers criticized P&G's use of European product managers for slowing the European launch of its Pampers brand of disposable diapers. In particular the change in reporting structure may have made national managers less interested in supporting Pampers. But, if true, that problem does not demonstrate the weakness of global organization or global marketing but of inadequate change in *all* the elements of global organization. P&G should also have changed the management evaluation and incentive process to support the new strategy. By the mid-1990s, P&G went beyond Unilever in globalizing its management structure by reorganizing away from a geographically dominated matrix to seven global business units. Furthermore, P&G located the headquarters of some of these business units outside the United States. For example, the global management of the detergents business moved to Brussels.

Dow Chemical has used a three-dimensional (function, business, and geography) matrix management since the 1960s to cope with its plants in over 30 countries and its 1,800 different products. After many changes, Dow settled on a flexible approach in which, depending on the nature and needs of a business sector, one of the three dimensions of the matrix is chosen to carry more weight than the other two. Lastly, perhaps most important, is that regardless of the organization structure, managers should think in matrix fashion.[14]

ABB'S GLOBAL MATRIX

By the early 1990s Asea Brown Boveri represented for many the "new model of competitive enterprise—an organization that combines global scale and world-class technology with deep roots in local markets."[15] According to Percy Barnevik, ABB's president and CEO, the "only way to structure a complex, global organization is to make it as simple and local as possible."

To build this "multidomestic" practice Barnevik implemented a matrix structure designed to optimize its global businesses by leveraging core technologies and economies of scale and maximizing local market performance and responsiveness. Ultimately, ABB became a "federation of national companies with a global coordination center." One dimension of the matrix was 50 "business areas," whose leaders were considered to be the experts for their product or service and were responsible for a specific global strategy and cost and quality standards. The other dimension is a country structure made up of national companies with independent profit and loss responsibility. By 1991 ABB had 1,100 local companies located around the globe with presidents who reported to two bosses. The first was the president of the national company, of which the local company is a subsidiary, and the second was one of 50 business area leaders who were typically located outside the country. By 1996, there were 1,300 local companies and 5,000 profit centers.

The multidomestic organization offered inherent strategic advantages for a company with businesses that are "super global" as well as some that are "super local." Globally, businesses can specialize in the production of components, technology managers can be rotated to share expertise, and economies of scale can be maximized. On the local level, the best talent can be drawn from the domestic community, a strong government relationship can be nurtured, and products can be designed to match specific tastes. As the 1990s developed, ABB began to place more emphasis on the business part of the matrix and less on the geographic part.

ABB's global matrix also illustrates the relationship among industry globalization drivers, global strategy levers, and global organization. Most of ABB's businesses operate in industries with strong cost globalization drivers, particularly in terms of economies of scale in R&D and manufacturing, and strong competitive globalization drivers in that most of its competitors are also global companies. On the other hand, given that ABB sells to many local, often state-owned, customers (e.g., utilities) in regulated industries (e.g., telecommunications), many of the market globalization drivers that it faces are local and the government globalization driver even more so. So both ABB's strategies and organization need to combine global and local elements—global in the upstream parts of the business system and organization, and more local in the downstream parts.

In a company pursuing a global strategy, the extent of integration within businesses needs to be very strong. At the same time, integration within each country is important in order to coordinate the activities of the different businesses and to be able to present a common front to host governments, suppliers, channels, customers, and community groups. In theory, strong integration along both business and country dimensions should be possible. In practice, the two efforts often conflict. Exhibit 8-3 illustrates some possible combinations of geographic and business integration. The situation in the top left box, "Fragmented Multilocal Strategies," illustrates the case of extreme global fragmentation, in which there is no organization structure integrating either businesses within a country or countries within a business. Senior executives in many large and

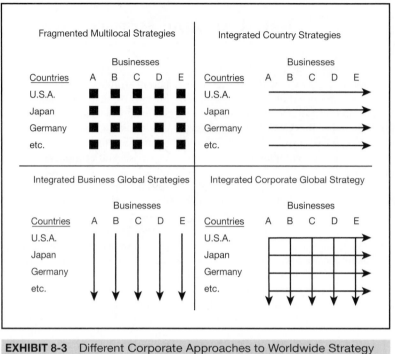

EXHIBIT 8-3   Different Corporate Approaches to Worldwide Strategy

small American multinational companies characterize (with embarrassment) their company that way.

The situation in the top right box, "Integrated Country Strategies," illustrates a historically very common form of multinational organization in which a country manager has great powers over all the businesses in his or her country. This form of integration was particularly popular in the early days of multinational expansion when communications and travel were far more difficult than today. European companies, with their heritage of colonial administration, probably developed the country manager role to its highest degree of power. The country managers of India in a British multinational company used to "rule like a rajah." Many corporate executives have complained of national and regional "fiefdoms" run by these highly independent country managers. Even Roger Enrico, who persuaded Michael Jackson to sing and dance for Pepsi-Cola, could not control the head of Pepsico in Latin America.[16] But the need for global strategy, and improvement in communications, is causing many companies to reduce the role of the country manager. *In one sense, the country manager has been made obsolete by the fax machine and the Internet.* In a major American financial service business the role of the country manager has changed a great deal. The country manager used to run the business in the country but is now more the titular head who represents the parent company in the country. It seems, however, that there will always be one role for the country manager. The Swiss chief financial officer of a European multinational said that his company would always need country managers, because "governments need one man to go after to put in jail"! On the other hand, the opening up in the 1990s of many emerging economies is recreating the need for country managers in those markets.

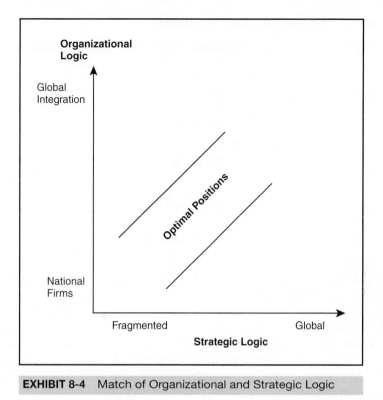

EXHIBIT 8-4   Match of Organizational and Strategic Logic

The bottom left box, "Integrated Business Global Strategies," illustrates the situation in which the organization structure provides strong global integration within each business across countries but provides little integration across businesses within each country. Only in the bottom right box, "Integrated Corporate Global Strategy," does the structure provide integration across both dimensions. When executives are asked which diagram best represents their corporation, few select this last box, but almost all say that their company is headed that way. Philips, the giant Dutch manufacturer of electrical products, provides an instructive example of a company that long had a much more powerful geographic dimension than a business one but is now striving hard to "tilt the matrix" toward the business dimension. Because of the Dutch colonial heritage and because the head office was cut off from the subsidiaries during World War II, the latter grew to operate very independently. But under global attack from Japanese electronics manufacturers in the 1980s, and facing the integration of Europe, Philips found that it needed a global rather than a multinational organization.[17]

Lastly, companies need not adopt just one of the four modes depicted in Exhibit 8-4. A mixture can be best, allowing some businesses (those in industries with low globalization potential) to be managed on a country-by-country basis, some countries (those with high barriers to trade) to operate independently with extensive control over the businesses in them, and other countries and businesses to be part of an integrated global matrix. This idea is summarized in Exhibit 8-4, which shows that the organizational logic has to match the strategic logic.

DESIGNATING STRATEGIC LEADERS

A less direct approach to globalization than changing the organization structure is to assign to a specific country the lead role in developing a product and to see to that product's spread into other countries and to its adaptation.[18] Thus some responsibilities are diverted from the other countries to the country acting as the strategic leader. One of the most effective ways of using this approach is to assign strategic leadership responsibility for different products to a number of different countries. In that way, each country has to cooperate with the others, and none is singled out. Assigning lead roles to subsidiaries helps to compensate them for the way in which global strategy reduces their scope and autonomy. Some researchers argue that subsidiaries can play a new role by bidding for "global mandates" to perform either internal roles (such as becoming a global regional activity center) or external roles (such as working with global customers).[19]

NATIONAL DIFFERENCES IN GLOBAL ORGANIZATION

Multinational companies from the three major business areas of the world—the United States, Western Europe, and Japan—tend to have differing organization structures and therefore face differing globalization challenges.[20] Because of the small size of their home markets and because of their nations' overseas empires, European companies were typically the most advanced in multinationalization whether measured by the percentage of their sales outside their home country or by their use of managers of different nationalities. More important, European multinationals—such as Unilever, Philips, and Nestlé—have probably given more autonomy to their foreign subsidiaries than have American or Japanese multinationals. Many European multinationals face, therefore, a greater need to reduce multilocal autonomy and increase global integration.

Because of the huge size of their home market, American companies were somewhat slower to go international than were comparable European and Japanese companies. From the 1980s there was increased pressure to internationalize because of increased foreign competition, slower growing domestic markets, and the new public recognition of America's trading problems. Although indirect, the last factor powerfully affected the attention paid to international business by corporate stakeholders (such as share owners, boards of directors, and employees) and, therefore, the attention of senior management. The size of the American domestic market has also created an issue that is more typical for American multinationals—the organizational and psychological division between the home country and other countries. Separate domestic and international organizations are common in American multinationals but rarer in European ones.[21] As a result American companies pursuing global integration face the dual challenge of confronting not just local country autonomy but domestic–international divisions as well.

Most Japanese companies operated until the late 1980s/early 1990s as exporters rather than as multinationals. Although they typically used an international division, the export emphasis of their businesses allowed very close links between their domestic and international businesses. Their rising domestic costs, plus the threat of protectionism in their foreign markets, spurred an increasing relocation of their production activities to the countries of their markets. Japanese companies now face the task of learning how to operate as multinational companies and to build the needed organization structure. In terms of global strategy, they face a challenge opposite to that for American and

European companies. Japanese companies have generally been highly effective in operating with an integrated global strategy. Now they face the task of retaining that global integration while allowing the local autonomy needed to operate as multinationals.

As multinationals arise from other economies—especially Korea, the rest of Asia, and Latin America—they all face the same issue of transition from national focus to a global one. By virtue of their relative lateness in internationalization, most of these companies will be able to bypass or accelerate through some of the earlier forms of international organization, such as multilocal, autonomous subsidiaries, and reach quickly for effective forms of global organization.

POTENTIAL FOR COST SAVINGS

Reorganizing along global rather than multilocal lines can produce major cost savings by reducing the extent to which activities are duplicated in multiple countries (as discussed in Chapter 5). The traditional way to cut costs in reorganization is to eliminate *horizontal* layers by cutting the number of levels in a company. Reorganization along global lines provides a *vertical* option for cost cutting, such as by eliminating nine out of 12 manufacturing sites in different countries. But companies need to beware of reorganizing globally just for the sake of cost savings. The reorganization must also make sense strategically, relative to industry globalization drivers and the type of global strategy needed.

MANAGEMENT PROCESSES

While organization structure has a very direct effect on management behavior, it is management processes that power the system. The appropriate processes and systems can even substitute to some extent for the appropriate structure. These processes and systems include the global strategy information system, cross-country coordination, global strategic planning, global budgeting, and global performance review and compensation.

GLOBAL STRATEGY INFORMATION SYSTEM

Information systems comprise the data that are collected, analyzed, stored, and communicated as well as the methods for performing those activities. Information systems go beyond hardware and software. Having information about the world is a minimum requirement for being able to formulate and implement a global strategy. Information needs to be specified at a global level as well as at regional and national levels. So the system needs to contain information about *global* market share as well as national market share, and so on. A useful test for managers is to ask whether the system has information about the company's global share of a particular customer's business. The system also needs to regularly collect strategic information in a common format for easy comparison. Information needs to be communicated to headquarters in a method that is as easy as possible for subsidiary managers. The information needs to be processed and analyzed for global strategy implications. *Perhaps most important, headquarters needs to disseminate its findings back to the countries so that they do not view the home country as a black hole, sucking in information but giving nothing in return.*

New information technology—enterprise resource planning systems (ERPs) such as SAP, the Internet, and CRMs (customer relationship management systems)—makes it much easier to create and maintain global strategy information systems. Dow

BARNEVIK'S EMPHASIS ON SHARING INFORMATION

When he was CEO of ABB, Percy Barnevik used an overemphasis on sharing information to combat any communications challenges and to avoid any bias toward one particular country or region.[22] To overcome these hurdles and really make an impact, he said that change needs to be "factual, quick and neutral." Barnevik also emphasized speed in decision making over accuracy, stating that the costs of making an occasional mistake are overshadowed by the costs incurred by a delayed decision.

Chemical globally interconnected the different parts of its organization by implementing SAP R2. By installing SAP throughout the world, Owens-Corning transformed its organization from a decentralized company into a centralized, global one. Many companies use CRMs to collect and manage information about their national and multinational customers. Intranets and extranets allow companies to share information across borders both internally and externally.

But the term "system" needs to be interpreted loosely and need not be equated with computers. Many companies have foundered in their initial attempts at building global strategy information systems by getting sidetracked into developing complex computer-based data entry and retrieval systems that never became usable. They forgot that the more difficult task in global information is getting the data in the first place. The way in which information gets sent by the subsidiaries should be made as simple as possible. A medium-sized industrial equipment company has developed a one-page form on which national sales representatives can report competitive intelligence. A major chemical company has done quite well by keeping its information on paper, updating with hand notations as needed. The company has also found that subsidiary managers are much more willing to fax information in fairly casual formats than to enter data into a computer terminal. One major international advertising agency used to collect global information by sending a senior executive traveling around the world. He would "beat the information out of the national managers." Today leading agencies use intranets instead: National offices place on the Net their local advertising so that all offices can see what is being done for a given client around the world.

CROSS-COUNTRY COORDINATION

Creating cross-country coordination mechanisms provides a way to make up for the lack of direct reporting structure, although its use seems limited to date. The lack of coordination can bring drastic consequences. In defending an advertising claim, an American drug manufacturer (better left unnamed) argued to the U.S. Federal Drug Administration that the recommended dosage of *two* tablets for its full strength analgesic product provided the maximum possible benefit. The regulatory agency accepted this argument until it discovered a television commercial by the same company in Canada recommending *three* tablets for severe symptoms. An industrial company fre-

DU PONT DE NEMOURS: OPEN SESSIONS TO SPAN THE GLOBE

With approximately 100 businesses and 1,200 different products, more than half of Du Pont's revenue in 1990 was derived from customers outside the United States.[23] That same year, the company established an Open Systems Program Office to help guide the introduction of open systems throughout the global organization. In the long term, open systems is fundamental to Du Pont's strategy to be a truly global company. The company is continuously striving to create a high degree of synergy across the corporation so that information would be available to "anyone in the corporation that needs it to do his or her job." The company realized it could not "create an integrated Du Pont information environment" based on proprietary solutions.

The corporate information systems function worked hard to increase Du Pont's global reach. Du Pont wanted technology based on international standards to build an interconnected worldwide network of open systems, and the company expected vendors to build systems based on that chosen technology. Other factors behind developing open systems at Du Pont included the need to respond more quickly to market needs, to develop closer partnerships with customers and suppliers, and to handle the mass of government regulations and paperwork.

Open systems is a long-term effort at Du Pont. The company planned to build the open systems implementation and expertise through the 1990s. An early priority was to focus on changing the culture and "develop an open, distributed mind-set" in the information systems people. This involved educating Du Pont's 6,000 information systems professionals worldwide about the benefits of open systems.

quently got into trouble with its global customers because businesses in different countries did not share their plans on pricing changes. In one instance, the business in France offered a temporary price reduction on a product line sold to a global customer that also bought from the United States. The customer then switched its purchases from the United States to France and shipped the product across the Atlantic—the price cut more than covering the additional transportation cost and duty.

Cross-country coordination mechanisms range from sharing of information—the least coercive—to setting direct requirements—the most coercive:

- Countries can *share information* about their strategic and operating plans. That alerts headquarters and other countries about opportunities and the possibility of conflicts.
- Countries can be required to *negotiate* their plans with headquarters and other countries that might be affected.
- Countries can be required to *clear* their plans with headquarters and other countries.
- Headquarters or some coordination group may *direct* countries to take certain actions. For example, all countries may be required to launch a particular new product. Giving direct orders verges on changing the organization structure to direct reporting. So management needs to be particularly cautious in setting down the path of directing countries' actions.

While informing, negotiating, clearing, and directing represent critical functions in cross-country coordination, their effectiveness is limited unless they are based on more

IMPLEMENTING GLOBAL SOFTWARE

As many businesses seek to consolidate local software packages and implement global software technology, companies realize that the strategic benefits must justify the large implementation costs.[24] Better access to worldwide data, the ability to service global customers, the integration of best practice procedures and common processes through a single interface, and lower costs due to centralized support and negotiated software costs can all add value to a company's global operation. However, many companies believe that these benefits cater to the center, and many subsidiaries suffer from a new global system. In many instances, local packages that solve the complexities of local markets will produce greater benefits. Implementing a new system may cause serious upheaval in a subsidiary that has little need for an integrated, cross-functional global package.

In practice, the decision to implement global software must be determined by the strategic nature of a company's business. Companies that have single integrated worldwide businesses are excellent candidates for global software packages. Gillette, with major clients positioned all over the world, is a good example. In response to customer needs, the company is implementing common processes worldwide, supported by SAP software. The implementation process is also very complicated and runs the risk of escalated costs if not done properly. Some of the major considerations in the process are as follows:

- Provide central, first-level support that encourages common standards and central control over versions and upgrades. Gillette, for example, has three separate daytime shifts in centers located in the United States, Europe, and East Asia.

- If possible, use an internal team to implement the software with the vendor's technical consultants. They already know the business and will be trained to support user needs once the software is implemented.

- Use change management practices to ensure cooperation from local managers whose responsibilities change due to the shift to central decision making.

- Quantify planned business benefits in order to justify the high costs of a global standardization project.

than paper being shuffled around the globe. Processes directly involving managers can greatly enhance cross-country coordination. The least formal approach is to have regular *global meetings*. Holding global groups and forums allows exchange of information and building of relationships across countries. This in turn makes it easier for country nationals to gain an understanding of whether the differences they perceive between their home country and others are real or imagined. It also facilitates the development of common products and the coordination of marketing approaches. While these meetings can be costly in travel time and expense, ways can be found to reduce such costs. For example, management training programs can be set up to double as global forums if participants are drawn from geographically mixed locations.

A more formal, and increasingly adopted, approach is to set up *global teams* (or regional, e.g., European, teams). These teams can take responsibility for specific programs or for all of the global strategy. A French manufacturer of security devices uses councils of country managers, with different countries playing the lead role for different products. While this approach is time-consuming, the company has found that this re-

3M's EUROPEAN TEAM

3M uses "European Management Action Teams," one for each of its 50 product lines. Each team has eight to 14 members representing many functions and different countries and is chaired by a Brussels-based product manager. The teams help to translate global strategic plans into pan-European business plans, and then into action plans for the subsidiaries; and to make decisions about resource allocation, performance targets, and subsidiary investment.

liance on line managers makes it easier for various countries to accept the input of other countries, and thus for global approaches to be pursued by all.[25]

In setting up the coordination process, top management needs to set a balance between doing too much and too little at the start. On the one hand, it is very tempting to appoint a powerful coordinator or even "czar." But such an appointment can immediately stimulate resistance from subsidiary managers who feel threatened by the new appointment. On the other hand, setting up a coordination committee with a weak leader where the real power lies with subsidiary managers can lead to little action.[26]

Going further, a business can appoint *global product managers* or *global account managers*. Although adding such managers might be viewed as a change in organization structure, their roles are typically more that of coordination. In both cases the global product managers or global account managers perform similar roles on a global (or regional) scale to those performed by their national equivalents.

Armstrong World Industries, a leading U.S.-based manufacturer of flooring and other building materials, established cross-country planning and management teams for those businesses where a global perspective is important. Team members are drawn from existing personnel of the parent company and its subsidiaries. These team members meet periodically to develop worldwide business plans that include the setting of strategic business choices, product development priorities, planning capital expenditures, and developing human resources.

GLOBAL KNOWLEDGE SHARING

Many argue that the main source of competitive advantage for multinational companies is being able to share knowledge and learn across their geographic subsidiaries. To benefit from global innovation, creativity, and superior customer service, vital knowledge and information from any part of the company should be systematically captured and made accessible in real time to all parts of the company around the world.[27] Being able to transfer knowledge can also be the most important determinant of subsidiary success.[28] But research to date shows the great difficulty in managing and transferring knowledge.[29]

GLOBAL STRATEGIC PLANNING

Multinational companies and their subsidiaries are now quite skilled at developing *corporate* and *national* strategic plans.[30] But most have yet to develop *global* strategic

HOW GENERAL ELECTRIC SHARES KNOWLEDGE

General Electric uses many methods to share global knowledge.[31] The company:

- Uses written and live case studies in its development program from many countries
- Deploys best-practice teams to codify best practices that can then be shared
- Uses groupware technology to connect people from different countries to share ideas
- Transfers people from one country to another either permanently or on temporary assignments to transfer knowledge

plans that integrate the strategies of the same business in different countries, let alone integrating strategies across multiple worldwide businesses. Too often, strategic plans are developed separately for each country and then summed to add up the numbers. But no real strategic integration has been planned. Failure to plan across countries makes it difficult to understand the business's competitive position worldwide and difficult to develop integrated strategic responses to competitors who do plan on a global basis.[32] This makes it difficult to design and implement global programs that need the cooperation of several countries. Ideally, there should be a global strategic planning process that involves the senior management from key countries and regions. Such a process would fit in with the corporate and national strategic planning cycles. Whether the global strategic planning process should precede or follow the national planning processes is less important than that it should be done at all. (Extensive research on formal strategic planning has shown that it needs to use a multilevel and multistage process. Agreement needs to be sought between levels—corporate, business, and function—at each of three stages—objective setting, program formulation, and budgeting—in contrast to a one-stage process in which the corporate level sets objectives and the business in turn responds with a complete plan that is a *fait accompli*.[33] For global strategic planning, a similar process can be used that involves corporate, global, and national levels.)

A key benefit of any strategic planning process is that it brings in the views of those who might not otherwise be heard. Such a benefit doubly applies in global strategic planning: It brings in the views of units that may be geographically distant but strategically critical. As the head of a multinational computer equipment business said, "Having a global strategic planning process helps give the 'outlanders' some say."

Having a formal global strategic plan provides a way to put teeth into cross-country coordination processes. Instead of coordinating with no particular end objective, managers in the different countries have to work together in producing the global plan. A global strategic plan needs to contain the usual plan information expressed at a global level. But, in addition, the global plan needs to contain strategies and programs that cut across countries and are, thus, inherently difficult to formulate without a cross-country planning effort.

GLOBAL BUDGETING

Having global strategies and programs implies having global budgets to implement them. Adding up the country budgets into a global total for each product line provides a first step in global resource allocation.[34] Surprisingly few companies do this thoroughly. Many companies do not even know how much profit they make worldwide in a particular business. Typically, the profit contribution is spread across many national and regional accounts. Most alarming is that many managers believe that the global numbers are readily available only to find otherwise when asked to produce them.

Beyond knowing the global numbers, companies need to do three other, difficult, things:

- First, companies need to be able to transfer resources from one country to another in order to be able to subsidize across countries. Such strategic subsidization is a crucial requirement of global strategy. But the accounting system frequently interferes with such efforts. For example, many companies set transfer prices rigidly. So, these companies cannot provide lower prices to countries that need them in order to strengthen their competitive position as part of the global strategy. If making a strategic move means incurring red ink, then many subsidiary managers will decline the invitation to participate in the global strategy. Some companies have found ways to have *flexible transfer pricing*—particularly where there is the opportunity to reduce taxes. Flexible transfer pricing includes the use of different margins and allows for different rates at which capital equipment is amortized.[35] So why not be flexible for the sake of global competitiveness? *Companies should not allow their accounting systems to prevent them from having a global strategy.*

- The second difficult accounting task is to cost out these activities in a globally neutral way. For example, as one executive put it, the French subsidiary should not be charged a low price for raw materials just because the plant it buys from happens to be in France. Thus the global budgeting process needs to provide for *geographically neutral costs* as the base point. These prices can then be adjusted as strategically necessary.

- The third difficult accounting task is to have *global budgets* that are available only for global programs. Typically, budgets are controlled by national and regional managers with limited amounts left to corporate. The drive against overhead has made large corporate budgets highly unpopular. But budgets for global programs do not provide for overhead. Instead, they can fund strategically vital activities, such as developing global products or subsidizing attacks on global competitors. Such activities are typically difficult for individual countries, or even regions, to undertake. Global budgets can provide a pot of money or "war chest" that managers with ideas for global activities can apply for. But protecting global budgets can be very difficult. Executives in one division of a diversified *Fortune* 500 company were worried that if they created a global budget for strategic contingencies, the money would be appropriated by corporate "the next day."

At its most extreme a global accounting system would charge companies the same cost for materials and products regardless of where they were shipped from. One of the largest companies in the world, a U.S.-based chemical company, is attempting to use

AT&T GLOBAL CUSTOMERS

In the telecommunications industry, customers are demanding service guarantees and smooth transitions to new technologies.[36] AT&T identifies global (business) customers as those who require worldwide services. AT&T provides its global customers with special services including a single point of contact for domestic and international operations (all operations handled by one party) and consistent worldwide service. The services AT&T provides to its global customers may differ, however, from country to country due to government regulations. Unlike in the advertising or computer industries, marketing plays a minor role in AT&T's approach to global account management. Once a sale is made, the sales manager provides only a limited amount of account service and support. The actual management of an account is handled by another party who is exclusively devoted to service.

such a transfer price approach. But the company has found its cost accounting system so inflexible that it has to make adjustments by hand in the businesses taking this approach. Executives at this company estimate that it will probably take them five to seven years to change the accounting system.

GLOBAL CUSTOMER MANAGEMENT

As discussed in Chapters 2 and 6, managing customers on a global basis has become increasingly necessary. Being able to do so effectively is in many ways a real test of a global company. It means that the company has to be able to deploy its resources and processes to serve global customers on an integrated and coordinate basis around the world. As discussed in Chapter 6, Hewlett-Packard's global account management program requires changes in all aspects of its organization.

Global key account management plays a critical part in ABB's matrix organization system. Each global account is managed by a global key account (GKA) executive, supported by a GKA team. Each team member represents its business area, company, or country. The team concerns itself with such issues as the global structure for dealing with the customer, major investments needed to serve the customer across regions and businesses, increasing sales potential, and running a centrally coordinated decision process.[37]

GLOBAL PERFORMANCE REVIEW AND COMPENSATION

The last and, in many ways, most important global management process involves the way in which managers are evaluated and rewarded. Getting these systems to support global strategy can go a long way to offsetting deficiencies in the other systems. If the financial reporting system cannot be changed, managers can still be motivated to undertake loss-incurring strategic actions if they are evaluated and rewarded appropriately. So, rewards, especially bonuses, need to be set in a way that reinforces the company's global objectives. If not, the global strategy never takes off. For example, an electronics manufacturer decided to start penetrating the international market by introducing a new product through its strongest division. The division head's bonus was based on the current year's worldwide sales, with no distinction between domestic and international sales. Because increasing his domestic sales was a lot easier—and had a much quicker payoff—than trying to open up new international markets, the division head did not worry much about his international sales. Predictably, the firm's market penetration strategy failed.

Most companies seem to have a long way to go. The head of international marketing and sales for an industrial controls business viewed the lack of global performance review as a major problem. To help remedy this defect, the company moved to basing a portion of incentive compensation for global team members on worldwide achievement. The head of business planning for a computer equipment company found that the difficulty of getting product managers to think globally was exacerbated by the lack of global reward systems. So it was all too common to not take the global job requirements as seriously as the domestic ones. Indeed, this executive believed that the product managers would like to be measured on a global basis and were willing to take their chances on that. In the same business, the director of international strategic planning also viewed the lack of global compensation as a major weak spot.

The last example shows the importance of rewarding those with global responsibility for global performance. Going further, companies also need to find ways to reward managers for performance in geographic areas *beyond their immediate control,* but that are influenced by their actions. Country managers need to be rewarded not just on the basis of their country's performance but on that of their region or the world. Thus, the French country manager needs to be given incentive to help and cooperate with the German country manager, and the German with the Italian. Performance review and compensation should depend not just on a manager's performance in his or her own region but on the performance of the rest of business globally, evaluations by global business managers, evaluations by managers of other regions, and the achievement of global objectives (e.g., the introduction of particular products into region, implementation of a global program, or creation of a information system to report back to headquarters).

GETTING GLOBAL COOPERATION

Each of the methods just described has the common aim of getting global cooperation. Each company has to find what works best for a particular business at a particular time. Typically, using multiple methods reinforces the benefits, as shown in the following example. Even as entrepreneurial a business as the music and recording industry has some need for global strategy. A leading multinational music company uses three different approaches for globalizing its programs. First, the company uses direction, by insisting on global adoption in the case of new albums by already established international recording stars. In the case of real superstars, the insistence is unspoken. National managers just know that they will get into serious trouble if they do not adopt the album. In other cases, a committee of regional heads agrees on artists and albums as global priorities, which all countries must then introduce. Unfortunately, getting agreement is seldom easy. Second, individual countries ("exporters") use flexible budgets to set up inducements for other countries ("importers") to adopt their national stars, by paying for such expenses as airfare and other tour and promotional expenses that would normally be the responsibility of the importers. Third, the company simply relies on voluntary adoption in other cases. This last approach has had its failures. When asked, each national manager was able to cite instances in which other countries incorrectly failed to adopt one of his or her artists or had waited too long, thereby missing the boat in this fast-changing business.

PEOPLE

Global strategy can be implemented only by the people in the organization. Developing managers and other members of the organization to think and behave globally requires many of the policies used by successful multinational companies, but it also needs to go beyond that. In particular, the "United Nations" model of multinational management has favored having local nationals take over all positions in their countries. But in the extreme, such an approach reduces the benefit from executives having experience in many countries. The ideal human resource policy for global strategy provides a mix of different national backgrounds represented in the management of each country's business. And in further violation of the United Nations spirit of equality, it is executives from globally strategic countries who should be favored for global careers. It is more important to spread their experience globally from these key countries than that of executives from strategically marginal countries. So while it might be easier to move a native of Liechtenstein around the world, it might help the global strategy more to move a Japanese.

In the early stages of internationalization, companies tend to rely on expatriates, while in the multilocal stage, companies aim to have as many local managers as possible. The global stage requires a balance of global, regional, and national managers. A global network can be operated if many members have had international experience and also have many interpersonal connections and shared experiences. Furthermore, individuals can take different roles at different stages of their career or family life cycle. Global companies need to invest in building a portfolio of needed capabilities, not just in technical or business terms but in terms of language and cultural capabilities and types of international experience. Japanese and Korean companies may find it difficult to incorporate foreign nationals into their management systems, but they also invest heavily in preparing their own nationals for foreign assignments. Samsung puts executives through a one-year program before they are sent abroad and also spends two months debriefing them upon return at its Global Management Institute. Statoil, the Norwegian oil company, finds that many of its international opportunities lie in Central Asia. Few Norwegians speak the languages of Kazakhstan or Uzbekistan! Perhaps it should fund students in Norwegian schools to learn those languages.

The development of global leaders requires the creation of an environment that fosters and promotes cooperation across borders, free exchange of information, and the development of creative managers capable of functioning effectively anywhere in the world.[38] Necessary programs include:

- Establishing successful leadership development programs for global organizations
- Empowering managers with the flexibility and creativity to transform and apply best practices on a global scale
- Strong commitment to recognizing, hiring, developing, and nurturing managers with the greatest global leadership potential
- Maintaining practices to encourage managers to boost global awareness, multicultural, and multilinguistic skills

DEVELOPING GLOBAL LEADERS

AMP, the U.S. producer of electrical connectors and related products, began an extensive program in 1992 to develop what it called "globe-able leaders."[39] These leaders must "demonstrate notable mastery of identified global business skills, and the internationalization of key globalization concepts, and global competitive and organizational dynamics as well as be able to function effectively corporate-wide anywhere in the world." AMP managers receive a variety of development programs that stress "global perspectives, knowledge base and skill sets" and are expected to remain current in global leadership areas from an extensive globe-able bibliography.[40]

General Electric's Medical Systems Group instituted its Global Leadership Program, a multiyear process in which selected managers from around the world devise an organized framework to solve problems on important global projects such as improving worldwide engineering productivity, sharing technical expertise, and a common strategy for a network of suppliers. One team is working on a worldwide employee integration plan to increase commitment and a sense of belonging.[41]

Unilever rotates managers through various jobs and moves them around the world, especially early in their careers. The company maintains four development lists that indicate the level of each manager and his or her potential. The progress of managers on the top "A1" list is tracked by Unilever's Special Committee, which includes the two chairmen, whose responsibility in part is to develop and nurture talented managers by providing opportunities for achievement, such as handling negotiations in a worldwide context.[42]

Colgate-Palmolive gives executives short-term assignments overseas to boost their global awareness; Aetna Insurance and Electrolux rotate managers between domestic and international assignments.[43]

USE OF FOREIGN NATIONALS

High-potential foreign nationals need to gain experience not just in their home country but at headquarters and in other countries. This practice has three benefits. It broadens the pool of talent available for executive positions, it visibly shows the commitment of top management to internationalization, and it gives talented individuals an irreplaceable development opportunity. U.S. companies have been slow to do this, particularly at the most senior ranks. Promoting foreigners, and using staff from various countries, has often paid off.

A French packaged goods manufacturer undertook some years ago to move its European staff from country to country. Today, of 15 staff working at headquarters, seven are French, three are English, three are German, and two are Italian. The company credits this practice, among others, for its remarkable turnaround. It can be particularly helpful to move national managers to headquarters early in their careers. The plastics division of a major U.S. chemical company has implemented a plan for moving foreign executives to headquarters early in their careers, placing them in market manager positions. These positions are ideal as they provide broad strategic exposure to the business in the home country but do not have direct selling responsibility, which typically poses the greatest cultural barriers. Companies should also use non–home country nationals not just at headquarters but in other countries as well. Indeed, companies should ideally never use the term "foreign national" or even "home country." American

ABB'S GLOBAL MANAGERS

A key success factor for ABB is the presence of a core group of global managers at the top of the organization.[44] These managers are remarkably open-minded and appreciate the differences between countries and cultures. The development of such managers is critical to the success of any global organization and can be done by rotating employees through line experience in multiple countries to gain a global perspective. ABB advocates strict decentralization. The company offers its managers the maximum degree of autonomy as well as well-defined accountability. In addition, the organization at the top is structured to facilitate quick decision making.

companies could refer to "non-U.S. nationals"; Japanese companies to "non-Japanese nationals" rather than to "gaijins"; and so on. Percy Barnevik would levy a fine of $10 on anyone at ABB's headquarters who used the word "foreign."

A global company also needs to have the courage and common sense to override local objections to foreigners. National managers are often nervous about bringing foreigners into their country. One of the more extreme examples concerns an American multinational professional services company. Its senior European managers recently held a meeting to select a new country manager for the Netherlands. When a Spanish manager was suggested, the Dutch executive present objected that Spain used to rule the Netherlands, so a Spaniard would not be welcome. Surprised, an American executive asked when that rule was. The Dutchman replied: "About four hundred years ago, but the Spanish are still very much resented." This objection was overruled, and the Spanish manager was appointed without subsequent problems.

MULTICOUNTRY CAREERS

Making work experience in different countries a necessity for progression, rather than a hindrance, is another important step that helps a company become truly global. An electronics manufacturer decided to make a major push into Japan, but a middle-level executive offered a transfer there was loathe to take it. He was concerned whether there would be a job for him when he came back. As he put it, "The road to the executive suite lies through Chicago, not Osaka." In contrast, Jacques Maisonrouge, the former head of IBM World Trade (then IBM's international arm), initiated a policy that no executive could rise to a general manager position without having taken a foreign assignment beforehand. Using home country nationals overseas has been a very common practice. Increasing costs of relocation and the problems of moving dual-career couples have made this more difficult. But companies need to take a longer term view of the benefits from such placements. Companies have to be willing to pay the cost of transferring executives around the world. A senior executive in a large American multinational company did not see the flaw in his company's position that it would pay American executives transferred overseas the higher of the American or local rate, but had trouble getting Swiss executives to come to the United States because of the lower American pay.

Percy Barnevik implemented many innovative global human resource management (HRM) practices at ABB.[45] He required that all employees read a short booklet that outlines company objectives and values, and he has made English the company language. In addition, he maintains a small headquarters staff that supervises the entire organization. An executive committee from different regions of the world, as well as a select number of global managers, supports the thin core. The global managers must be experienced and willing to move with their families. Their responsibilities include the transfer of expertise around the world, the task of keeping the organization closely bound together, and the continuous communication to leadership of different perspectives from the field.

To encourage multicountry careers, companies may need to set tough rules such as the following:

- No advancement occurs beyond a certain level without two years outside the home country of the national.
- Transfers occur at an early stage of a manager's career.
- A target of all positions at a certain level and above held by nonnationals is set at 10 percent.
- The best performers get transferred overseas.
- Transferees are guaranteed a position back home, but its level depends on performance overseas.
- Veterans of foreign assignments get job preference.
- The human resources department tracks and takes responsibility for the careers of overseas transferees.

Using foreign nationals and multicountry careers has the important additional benefit of gradually creating a group of subsidiary managers who are likely to be more sympathetic to global strategy. As managers gain multicountry experience, they are less likely to focus on the unique differences of the particular country in which they operate and more able to appreciate the benefits of also looking for global commonality. This greater sympathy for global strategy becomes more important as the role of subsidiary managers changes with globalization—from that of running their own show to that of integrating into a larger global effort.[46]

FREQUENT TRAVEL

Senior managers must spend a large amount of time in foreign countries. The CEO of a large grocery products company spends half his time outside the United States—a visible demonstration of the importance and commitment of the company to its international operations. Also important, senior managers should spend more of their time in the strategically important countries rather than in countries with operational difficulties but that are not important in the global strategy. Such countries represent black holes for senior management time.

STATEMENTS AND ACTIONS OF LEADERS

The senior management of a company that wants to globalize its strategy needs to constantly restate that intention and to act in accordance with it. Otherwise, the rank and file will not believe that the globalization strategy is for real. One test among many is

HOW ROYAL DUTCH/SHELL GROUP ENCOURAGES EXPATRIATE ASSIGNMENTS

With more than 5,500 expatriates of 70 nationalities located in more than 100 countries around the globe, Shell recognizes the importance of making its employees internationally mobile and implementing an expatriate program.[47] Shell's human resource managers sensed that there were problems discouraging candidates from accepting international assignments. In 1993, the organization conducted the "Outlook Survey," a wide-reaching internal survey that was successful in determining which stumbling blocks in Shell's expatriate program were the most problematic. The resulting underlying message was that "the family is the basic unit of expatriation, and Shell could do more to show that it recognized this." The two issues that emerged as key detractors from international mobility were the separation from children during secondary education and the loss of a spouse's and partner's careers. Shell's HR managers assembled six task forces in 1994 to look closely at these concerns.

Policy changes and programs implemented based on the results of the survey include the following: Shell instituted two options for elementary school children—build a company school and, where the numbers aren't feasible, strengthen existing ones. For secondary education, Shell supports the Swiss-based International Baccalaureate Organization[48] and contributes $50,000 annually to ensure that a growing number of high-quality schools are available to its employees around the world. The company maintains a database of 11,000 volunteers made up of families who have agreed to discuss informally their experiences with another family about to relocate to an area where they have lived. And finally, spousal support programs include vocational assistance for job search fees, professional skills management, course fees, and career counseling. Since the implementation of programs such as these, Shell "experiences less resistance from first choice candidates to accepting assignments."

the prominence given to international operations in formal communications such as the chairman's letter in the annual report or statements to stock analysts.

GLOBAL BOARDS OF DIRECTORS

Another increasingly important test of globalization is the extent to which the board of directors has been globalized. A global company must have a board that reflects its global operations. Excellence in global governance and leadership means getting the best top executives and board members from anywhere in the world. Few of even the largest multinational companies have representation of all continents on their boards, even though nonexecutive directors provide an easy source of such expertise. Companies that cannot quickly change their legal boards are instituting global advisory boards as a first step at tapping into a broader global base of advice. Japanese companies have found it particularly hard to change their boards. Sony has been an exception to the rule. The company has heavily recruited non-Japanese, added outside directors to its board, and created regional boards that include local nationals. Portugal's innovative Sonae group has set up global advisory boards to help its globalization strategies.

GLOBAL COMPANIES NEED TRANSNATIONAL MANAGERS

The 1990s saw companies shift decision-making authority from regional or geographic structures to "global" product divisions.[49] Ford consolidated its separate worldwide operations into five program centers each responsible for all product development efforts. IBM recognized the need to be responsive to customer segments with similar needs in different locations and restructured its sales and marketing organization from a geographic focus to one focused on industry-specific needs. Even companies as diverse as Philips, ABB, Honda, and Mitsubishi Electric have combated the common need to coordinate complex activities by setting up cross-national task forces and breaking down operations into small units with global responsibilities. The common dilemma has been to balance the need for a global approach with local demands.

Global companies have responded by transferring best practices throughout their organizations and by nurturing global managers who are sensitive to different cultures, have a better understanding of the global business environment, and are armed with language and communication skills to work effectively in multicultural teams. Companies are responsible for developing "*trans*patriates," rather than expatriates, and are putting systems into place that offer their managers international experience. At Squibb, the decision to hire the head of the Chinese language department at Cornell, with none of the pertinent technical experience, to head its new subsidiary in Shanghai proved to be a success. His knowledge of the language and culture coupled with the strong support of a U.S. staff produced a winning team. Even top U.S. corporations such as Ford, Coca-Cola, Citibank, Salomon Brothers, Compaq, Intel, 3M, and Apple have seen an increase in the number of foreign-born CEOs.

LEADING TO MAKE NESTLÉ MORE GLOBAL[50]

In the early 1980s Nestlé was commonly viewed as a sluggish and reserved albeit global giant in the food industry tightly controlled by its predominantly Swiss management. Feeling the pressures of competition in the early 1990s from rivals such as Procter & Gamble and Philip Morris Nestlé's German-born chairman, Helmut Maucher, recognized the need to restructure Nestlé's conservative, centralized bureaucracy. He transformed the top ranks at Nestlé, and now the company's executive board resembles "a mini-U.N. that conducts business in English." He reduced the power held by the headquarters bureaucrats and pushed it down to globally minded operating executives of the company's seven strategic business units. Nestlé also initiated a program to move rising managers around Europe and insisted that all management trainees be at least bilingual. The result was 80 executives who "react like Europeans rather than Germans or French."

CULTURE

Culture is the most subtle aspect of organization, but it can play a formidable role in helping or hindering a global strategy.

BUILDING A GLOBAL IDENTITY AT READER'S DIGEST

Reader's Digest made a strategic shift in the 1990s to become a global organization.[51] It now uses intensive training programs, the sharing of ideas across continents, and the immersion of local talent in the organization's corporate values and strong culture. Reader's Digest makes a very conscious effort to keep a global perspective in its communications. Semantics that infer arrogance by U.S. offices—such as using the words "domestic," "abroad," and "overseas"—are avoided. This helps create a sense of equality and fairness within the organization.

GLOBAL IDENTITY

A strong national identity can hinder the willingness and ability to design global products and programs. It can also create a "them or us" split among employees. One firm was making a strong global push, and yet many of its corporate executives wore national flag pins! European companies are generally well in advance of both American and Japanese firms in adopting a global identity. Having multiple national identities—a different one in each country—is more international than having just the identity of the home country, but it is not global. Instead a truly global culture would transcend the nationality of the home and other countries.[52] At the same time, each national business still needs to be rooted in its local culture, or at least some of the executives, depending on their jobs, need such roots. Building a global identity is helped if nationalistic displays are avoided. Similarly, it helps if important meetings are not always held in the home country. Having foreign nationals on the corporate board also helps foster a global identity as well as bringing the substantive knowledge of these board members.

Percy Barnevik of ABB had probably the best comment on culture: "We need to be sensitive to national cultures, but not paralyzed by them."

Partly to help foster a global identity, Procter & Gamble now seeks to instill a global perspective in all of its employees. P&G wants to establish the mindset of seeing the world as the company's marketplace. To do so, P&G is cultivating two attitudes in its people. The first is to search for ideas that can be applied to its business around the world. The second is to find reapplications for good ideas that have already been developed. In 1990, P&G made another major commitment to globalization when the company appointed as its new chief executive the head of its international division—jumping him over a more senior executive in the U.S. business.

COMMITMENT TO WORLDWIDE NOT DOMESTIC EMPLOYMENT

Many companies view their domestic employees as somehow more important than their foreign employees and are much more committed to preserving domestic employment than to developing employment regardless of location. This often leads them to decide to keep expensive manufacturing operations in the home country rather than relocate them in lower cost countries—thereby putting them at a competitive cost disadvantage and threatening their overall competitive position. Of course, there may be

BUILDING A GLOBAL CULTURE IN
CROSS-BORDER MERGERS

As companies undertake more cross-border mergers, creating a combined global culture in the aftermath is becoming a major challenge. In recent years, BP Amoco and DaimlerChrysler have faced these issues, and cross-cultural problems in the latter merger are cited as one of the major causes of the disastrous performance of Chrysler after the merger. In contrast, the BP Amoco merger went much more smoothly, perhaps because BP had already moved to an American-style business culture.

Pharmacia & Upjohn suffered major cultural drawbacks that offset the expected synergies of its merger.[53] After the merger of these two companies—with headquarters located in different countries (the United States and Sweden) and operations located in a third country (Italy)—communications problems slowed coordinated product launch efforts, the departure of top researchers reduced R&D efforts, and cultural tensions forced the resignation of the former chief executive. Executives struggled to create a hybrid of management styles and work policies that do not emanate from nationalistic overtones. Although the merger cut costs by approximately $200 million, refocused research operations, and strengthened the balance sheet, the company suffered overall.

The issue of the company headquarters exemplified the difficulties in forming a global company out of two medium-sized companies. Although the newly formed company had to be registered in the United States, both Swedish and Italian executives feared that a U.S.-headquartered company would wrest control from Europe. A compromise solution was to create a "global center for a global company." London was picked as the new site. The new structure proved to be a disaster. The extra layer of management slowed approvals, product launches, and staffing decisions; and the London staff became frustrated with the cultural differences of the separate branches. Work rules such as drug testing, summer vacation conflicts, and computer incompatibilities made coordination very difficult for London staffers.

More evident, though, were the different management styles and business practices that slowed progress. In Sweden, big decisions are made by gaining an entire group's approval, and the Swedish open system allows for small teams to be left on their own. The American approach clashed with this system. Upjohn's culture kept managers on a tight leash, requiring frequent updates and reports on the separate business units. The Italian system, however, proved to be the most volatile. The Italians had a hierarchical structure, placed a higher value on families, recorded inaccurate data and accounting history, and had confusing laws. The many conflicting practices ultimately made simple tasks more complicated. Consequently, senior executives have had to take cultural differences and practices much more seriously.

good defensive reasons for maintaining higher cost facilities in the home country. But cultural bias should not be one of them.

INTERDEPENDENCE OF BUSINESSES

A culture of local business autonomy, when carried too far, can also be a barrier to globalization. The culture needs to balance the celebration of autonomy with the recognition of interdependence. Achieving such a balance is not easy. Country managers are masters at ignoring directives from the head office. Like Admiral Nelson at the Battle of Copenhagen, they delight in putting the telescope to their blind eye. Top management can help foster a sense of country interdependence by educating staff in each country, particularly the home country, about achievements of operations in other countries.

MATCHING CULTURE TO GLOBALIZATION NEEDS

Companies pursuing global strategy need to develop not just a generally favorable culture but also specific cultural characteristics to support specific strategies. A large U.S. manufacturing company's culture included the following characteristics:

- A high degree of responsiveness to customers' requests for product tailoring
- A strong emphasis on letting every business and every country be highly autonomous
- A desire for 100 percent control over foreign operations
- A commitment to preserving domestic employment

Not surprisingly, the company found it very difficult to implement a global strategy. Senior management was able to understand its difficulties more clearly only after it spelled out the cultural change implications in global strategy. Specifically, the CEO came to realize that rapidly implementing a pure global strategy would require an organizational revolution. In contrast, a culturally less risky option would be to make a series of incremental changes in both strategy and organization, leading to a mixed strategy of globalization and national responsiveness. The CEO also considered an explicit rejection of globalization, which would require a conscious decision to build on the company's existing organizational and cultural characteristics to develop a pure national responsiveness strategy. Thinking through these cultural implications helped the company to make fundamental and realistic choices rather than assuming the unavoidable dominance of strategy over organization and of globalization over national responsiveness. Aided by this analysis, the company chose the second, mixed option of incremental change and has had satisfying results to date.

MINIMIZING THE DRAWBACKS OF GLOBAL ORGANIZATION

Globalization can incur organizational as well as strategic drawbacks. Costs may rise because of increased coordination, reporting requirements, and even added staff. Globalization can also reduce management effectiveness in individual countries if overcentralization hurts local motivation and morale. But some approaches can minimize these problems. Costs can be held down if new global functions replace rather than add to national functions. When a manufacturer of chemical and refining process equipment reorganized its separate European businesses into one, the company was able to eliminate some of the general management and administrative support positions. Those savings more than paid for the positions related to the new office of the general manager for Europe.

Political infighting can be minimized if global responsibilities are shared by many executives, each of whom retains some national (regional) roles. The "two hat" approach is particularly helpful. For example, the general manager of one country takes on the role of global marketing chief, while the general manager of another country becomes the global manufacturing chief. So each executive has to cooperate with the other. Resentment of headquarters can be assuaged if lead responsibilities get spread around the world. Thus different countries can be given the lead for different strategic thrusts.[54] Companies may even go so far as to relocate business headquarters out of the home country. IBM recently took this step, moving the management of its worldwide telecommunications business from the United States to Europe. Lastly, headquarters executives should try to be psychologically equidistant from any part of the world, making decisions on the basis of strategic advantage rather than emotional attachment.[55]

EFFECTS OF THE INTERNET ON GLOBAL ORGANIZATION

The Internet is just starting to change the ways in which global companies organize and manage. As with global strategy levers, the Internet should make it easier for companies to be both global and local. The Internet certainly improves global coordination, the running of global teams, and the global sharing of information. As yet we do not know whether the Internet will also affect global organization structures, but the potential is there. The Internet and the Web are consolidating the dominance of the global network as the dominant model of multinational companies for the foreseeable future.[56] This model seeks to reduce duplication of activities. As an electronic network, the Web, through both intranets and extranets, offers the potential to complete this process of de-duplication. This model is, therefore, also ideal for Internet-based new-economy companies, many of which are "born global."

COMBINING STRATEGIC AND ORGANIZATIONAL ANALYSIS

In sum, the four organization factors—organization structure, management processes, people, and culture—play a key role in facilitating or hindering a company's move toward globalization. For example, take a company with a strong structural split between domestic and international activities, management processes that are country-driven rather than business-driven, people who work primarily in their home countries, and a parochial culture. Implementing global strategy in the company is likely to prove exceedingly difficult. If the analysis of industry globalization drivers has shown that such strategies are necessary for market, cost, or competitive reasons, top managers need to make a tough choice. Either they undertake a major change effort aimed at making the internal environment better adapted to the strategic moves the company needs to make, or they have to decide that the profound organizational changes needed to adopt a global strategy are too risky and that the company should avoid globalization and compete based on its existing organizational strengths.

This chapter ends with two examples of how to combine the analysis of all three elements in the globalization triangle: industry globalization drivers, global strategy levers, and global organization capability. The examples come from the experiences of two companies, both of them multi-billion-dollar multinationals. One company, disguised as TransElectronics, is a U.S.-based concern operating in many aspects of electronics. The other company, disguised as Persona, is a European-based manufacturer and marketer of consumer packaged goods. The two companies provide different views of the challenge of global strategy. TransElectronics is still developing as a fully multinational company and faces the challenge of accelerating that process to become a global competitor. Persona, on the other hand, has long been thoroughly multinational, with many highly autonomous companies operating around the world. Its challenge is to temper some aspects of that multinational autonomy in order to compete more effectively on a global basis.

TRANSFORMING TRANSELECTRONICS

The communications sector of TransElectronics had one division, Electron, based in the United States, that sold "transcramblers" against fierce European and Japanese competition. A major market, Japan, closed until recently to foreign competition, was beginning to open through a combination of TransElectronics' efforts and U.S. government pressure on Japanese trade barriers. So developing a global strategy for transcramblers was a high priority for TransElectronics. A complication was that Electron was not a stand-alone business unit: Other units had related responsibilities. As will be described, this split of responsibilities was one of the major barriers to Electron's implementation of a global strategy.

Analyzing Industry Globalization Potential

Electron's managers were unsure as to how much potential for globalization there was in the transcrambler industry. A step-by-step analysis made this much clearer. First, *market* drivers pushed for globalization: There were few differences among countries in what they wanted from transcramblers. On the other hand, few global customers existed: National public sector telecommunications companies (PTTs) accounted for a large part of the market in each country. *Cost* drivers also strongly pushed for globalization: There were substantial scale economies and learning effects; sourcing efficiencies could be gained by consolidating manufacturing; and Electron's labor costs — a significant part of the product's total cost — were much lower in Puerto Rico and Taiwan than they were in the United States. *Government* drivers favored globalization: The privatization of some national PTTs was opening up previously closed markets, and products were becoming more standardized in Europe around a common format. An offsetting factor was local content requirements in many countries. Lastly, *competitive* forces were also pushing for globalization: Electron's major competitors (European and Japanese) took a global product approach with fewer price levels and with minimum product customization. The competitors had also largely centralized their manufacturing activities in just one or two countries each. In summary, strong external forces pushed the transcrambler industry to globalization. Not only was globalization already high, but it was likely to continue increasing.

Evaluating Use of Global Strategy

The Electron managers next evaluated how much the business actually used global strategy. Electron was quite global in its *market participation* — its sales split among countries closely matched that of the industry. Electron's *product line* was highly standardized — in fact, more than its executives realized. Electron's R&D and purchasing *activities* were specialized in the United States, but much of its manufacturing was dispersed across the United States, Puerto Rico, Taiwan, and Europe. *Marketing* was primarily done in the United States. Selling, distribution, and service were by necessity done locally, but were not at all coordinated across countries. Electron's competitors were all much more centralized and coordinated. The product positioning of transcramblers was consistent across countries, as was that of Electron's competitors. If anything, TransElectronics' marketing policies were too uniform, with a rigid pricing policy that did not allow Electron to adapt to the wide variations in price across countries. As a result, Electron did not use price as a strategic weapon. Lastly, Electron did not integrate its *competitive moves* across countries, but, fortunately, neither did its competitors.

From the previous analyses, the Electron managers concluded that their extent of globalization was significantly lower than the industry potential, and lower than that of their competitors. The industry potential for globalization was steadily increasing. It was clear that Electron had a strong need to develop a more global strategy than it had been pursuing. The next issue was whether Electron would be able to implement such a strategy.

Evaluating Organizational Capability

Having understood the strategic changes needed, the Electron managers now had to understand the organization factors that might affect implementation. They diagnosed that TransElectronics' *organization structure* worked in two major ways against a global strategy. First, TransElectronics operated with a strong domestic–international split within each sector. Second, worldwide responsibilities for Electron's business were scattered throughout the organization. The Electron division itself had responsibility for some product development, some manufacturing, and some marketing. Other divisions in the United States and overseas shared these responsibilities. Selling was the responsibility of both local non-U.S. countries and in the United States of a totally separate distribution group for the entire communications sector. In effect, there was no manager below the sector head who had global authority over transcramblers.

Management processes did not help global strategy much. The budget process worked against a global approach in that the Electron division budgeted only a total number for overseas sales, without country targets. The International Group in the communications sector set country quotas for the entire sector, without product quotas or product-by-country quotas. The strategic planning process did not help either: The Electron Division and the International Group developed separate plans simultaneously. In terms of compensation, there were no international components in the bonus formula for domestic managers. In addition, Electron's strategic information systems provided only spotty coverage of key markets and key competitors.

TransElectronics' use of *people* worked against a global approach. There were few foreign nationals in the United States at either corporate or divisional levels. There were many foreign nationals overseas, but these were mostly in their home countries, and there was little movement between international and domestic jobs. In particular, the U.S. divisions were reluctant to give up people, and overseas assignments were not seen as being a desirable career track.

Lastly, TransElectronics' corporate *culture* worked against a global view in both obvious and subtle ways. At the obvious level, TransElectronics was very much an American company with a "them-and-us" mentality. Indeed, the CEO had made speeches calling for increased trade barriers against Japanese firms. More subtly, TransElectronics had a very strong culture of being responsive to customer requests for product tailoring, born of a heritage of selling exclusively to a very small number of automotive customers. This culture worked strongly against attempts to standardize globally.

So, TransElectronics clearly had a very low organizational ability to develop a global strategy for transcramblers. It had certainly experienced many difficulties in its fitful attempts at doing so.

Changes Needed

The globalization analysis, just described, convinced the Electron managers that the most important business changes they had to make were to exploit more opportunities for product standardization and to specialize somewhat more as to where different activities (particularly manufacturing) were conducted. More widespread changes were needed in terms of management and organization. While many aspects of these needed to change, the most implementable change was in terms of management process. TransElectronics adopted for the transcrambler business a global strategic planning process and globally based evaluation and compensation. These relatively modest changes would pave the way for future acceptance of the more radical changes needed in organization structure, people, and culture.

REPOSITIONING PERSONA

Persona had operating companies around the world that sold many kinds of personal care as well as other household products. The global strategy analysis was conducted for one particular product, "hairfloss," that was sold worldwide.

Analyzing Industry Globalization Potential

Persona's managers had always assumed that there were major differences in customer needs and trade practices across countries, such that the hairfloss category did not have much globalization potential. But the systematic globalization analysis revealed some surprises. *Market* drivers pushed strongly for globalization: Market needs were very much the same around the world within income categories—higher income countries were earlier users of the new variants and ingredients that were introduced every few years. Brand names and advertising were also widely transferable: Some competitors used just one major brand name around the world and essentially the same advertising campaign. *Cost* drivers were less important, given that product costs were only about 25 percent of total costs, economies of scale were low, and price was not a major basis of competition. Also the low value-to-weight ratio of hairfloss made it uneconomical to ship it far. Nonetheless, there was some centralized manufacturing on a multicountry regional basis in parts of Western Europe, Southeast Asia, and Africa.

Government drivers did not particularly favor globalization. In Western Europe, however, the increasing importance of multicountry media, particularly satellite television with wide reception, and of the European Community pushed for regional, if not global, approaches. It was *competitive* behavior that was the major force pushing the industry to globalization. Persona faced three major worldwide competitors, multinationals like itself. Two of these competitors took a much more standardized approach than Persona: They concentrated their resources behind the same one or two brands of hairfloss in each country. In contrast, Persona tended to market three or four brands in each country, and furthermore, these brands were different among major countries. Persona's competitors were also quick to transfer successful innovations from one country to the next, while Persona's brand fragmentation hindered its efforts. This global fragmentation seemed to be a major reason behind Persona's slipping share and profitability.

Persona concluded that there were strong external forces pushing the hairfloss industry toward globalization—at least to the extent of requiring coordinated regional operations—and this push toward globalization was likely to increase in the future.

Evaluating Use of Global Strategy

Although Persona had plenty of market and competitive information from virtually all the countries in which it operated, its managers did not make much use of that information to evaluate its global, as opposed to national, strategies. Using this information for global purposes revealed a new view of the worldwide hairfloss business. Persona's *global market participation* was very strong: It sold hairfloss in markets that accounted for almost 90 percent of worldwide category volume (excluding communist countries). Its largest competitor participated in almost 100 percent. Persona's hairfloss *product line* was quite highly standardized around half a dozen variants. Persona generally marketed a larger number of variants in wealthier countries, but the variants were still basically the same across countries. Like most consumer packaged-goods multinationals, Persona practiced very little specialization of *activities* by country: It fielded a full business operation in most countries. In terms of *global marketing,* Persona was severely lacking because of its multiple brands, multiple product positionings, and multiple advertising campaigns. Lastly, Persona did not do much to integrate its competitive moves across countries, although it had recently begun to experiment with such attempts. Overall, Persona's actual extent of globalization was somewhat lower than that of its competitors.

While Persona's worldwide hairfloss strategy was quite global in some respects, it was the lack of global marketing that was the biggest problem. The key variables that Persona could operate on were brand name and positioning. First, to increase local marketing muscle, Persona needed to reduce the number of brands in each country to two. Second, to achieve the benefits of global market uniformity, they had three broad alternatives:

- A different brand but common positioning for each product variant in each country
- A common regional brand and positioning
- A common global brand and positioning

Because Persona already had strong brand names around the world that it did not want to abandon, and because a common positioning would achieve most of the benefits of uniformity, the company concluded that the second alternative was best. The next issue was whether Persona would be able to implement such a strategy.

Evaluating Organizational Capability

The Persona managers conducting the globalization analysis were the most discouraged by what they found about organization capability. Persona's *organization structure* made it very difficult to develop and implement a global strategy. Persona operated with a strong geographic structure that was overlaid with a worldwide product direction function at corporate. This function, however, had advisory rather than direct authority over the individual country businesses. Furthermore, the direction function did not include the United States. *Management processes* were of limited help. The budget and compensation systems worked against global strategy: These were done on a strictly local basis, although aggregated geographically. But there was no mechanism to encourage local participation in a worldwide effort. A strategic plan was developed globally, but local acceptance was voluntary. Persona did, however, have an excellent strategic information system. Each year the subsidiaries provided detailed and accurate data for products, markets, and competitors. For example, Persona knew how much each global competitor spent on advertising on each product category in each country and even had fairly accurate estimates of each competitor's profitability in each country. Persona also scored highly on the global capability of its people. Managers were drawn from all over the world, and transfers both among countries and to and from corporate were common. Culture was really the biggest organization barrier. Persona had a very strong culture of giving autonomy to its local managers. Although corporate increasingly wanted to give direct orders on strategy, the firm was loath to risk the possible loss of local accountability and commitment. So, like TransElectronics, Persona also had a low organizational capacity for global strategy, but for somewhat different reasons.

Changes Needed

As a result of the globalization analysis, Persona managers realized that the most important business changes they had to make in hairfloss were to reduce the number of brands in each country and develop a common brand by region and common positioning for each major product variant. Organizationally, it was too huge a disruption to change the structure. What was needed was a greater willingness by corporate to push for countries to adopt a global approach. A first step was a directive that all countries should launch the new "high-gloss" variant within a six-month period. Persona hoped that a successful experience of common action would start moving the culture toward greater acceptance of global strategies.

GUIDELINES FOR BUILDING THE GLOBAL ORGANIZATION

In building the global organization, managers should keep in mind the following guidelines:

- A global strategy cannot succeed in the face of organization barriers and resistance.
- Different aspects of organization—whether organization structure, management processes, people, or culture—will be more difficult to globalize depending on the history and circumstances of the company. Managers may find it best to work on the most easily changed aspects first, in order to prepare the way for the more difficult changes.
- As with the elements of global strategy, different aspects of organization can have different levels of being global.
- But globalization will not work fully unless all aspects of organization complement each other to support the desired global strategy.
- Changing the organization, particularly toward globalization, can take a great deal of time. Senior management needs to instill a sense of urgency to drive toward the desired changes.

CONCLUDING THOUGHTS

Global strategy in the twenty-first century sets very tough challenges for companies. They need to be globally excellent in nearly every activity and find the right balance of global, regional, and national solutions. This concept is best summed up in the philosophy at Beiersdorf: "As global as possible, as local as necessary." The global company does not have to be everywhere, but it has the capability to go anywhere, deploy any assets, and access any resources, and it maximizes profits on a global basis. Now global companies also need to do it all very fast—at Internet speed. And if they do not do all this, their competitors will. Globalization means there is no place to hide.

Discussion and Research Questions

1. What are the key elements of a global organization?
2. What are the ways in which organization structure can be used to implement global strategy?
3. What are the ways in which management processes can be used to implement global strategy?
4. What are the ways in which human resource policies can be used to implement global strategy?
5. What are the ways in which culture can be used to implement global strategy?
6. Select one company that has made significant changes in its organization in order to globalize. Describe and critique the changes that this company has made.
7. How can companies use the Internet to enable global organization and management?

Notes

1. This chapter is based in part on George S. Yip, Pierre M. Loewe, and Michael Y. Yoshino, "How to Take Your Company to the Global Market," *Columbia Journal of World Business,* Vol. 23, No. 4, Winter 1988, pp. 37–48. For a recent review of the academic literature on multinational organization, see D. Eleanor Westney and Srilata Zaheer, "The Multinational Enterprise as an Organization," in *The Oxford Handbook of International Business,* Alan M. Rugman and Thomas L. Brewer, Eds. (Oxford, England: Oxford University Press, forthcoming 2001), Chapter 13, pp. 349–79.

2. A stream of work has described and characterized this dilemma as the integration-responsiveness grid. See C. K. Prahalad, "The Strategic Process in a Multinational Corporation." Unpublished doctoral dissertation, Harvard Business School, 1975; C. K. Prahalad and Yves L. Doz, "An Approach to Strategic Control on MNCs," *Sloan Management Review,* Summer 1981, pp. 5–13; Yves L. Doz, Christopher A. Bartlett, and C. K. Prahalad, "Global Competitive Pressures vs. Host Country Demands: Managing Tensions in Multinational Corporations," *California Management Review,* Vol. 23, No. 3, 1981, pp. 63–74; C. K. Prahalad and Yves L. Doz, *The Multinational Mission: Balancing Local Demands and Global Vision* (New York: The Free Press, 1987).

3. The importance of global learning has been particularly stressed by Sumantra Ghoshal, "Global Strategy: An Organizing Framework," *Strategic Management Journal,* Vol. 8, No. 5, September–October 1987, pp. 425–40; and Christopher A. Bartlett and Sumantra Ghoshal, *Managing Across Borders: The Transnational Solution* (Boston: Harvard Business School Press, 1989). See also Anil K. Gupta and Vijay Govindarajan, "Knowledge Flows Within Multi-national Corporations," *Strategic Management Journal,* Vol. 21, No. 4, 2000, pp. 473–96; Karl Moore and Julian M. Birkinshaw, "Managing Knowledge in Global Service Firms: Centres of Excellence," *Academy of Management Executive,* December 1998; and Julian Birkinshaw, "Why Is Knowledge Management So Difficult?" *Business Strategy Review,* Vol. 12, No. 1, Spring 2001, pp. 11–18.

4. This view is particularly stressed in the literature on foreign direct investment, for example, John H. Dunning, "The Eclectic Paradigm of International Production: A Restatement and Some Possible Extensions," *Journal of International Business Studies,* Spring 1988, and on internalization theory, for example, Peter J. Buckley and Mark Casson, *The Future of the Multinational Enterprise* (New York: Holmes and Meier Publishers, Inc., 1976); Alan M. Rugman, *International Diversification and the Multinational Enterprise* (Lexington, MA: Lexington Books, D. C. Heath, 1979); and Peter J. Buckley, *The Theory of the Multinational Enterprise,* Acta Universitatis Upsaliensis, *Studia Oeconomiae Negotiorum* 26, Uppsala, Sweden, 1987. See also Henry P.

Conn and George S. Yip, "Global Transfer of Critical Capabilities," *Business Horizons,* Vol. 40, No. 1, January–February 1997, pp. 22–31.

5. This incremental approach to strategic change has been advocated by many management theorists. See, for example, C. E. Lindblom, *The Policy-Making Process* (Upper Saddle River, NJ: Prentice-Hall, 1968); Henry Mintzberg, *The Nature of Managerial Work* (New York: Harper & Row, 1973); and James Brian Quinn, "Strategic Goals: Process and Politics," *Sloan Management Review,* Fall 1977, p. 22.

6. Much early research on MNC management has confirmed the critical role of formal organization structure in influencing both parent and subsidiary strategy. Clee and di Scipio (1959) and Clee and Sachtjen (1964) were among the first to point out the shortcomings of the international structures adopted by MNCs and to recommend the implementation of global organization structures. See G. H. Clee and A. di Scipio, "Creating a World Enterprise," *Harvard Business Review,* November–December 1959, pp. 77–89; and G. H. Clee and W. M. Sachtjen, "Organizing a Worldwide Business," *Harvard Business Review,* November–December 1964, pp. 55–67. Fouraker and Stopford (1968), Stopford and Wells (1972), and Franko (1976) conducted a series of studies aimed at confirming Chandler's (1962) strategy-structure fit thesis with respect to international business, as did Egelhoff (1982 and 1988) and Daniels, Pitts, and Tretter (1984). See Lawrence E. Fouraker and John M. Stopford, "Organization Structure and Multinational Strategy," *Administrative Science Quarterly,* Vol. 13, 1968, pp. 57–70; John M. Stopford and Louis T. Wells, Jr., *Managing the Multinational Enterprise* (New York: Basic Books, 1972); and Larry G. Franko, *The European Multinationals* (Greenwich, CT: Greylock Press, 1976); Alfred D. Chandler, Jr., *Strategy and Structure* (Cambridge, MA: The M.I.T. Press, 1962); William G. Egelhoff, "Strategy and Structure in Multinational Corporations: An Information Processing Approach," *Administrative Science Quarterly,*

Vol. 27, 1982, pp. 435–58; ——, "Strategy and Structure in Multinational Corporations: A Revision of the Stopford and Wells Model," *Strategic Management Journal,* Vol. 9, 1988, pp. 1–14; J. D. Daniels, R. A. Pitts, and M. J. Tretter, "Strategy and Structure of U.S. Multinationals: An Exploratory Study," *Academy of Management Journal,* Vol. 27, 1984, pp. 292–307. But that stream of research focused on dimensions of international strategy (foreign product diversity and percent of foreign sales) that do not relate directly to global strategy. More directly relevant to the latter, Davidson and Haspeslagh (1982) examined the role of global product and global matrix approaches and found that global product organizations had many disadvantages. (See William H. Davidson and Philippe Haspeslagh, "Shaping a Global Product Organization," *Harvard Business Review,* July–August 1982, pp. 125–32.)

Focusing on global strategy, Bartlett and Ghoshal (1987 and 1989) argued for a network structure that facilitates global learning. See Christopher A. Bartlett and Sumantra Ghoshal "Managing Across Borders: New Strategic Requirements," *Sloan Management Review,* Summer 1987, pp. 7–17; and ——, *Managing Across Borders: The Transnational Solution* (Boston: Harvard Business School Press, 1989). Ghoshal (1987) argued that the tendency of global strategy toward a centralized global authority, and the potential corresponding erosion of global learning benefits, is one of the "strategic trade-offs" associated with pursuing a global strategy. (See Sumantra Ghoshal, "Global Strategy: An Organizing Framework," *Strategic Management Journal,* Vol. 8, No. 5, September–October 1987, pp. 425–40.)

7. This example is based on Simon Caulkin, "Ford Tunes Up Europe," *Management Today,* July 1988, pp. 38–44.

8. *The Economist,* March 30, 1996.

9. In a study of 180 leading U.S.-based multinationals, the Harvard Multinational Enterprise Project found that 163 initially created a separate international division to

manage foreign operations. See William H. Davidson, *Global Strategic Management* (New York: John Wiley & Sons, 1982), p. 274. This study covered the period up to 1979.

10. "Coke Drops Domestic and Goes One World," *New York Times,* January 13, 1996, p. 17.

11. According to the stages theory of multinational organization design, many firms evolve through either a product dominated or geography dominated structure toward some form of matrix organization (Stopford and Wells, *Managing the Multinational Enterprise*).

12. Bartlett and Ghoshal define the transnational as follows: "In contrast to the global model, the transnational mentality recognizes the importance of flexible and responsive country-level operations—hence the return of *national* into the terminology. And compared to the multinational approach, it provides for linking and coordinating those operations to retain competitive effectiveness and economic efficiency—as indicated by the prefix *trans*. The resulting need for intensive organization wide coordination and shared decision making implies that this is a much more sophisticated and subtle approach to MNC management." See Christopher A. Bartlett & Sumantra Ghoshal, *Text, Cases, and Readings in Cross-Border Management,* 3rd ed. (Boston: McGraw-Hill, 2000), p. 13. See also Nitin Nohria, Sumantra Ghoshal (contributor), and Cedric Crocker (editor), *The Differentiated Network: Organizing Multinational Corporations for Value Creation* (San Francisco: Jossey-Bass Business and Management Series, 1997).

13. "Perestroika in Soapland," *The Economist,* June 10, 1989, pp. 95–7.

14. Christopher A. Bartlett and Sumantra Ghoshal, "Matrix Management; Not a Structure, a Frame of Mind," *Harvard Business Review,* July–August 1990, pp. 138–45.

15. This example is based on William Taylor, "The Logic of Global Business: An Interview with ABB's Percy Barnevik," *Harvard Business Review,* Vol. 6, No. 2, March–April 1991, pp. 91–105.

16. See Roger Enrico and Jesse Kornbluth, *The Other Guy Blinked: How Pepsi Won the Cola Wars* (New York: Bantam Books, 1986).

17. See Gerrit Jeelof, "Global Strategies of Philips," *European Management Journal,* Vol. 7, No. 1, 1989, pp. 84–91; and Francis J. Aguilar and Michael Y. Yoshino, "The Philips Group: 1987," Case No. 9-388-050 (Boston: Harvard Business School).

18. See also Roderick E. White and Thomas A. Poynter, "Strategies for Foreign-Owned Subsidiaries in Canada," *Business Quarterly,* Summer 1984, pp. 59–69, on the different strategic roles that national subsidiaries can play.

19. Julian Birkinshaw and Nick Fry, "Subsidiary Initiatives to Develop New Markets," *Sloan Management Review,* Vol. 39, No. 3, 1998, pp. 51–62.

20. See Johny K. Johansson and George S. Yip, "Exploiting Globalization Potential: U.S. and Japanese Strategies," *Strategic Management Journal,* Vol. 15, October 1994, pp. 579–601; and George S. Yip, Johan Roos, and Johny K. Johansson, "Effects of Nationality on Global Strategy," *Management International Review,* Vol. 37, No. 4, October–December 1997, pp. 365–84.

21. Most companies, whatever their nationality, begin their international activities with separate domestic and international organizations. But the typical pattern has been an evolution to a multinational form of organization in which the uniqueness of the domestic market disappears. American companies seem to be slower than European companies in making this transition.

22. William Taylor, "The Logic of Global Business: An Interview with ABB's Percy Barnevik," *Harvard Business Review,* Vol. 6, No. 2, March–April 1991, pp. 91–105.

23. Adapted from Johana Ambrosio, "Opening Sessions to Span the Globe," *Computerworld* Vol. 25, No. 25, June 24, 1991, pp. 75, 78–9.

24. Adapted from "International Software," *Financial Times,* February 25, 1998, p. 10.

25. The author thanks Pierre M. Loewe of The MAC Group, San Francisco, for this example.

26. See Yves L. Doz, "Managing Manufacturing Rationalization Within Multinational

Companies," *Columbia Journal of World Business,* Fall 1978, pp. 82–94.

27. Deloitte & Touche, *Leaders in Innovative Globalization Program,* report, London, 1998.

28. Henry P. Conn and George S. Yip, "Global Transfer of Critical Capabilities," *Business Horizons,* Vol. 40, No. 1, January–February 1997, pp. 22–31.

29. See Karl Moore and Julian M. Birkinshaw, "Managing Knowledge in Global Service Firms: Centres of Excellence," *Academy of Management Executive,* December 1998; Julian Birkinshaw, "Why Is Knowledge Management So Difficult?" *Business Strategy Review,* Vol. 12, No. 1, Spring 2001, pp. 11–18; and Johan Roos, Georg von Krogh, and George S. Yip, "An Epistemology of Globalizing Firms," *International Business Review,* Vol. 3, No. 4, pp. 395–409, special issue on Organization's Knowledge, Knowledge Transfer, and Cooperative Strategies, November–December 1994.

30. They have had plenty of help from both academics and consultants. For guides to strategic planning, see, for example, George A. Steiner, *Strategic Planning: What Every Manager Must Know* (New York: The Free Press, 1979); Peter Lorange, *Implementation of Strategic Planning* (Upper Saddle River, N.J.: Prentice-Hall, 1982); and Arnoldo C. Hax and Nicolas S. Majluf, *Strategic Management: An Integrative Perspective* (Upper Saddle River, NJ: Prentice-Hall, 1984).

31. J. Stewart Black and Dave Ulrich, "The New Frontier of Global HR," in *The Global HR Manager,* Pat Joynt and Bob Morton, Eds. (London: Institute of Personnel and Development, 1999), Chapter 2, pp. 12–38.

32. C. K. Prahalad and Yves L. Doz, *The Multinational Mission: Balancing Local Demands and Global Vision* (New York: The Free Press, 1987), have argued for using global strategic planning. For a discussion of different types of global strategic planning, see Balaji S. Chakravarthy and Howard V. Perlmutter, "Strategic Planning for a Global Business," *Columbia Journal of World Business,* Summer 1985, pp. 3–10; and David C. Shanks, "Strategic Planning for Global Competition," *Journal of Business Strategy,* Winter 1985, pp. 80–9.

33. See Richard F. Vancil and Peter Lorange, "Strategic Planning in Diversified Companies," *Harvard Business Review,* January–February 1975; and George S. Yip, "Who Needs Strategic Planning?" *The Journal of Business Strategy,* Vol. 6, No. 2, Fall 1985, pp. 30–42.

34. See the discussion of global management control in John J. Dyment, "Strategies and Management Controls for Global Corporations," *Journal of Business Strategy,* Spring 1987, pp. 20–6.

35. For an in-depth discussion see Robert G. Eccles, *The Transfer Pricing Decision* (Lexington, MA: Lexington Books, 1985); and Lorraine Eden, "Taxes, Transfer Pricing, and the Multinational Enterprise," in *The Oxford Handbook of International Business,* Rugman and Brewer, Chapter 21, pp. 591–622.

36. George S. Yip and Tammy L. Madsen, "Global Account Management: The New Frontier in Relationship Marketing," *International Marketing Review,* Vol. 13, No. 3, pp. 24–42, special issue on Global Marketing Implementation, 1996.

37. Anton Fritschi, "Global Key Account Management bei ABB: Erfolg kennt keine (Lünder-) Grenzen," *Thexis,* Vol. 4, 1999, pp. 26–9.

38. Deloitte and Touche, *Leaders in Innovative Globalization Program.*

39. Ibid.

40. M. Marquardt and A. Reynolds, *The Global Learning Organization: Gaining Competitive Advantage Through Continuous Learning* (Homewood, Illinois: Irwin, 1994).

41. R. T. Moran, P. R. Harris, and W. G. Stripp, *Developing the Global Organization: Strategies for Human Resource Professionals* (Houston: Gulf Publishing Co., 1993).

42. P. Barnevik and R. M. Kanter, Eds., *Global Strategies: Insights from the World's Leading Thinkers* (Boston: *Harvard Business Review,* 1994).

43. Marquardt and Reynolds, *The Global Learning Organization: Gaining Competitive Advantage Through Continuous Learning.*

44. Taylor, "The Logic of Global Business: An Interview with ABB's Percy Barnevik."

45. Ibid.

46. White and Poynter have written extensively on the role of subsidiary management. See Roderick E. White and Thomas E. Poynter, "Strategies for Foreign-Owned Subsidiaries in Canada," *Business Quarterly,* Summer 1984, pp. 59–69; and ——, "Organizing for Worldwide Advantage," in Christopher A. Bartlett, Yves L. Doz, and Gunnar Hedlund, Eds., *Managing the Global Firm* (London: Routledge, 1990).

47. Valerie Frazee, "Tearing Down Roadblocks," *Workforce,* Vol. 77, No. 2, February 1998, pp. 50–1.

48. A nonprofit group that provides schools worldwide with a set of rigorous, internationally recognized academic standards.

49. Adapted from José de la Torre, *Los Angeles Times,* Sunday, July 24, 1994, p. D2.

50. Adapted from *Business Week,* March 22, 1993, pp. 38–40.

51. "Going Global: How to Expand Your Horizons While Avoiding the 'Ugly American' Syndrome," *Executive Speeches,* December 1, 1997, p. 29.

52. See Howard V. Perlmutter, "The Tortuous Evolution of the Multinational Corporation," *Columbia Journal of World Business,* January–February 1969, pp. 9–18, for the distinction between ethnocentric (national), polycentric (multinational), and geocentric (global) corporate cultures.

53. Adapted from "Side Effects: Cross-Border Merger Results in Headaches for a Drug Company," *The Wall Street Journal,* February 4, 1997, p. A1.

54. For example, Bartlett and Ghoshal, *Managing Across Borders: The Transnational Solution* (p. 106), describe how Philips assigned responsibility for developing the teletext TV business to its U.K. subsidiary.

55. Kenichi Ohmae, *The Borderless World: Power and Strategy in the Interlinked Economy* (New York: Harper Business, 1990), p. 17.

56. George S. Yip, "Global Strategy in the 21st Century," in Stuart Crainer and Des Dearlove, Eds., *Financial Times Handbook of Management,* 2nd ed. (London: Financial Times/Prentice Hall, 2001), pp. 150–63.

9
REGIONAL STRATEGY

So far this book has focused on industry globalization drivers and global strategies that apply on a worldwide basis. But the same drivers and strategies also apply on a regional basis.[1] For example, as discussed in Chapter 2, there can be drivers and strategies that apply across the European Union. Indeed, because regions (defined here as multicountry, rather than subcountry, areas) are smaller, the forces for regional integration in any given industry are usually stronger than for global integration. The word *usually* is applied here, rather than *always,* because some geographically contiguous regions can be so diverse (from the perspective of a particular industry) that it makes little sense to develop common strategies within that region. For example, Gillette groups its regions by socioeconomic/usage criteria and not geography. One of its regions encompasses Canada, the United States, Britain, Australia, and New Zealand.

REGIONAL STRATEGY IN THE CONTEXT OF GLOBAL STRATEGY

Regional strategies should be developed in the context of an overall global strategy:

- *Overall global strategy.* Before deciding whether and how to do business in a region of the world, a company needs to have a clear global strategy. As developed in earlier chapters, key elements of this strategy include the core business strategy, the competitive objectives for the business, and the extent to which the business will be operated as one integrated business or a looser collection of geographically independent units.
- *Regional strategy.* Next, a company needs to decide on the overall role of the region within the global strategy. Should the region be a source of growth, of profit, or of both? Should the region be primarily a source of supply or a locus of markets? Or should different countries play differing roles? In which countries in Asia should the company do business?
- *Country strategy.* Having selected the countries in which to be involved, the company needs to develop a country strategy that includes the mode of entry, partner selection, and the usual elements of a business strategy (what activities to conduct including what parts of the value chain to locate in the country, and how activities in the country will relate to those in the rest of the region and the world).
- *Country operations.* Lastly, the company has to be concerned with implementation at the operational level. Here the company has to deal with detailed matters such as how to adapt to local culture and business practices, how to develop the right kinds of contacts, how to find customers, and how to cope with the country's written and unwritten regulations.

DEFINING REGIONS

Regions are not synonymous with continents. An increasing number of regional organizations now provide some degree of macroeconomic and/or political integration for many countries. Broadly speaking, these entities, in increasing degrees of integration, are customs unions (e.g., European Community from 1965), border unions (e.g., the Schengen Agreement countries within the European Union that have agreed to drop all border controls among themselves), monetary unions (e.g., the Euro zone), and political unions (a declared long-term objective of many leaders in the European Union). Some countries belong to multiple regional entities, and many regions offer multiple organizations. For example, the United Kingdom belongs to most, but not all, aspects of the European Union, NATO, the World Trade Organization, Group of Eight, and others. Asia-Pacific boasts a wide variety of trade entities: ASEAN, APEC, AFTA, PECC, ANZERTA, among others.[2] The task of the multinational company is to make the best use of these formal (e.g., trade pacts) similarities and integrating forces as well as others (e.g., culture, contiguity) to develop effective regional strategies analogous to the global strategies discussed in the rest of this book.

Regions can be defined in many ways depending on the purpose of the definition. For multinational companies (MNCs), geographic proximity is usually the default basis of definition, if only because of the extensive travel involved in running a global business. A region defined for strategic reasons is also easier to administer if it has geographic coherence or even just spans the same band of time zones. But, in addition, a region defined for the purposes of business strategy should have a high degree of commonality in as many as possible of the following other characteristics:

- Culture
- Physical environment
- History
- Language
- Way of doing business
- Form of government
- Institutional arrangements
- Cross-investment
- Intraregional trade
- Trade policies and agreements
- Economic performance and prospects
- Infrastructure, such as airline connections

While taking geography into account, a region is also defined by less tangible characteristics. A multinational company must consider all these characteristics to develop a successful long-term strategy.

EXAMPLES OF MAJOR REGIONS

A number of major regions are so frequently used by multinational companies that they are worth noting here. They include the European Union, Central and Eastern Europe, Asia-Pacific, North America, and Latin America.

EUROPEAN UNION AS A REGION

From the viewpoint of multinational companies, the European Union provides the most clear-cut region in the world. Its membership and conditions are clearly defined, and it provides a number of increasingly integrated mechanisms. With the adoption of the Euro currency by most member states in 1999 (and Euro notes and coins in 2002), this region became even more integrated. Planned expansion eastward will probably reduce integration and homogeneity.

CENTRAL AND EASTERN EUROPE AS A REGION

The former members of the Soviet bloc other than the U.S.S.R. (the Baltics, Poland, the Czech and Slovak Republics, Hungary, the Balkan states, Romania, and Bulgaria) shared many common experiences and became free of Soviet domination all at about the same time around 1990.[3] On the other hand, these economies have huge discrepancies in wealth and economic strength. But all are undergoing a rapid period of transition and opening to free markets and globalization, albeit at different speeds. Most of these states have also applied to join the European Union. Consequently, most multinational companies tend to treat them as one region, partly because few are large enough to merit stand-alone strategies.

In terms of social makeup (culture, history, religion, language, and ethnic groups) the region is diverse and varied. Many existing social divisions do not correspond to constructed political and geographic boundaries. For example, there is a large population of ethnic Hungarians in Romania and the former Yugoslavia, Slovaks in Hungary, Ukrainians in the Slovak Republic and Poland, and Russians in the Ukraine and the Baltic Republics. Throughout the region large minority groups co-exist within a shared geographical area.

THE FORMER SOVIET UNION AS A REGION

Some companies include Russia and other former parts of the Soviet Union as part of an Eastern European region. Others treat them separately. Arguments for the latter include the much longer history of communism (from 1917 to 1991 for Russia rather than from 1945 for Central and Eastern European nations) and/or a lower level of economic development and political stability. In addition, the sheer physical size and diversity of Russia make it almost a region unto itself.

THE MIDDLE EAST AND ISLAMIC COUNTRIES AS A REGION

The Middle East scarcely exists as an economic region. A common language, religion, and culture cover most of the territory from the Atlantic coast of Morocco to the Sultanate of Oman on the Arabian Sea. Beyond the Middle East, the Islamic religion stretches as far as Indonesia in the Pacific and as far north as Kazakhstan in the heart of the former Soviet Union. But the economies remain highly separated with high trade barriers, the exception perhaps being among the six members of the Gulf Co-operation Council where stronger economic integration includes lower trade barriers. So multinational companies face many limitations in how far they can apply regional strategies.

NORTH AMERICA AS A REGION

Most multinational companies have long grouped Canada and the United States together. Indeed, the economic ties north-south between Canada and the United States are in many ways stronger than the east-west ties within Canada, a function of the distribution of Canada's population in a string along its U.S. border. The advent of the North American Free Trade Agreement (NAFTA), with Mexico as a third member, increasingly pulled Mexico into closer economic ties with its northern neighbors. Both Canada and Mexico now have over 80 percent of their trade with, and over 60 percent of their foreign direct investment stocks in, the United States.[4] Several industries, such as automotive, increasingly operate on an integrated basis within NAFTA. Interestingly, geographic proximity has created a business region out of a group of very diverse countries, particularly in terms of the cultural and economic differences between Mexico and its neighbors.

LATIN AND SOUTH AMERICA AS A REGION

The countries of Latin and South America share a common language, Spanish (in all cases except for Brazil, whose native Portuguese is closely related to Spanish), a similar history and culture, and similar stages of economic development. On the other hand, attempts at trade and economic integration have met only limited success. Neither Mercosur (the pact among Argentina, Brazil, Paraguay, and Uruguay) nor the Andean Pact (Bolivia, Colombia, Ecuador, Peru, and Venezuela, Chile having withdrawn in 1977) has had a huge impact. Mexico has now moved into the North American orbit by joining NAFTA, and Chile is negotiating with NAFTA. But increasing liberalization and deregulation are creating more opportunities for multinational companies to use integrated strategies in this region.

AFRICA AS A REGION

Most multinational companies treat Africa as one region, although some split sub-Saharan Africa from the Arab countries of North Africa. The continent enjoys few trade pacts, but that is not of great relevance as few MNCs currently locate production activities on the continent. Most MNCs operate in Africa through a strategy of direct export. There are sufficient similarities in economic development and culture that in many cases companies are able to offer regionally standardized products and services. Furthermore, the low level of development of most markets means that those customers cannot indulge in preferences for national versions of foreign products. Most MNCs are waiting to see if the transformation of South Africa, combined with increasing democratization and liberalization in some other countries, can spill over to produce real growth on the continent.[5]

ASIA-PACIFIC AS A REGION

Asia-Pacific is the largest, most populous, and most diverse of the regions commonly used by MNCs.[6] The region can encompass the countries and economies in the triangle from Japan to India to New Zealand, and it may sometimes extend beyond India to include Pakistan and contiguous countries. The trade policies in the region vary tremendously from nearly totally open markets in Hong Kong and Singapore to heavily

226 Total Global Strategy

controlled markets in Vietnam. But all these economies are moving in the direction of greater openness. Furthermore, there is rapid growth of many intraregion mechanisms to reduce trade barriers. Several regional institutions—particularly ASEAN (Association of South-East Asian Nations) and its AFTA (ASEAN Free Trade Area) program, APEC (Asia-Pacific Economic Cooperation forum), and "growth triangles" or "growth polygons"—play increasingly important roles in fostering regional trade, although APEC includes countries on the other side of the Pacific.

Including Australia and New Zealand is somewhat of a stretch, but they exhibit a number of qualifying characteristics. Both have now deemphasized their British heritage and have committed themselves to becoming a part of Asia. Most important, they have opened their borders to immigration from Asia. One of the ASEAN leaders, the prime minister of Singapore, has made an open invitation for Australia to join ASEAN. So the links northward will continue to strengthen. Many Hong Kong entrepreneurs have emigrated to Australia and New Zealand, bringing these countries into the overseas Chinese network. In addition, a large number of Australian nationals and, to a lesser extent, New Zealanders have spread throughout Asia in the role of expatriate managers.

DIAGNOSING INDUSTRY REGIONALIZATION POTENTIAL

The industry globalization drivers framework described in Chapter 2 can be adapted to diagnose the opportunities for regional strategies, as opposed to either national or global strategies. The potential will vary from region to region: In some industries some regions will be open to global strategies while other regions will be more hospitable to regional strategies. The European Union, as the world's most integrated region, generally offers the most opportunities for regional strategies in most industries. A very interesting question is whether the European Union will be able to nurture new pan-European companies that will evolve into global winners. Finland's Nokia is so far the most dramatic example of a company that used an initial European strategy to achieve global leadership (in mobile phone handsets). In contrast, most other Europe-based global companies achieved global scale before the advent of the European Union.

MARKET REGIONALIZATION DRIVERS

Each market *globalization* driver can act as a market *regionalization* driver.

Common Customer Needs and Tastes
The earlier list of potential regional commonalities (culture, history, etc.) can drive strongly to create regionally common customer needs and tastes. Products and services that have strong cultural roots in their use can be candidates for cultural commonality. Companies should, of course, make use of any existing cultural commonalities, such as a traditional value for gold in Middle Eastern, Arab, and Indian cultures; for olive oil in the Mediterranean region; and for cream in Northern Europe. More interesting, companies can make use of growing regional identities to pioneer pan-regional products or services. The European Union, in particular, offers many opportunities to get ahead of the curve. As increasing numbers of EU inhabitants, especially younger ones, include being European in their self-identity, savvy companies such as Benetton, Ikea, and Zara actively promote their European as opposed to national identities. Britain even has a popular television program called "Eurotrash." A growing sense and pride in being

Asian supports emerging Asian media and fashion companies, such as Star TV and Shanghai Tang.

Similarity in the physical environment (including climate) also provides many opportunities for regional offerings in categories as varied as housing, automobiles, clothing, and appliances.

Regional Customers and Channels

In many industries it is easier for regional rather than global customers and channels to emerge. Transportation, trade, or other barriers can prevent many customers and channels from going fully global. For example, most construction-related businesses tend to buy on a national or regional basis. In such industries, the existence of companies that operate around the world does not necessarily mean that they act as global customers. In general merchandise retailing, including supermarkets, companies have found it far easier to expand regionally than globally (because of the large need to adapt to local customer tastes and the limited transportability of bulky, low-value merchandise). But managers must be careful to recognize and treat differently *global* customers who make purchase decisions on a global basis, even if they get deliveries on a regional basis. Lastly, as discussed in Chapter 6, suppliers can convert multilocal customers into regional ones by changing the way in which they service the customers.

Regionally Transferable Marketing

Most industries should offer more opportunities for regionally, rather than globally, transferable marketing. Transferability depends on an absence of inhibiting differences such as in culture, language, market and distribution structures, legal restrictions, currency, and the norms for doing business. Fewer such barriers can exist within regions, although each region tends to offer different opportunities. The European Union lacks legal and currency barriers (in most cases) and has falling cultural and distribution barriers to marketing transferability, but language barriers remain. In contrast, Latin America faces only limited language barriers (different versions of Spanish, and the difference between Spanish and Portuguese), limited cultural barriers, but many legal and distribution barriers to marketing transferability. In much of Asia, a converging lifestyle for the educated, younger elite is enabling English-language, American-style marketing in many industries.

Regional Lead Countries

Lead countries can emerge, or be created, more easily on a regional than global basis. Japan has become a fashion leader for younger consumers in much of Asia, but much less so in the rest of the world. The United States acts as a lifestyle leader for many consumers all over the world, but even more so in Latin America, especially with lifestyles from Miami or Los Angeles. Western Europe, especially Germany, acts as a lead country for most of Central and Eastern Europe. Interestingly, individual Western European countries seem to resist taking the lead from anyone else. Indeed, European countries seem to have a number of "antilead" countries, at least as perceived by their cultural elites: for example, the United States for France, France for Britain, Spain for Portugal, and Sweden for Norway.

COST GLOBALIZATION DRIVERS

Most industry cost drivers can have strong regionalization effects.

Regional Scale Economies

In many industries, direct activities, such as production, achieve the minimum efficient scale at regional rather than global levels. For example, most automobile assembly plants can operate economically while serving regional-size markets, such as Europe or North America. Operating at a global scale can bring further cost reductions but not dramatically so, and often not enough to offset the other benefits of regional location (such as getting behind tariff walls). In contrast, some support activities, such as research and development and information systems, typically continue to benefit from increasing scale. On the other hand, in most industries these support activities represent relatively small proportions of total costs.

Regional Experience Curve

The experience curve effect is perhaps the only driver that always benefits significantly from expanding to global rather than regional scale. Assuming a constant decline in unit costs from increasing accumulated experience, there is no reason why the effect should stop at regional borders. But that assumption depends on not having to change the product that is being produced. Once a company shifts from global to regional products, a significant part of accumulated experience can be lost.

Regional Sourcing Efficiencies

Companies operating regional production sites can usually also benefit by sourcing regionally. But at the same time, they need to think about which supplies can best be sourced locally, nationally, regionally, or globally.

Regionally Favorable Logistics

Transportation costs limit many industries to regional rather than global movement of products. Products with logistic costs that are high relative to prices and margins — such as steel, wood panels, and other bulky, heavy, or perishable items — impose a regional restriction on manufacturing. At the same time, the product designs could be global and the companies can operate globally. It is just the manufacturing stage of the value chain that has to stay regional. For example, the top three or four European steel companies operate mainly as regional producers and account for only about 10 percent of market share. In wood panels, top global firms, such as Portugal's Sonae Industria, hold only a few points each of global market share. In such logistically challenged industries, direct global competition occurs only in periods of severe excess supply or demand. Excess supply may drive some producers to export out of their region at marginal costs low enough to offset the additional transportation costs. Excess demand may generate prices and margins high enough to cover extraregional transport.

Differences in Regional Costs

Differences among regions in production or activity costs may become so great that some regions become prohibitively expensive and other regions may sweep the board. In the production of consumer electronics, Western Europe has long since lost its viability, and North America except for Mexico has followed. South and Far East Asia have become dominant as location sites for production and support activities in many industries.

GOVERNMENT REGIONALIZATION DRIVERS

Most industry government drivers have even stronger effects at the regional level than at the global level.

Favorable Trade Policies

Regional trade arrangements continue to grow: the deepening and broadening of the European Union; continuing expansion of NAFTA to cover more categories of trade; Mercosur in South America; U.S. proposals to create a free trade area of the Americas covering all of North and South America; the widening role of ASEAN; other emerging regional pacts; and special multicountry free trade zones such as the SIJORI growth triangle of Singapore, the Malaysian state of Johore Bahru, and the Riau Islands in Indonesia.[7] Within each region covered by special trade and investment arrangements, most industries will face more favorable trade policies. Negotiations with governments are also easier, as companies can go to the relevant regional body to argue their case for market, trade, or investment access. For example, from 1998, deregulation in the European Union allowed any telephone company in the EU to offer services across national boundaries.[8] Resistance to change, however, may slow down the expected benefits of deregulation. Many countries are not adhering to market-opening rules. Thus for deregulation to take root in Europe's telecommunications market, regulators will play a large role in ensuring that the new rules are followed by all participating countries.

Regionally Compatible Technical Standards

Regional pacts can also make technical standards more compatible within the region, thereby creating significant opportunities. In mobile phones, Europe adopted the technology known as Global System for Mobile Communication (GSM) in 1987 and has used the common standard since then. In the third generation (3G) of cellular systems, Europe has also agreed to adopt a common standard. The United States, on the other hand, has three separate digital systems. For 3G, the United States appears intent on allowing for a multitude of incompatible digital standards. European compatibility has allowed European handset manufacturers such as Finland's Nokia and Sweden's Ericsson to become global leaders.

Regionally Common Marketing Regulations

Regional agreements that create common marketing regulations can have powerful implications in specific industries. For example, as already discussed in Chapter 2, the European Union is developing a set of common regulations to regulate marketing on the Internet.

Regional Government-Owned Competitors and Customers

Competitors and customers owned by national governments can cause enough problems for the global strategies of private multinational companies. Those owned or supported by multicountry regional entities pose even bigger problems. As yet, only Europe has produced a significant regionally owned competitor—Airbus. This consortium—supported by the French, German, British, and Spanish governments—has reached parity with Boeing in commercial aircraft. It may represent a forerunner of future regionally sponsored global competitors.

Regional Host Government Concerns

Regional entities can be just as protectionist as national governments, and with even more power. The European Union has used its greater muscle again and again in bilateral trade disputes and in setting rules that affect the behavior of multinational companies. Most recently, EU concerns about anticompetitive effects in *Europe* have stopped would-be mergers between *U.S.* companies, as in the case in 2001 of General Electric and Honeywell.

COMPETITIVE REGIONALIZATION DRIVERS

Regional groupings can create strong competitive effects within them and usually more quickly than effects from global competitors coming from outside a region.

Regional Exports and Imports
The main purpose of regional trade pacts is to increase intraregion trade relative to interregion trade. In 1997, intraregional exports was 49 percent of total exports in NAFTA, 53 percent in Asia, and 61 percent in the European Union.[9] In consequence, multinational companies face significant competition from within their own regions.

Regional Interdependence of Countries
A major consequence of regional groupings is for multinational companies to create regional activity networks. Consequently, industries rapidly become regional rather than national, at least on the supply side.

Regionally Transferable Competitive Advantages
As discussed in Chapter 2, industries that depend on locally based advantages, such as local knowledge and local relationships, tend to be multilocal rather than global. But advantages can also be regionally based or extended to a regional level as a consequence of regional integration. Many European companies thought that their industries were inherently national until European integration revealed opportunities to transfer their advantages regionally. For example, many food categories, thought to be based on national tastes and hence advantages, have turned out to have broad regional appeal, allowing previously national European companies to go pan-European.

SUMMARY

Analysis of industry regionalization drivers may show potential for regional strategies, especially for regional players. But larger MNCs may choose to stay with global strategies. Industries with strong regionalization drivers will not allow dominance by a small number of global firms. Global strategies are blocked from their full potential. For example, the car rental industry has sufficiently strong regionalization drivers that it allows for global, regional, and national players.

THE CASE OF THE EUROPEAN UNION

The European Union provides an intriguing and highly important example of how industry globalization drivers can be analyzed for an entire region across all its industries.[10] The Europe 1992 program increased the strength of all globalization (or Europeanization) drivers within the EU and also affected overall globalization drivers for any industry of which Europe is part of the world market.

CHANGES IN EU GOVERNMENT GLOBALIZATION DRIVERS

The legislation creating Europe 1992 can be viewed as direct changes of each of the government globalization drivers in Europe:

- *Trade policies* were made fully favorable among all member countries by eliminating all tariff and nontariff barriers and all subsidies. "Mutual recognition," whereby (with few exceptions) products accepted for sale in any member country will have to be accepted by all member countries, represents a very powerful weapon against nontariff barriers. Consequently, Germany could no longer rely on its "beer-purity" laws to keep out British and other European beers.

- *Subsidies* were outlawed. When Mercedes wanted to set up a plant in Baden-Wurttemberg, the wealthiest state in Germany, the European Commission prevented the state government from offering a subsidy.
- *Technical standards* are becoming compatible through harmonization of each industry's standards, although each industry is proceeding at its own pace. The European Union distinguishes between those areas where European harmonization is needed and those where mutual recognition of national standards is sufficient. The European Commission is restricting itself to laying down essential health and safety requirements that are obligatory in all member states.[11] Adoption by most EU member states of a common currency, the euro, from 1999 can be considered a special and very important case of harmonizing a technical standard. Full conversion from 2002 (use of euro notes and coins) will make it far easier for consumers to see cross-European price differences and will put enormous pressure on many companies to reduce arbitrary price differentials.
- *Marketing regulations* may, however, take somewhat longer to become compatible because of the strong cultural attitudes toward the role of advertising and other forms of promotion.
- *Government-owned competitors* can remain, but will lose much of their subsidy-based advantages when competing within the community.
- *Government-owned customers* will lose their ability to favor national suppliers, openly so at any rate. Given that public procurement now accounts for about 15 percent of the community's gross domestic product, this is a particularly powerful change.[12]

CHANGES IN COMPETITIVE GLOBALIZATION DRIVERS

Europe 1992 increased the strength of each of the competitive globalization drivers. *Exports* and *imports* within the EC increased. By 1996, intra-EU exports accounted for 61 percent of all EU exports.[13] The number of *competitors from different (European) countries* in each single country increased. The large size of the integrated European market has also attracted more *competitors from different continents.* Both American and Japanese companies geared up to participate more in Europe. The competitive *interdependence of countries* also increases as companies build manufacturing and distribution networks that are continental in scope rather than national. By 1997, 41 percent of the stock of foreign direct investment was intra-EU.[14] But there has also been a surge of investment from outside the EU, with the United Kingdom being the largest recipient. As a result, competitive battles are becoming Europe-wide in scope. Lastly, *Europeanized competitors* are increasing in number and scope, as companies increasingly adopt pan-European strategies.

CHANGES IN MARKET GLOBALIZATION DRIVERS

Market drivers for globalization or Europeanization increased. *Customer needs* and tastes are becoming more common across countries through exposure to other products. This is not to say that needs and tastes will reduce in number and variety. Rather, in most markets there is arising both a large "Euromass" segment and smaller national segments at the fringe, instead of the current largely separate national segments to one large European (global) segment with fringe national segments. *Europe-wide customers and channels* will increase in importance. Many previously national European retailers now operate throughout the continent, including France's Carrefour/Promodès and Intermarché, Germany's Metro and Rewe, and the Netherlands' Ahold.

Companies increasingly search all of the EU for suppliers. Distribution channels are already merging and forming alliances in order to provide pan-European coverage. *Transferable marketing* is increasingly becoming the norm, as buyers get more exposed to multilanguage packaging, to German sales representatives in France and vice versa, and to pan-European advertising created by pan-European marketing teams. The Spanish retailer of fashion clothing, Zara, started in the mid-1990s to attach labels that show the prices in each European country in each separate currency. Furthermore, *lead countries* now play a greater role with the freer movement of products and services. In the 1990s, London became the trend capital of not just Europe but the world. For example, the head of Ford's luxury-car group (which includes the Aston Martin, Jaguar, Land Rover, Lincoln, and Volvo marques) locates himself in London, as does the head of Switzerland's Richemont Group (owners of Montblanc pens and Cartier watches).

CHANGES IN COST GLOBALIZATION DRIVERS

Lastly, strengthening of cost globalization drivers is a major objective of Europe 1992. The potential for *European scale economies* greatly increases because the elimination of barriers to trade will allow the concentration of production, and the harmonization of standards enhances the potential for standardized products. Similarly, the increasing acceptability of pan-European products makes *experience curve* strategies more viable. One of the strongest cost drivers will be *favorable logistics* as the elimination of frontier checks speeds the flow of trucks from their previous average of 15 mph or so.[15] Combined with the elimination of tariff and nontariff barriers, these favorable logistics now make *sourcing efficiencies* from centralized purchasing more achievable. In the short term, *differences in country costs* are becoming more significant in the absence of trade and logistical barriers, as companies find it easier to shift from high-cost to low-cost countries, such as Spain and Ireland. In the longer term, such movements will push costs closer together. But the next projected round of expansion to include Poland and other Eastern European economies will bring in many new locations of low-cost labor. Companies now feel encouraged to invest in high-cost pan-European *product development* efforts because there will be larger markets for the results.

USING REGIONAL STRATEGIES

Each global strategy lever obviously can be used at the regional level as well or instead. Some researchers have cited the many difficulties of implementing global strategies and therefore favor regional solutions.[16]

REGIONAL MARKET PARTICIPATION

Expansion within a region has been the traditional first route for internationalizing companies, often on the basis of convenience and familiarity. Regional integration adds an extra dimension—perhaps the need to expand rapidly to all major markets in a region for both offensive and defensive reasons. A key question is whether a company needs to expand first within its region or hopscotch around to key markets around the globe. The answer depends on the relative strength of regionalization as opposed to globalization drivers, the potential benefits of first mover advantages, and the starting position of the company. For example, Nokia, then unknown outside Finland, had to first establish a position and reputation in Europe, where it was relatively easy to do so, before going global. In contrast, many already established European companies often target the U.S. market for new products before rolling out to the rest of Europe. For example, the United States is a more important market for Ferrari cars than the rest of Europe outside Italy. Sweden's Hennes and Mauritz (H&M), a clothing retailer, is using European integration and convergence to expand into the rest of Europe from its Nordic and Germanic base.

Many industries have patterns of regional dominance. In the express delivery industry, FedEx dominates the Americas, while DHL does so for Europe, and TNT to a lesser extent for Asia-Pacific. Many companies struggle as they expand outside their home region. Wal-Mart has had to deal with being considered too "all-American" for the Latin American market despite its partnerships with important local store chains. Wal-Mart does not accept postdated checks, which are commonplace in Brazil, and its huge inventory has not gone over well in Argentina, where customers care more about "creatively priced and promoted specials" than a large selection. Within its own region, the Jollibee chain of fast-food restaurants is successfully expanding beyond its home base of the Philippines. America's MTV is working hard to invade the Asian regional home market of Star TV's rival Channel [V].[17] MTV has started 24-hour service in some areas and launched Indian, Chinese, and Southeast Asian versions of its basic format. Each week MTV produces programs with local partners as well as importing the latest music from the United States.

REGIONAL PRODUCTS AND SERVICES

Designing regional rather than global products and services requires fewer complexities and is more appropriate when there are strong interregional differences in customer needs and tastes. For example, U.S. and Canadian drivers prefer wider, bigger cars than do Europeans and Asians, while in most emerging markets most customers can afford only basic versions of models sold in the developed world. Consequently, despite the large economies of scale in both R&D and production, many but not all mass market automobile producers offer separate lines for different regions. It would be even better to develop global product platforms that can be adapted relatively easily for regional markets, as Honda has now done with its adjustable width platform. In the service sector, Club Med bends its philosophy of maximal standardization to cater to the North American market by offering greater comfort (including in-room phones and TV sets) and fewer public announcements in French (a key part of its French ambience). Indeed, the brochures sent to North American clients exclude various Club Meds that are too basic or French for the tastes of these vacationers.

Managers also need to beware of overadapting to regional markets. At first glance, it might seem obvious that multinationals serving the emerging markets of Central and Eastern Europe need to make significant product adaptations. But a recent study found that most multinational companies market globally standardized products quite successfully in that region.[18] On the other hand, managers need to recognize the limits of regional standardization. For example, continuing European diversity means that European hotel chains cannot push as far in pan-European standardization as can their U.S. competitors, who cater more for American customers.

REGIONAL ACTIVITY LOCATION

Many companies now build regionwide activity networks. Staying within a limited number of time zones and limited geographic distances, and within regional tariff barriers, such networks can be much easier to operate than global ones. Again, it is the relative strength of industry regionalization as opposed to globalization drivers that determines the optimum strategies. The automotive industry has many strong regionalization drivers as well as globalization ones.[19] Toyota spent $13.5 billion on global expansion through the year 2000 in an aggressive effort to become the first car manufacturer with major manufacturing hubs in the three major markets (North America, Europe, and Asia).[20] Toyota now has the ability to customize vehicles for regional markets. Such extensive coverage allows Toyota to react quickly to regional tastes, bypass regional trade barriers, and use regionally based suppliers to increase cost efficiencies. A new plant in France will allow Toyota to bypass tariffs and locally produce Toyota's "Europe Car." In Asia, a local network of suppliers and assembly hubs will allow Toyota to build sturdy, simply designed, low-priced cars that appeal to the Asian consumer.

ASEAN offers a "brand-to-brand complementation" (BBC) scheme whereby imports and exports of components or final products of the same brand (e.g., Toyota) are tariff free. Companies can benefit by production networks that have sites in different countries in the region specializing in particular components or production stages.

In logistics, European integration allows more and more companies to create centralized distribution systems, as has been done by both European and foreign companies.

REGIONAL MARKETING

Convergence of regional needs and tastes, growth of regional media and channels of distribution, and harmonization of regional marketing regulations can all make regional marketing feasible relative to multilocal marketing and much easier than global marketing. Again, European companies have the chance to pioneer with regional marketing.

REGIONAL COMPETITIVE MOVES

Strengthening competitive regionalization drivers, such as increased intraregional trade and the rise of regional competitors, spurs companies to pay attention to regional competitive moves. Such moves, relative to national or global ones, are particularly necessary when the weakening of a regional market position will have serious global repercussions. For example, Nokia's global success depends first on the maintenance of its European regional base, as do DHL's and IKEA's global positions.

REGIONAL STRATEGY AS A PARTIAL OR TEMPORARY SOLUTION

In many cases, the use of regional as opposed to global strategies should be viewed as partial or temporary solutions. A multiindustry study found that companies employing regional strategies had poorer performance than those using global strategies.[21] A recent study of the automotive industry found that the more successful companies deployed regional strategies in the context of global strategies rather than instead of.[22] Industry drivers can also change. In the 1980s, the major appliance industry faced very strong regionalization drivers in Europe, favoring those companies that used regional rather than global strategies.[23] But by the 1990s, changes in the EU and in the industry seemed to strengthen industry globalization drivers and favor global strategies.[24]

REGIONAL ORGANIZATION AND MANAGEMENT

Each of the global organization structures and processes discussed in Chapter 8 can apply at the regional level. Decisions on these organizational issues should follow the analysis of the need for regional strategies and balance the strategic and organizational logic. Three critical issues arise in terms of regional organization structure—the autonomy of the regions and the role and location of the regional headquarters.

Autonomy of Regions MNCs need to decide how much autonomy each regional operation should have. This decision depends mainly on the integration of the region with the overall global strategy and also on the level of experience of the subsidiaries in the region and their managers.

Role of Regional Headquarters As a company builds its presence in a region, the role of the regional headquarters needs to change. One researcher suggests that there are three evolving roles:[25]

- *Explorer:* exploit local opportunities, with limited self-contained operations and only an ambivalent commitment to the region.
- *Mover:* build regional presence through regional linkages and a strong regional headquarters, with a very high commitment to the region.
- *Consolidator:* run a balanced role for the region within the global portfolio, using global linkages and a reduced but still high commitment to the region.

Location of Regional Headquarters Often the most important issue is whether and where to have regional head offices. That decision inevitably has an influence on the emphasis placed within the region. For example, in the Asia-Pacific region, the currently most popular cities for regional headquarters are Hong Kong, Singapore, Tokyo, and Sydney. Companies also shift their headquarters around a region as they change their priorities within the region.

GUIDELINES FOR DIAGNOSING REGIONALIZATION POTENTIAL AND DEVELOPING REGIONAL STRATEGIES

- Do not assume that industries are either regional or not regional. Instead, nearly every industry has regionalization potential in some aspects and not others.
- Different industry regionalization drivers can operate in different directions, some favoring regionalization and others making it difficult and inadvisable.
- Businesses can respond selectively to industry regionalization drivers, by regionalizing only those elements of strategy affected by favorable drivers.
- The level of regionalization potential changes over time.

- Regional strategies need to be developed in the context of global and national strategies and work with them.
- Regional trade agreements and blocs can be particularly important as a focus for regional strategies.

Discussion and Research Questions

1. Research and evaluate the different regional trade and trading bloc agreements—the European Union, the North American Free Trade Agreement, Mercosur, ASEAN, APEC, and so on—in terms of how they affect global and regional strategies.
2. Select an industry and analyze its regionalization drivers as they were five years ago, as they are today, and as they are likely to be in five years' time.
3. How should a company decide when to use regional rather than global strategies?
4. What are the most globally successful companies from your region? Why?

Notes

1. This chapter draws on George S. Yip, *Asian Advantage: Key Strategies for Winning in the Asia-Pacific Region* (Reading, MA: Addison Wesley, 1998); *Updated Edition—After the Crisis* (Cambridge, MA: Perseus Publishing, 2000).
2. Mari Kondo and George S. Yip, "Regional Groups—ASEAN, AFTA, APEC, Etc.," in Yip, *Asian Advantage*, Chapter 16.
3. This section is drawn from Andrzej Kozminski, George S. Yip, and Anna M. Dempster, "Evaluating the Central and Eastern European Opportunity: Eastern Promise," in Andrzej K. Kozminski and George S. Yip, Eds., *Strategies for Central and Eastern Europe* (Basingstoke, England: Macmillan, 2000). Chapter 1, pp. 1–32.
4. Alan M. Rugman, *The End of Globalization* (London: Random House Business Books, 2000), Chapter 6, p. 96.
5. See also John A. Quelch and James E. Austin, "Should Multinationals Invest in Africa?" *Sloan Management Review*, Vol. 34, No. 3, Spring 1993, pp. 107–19.
6. See George S. Yip, *Asian Advantage: Key Strategies for Winning in the Asia-Pacific Region (Updated Edition—After the Crisis)* (Cambridge, MA: Perseus Publishing, 2000).
7. Kondo and Yip, "Regional Groups—ASEAN, AFTA, APEC, Etc."
8. Adapted from "In the Shark Pond," *The Economist*, January 3, 1998, pp. 59–60.
9. From Rugman, *The End of Globalization*, p. 116.
10. For a detailed explanation of Europe 1992, see, among others, Paolo Cecchini, *The European Challenge: 1992, The Benefits of a Single Market* (London, England: Wildwood House, 1988); and John A. Quelch, Robert D. Buzzell, and Eric R. Salama, *The Marketing Challenge of 1992* (Reading, MA: Addison-Wesley, 1990). For a quantification of how much EC 92 might improve business profitability, see George S. Yip, "A Performance Comparison of Continental and National Businesses in Europe," *International Marketing Review*, Vol. 8, No. 2, 1991, pp. 31–9.
11. See Chris C. Burggraeve, "Meeting Product Standards in the Single Market," *The Journal of European Business*, May/June 1990, pp. 22–6.
12. Speech by Peter Sutherland, former commissioner of the European Community, to the Planning Forum Conference on "The Challenge of Europe 1992," Boston, October 16, 1989.
13. International Monetary Fund, *Direction of Trade Statistics, 1999*, reported in Rugman, *The End of Globalization*, Figure 7.2, p. 116.
14. Rugman, *The End of Globalization*, Figure 7.4, p. 120.
15. Estimate by McKinsey & Company.
16. Allen J. Morrison and Kendall Roth, "The Regional Solution: An Alternative to

Globalization," *Transnational Corporations,* Vol. 1, No. 2, 1992, pp. 32–55; A. J. David, Allen J. Morrison, David A. Ricks, and Kendall Roth, "Globalization Versus Regionalization: Which Way for the Multinational?" *Organizational Dynamics,* Vol. 19, No. 3, 1991, pp. 17–29.

17. "MTV Cranks Up the Volume in Asia," *Business Week,* June 23, 1998, p. 23.

18. Arnold Schuh, "Global Standardization as a Success Formula for Marketing in Central Eastern Europe?" *Journal of World Business,* Vol. 35, No. 2, Summer 2000, pp. 133–48.

19. Erik Schlie and George S. Yip, "Regional Follows Global: Strategy Mixes in the World Automotive Industry," *European Management Journal,* Vol. 18, No. 4, August 2000, pp. 343–54.

20. Adapted from "Toyota's Crusade," *Business Week,* April 7, 1997, pp. 104–14.

21. Henry P. Conn and George S. Yip, "Global Transfer of Critical Capabilities," *Business Horizons,* January–February 1997, Vol. 40, No. 1, pp. 22–31.

22. Schlie and Yip, "Regional Follows Global."

23. Charles W. F. Baden Fuller and John M. Stopford, "Globalization Frustrated: The Case of White Goods," *Strategic Management Journal,* Vol. 12, No. 7, 1991, pp. 493–507.

24. S. Segal-Horn, D. Asch, and V. Suneja, "The Globalization of the European White Goods Industry," *European Management Journal,* Vol. 16, No. 1, 1998, pp. 101–9.

25. Helmut Schütte, "Strategy and Organisation: Challenges for European MNCs in Asia," *European Management Journal,* Vol. 15, No. 4, August 1997, pp. 436–45.

10
MEASURING INDUSTRY DRIVERS AND STRATEGY LEVERS

The previous chapters have discussed globalization concepts without specifically explaining how to measure them. Being able to measure industry globalization drivers and global strategy levers greatly increases the usefulness of these concepts. Usable measures allow management to compare the globalization potential of different industries at the same time, of one industry over time, of the extent of globalization of different businesses within a company, and of a business and its competitors. Measures also facilitate implementation by making it clearer what needs to be changed and by how much. Instead of deciding to "increase the extent of global products," which is a very vague goal, it is far better to be able to decide to "increase the proportion of revenues in global products from 60 to 80 percent."

Good measures encourage implementation by exploiting the familiar idea that executives manage what is measured. So this chapter provides a series of practical measures of globalization. These measures have been developed and tested on over 50 American, European, and Japanese businesses and their executives in both research and consulting settings. Those who wish to undertake the step-by-step global strategy analysis described in the next chapter should use the measures described in this chapter. Users should also feel free to adapt the measures suggested here and to develop their own. The important thing is to make some measurement.

GEOGRAPHIC BASIS FOR MEASUREMENT

Measures can be made at both global and subglobal (e.g., regional) levels. Often, a global measure may be less useful than separate regional measures. For example, in measuring common customer needs, there may be significant commonality within regions (Europe, North America, etc.) but major differences among regions. So the commonality of customer needs should be measured at both levels—between countries within a region and between regions. Also, the definition of the world varies. The definition should usually exclude markets that are effectively closed to Western (and other market economy) multinational companies.

WHO SHOULD DO THE MEASURING

Because the measures of industry globalization and business global strategy cut across countries, it is important to get input from representatives of the major regions or countries in a business. While one manager (or team) should be responsible for assembling and updating the measurements, he or she should involve managers from different geographic locations, as well as different functions, in developing and checking the measures. Chapter 11 will describe further how to assemble a global team to diagnose globalization potential and to develop global strategy.

MEASURING INDUSTRY GLOBALIZATION DRIVERS

As each of the four types of industry globalization drivers—market, cost, government, and competitive—differs in its nature, measures for them vary. Many, but not all, of the measures can be quantified.

SUMMARY OF GLOBALIZATION MEASURES

DRIVER	MEASURE
Market Drivers	
Common customer needs and tastes	Extent to which customer needs and tastes are common around the world
	Percentage (by cost) of the components of a global product or service that can be common worldwide
National global customers	Share of worldwide market sales to customers who search the world for vendors
Multinational global customers	Share of worldwide volume accounted for by customers who purchase or select centrally
Global channels	Share of worldwide volume accounted for by channels that purchase centrally
Transferable marketing	For each element, share of world market accounted for by countries where foreign element is acceptable
Lead countries	Number of countries that account for the most important product innovations
Cost Drivers	
Global scale economies	Percentage of world market needed for minimum efficient scale production or service operation
Steep experience effects	Percentage decrease in unit production costs with each doubling of accumulated capacity
Sourcing efficiencies	Potential percentage savings in purchase expenditures from making all purchases centrally
Favorable logistics	Transportation cost over a standard intercontinental route, excluding customs and duties, as a percentage of the selling price
Differences in country costs	Ratio of lowest to highest cost countries in the industry for (1) fully loaded hourly cost of the most common form of production labor and (2) total unit production cost
High product development costs	Total cost of developing (but not marketing) a major new product or service, as a percentage of the expected lifetime sales of the product or service
Fast-changing technology	Market life of typical new product
Government Drivers	
Tariffs	Percentage of the pretariff selling price, averaged globally
Subsidies	Percentage of the presubsidy selling price, averaged globally
	Net percentage effect on selling prices of subsidized competitors
Nontariff barriers	Percentage of the world market that is blocked from imports
Compatible technical standards	Percentage, in cost, of the typical product that is in components that are technically compatible worldwide

(continued)

Continued	
DRIVER	*MEASURE*
Government Drivers (continued)	
Common marketing regulations	Proportion of the industry's worldwide marketing expenditures that are in activities allowed in every country
Government-owned competitors	Combined global market share of all government-owned competitors
Government-owned customers	Combined share of global industry purchases made by government-owned customers
Competitive Drivers	
Exports	Exports as a percentage of the world market
Imports	Imports as a percentage of the world market
Competitors from different continents	Number of continents that are the home of global competitors
Interdependent countries	Amount of volume sold in each country that is dependent on production facilities that supply more than one country, averaged across competitors
Competitors globalized	Extent to which competitors use global strategy levers
Transferable competitive advantage	Extent to which competitive advantages in the industry are transferable globally

MARKET GLOBALIZATION DRIVERS

Measuring market globalization drivers requires making some qualitative judgments in addition to quantitative estimates.

Common Customer Needs Driver

Common customer needs and tastes represent perhaps the most difficult driver to measure, because customer need in a product or service category is actually a bundle of different needs. For example, in a passenger automobile, safety is one kind of need and comfort is another kind. The only common yardstick is to measure the proportion of total cost accounted for, in a typical product, by the product or service components that satisfy each individual need. In an automobile, components such as brakes and caging provide safety, while components such as seating and shock absorbers provide comfort. If these safety and comfort components account for about 10 percent of the total cost of a typical vehicle, and if safety and comfort needs are the only ones to vary by country, then needs are 90 percent common. Of course, what customers consider a comfort need in one country may be considered a safety need in others (for example, rust on automobiles is viewed as a safety hazard in Germany[1]). But such differences do not matter. What matters is the sum of the costs for all components that need to differ between countries.

   An important consideration is to distinguish between changeable and unchangeable differences in country needs. Changeable needs arise from differences in customer tastes and preferences. For automobiles these changeable needs include styling and comfort. Unchangeable needs arise from legal, technical, or physical differences. For automobiles, unchangeable needs include the side on which the steering wheel is placed, emission control systems, heavy-duty batteries in cold countries, and air conditioning in hot ones. A manufacturer has to adapt its products to meet unchangeable needs but may be able to alter or offset changeable needs through marketing. Volkswagen used innovative advertising in the late 1960s and early 1970s in changing some American consumers' previous preference for large automobiles. Clearly, there are gray areas that fall somewhere between changeable and unchangeable needs. For example, the size of vehicles is affected both by preferences (a changeable factor) and by road and traffic conditions in a country (an unchangeable factor).

Managers using the type of measure just described usually find that customer needs are much more common than they might have seemed before applying the measure. Managers, particularly those with single-country responsibilities, tend to focus on the differences between countries, because it is the differences that require effort in adaptation. But when taking a global view, it is helpful to use this measure to get a better understanding of the extent of commonality.

The measure can also be applied to separate product categories where there is more than one, and to separate features of an individual product. In the latter case the ratings of the separate features can be summed into a composite for the entire product.[2]

Global Customers and Channels

There are two types of global customers: national and multinational. For industries that sell to organizations, the extent to which there are *national* global customers can be measured by the share of worldwide market sales to customers who search the world for vendors. The extent to which there are *multinational* global customers can be measured by the extent to which these customers buy or select centrally for global use. These multinational global customers may do all of the buying at one or a small number of central points or may make centrally major decisions such as the selection of vendors. An analogous measure is for regional customers. For industries that sell to consumers or individuals, the measure applies to purchases made outside the home country.

The extent to which there are *global channels* can be measured by the share of worldwide sales through channels of distribution that buy or select centrally. An analogous measure is for regional channels.

For both global customers and global channels, it may be worth repeating that mere multinationality does not qualify: The customers and channels have to make central purchase or selection decisions. Only then does the selling business need to respond with global programs for selling to and servicing these customers and channels.

Transferable Marketing

Marketing transferability can be measured by analyzing the extent to which customers around the world accept or would accept a foreign element of the marketing mix (e.g., a foreign brand name or sales representative). This measure should be applied to all elements of the marketing mix—company name, brand name, packaging, advertising, promotion, and sales representatives. For company and brand names, being foreign means having a name that is generally recognized as being from another country, for example, McDonald's, in non–English-speaking countries or Louis Vuitton in non–French-speaking countries. For packaging, being foreign means using a nonlocal language for the pack copy, including multilanguage packs. For advertising, being foreign means not just using a foreign language (which is usually, but not always, undesirable) but also using recognizably foreign situations, scenery, or characters. To be more precise, transferable marketing can be measured for each marketing element by the share of the world market accounted for by countries where a foreign element is acceptable.

Lead Countries

Lead countries can be easily identified as those in which the most important product or process innovations occur. The measure can be made more precise by identifying the countries that accounted for the last 10 major innovations in the industry. In some industries the last 10 major innovations will have occurred over a short time span, such as one year or less. In other, slow-changing industries the time span may cover decades.

COST GLOBALIZATION DRIVERS

Cost globalization drivers are probably both the easiest and the most difficult to measure. They should be the easiest because they can be quantified. They can be the most difficult because most companies seem to collect little cost information that applies on a global basis. Yet, understanding the fundamental cost economics of a global business is critical for efforts to improve its global strategy.

Global Economies of Scale and Scope

Managers can measure global economies of scale by the share of the worldwide market needed to support a minimum efficient scale production or service operation. The extent of global economies of scope is usually more difficult to measure. It is indicated by the minimum global market share needed for a viable worldwide business. Global economies of scale or scope are typically significant when a global market share of 5 percent or more is needed to achieve the minimum efficient scale. In the passenger automobile business, the fifth and sixth largest global competitors, Nissan and Chrysler, had global market shares of only just over 5 percent in 1990. It can also be important to measure where in the value chain these scale economies occur.[3] In many industries, such as pharmaceuticals and electronics, it is in R&D rather than in manufacturing that world-scale economies occur.

Steep Experience Effects

The extent to which there are learning and experience effects is measured by the percentage decrease in unit production costs for each doubling of accumulated experience. This is the standard measure of the experience effect popularized by the Boston Consulting Group.[4]

Sourcing Efficiencies

Managers should keep in mind that the extent of sourcing efficiencies is more easily measured for an individual competitor within an industry than for the industry as a whole. The measure is the potential percentage savings in purchase expenditures from making all purchases centrally.

Favorable Logistics

The extent to which there are favorable logistics can be measured by the transportation cost over a standard intercontinental route in the particular industry, such as Tokyo to Chicago, or Chicago to Frankfurt, excluding customs and duties, as a percentage of the selling price. Transportation costs below 10 percent of the manufacturer selling price seem to be generally favorable for globalization. On the other hand, managers need to keep in mind that transportation, other logistical costs, and tariffs need to be related to margins and to the competitive price range. In general, the total transportation and tariff cost as a percentage of price needs to be at most half that of the competitive price range in most countries; that is, if the competitive price range is from 90 to 110 as an index, for a spread of 20 percent, transportation and tariff costs need to be no more than about 10 percent. For example, gourmet foods are globally competitive while basic foods are not, because the former's transportation cost is low relative to their price and the competitive price range. In addition, the availability of local products and trade barriers has the major influence on whether final products are shipped between countries.

Differences in Country Costs
The extent to which there are differences in country costs is measured in two ways. Each involves a comparison between the highest cost country and the lowest cost country in which there is production in the industry. In addition, managers may find it necessary to include countries that are potential producers. One measure of the differences in country costs is to compare fully loaded hourly cost of the most common form of production labor in the industry. The other measure is more complete but also more difficult and may require making hypothetical estimates. It is to compare the total unit cost of production between the highest and lowest cost countries.

High Product Development Costs
The extent to which product development costs affect industry globalization potential is measured by the total cost of developing (but not marketing) a major new product or service, as a percentage of the expected lifetime sales of the product or service. Both parts of this measure are difficult to estimate. Managers will need to make intelligent projections from past experience in most cases.

Fast-Changing Technology
The rate of change of technology can be measured by the market life of typical new products. It can be particularly helpful to measure this over time to see if the pace of technology change is accelerating (as Philips did for the telecommunications industry— described in Chapter 2).

GOVERNMENT GLOBALIZATION DRIVERS

Measuring government globalization drivers requires a good understanding of the worldwide trade and other government policies and practices that affect a particular industry.

Favorable Trade Policies
Managers can use several different measures of the extent to which trade policies are favorable to industry globalization:

Tariffs The importance of tariffs is measured by their charge as a percentage of the pre-tariff selling price. Usually it is just the individual country tariffs that matter when making decisions about single country-markets. But when taking a global view managers will find it helpful to calculate a single global number that represents the average worldwide extent of tariffs in a particular industry. A global average can be calculated by averaging tariffs across all countries, weighted by the share of the worldwide market accounted for by each country and adjusted for the universality of the tariff (i.e., a tariff may be levied against imports from some countries and not others). The latter adjustment can be made for each tariff-imposing country by weighting by the share of imports. For example, if France imposes a 10 percent tariff on electronics products from countries outside the European Community, and these countries account for 70 percent of electronics imports into France, the weighted tariff for France is 10 percent times 70 percent (.10 X .70), which equals 7 percent.

Subsidies The level of government subsidies is measured by their effect as a percentage of the selling price (including the full terms of sale such as financing and warranties). This effect is what matters to competitors rather than the effect on profitability. Estimating the effect on the selling price can be complicated, as subsidies are often in the form of a flat amount. It is their effect on the selling price that matters, not the total amount of the subsidy. For example, Airbus Industrie, the European aircraft consortium, is estimated to have received over $10 billion in subsidies from its start in 1970 to mid-1989, but to have delivered only 500 units over that period. If the full amount of the subsidy were allocated, the per aircraft amount would be $20 million, equivalent to about 50 percent of the average selling price. Even Boeing and McDonnell-Douglas, vociferous complainers about the Airbus subsidies, would not claim that their rival underprices by that amount. More relevant is the much smaller percentage price discount, of the order of 10 to 20 percent, that Airbus Industrie has in effect offered to customers. As in the case of tariffs, it is useful to be able to calculate one global number. A global average can be calculated by averaging subsidies across all competitors weighted by their global market share.

Nontariff Barriers The strength of quotas and other nontariff barriers is measured by the share of a country's market that is blocked from imports. For example, France's nontariff restrictions on Japanese automotive imports have restricted the latter's share to less than 5 percent. Without these restrictions Japan's share of the French automotive market might be closer to 20 percent (the level in the United Kingdom). The effect is, therefore, 15 percent. Local content requirements can be accounted for by using an analogous procedure to estimate the market value of the foreign content that is kept out. To calculate an overall global number, the national estimates should be summed and weighted by each country's market size as a percentage of the world total.

Compatible Technical Standards
Whether technical standards are globally compatible is measured by the percentage, in cost, of the typical product that is in components that are technically compatible worldwide. For example, in a television receiver, a large percentage of the product cost is in components that need to meet different technical specifications in different countries.

Common Marketing Regulations
The degree to which there are common marketing regulations cannot be easily quantified. One approach is to estimate the proportion of the industry's worldwide marketing expenditures that are in activities allowed in every country. For example, in the cigarette industry, television advertising is banned in many, but not all, countries. So worldwide TV advertising as a proportion of industry marketing expenditures accounted for by advertising in *any* medium is the measure of marketing regulations not being common.

Government-Owned Competitors and Customers

The extent of government-owned competitors or customers can simply be measured by their combined global market share.

COMPETITIVE GLOBALIZATION DRIVERS

Measuring competitive globalization drivers requires an effective global competitive intelligence system.

High Exports and Imports

The level of exports and imports is simply measured by the sum of world exports and imports as a percentage of the world market size.

Competitors from Different Continents

The extent to which there are competitors from different continents is measured by counting the number of continents that are the home of global competitors. A global competitor is a multinational business that has significant and extensive selling and/or production presence on more than one continent. The specifics of the latter definition will vary from industry to industry, but not its spirit.

Interdependent Countries

Whether countries are competitively interdependent can be measured by the degree to which individual competitors share activities within a global network. The key activity is production. For each competitor the extent of sharing is measured by the amount of volume sold in each country that is dependent on production facilities that supply more than one country. For example, an American business may have 50 percent of its U.S. volume supplied from Taiwan and 30 percent of its volume in Italy also supplied from Taiwan. Summing up the total volume dependent on shared facilities and dividing by the competitor's global volume yields that competitor's country interdependence. For the industry as a whole, interdependence of countries is simply calculated by averaging across all competitors weighting by their global market share.

Globalized Competitors

Managers can measure the globalization of competitors by first estimating the extent of globalization for each individual competitor, using the measures described later in this chapter for global strategy levers. To get the industry average, weight by each competitor's global market share.

Transferable Competitive Advantage

Measures of the transferability of competitive advantage include how long it would take for companies in the industry to re-create advantages in new countries and how much it would cost to make the transfer.

MEASURING GLOBAL STRATEGY LEVERS

In addition to measuring the globalization potential of the industry in which a business participates, its managers also need to measure where the business is in terms of the use of global strategy levers. Only then can the managers know whether they are adequately exploiting the industry's globalization potential. In addition, it helps to make three kinds of comparisons:

- Comparative measurement over time helps to identify the speed and direction of change in the business's globalization strategy.
- Measurement of competitors' strategies helps to provide both a guide to what might be done in this business and an indication of competitive opportunities and threats.
- Comparing measurements for multiple businesses in the same company helps to set benchmarks for what each business should target in the use of global strategy levers.

SUMMARY OF MEASURES OF GLOBAL STRATEGY LEVERS

LEVER	MEASURE
Global Market Participation	
Global market share	Business's global volume (units or revenues) divided by the total volume of the worldwide market
Globally strategic market share	Business's volume in globally strategic country-markets only, divided by the total volume in those markets
Global share balance	Index of the worldwide business's geographic split of revenues compared with that of the worldwide market
Market presence	
*Number of selling countries	Number of countries in which the worldwide business sells
*Global coverage	Share of global volume accounted for by the countries in which the worldwide business sells
Global Products and Services	
Mix standardization	Percentage of worldwide revenues in a common product or service mix
Content standardization	Percentage of cost of product or service that is in components that are standardized
Global Location of Activities	
Concentration of individual activity	(1) Share of global spending on activity in the country with the most of that activity
	(2) Index of concentration across all countries
Concentration of entire value chain	Weighted average of the concentration indices of individual value activities
Global Marketing	
Comparative marketing intensity	Standard deviation of marketing intensity by country, for advertising, promotion, and selling
Marketing element uniformity	(1) Share of the business's worldwide revenues accounted for by the countries that have a uniform approach
	(2) Degree of similarity of each country's marketing element to that in a base country
Overall marketing uniformity	Score on each element weighted by each country's share of the business's worldwide revenues and by each element's importance
Global Competitive Moves	
Multicountry competitive moves	Moves that involve three or more major countries
Counterparry moves	Response to a competitive attack in one country with a move in a different country; number out of last 10 responses

GLOBAL MARKET PARTICIPATION

Global market participation can be measured in several ways. Each measure provides a different perspective on the extent of global market participation.

Global Market Share

Global market share is measured by the worldwide business's global volume (units or revenues) divided by the total volume of the worldwide market. Managers should also consider an important variant—*globally strategic market share*—measured by the worldwide business's volume in globally strategic country-markets only, divided by the total volume in those markets. *Globally strategic countries* can be identified simply by reviewing the key characteristics discussed earlier:

- Large source of revenues or profits
- Home market of global customers
- Home market of global competitors
- Significant market of global competitors
- Major source of industry innovation

Global Share Balance

Global share balance can be measured by managers in a number of ways. The simplest approach is to compare the percentage split of the worldwide business's revenues accounted for in each country with the percentage split of the world market accounted for in each country. A business with a "perfect" global share balance would have its percentages match the market's exactly. For example, if 30 percent of the world market were in the United States, 20 percent in Japan, and 50 percent in Europe, the business would have 30 percent of its revenues in the United States, 20 percent in Japan, and 50 percent in Europe.

To calculate the global share balance, count the business's split in each country only to the extent that it does not exceed the market's split in that country. Using the previously mentioned market split, if the business's split were 60 percent in the United States, 10 percent in Japan, and 30 percent in Europe, its global share balance would be 0.7 (30 percent U.S. +10 percent Japan +30 percent Europe). One way to think about this balance is that it represents the portion of the business's revenues that are in the right countries relative to the location of the worldwide market. An index value of 1.0 indicates that the worldwide business's sales are in perfect balance with the market's. An index value of 0 indicates the limiting case where 100 percent of the worldwide business's volume is in a country that accounts for 0 percent of the world market volume.[5]

Market Presence

The extent of *market presence* can be measured by the *number of selling countries* (the number of countries in which the worldwide business sells) and by *global coverage*. The latter is the share of global volume (units or revenues) accounted for by the countries in which the worldwide business sells. This is not the same measure as the business's global market share.

GLOBAL PRODUCTS AND SERVICES

Managers can measure the use of global products and services by examining the level of standardization across countries. This standardization needs to be measured at two levels: mix standardization and content standardization.

Mix Standardization

A business may sell a different mix of product types or models in different countries. For example, Volvo does not sell its smaller automobiles in the United States. If these smaller models account for 30 percent of Volvo's worldwide automotive revenues, only 70 percent of its mix is global. Within this global mix, the products themselves have varying levels of standardization. So a complete measure of product or service standardization would read as follows: "This business sells a product (or service) mix that is 80 percent globally common. Of that common mix, products are 70 percent standardized in countries that account for 90 percent of world market volume."

Content Standardization

Managers will find that measuring the extent of content standardization is complex because of the multidimensional nature of a product. Cost is the most common denominator, and is, therefore, the best basis for measurement. Content standardization is measured by the percentage of the product's cost in components that are the same in each country. If the worldwide business sells more than one product, a composite measure can be used weighted by the worldwide sales volume of each product. An electronics business, part of an American multinational company, had a product line that was highly standardized—in fact, more than its executives realized. They initially thought that their product was not standard across countries, because 40 percent of the product cost was in a decoder that was different in each country. But digging deeper, however, they discovered that within the decoder, only the software was unique. Furthermore, the software was embodied in purchased parts (masked ROMs). Therefore, there was no difference in the manufacturing process, only in the inventory to be kept. Also, the cost of developing the unique software was amortized over a large sales base. As a result, what initially appeared to be 40 percent nonstandard turned out to be only 3 percent nonstandard.

The foregoing measure may need to be adjusted for major countries only, or particular groups of countries. This adjustment is particularly necessary if the worldwide business sells a highly standardized product in some but not all countries. With the geographic adjustment the measure has two numbers, as follows: "The worldwide business sells products that are X percent standardized in countries that account for Y percent of world market volume." The product XY (X times Y) can be used if a single statistic is desired.

The measure cannot adequately handle all possibilities. For example, the statistic XY would be the same for a worldwide business with 90 percent standardization in countries accounting for 55 percent of worldwide volume and no standardization in the remaining countries, and for another worldwide business that also had a different standardized product for the remaining countries.

GLOBAL LOCATION OF ACTIVITIES

As with the other global strategy levers, companies need to have an idea of where they are in their use of global activity location before they can decide whether and how to change it. Some useful measures include the following:

Concentration of Individual Activity Each activity should be analyzed in terms of how the geographic share of expenditure on that activity compares with the geographic share of the worldwide business's revenues. This can be done visually via comparative bar charts, numerically by comparing the percentage of the activity in key countries with the percentage of the world market or of the business's revenues in the same countries, or via concentration indices.[6] These comparisons then provide some of the basis for deciding whether the pattern of location is out of line with what it should be.

Concentration of Entire Value Chain One measure can be developed for the concentration of the entire value-adding chain by using the weighted average of the concentration indices of individual value activities.

Production Location Matrix Managers can better understand their global strategy for production location by creating a matrix of where products are produced versus where they are sold. Such a matrix helps to identify the flow of products and also shows the extent of reliance on local manufacture. Exhibit 11-4 in Chapter 11 provides an example of such a matrix.

GLOBAL MARKETING

Much of marketing is qualitative so that precise quantification of the extent of globalization will be difficult. But a number of measures can be applied to global marketing. These measures include the following:

Comparative Marketing Intensity This measures the degree to which spending on each element of the marketing mix—such as advertising, promotion, and selling—varies by country. It is measured by the standard deviation of the expenditure-to-sales ratios in each country for each marketing element.

Marketing Element Uniformity This can be measured in two ways: (1) by the share of the business's worldwide revenues accounted for by the countries that have a uniform approach and (2) by the degree of similarity of each country's marketing element to that in a base country.

Overall Marketing Uniformity Lastly, an overall measure of global marketing can be created by the similarity score on each element weighted by each country's share of the business's worldwide revenues and by each element's importance.

GLOBAL COMPETITIVE MOVES

Chapter 7 described six key types of global competitive moves:

- Cross-subsidization of countries within the same business
- Use of counterparries
- Globally coordinated sequence of moves
- Targeting of actual and potential global competitors
- Developing plans for each major country-competitor combination
- Preemptive use of global strategy

Each of these six key moves can be used to measure how much this global strategy lever is used by a business or by its competitors. But two of these features are more easily quantified than the others—the use of counterparries and the use of a globally coordinated sequence of moves. The use of counterparries can be measured by how often a business responds to a competitive attack in one country with a move in a different country. The use of a globally coordinated sequence of moves can be measured by the number of countries involved in each sequence of moves.

MEASURING GLOBAL ORGANIZATION

Measuring the extent to which management and organization help global strategy involves more subjectivity than measuring industry globalization potential and the use of global strategy levers. Because the effects of organization are so specific to individual companies, corporate managers might find it particularly helpful to measure global organization in their different worldwide businesses. They are likely to find that some elements are common across businesses, while others differ. Then they can investigate if these differences have helped or hurt the globalization efforts of each business. These measures are as follows:

ORGANIZATION ELEMENT	MEASURE
Organization Structure	
One global head	Whether there is one person whose primary job is to be head of the worldwide business
International division	Whether there is an international division that does not contain the domestic business
Functional line heads	Whether there is a single head with line authority for each function
Functional staff heads	Whether there is a single staff coordinator for each function
Strength of business dimension	In a matrix structure, the strength of the business dimension relative to the geographic and functional dimensions
Management Processes	
Global strategic information system	Extent to which the business collects strategic information, such as market share and competitor data, from around the world in a consistent format on a regular basis
Cross-country coordination	Extent to which the business has processes for coordinating strategy across countries—*sharing information, negotiating plans, clearing plans with headquarters,* and *direction by headquarters*
	Frequency and extent of *global meetings*
	Number and extent of *global teams*
	Number of *global product managers* or *global account managers*
Global knowledge sharing	Extent to which a company shares knowledge and information across borders
Global strategic planning	Extent to which the business uses an effective strategic planning process that integrates across countries rather than just adding up the national plans
	(continued)

Continued

ORGANIZATION ELEMENT	MEASURE
Management Processes (continued)	
Global budgeting	Extent to which the business has global budgets that are used for global programs, as opposed to national budgets for national programs
Global customer management	Extent to which the business manages multinational customers on a globally integrated basis, including the percentage of revenues from customers managed this way
Global performance review and compensation	Extent to which senior managers are evaluated and compensated on the basis of global and not just regional or national performance; percentage of compensation tied to global performance
People	
Foreign nationals in home country	Percentage of senior managers in home country who are foreign nationals
Home country nationals in other countries	Percentage of senior managers in other countries who are home country nationals
Foreign nationals in other countries	Percentage of senior managers in other countries who are non–home country foreign nationals
Global boards of directors	Percentage of board that are not nationals of the home country; geographic coverage represented by board members
Culture	
Global culture	Extent to which corporate or business culture is global rather than national
Interdependent culture	Extent to which culture favors interdependence rather than autonomy

---

Discussion and Research Questions

1. What are the benefits of measuring globalization and global strategy?
2. Which industry globalization drivers are the easiest to measure, and which the most difficult and why?
3. How often should measures of globalization and global strategy be made? and by whom?
4. Select one company and its product line. Describe how you would measure that product line's extent of global standardization. Also, how would you get the necessary information?

Notes

1. The author thanks Ed Davis, University of Virginia, for this example.
2. The composite can be derived by weighting the individual features according to their share of product cost, as follows:

$$H_i = \Sigma \, S_j \, C_j$$

where

H_i = the homogeneity index of product i
S_j = the similarity score for feature j
C_j = the percentage of product i's cost accounted for by feature j

3. See Michael E. Porter, *Competitive Advantage* (New York: The Free Press, 1985).
4. See Arnoldo C. Hax and Nicolas S. Majluf, *Strategic Management: An Integrative Perspective* (Upper Saddle River, NJ: Prentice-Hall, 1984), Chapter 6.
5. This measure of global share balance can be somewhat tedious to calculate if there are a large number of countries. The same index can be developed more easily by applying a computer spreadsheet program to the following formula:

$$\text{Index} = 1 - \Sigma(|\, BS_i - MS_i \,|)/200$$

where

BS_i = the percentage share of the world-wide business's volume in country i

MS_i = the percentage share of the world-wide market's volume in country i

The index will range from 0 to 1.0 in value.
6. The following index for activity concentration can be used:

$$\text{Index} = \sqrt[2]{\Sigma\, S_i^2}$$

where S_i is the ith country's share of global expenditure on the activity

11

CONDUCTING A GLOBAL STRATEGY ANALYSIS

—◈◈◈—

This last chapter provides a guide to the more practical aspects of applying the global strategy framework and conducting the necessary analyses. It also provides a number of forms that have proved useful in guiding executives through the analysis. One of the greatest challenges for the would-be global manager is acquiring the information that is needed both to formulate and to implement a global strategy. Surprisingly few companies have complete and readily accessible information about the products and services they offer worldwide. Often, complete information by country exists only at the country level. Some companies even get trapped in a circular dilemma: They cannot collect information about a particular country because they do not participate in it, and they do not participate there because they do not have any information about the country.

WORKSTEPS

A global strategy analysis can range in effort from a one-day brainstorming exercise to a multimonth study. The analysis can also cover an entire business, or even the entire company, or be restricted to a narrow range of issues, such as developing a global pack design or a global purchasing policy. The following list (depicted in Exhibit 11-1) sets out the steps for a comprehensive effort:

A. Assembling the global team
B. Defining the business
C. Identifying key markets
D. Identifying key competitors
E. Checking the core strategy
F. Checking country selection
G. Diagnosing industry globalization potential
H. Evaluating current and potential use of global strategy levers
I. Evaluating organization capability
J. Developing global programs

Also, as shown in Exhibit 11-1, feedback should be provided at each step to earlier steps. For example, discovering an opportunity to use global strategy at step H may generate a need to reconsider the core strategy checked earlier in step E.

A. ASSEMBLING THE GLOBAL TEAM

Involvement of managers from different functions and locations is absolutely crucial to the success of a global strategy. So selecting the team to participate in the global analysis is a key decision. The team needs to be selected from the following:

• Head of the worldwide business, if there is one
• Senior representatives from related businesses (that share facilities or staff)

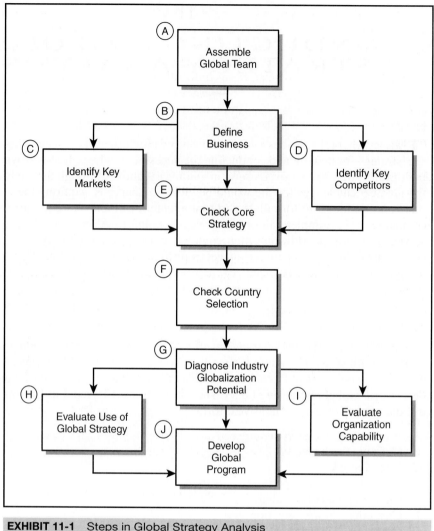

EXHIBIT 11-1 Steps in Global Strategy Analysis

- Senior corporate executive
- Heads of major regions/countries
- Heads of key functions

Ideally, the team should consist of no more than six to eight regular members. If choices have to be made, full geographic representation should be favored over full functional representation. In addition, the team needs support staff, such as from the planning function, or staff from the organization of the individual members. The invitation to join the global team should come from the highest possible level, ideally from the CEO. The inviter needs to stress the importance and relevance of the effort and indicate the hoped for outcome. The team should have a leader, who should be the head of the worldwide business or the nearest equivalent.

Although perhaps obvious, the most difficult practical problem is often setting up a meeting schedule. So that should be done at the first meeting. Because each of the executives is extremely busy, it is better to establish a set schedule even though the work may not fit exactly. At least three meetings should be set up, between one and two months apart, perhaps piggybacking onto other events such as corporate planning meetings. It is also very helpful to move the location of the meeting around the world— anything to avoid the appearance of a head office/home country driven project helps. In addition, rotating the location helps the team members to undertake the travel needed in a global business and allows local staff to participate.

The schedule should also allow enough time between meetings to collect and analyze information and to develop strategies and reports. Having new input greatly enhances what can be achieved in each meeting.

B. DEFINING THE BUSINESS

The leader of the global team needs to have a good idea of what business will be analyzed before he or she can assemble the global team, but developing a complete definition needs the input of the team. *Business definition is an important issue, because a global strategy analysis is often more effective by starting out with a piece of the business rather than with the entire business.* Experience with analyzing this part of the business can then be transferred to subsequent expanded efforts. Perhaps as important, the first global analysis needs to achieve usable results within a short time span, say, six months at the most. Classically, business definition has focused on the three dimensions of product (or service) function, technology employed, and customer groups served.[1] In the context of global strategy, the fourth dimension of geography must, of course, be added. Taking account of the geographic dimension will make it clearer which businesses face broader global issues and, therefore, have a greater need for global strategy. In addition, the team may wish to restrict the analysis to just one region, such as Europe. So, for example, a manufacturer of medical equipment may have several options in defining the business to study:

- The entire medical equipment division (and the industries in which it participates)
- The worldwide hospital equipment business
- The worldwide hospital radiography equipment business
- The European hospital radiography equipment business

Another concern is to define the business sufficiently broadly to encompass competition from actual and potential substitutes.

C. IDENTIFYING KEY MARKETS

The global team cannot collect and analyze information about every country in which the business operates or might operate, because of both the time and effort needed for collection and the resultant information overload. One approach is to split the analysis into two levels, first by region and then by country within each region. The choice of regions is usually easy—North America, South America, Europe, Far East, or Pacific Rim being the most common. Matching the region definitions to the way in which the company is organized may not be the purest approach, but is usually the most practical for data gathering and for subsequent implementation. Some companies use unusual regional groupings. Gillette has organized a North Atlantic region, because of the similarity in income levels and lifestyle among the United States, Canada, and Western Europe. Sterling Drug has used a JCAP region, combining Japan, Canada, and other Pacific Rim countries, managed out of New York. Citibank also has an unusual grouping for its global finance business—JENA, an acronym for Japan, Europe, North America, Australia, and New Zealand; in short, most of the developed world. When selecting countries within regions, the definition of a country is flexible, as described in Chapter 1. For example, a "country" can be Benelux or Scandinavia. As with regions, only the most important countries should be chosen. Criteria for country selection should include the largest country-markets, the countries in which the company has the largest businesses, and globally strategic countries.

Splitting the analysis into two levels—global and regional—reduces the number of geographic entities that need to be considered at one time. *It is surprisingly important to be able to view all key markets spread across one exhibit as a comparative chart.* Executives are able to generate new understanding and insight when they can compare and contrast across regions and countries. Furthermore, when the members of the global team view these comparative charts *together,* they stimulate each other in developing ideas. So a total of no more than 10 geographic entities plus "all other" and "total world (region)" columns should be used. At the country level, markets should be selected for analysis using the criteria in Chapter 3 on global market participation. The list should include the six or so largest markets in which the business participates, any other country-markets among the largest six in the world even if the business is not there, any other markets that are strategically important, and any other markets in which the worldwide business has its largest country-businesses. This combination will usually result in a list of eight to 10 countries. In deciding on the "all other" category, the team needs to define the world. As stated in Chapter 1, the world market includes only country-markets that are accessible to multinational companies. Such accessible countries vary from industry to industry and also change over time. Until the changes of regime in 1989, most countries in Eastern Europe might have been excluded. Similarly, the breakup of the Soviet Union added new countries to the list of accessible markets. In some industries, it may be useful to add a column combining the countries that are not accessible to the business. Having such a column will give a better perspective on the total market and may help the global team avoid being blindsided by developments coming out of inaccessible countries.

The global team should then use the list of countries as the basis on which most of the information will be collected and displayed.

INFORMATION TO BE COLLECTED FOR EACH REGION/COUNTRY

In conducting analysis of individual countries in order to make an entry decision, for example, a large amount of information needs to be collected (some of which will be identified in step F). But for this step of identifying key markets, much less information is needed. The following basic set of information needs to be known for each country-market:

- Market size in units and revenues
- Stage of product life cycle

- Number of global competitors
- Number of regionwide competitors
- Number of national or local competitors
- Percentage of country production (in the industry) exported
- Percentage of country consumption imported
- Local content requirement
- Labor cost
- Government share of customer purchases
- Tax rate for local and for foreign companies
- Percentage of foreign ownership allowed

Coping with Exchange Rates

Currency exchange rates obviously have a very crucial role in globalization decisions. To make data collection simple and to ease subsequent analysis, all data should be reported in the currency of the headquarters country at historical exchange rates, that is, using the same exchange rates that were applied by the local businesses when they reported to headquarters in each time period in the past. Typically, that means the annual average exchange rate for revenue and profit items and year-end exchange rates for balance sheet items. The key reason for converting to the home currency is that most owners or shareholders care about the worldwide business's contribution to revenues and profits in their home currency. Similarly, the key reason for using historical exchange rates is that for a globalization analysis, the need is to know how each country-business contributed to the total business. So, a depreciating local currency, for example, needs to be recognized for its impact on the role that the local business can play. (In contrast, evaluating the performance of local managers should generally be done using figures in their local currency.)

D. IDENTIFYING KEY COMPETITORS

Just as every country cannot be analyzed, neither can every competitor. So the global team needs to select the most important competitors to study. Competitors that need to be analyzed include the following:

- All global competitors, as defined by all competitors that have significant market presence in North America, Europe, and Asia and have at least 5 percent global market share. (This definition may need to be adapted in industries where the key continents are different from those listed.)
- The largest competitors based in each lead country and major region, even if they are not global.
- Potential global competitors.

If possible, the list of all competitors should be kept to 10 or fewer.

The list of key competitors combines with the list of key markets to make a very powerful organizing framework for displaying and analyzing information. Exhibit 11-2 illustrates the different kinds of data matrices that are useful to develop for this market-competitor combination—such as global and European matrices for competitors' market share, relative prices, relative costs, and relative quality.[2]

Markets / Competitors	N. America	S. America	Europe	Asia	All Others	Total
Our Company						
Competitor A						
Competitor B		Market Share %				
Competitor C		* 3 Years Ago				
Competitor D		* This Year				
Competitor E		* 3 Years in Future				
All Others						
Total						

Markets / Competitors	Germany	France	U.K.	Italy	All Others	Total
Our Company						
Competitor A						
Competitor B		Market Share %				
Competitor C		* 3 Years Ago				
Competitor D		* This Year				
Competitor E		* 3 Years in Future				
All Others						
Total						

Create Also for: Relative Prices | Relative Costs | Relative Quality

EXHIBIT 11-2   Example Data Matrices for Analyzing Competitors

E. CHECKING THE CORE STRATEGY

In conducting a global strategy analysis, it is common for the members of the global team either to not know what the business's core strategy is or, more commonly, to hold differing views on what it is. So the global team will find it very helpful to check its core business strategy early in the process. The best way to conduct this check is to have executives from both headquarters and each major region or country write down the core strategy. Doing so has two benefits. First, if the core business strategy is not already specified in some document, this procedure helps make explicit what may have been implicit. In addition, many statements of business strategy are typically less detailed than they should be and often consist of what Americans like to call "apple pie and motherhood" statements, such as "this business will profitably offer the highest quality products and provide the best value to our customers." Such statements can be very helpful in motivating organization members and reassuring shareholders but provide little strategic guidance. The essence of a strategy is that it makes choices, something that the previous example does not. After all, who would choose the opposite: "This business will unprofitably offer the poorest quality products and provide the worst value to our customers"? Andrall E. Pearson, then president of Pepsico, very succinctly captured the importance of strategic choice when he said, "A strategy is something that someone else would not be stupid not to choose."[3] So managers should write out their core business strategy in some detail and in a format that makes choices explicit.

The statement of core strategy should include:

- Business definition
- Strategic thrust
- Financial targets
- Sources of competitive advantage
- Strategy elements
- Value-adding activities
- Competitive strategy

Exhibit A-1 in the Appendix provides forms that are useful for specifying the core strategy.

The second benefit of having each major region or country specify its view of the core business strategy is that differences among the regions and countries can then be identified. Identifying these differences is facilitated by summarizing and combining the strategy statements into comparative charts such as those in Exhibit A-2 in the Appendix.

F. CHECKING COUNTRY SELECTION

Country selection is one of the most important elements in both internationalization and globalization. It is also a decision for which analytical techniques can be particularly helpful. Traditional analytical approaches to selecting countries for entry have focused entirely on stand-alone attractiveness.[4] But managers need to consider the global strategic importance of a country. Of additional relevance is the potential for synergy between the business under consideration and sister businesses in each country. For example, a leading American forest products company finds that a key factor in deciding whether or not to expand a particular business into a new country is that business's potential for absorbing paper production capacity already in place in the country. So three sets of overall factors should determine country selection:

- Stand-alone attractiveness
- Global strategic importance
- Synergy

The global team should evaluate country selection using the following steps:

1. Identify countries/regions for analysis
2. Develop a list of subfactors for each of the three sets of overall factors
3. Assign weights to each subfactor
4. Rate each country/region on each subfactor
5. Combine the weights and ratings to arrive at a total score for each country or region
6. Adjust the total score for country risk

1. IDENTIFY COUNTRIES/REGIONS

The global team should identify all countries or regions in which the business already participates or might do so. Existing countries should be analyzed in order to help determine the level of effort that should be devoted to them and to provide a benchmark for evaluating new countries. It is particularly important to include countries that may be difficult to enter but that are globally strategic or potentially so.

2. DEVELOP LIST OF SUBFACTORS

The global team should develop its own list of subfactors to assess each of the sets of factors. Such a list might include the following:

Stand-Alone Attractiveness of Country/Region

- Size of market
- Growth rate of market
- Barriers to entry
- Competitive situation
- Price levels
- Tax rates
- Macroeconomic conditions
- Political risk
- Cost of adaptation

Global Strategic Importance of Country/Region

- Home market of global customers
- Home market of global competitors
- Significant market of global competitors
- Major source of industry innovation
- Home of most demanding customers

Synergy with Other Businesses in Country/Region

- Shares activities with other company businesses
- Uses upstream (e.g., raw material production) capacity
- Uses downstream (e.g., final assembly or distribution) capacity
- Proximity to other markets

For countries in which the business is not already present, *potential* synergy is what should be evaluated.

3. ASSIGN WEIGHTS TO EACH SUBFACTOR

The global team should next assign a weighting to each subfactor such that the total for all subfactors sums to 100 points. One approach is to first split the 100 points among the three overall factors of stand-alone attractiveness, global strategic importance, and synergy with other businesses. For example, these three overall factors might be assigned 40, 40, and 20 points, respectively. Then the points for each overall factor can be split among the individual subfactors.

4. RATE EACH COUNTRY/REGION ON EACH SUBFACTOR

The global team should then rate each country or region on each individual subfactor on a scale from 0 to 10. A practical way to do this is to set benchmarks by giving a rating of 10 to the country or countries with the strongest showing on each particular factor. For example, on the market size subfactor, the largest market can be assigned a score of 10 and all other countries scaled in proportion. In some other cases no country may qualify for the maximum score, so the global team needs to consider what would rate a maximum score, and scale the countries accordingly. The exact approach used is not as important as the end result of differentiating among the countries on the various subfactors.

5. COMBINE THE SUBFACTOR WEIGHTS AND COUNTRY RATINGS

To arrive at a total rating for each country, the weights and ratings should be multiplied together and summed (and divided by 10 to get a total country rating that is out of 100).

6. ADJUST FOR COUNTRY RISK

Finally the total country ratings should be adjusted for country risks such as political instability, the risk of expropriation, and the risk of currency devaluation. Traditionally, country risk has been included with other factors in evaluating stand-alone attractiveness, rather than being considered separately as done here.[5] This separate approach is preferable for three reasons. First, it separates the business factors from the political ones. For example, both Brazil and Japan are large markets that may be highly attractive in particular industries. But the level of country risk has been much higher in Brazil than in Japan. Mixing the two types of factors makes it difficult to recognize two fundamentally different sources of uncertainty that need to be managed in different ways. Second, risk can be viewed as a discount factor applied to expected returns from participating in a country. Third, country risk changes much more quickly than business attractiveness, as it did for China in 1989, the Middle East in 1990, Mexico in 1994, and Russia and Indonesia in 1998. Various services such as Political Risk Services (formerly the Frost & Sullivan Political Risk Letter) provide relatively low-cost and comprehensive ratings of country risk.[6] The ratings provided by these services should be converted into a risk adjustment factor scored from 0 as hopelessly risky to 1.0 as no risk at all.

USING THE RATINGS

The resultant ratings should be used as one input to the decision on country selection and should not be used in a mechanistic way. The global team should solicit the input of managers familiar with the individual countries as well as use their own individual judgment. Although a lot of work, this kind of comprehensive analytical process can be helpful in dispelling myths or clearing up ignorance about the attractiveness of particular countries. The process can also force companies to recognize the importance of entering countries that have been avoided for their difficulty. In summary, the benefits of this technique include identifying relevant data, reducing complexity, encouraging a systematic approach, providing quantitative measurement, and complementing intuition.

At the same time, users have to be cautious of its weaknesses, which include oversimplifying, requiring subjective evaluations, and needing modification for each application. Most important, this technique must not be used blindly.

G. DIAGNOSING INDUSTRY GLOBALIZATION POTENTIAL

Diagnosing industry globalization potential can best be done in two stages. In the first stage, the global team can make preliminary assessments through group discussion at one of its meetings, using the measures summarized in Chapter 10. These assessments should be written up so that they can be verified by country managers and staff in a second stage. A typical assessment might be as follows:

> The globalization driver of global customers rates a moderate score today and is increasing in strength. Global customers now account for about 20 percent, up about 5 percentage points from three years ago, and regionwide customers a further 35 percent, up about 10 points from three years ago. We expect both global and regionwide customers to increase their share of purchases. Showa K.K. behaves the most globally as a customer. In its last request for proposal, it required a bid with standard prices for each country. Duvall & Cie. is starting to behave as a global customer and now requires all products to be approved in Paris even though its local subsidiaries make their own purchase decisions. We are not sure what Schmidt AG is doing and want each country manager to report back with an assessment.

Next, the global team should identify how industry globalization drivers give rise to opportunities to use global strategy levers. For example, what does the diagnosis of global customers indicate for the use of global marketing such as global account management?

H. EVALUATING CURRENT AND POTENTIAL USE OF GLOBAL STRATEGY LEVERS

Identifying changes to be made in the use of global strategy levers requires a diagnosis of both their current and their potential use. There are three major sources of ideas for diagnosing the potential use of global strategy levers:

- Analysis of the potential benefits from using global strategy
- Analysis of the industry globalization drivers
- Analysis of what competitors are doing

Various analytical and display techniques can help diagnose the individual global strategy levers, as explained next.

GLOBAL MARKET PARTICIPATION

A key aspect of a global approach to market participation is the extent to which the business's revenues are in geographic balance with those of the market as a whole. It can be very helpful to depict graphically the global share balance to compare where the

Reducing the number of products worldwide by 33% would save:

	% of Sales
• Manufacturing	3% to 4%
• Inventory (14% of sales times 20% carrying cost)	2.8%
• Out-of-stock and orders not pushed from fear of out-of-stocks (10% of sales times 40% gross margin)	4.0%
Total	10% to 11%

These potential savings can be compared with a pretax margin of 8% and a media budget of 12%.

EXHIBIT 11-3   Example Calculation of Potential Savings from Product Standardization

business has its revenues with the overall global market. A comparative bar chart might show, for example, that a business has far too much of its revenues concentrated in the United States and not nearly enough in Japan, and that this imbalance will worsen in the next five years.

GLOBAL PRODUCTS AND SERVICES

The key analysis needed for product standardization decisions is the calculation of potential cost savings. Potential cost savings from product standardization can be small for individual factors but can add up significantly. Exhibit 11-3 illustrates the type of analysis needed.

GLOBAL ACTIVITY LOCATION

As with market participation, the analysis of activity location can be enhanced through the use of visual display. Working with an industrial supplies company, this author found one such display helped to highlight the dominance of Germany in R&D and manufacturing relative to its share of the business's global revenues. The implications depend, of course, on the specific situation of the business. In this example, the business's high level of concentration helped to achieve economies of scale in R&D and manufacturing. But the business also suffered from a lack of R&D facilities in two of the most innovative markets—the United States and Japan.

The location of manufacturing is typically the most difficult issue in global strategy. It helps to start with a good understanding of where products are produced and where they are shipped. Exhibit 11-4 provides an example of a *production location matrix* that helps managers understand their current production location strategy. In Exhibit 11-4 the shaded boxes indicate units that are sold in the country of production. So in this example, 51 percent of production is for local sale, which in most cases is probably greater than it should be under a globally integrated strategy.

Having evaluated each value-adding activity, the team should summarize the actual and target location of each activity in terms of whether it is, or should be, mostly local

Units in Millions

Produced in \ Sold in	U.S.A.	Germany	France	U.K.	Japan	Brazil	Others	Total Units Produced
U.S.A.	1,320						230	1,550
France		380	250	210			130	970
Brazil						140		140
Taiwan					470		220	690
Total Units Sold	1,320	380	250	210	470	140	580	3,350

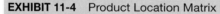 = Produced and Sold in the Same Country

51% of Production is for Local Sale (U.S.A., France, and Brazil = 1,710 Million Units out of 3,350 Million Total)

EXHIBIT 11-4 Product Location Matrix

or mostly central. In addition, the team should decide on the nature of headquarters co-ordination and control needed for each activity (Exhibit 11-5).

GLOBAL MARKETING

As with value-adding activities, it can be useful to summarize the actual and target use of global marketing. Exhibit 11-6 provides a format for summarizing conclusions on which marketing element to globalize and to what extent. It can provide a useful focus on the end objective of the analyses of industry globalization drivers, potential benefits of global strategy levers, and competitors' approaches.

The global team can also use a *relative price map* to deal with the one marketing element that is easy to quantify—pricing. Such a map shows the business's pricing in each country indexed relative to the home country (or any one reference country). This index can be constructed in a number of ways. The easiest way is if there exists a typical product that is sold in every country or region being analyzed. If no one product

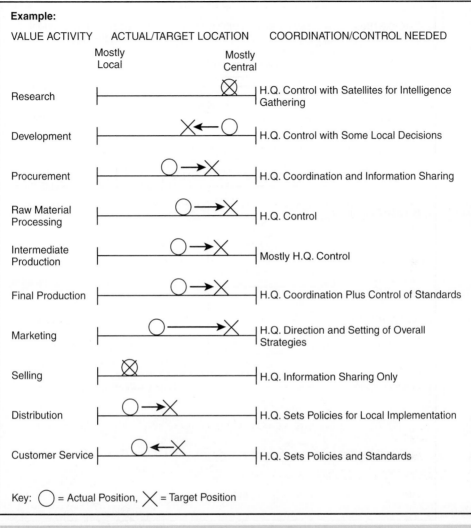

EXHIBIT 11-5 Actual and Target Globalization by Activity

meets this criterion or if different products have different patterns of international pricing (e.g., one major product may be priced in Europe above the company's home country price, while another major product may be below the home country price), then the global team needs to create either a number of different charts or a single weighted composite.

GLOBAL COMPETITIVE MOVES

Most companies have very poor information about their competitors' moves. If the information exists, it is usually scattered around the company with different people and in different countries. Historical information about competitors' moves is even scarcer.

MARKETING ELEMENT	ACTUAL/TARGET UNIFORMITY	COORDINATION/CONTROL NEEDED
	Mostly Different ————————— Mostly Uniform	

Positioning	○ ——→ ✕	H.Q. Specifics for Major Brands
Brand Name	⊗	No Changes in Major Brand Names
Packaging Design	○ ——→ ✕	H.Q. Guidelines
Absolute Pricing	○ ——→ ✕	Local Decisions Coordinated Regionally
Relative Pricing	○ ——→ ✕	H.Q. Guidelines
Advertising Strategy	○ ——→ ✕	H.Q. Sets for Major Brands
Advertising Execution	⊗	Local Adaption of Core Campaigns, Plus Create Own Other Campaigns
Sales Promotion	⊗	H.Q. Information Sharing Only
Selling Approach	⊗	Region Sets Policies for Local Implementation
Sales Personnel	⊗	Local Selection and Standards
Distribution	○ ——→ ✕	Regional Coordination
Customer Service	○ ——→ ✕	H.Q. and Regions Set Policies

Key: ○ = Actual Position, ✕ = Target Position

EXHIBIT 11-6   Summary of Global Marketing Strategy

But collecting and maintaining such information is crucial for understanding and pre-dicting the pattern of competitors' global moves.[7] For example, mapping the history of each major competitor's moves, as in Exhibit 11-7, helps to identify the extent to which they globally integrate their competitive moves. In the example in Exhibit 11-7, "Haneda K.K." seems to make its price and product moves in North America first, closely followed by the other regions. In contrast, new advertising campaigns seem to start in Asia. It is also helpful to map the history of competitors' global responses to your business's moves.

Example:

COMPETITOR: Haneda K.K.

Period \ Market	N. America	S. America	Europe	Asia	Other
2000 Q1	▲ Raised Price on T29 Model				
2000 Q2			▲ Raised Price on T29 Model		
2000 Q3				▲ Raised Price on T29 Model	
2000 Q4					
2001 Q1		▲ Raised Price on T29 Model			▲ Raised Price on T29 Model
2001 Q2				◯ New Ad Campaign	
2001 Q3	◼ Introduced S32 Line		◼ Introduced S32 Line		
2001 Q4			◯ New Ad Campaign		
2002 Q1				◼ Introduced S32 Line	
2002 Q2	◯ New Ad Campaign				
2002 Q3	▲ Raised Price on S32 Line				◼ Introduced S32 Line
2002 Q4			▲ Raised Price on S32 Line		

Key: ▲ = Pricing Move   ◼ = Product Move   ◯ = Advertising Move

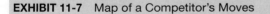

EXHIBIT 11-7   Map of a Competitor's Moves

SUMMARY OF BUSINESS AND COMPETITORS

Having evaluated the use of each individual global strategy lever and its elements, it is helpful to summarize the total use of global strategy by the business and its major competitors. The example in Exhibit 11-8 illustrates the position of the business and its three major competitors in terms of their use of each of the five global strategy levers.

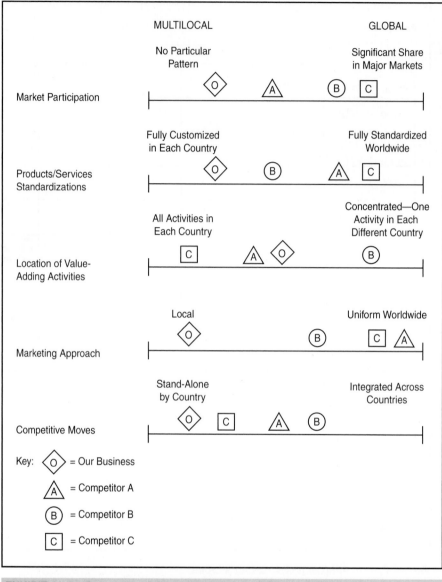

EXHIBIT 11-8   Summary of Competitors' Use of Global Strategies

I. EVALUATING ORGANIZATION CAPABILITY

Organization and management factors make a crucial difference to how well global strategy can be developed and implemented. So it is also essential to evaluate the organization's capability for global strategy and to diagnose the necessary changes. Chapter 8 discussed each of the sets of factors and their individual elements to determine together the organization's capability for global strategy. The global team should systematically evaluate each of these factors and elements using the measures described in Chapter 10. Typically, the methodology for this step should include getting the views of both headquarters and subsidiary managers through interviews, group discussions, and surveys. In this data gathering process, the global team should not just collect information about problems (which managers are usually happy to talk about) but also find out about possible solutions, as well as test for reactions to solutions devised by the team. To help find the best solutions, the global team should try to discover how other effective companies in the same industry or comparable industries organize and manage for global strategy.

J. DEVELOPING GLOBAL PROGRAMS

The last task in a global strategy analysis is to specify plans for global programs in sufficient detail that they can take on a life of their own. In other words, this last step ensures the transition to implementation. The previous analyses will typically have identified a large number of global programs. For example, one company that conducted a global strategy analysis concluded with the following programs that needed to be implemented:

- Global Products
- Global Technology Management
- Global Materials Procurement
- Global Marketing Management
- Global Account Management
- Global Pricing
- Global Identification
- Global Trade Show Coordination
- Global Market Intelligence

To move to implementation, the company developed plans for each program. The following summary illustrates the plan for the global products program:

GLOBAL PRODUCTS PROGRAM

Product and process are so interlinked that we need to treat them together. Our ability to develop highly customized products for key customers is a key competitive advantage. At the same time global customers expect to be able to purchase consistent/uniform products wherever they operate sophisticated equipment. But consistent products require a consistent manufacturing process, which we do not have. There is now wide variation from region to region in our manufacturing approach, arising from a combination of raw material availability, equipment, customers' expectations, and local economic conditions. The result is that products are not as standardized as they could or should be.

OBJECTIVE

Maintain and augment our competitive advantage of being able to provide consistent/uniform products around the world to those customers who require consistency. In addition, cut costs.

OVERALL STRATEGY

Increase standardization across countries by individual characteristics at tighter specifications that provide added value to customers. We will standardize only when the additional cost is low or is recoverable from customers.

POTENTIAL BENEFITS

- *Cost savings for the company*
- *Improved quality or performance for the customer*
- *Increased barriers to competition*
- *Improved trust of the company by customer management*
- *Training efficiencies*

POTENTIAL DISADVANTAGES

- *Possibly easier for customers to copy*
- *May be too expensive in many cases*
- *Impact on upstream product profitability and availability*
- *Customer perception of reduced flexibility*

IMPLEMENTATION

1. *Use the strategic account management programs in the various regions to develop an information base on the types of products required by key accounts throughout the world: type of equipment, product specifications, performance criteria, quality, and so on. This activity will be managed by the global marketing manager.*
2. *Develop a complete database on our manufacturing capabilities for sophisticated textile tubes worldwide. This activity will be managed by the global technical manager. An attachment shows a partial and preliminary analysis for the XYZ product and lists the key variations across countries.*
3. *Decide on which products and characteristics to standardize, and develop a cost-benefit analysis to justify each recommendation. This will be done jointly by the global marketing and technical managers.*

Next Steps: Complete analysis of worldwide capabilities for all high-end products
Responsibility: John Poulenc and Maria Suzuki
Timing: By end of June 2002

FURTHER STEPS

The global strategy analysis described in this chapter provides four concrete outputs:

- An assessment of how global an industry is today and is likely to become in the future
- An understanding of how global a company's approach is today, and how it compares to its competitors and to the industry potential for further globalization
- An identification of the organizational factors that will facilitate or hinder a move toward globalization
- A broad action plan, specifying strategic and organizational change priorities

The analysis in and of itself does not provide the details of a global competitive strategy. If its output has shown that adopting some form of global strategy is indeed desirable, the analysis needs to be followed by another effort aimed at developing a detailed total global and competitive strategy. Among the decisions that will need to be made are the definition of a competitive posture in various countries (i.e., in what part of the world should we compete on our own and in what part should we form alliances?), the articulation of specific functional strategies (manufacturing, marketing, financial, etc.), and the adoption of organizational mechanisms aimed at reinforcing the strategic objectives sought.

SOME GUIDING IDEAS FOR IMPLEMENTING A TOTAL GLOBAL STRATEGY

In conducting a global strategy analysis and then globalizing a business's strategy, the reader may wish to keep in mind a number of guiding ideas that summarize the concepts in this book:

1. Do not assume that "it cannot happen here." Almost any industry has the potential for globalization and global competition.
2. Global industries are not born but are created by global companies. The rewards of globalization go to the first movers.
3. Globalization requires a clear vision of the firm as a global competitor. It also requires a long-term time horizon and a commitment from top management.
4. Globalization is not all or nothing. A business can be global in some elements of its strategy and not in others.

Discussion and Research Question

1. Using the framework in this chapter, select a company and one of its worldwide businesses and conduct a complete global strategy analysis.

Notes

1. See Derek F. Abell, *Defining the Business: The Starting Point of Strategic Planning,* (Upper Saddle River, NJ: Prentice Hall, 1980).
2. Evaluating relative quality is a very difficult task. The PIMS program has developed some useful techniques. See Robert D. Buzzell and Bradley T. Gale, *The PIMS Principles: Linking Strategy to Performance* (New York: Free Press, 1987), Chapter 6.
3. He made this statement at a presentation at the Harvard Business School in 1982. See also George S. Yip, "Planning at Pepsi (B)," Case No. 9-583-051 (Boston: Harvard Business School, 1983).
4. For example, Franklin R. Root, *Entry Strategies for International Markets* (San Francisco: Jossey-Bass, 1994), provides a thorough method for scoring country attractiveness.
5. See Root, *Entry Strategies for International Markets* for a discussion of country risk.
6. Some observers have commented that the level of political risk varies by company. Companies with good ties to local power groups (such as via the prime minister's brother-in-law's cousin) face less risk of expropriation and other forms of risk affected by government actions.
7. There are now many guides on how to collect competitive intelligence. See, for example, Leonard Fuld, *Competitor Intelligence: How to Get It—How to Use It* (New York: John Wiley & Sons, 1985).

APPENDIX

—◦⧟◦—

WORKSHEETS FOR EVALUATING CORE STRATEGY

BUSINESS _____

REGION/COUNTRY _____

Date Completed _____

1. BUSINESS DEFINITION

The essence of both business definition and strategy formulation is choice. By defining your business in a certain way, you are choosing to do some things and not others. Similarly a strategy involves selecting certain customer groups and not others, offering some types of products and not others, and so on. MENTION ANY CHANGES THAT YOU PLAN TO MAKE IN YOUR BUSINESS DEFINITION, for example, shift from one type of customer to another type.

Customer Needs Addressed:

_____

Technologies Used:

_____

_____

Customer Segments Served:

_____

_____

_____

Products Offered:

_____

_____

_____

Geographic Scope:

_____

EXHIBIT A-1 Specification of Core Business Strategy

2. STRATEGIC THRUST

State whether you are trying to grow, maintain, or shrink the size of this business and at what rate.

State your short-term performance priorities in terms of market share, revenues, and profitability.

Direction:

Rate:

Performance Priorities:

1st _____

2nd _____

3rd _____

3. FINANCIAL TARGETS

4. SOURCES OF COMPETITIVE ADVANTAGE

State your major sources of competitive advantage. These sources both must be important to customers and must give you a significant advantage over competitors. The following list provides categories of advantage: You need to add more detail to the ones you specify:

- Patents
- Research capability
- Development capability
- Product or service quality
- Alignment of offerings with critical needs of customers
- Breadth of product line
- Customer relationships
- Access to lower cost or more effective factors of production
- Location of manufacturing near customers or sources of supply
- Unique manufacturing technology
- Vertical integration
- Operating efficiency

- Access to distribution channels
- Physical distribution capability
- Marketing skills
- Reputation of company
- Strength of brand name
- Sales force effectiveness
- Technical support strength
- Customer service
- Government support or protection
- Size of business
- Superior financial resources
- Lower cost finance
- Cross-business synergy
- Corporate support

Describe in order of importance your most important sources of competitive advantage:

_____

_____

_____

EXHIBIT A-1   *Continued*

5. STRATEGY ELEMENTS

For each strategy element specify the nature of your strategy:

Technology:

_____

_____

Manufacturing:

_____

_____

Product Line:

_____

_____

_____

Pricing:

_____

_____

Selling Approach:

_____

_____

Marketing Communications:

_____

_____

Distribution:

_____

_____

Customer Service:

_____

_____

EXHIBIT A-1 *Continued*

6. VALUE-ADDING ACTIVITIES

Specify the location of each value-adding activity in your business. Examples of value-adding activities include:

- Research
- Development
- Procurement
- Raw material processing
- Intermediate production/subassembly
- Final production/final assembly
- Marketing
- Selling
- Distribution
- Customer service

Activity   Location

_____   _____
_____   _____
_____   _____
_____   _____
_____   _____
_____   _____
_____   _____
_____   _____
_____   _____
_____   _____
_____   _____
_____   _____

7. COMPETITIVE STRATEGY

Identify your major competitors and specify your strategy versus each of them. Examples of competitive strategy are as follows:

- To keep competitor A as the second choice vendor by maintaining closer relationships with our customers
- To be a fast follower of innovations by competitor B
- To avoid head-to-head price competition with competitor C
- To restrict competitor D to its current segment of customers
- To gain five points of share in the next three years from competitor E

Competitor   Strategy vs. Competitor

_____   _____
_____   _____
_____   _____
_____   _____
_____   _____
_____   _____

EXHIBIT A-1   *Continued*

BIBLIOGRAPHY

BOOKS

Abegglen, James C., and George Stalk, Jr. *Kaisha: The Japanese Corporation.* New York: Basic Books, 1985.

Abell, Derek F. *Defining the Business: The Starting Point of Strategic Planning.* Upper Saddle River, NJ: Prentice Hall, 1980.

Avery, Christopher. *Business and Human Rights in a Time of Change.* London: Amnesty International Publications, 2000.

Baden Fuller, C., C. P. Nicolaides, and J. Stopford. "National or Global? The Study of Company Strategies and the European Market for Major Appliances." *London Business School Centre for Business Strategy Working Paper Series,* No. 28, 1987.

Baldwin, Carliss Y. "The Capital Factor: Competing for Capital in a Global Environment." In Michael E. Porter, ed. *Competition in Global Industries.* Boston: Harvard Business School Press, 1986.

Bartlett, Christopher A., "Building and Managing the Transitional: The New Organisational Challenge." In Michael E. Porter, ed. *Competition in Global Industries.* Boston: Harvard Business School Press, 1986, pp. 367–404.

Bartlett, Christopher A., Yves L. Doz, and Gunnar Hedlund, eds. *Managing the Global Firm.* London: Routledge, 1990.

Bartlett, Christopher A. and Sumantra Ghoshal. *Text, Cases, and Readings in Cross-Border Management,* 3rd ed. Boston: McGraw-Hill, 2000.

Bartlett, Christopher A., and Sumantra Ghoshal. *Managing Across Borders: The Transnational Solution.* Boston: Harvard Business School Press, 1989.

Beamish, Paul, and J. Peter Killing, eds. *Cooperative Strategies.* Lanham, MD: Lexington Books, 1997.

Beamish, Paul W., J. Peter Killing, Donald J. Lecraw, and Harold Crookell. *International Management: Text and Cases.* Homewood, IL: Irwin, 1991.

Beamish, Paul W., Allen J. Morrison, Philip M. Rosenzweig, and Andrew C. Inkpen. *International Management: Text and Cases,* 4th ed. New York: Irwin McGraw-Hill, 2000.

Black, J. Stewart, and David Ulrich. "The New Frontier of Global HR." In Pat Joynt and Bob Morton, eds. *The Global HR Manager.* London: Institute of Personnel and Development, 1999, Chapter 2, pp. 12–38.

Brandenburger, Adam M., and Barry J. Nalebuff. *Coopetition.* New York: Currency Doubleday, 1996.

Buckley, Peter J., and Mark Casson. *The Future of the Multinational Enterprise.* New York: Holmes and Meier Publishers, Inc., 1976.

Buzzell, Robert D., and Bradley T. Gale. *The PIMS Principles: Linking Strategy to Performance.* New York: Free Press, 1987.

Cecchini, Paolo. *The European Challenge: 1992, The Benefits of a Single Market.* England: Wildwood House, 1988.

Chandler, Alfred D., Jr. *Strategy and Structure.* Cambridge, MA: The M.I.T. Press, 1962.

Committe for the Study of the Causes and Consequences of the Internationalization of U.S. Manufacturing, Manufacturing Studies Board, Commission on Engineering and Technical Systems, National Research Council. *The Internationalization of U.S. Manufacturing: Causes and Consequences.* Washington, D.C.: National Academy Press, 1990.

Contractor, Farok J., and Peter Lorange. *Cooperative Strategies in International Business.* Lexington, MA: D.C. Heath and Company, 1988.

Cvar, Marquise R. "Case Studies in Global Competition: Patterns of Success and Failure." In Michael E. Porter, ed.

Competition in Global Industries. Boston: Harvard Business School Press, pp. 483–516.

Czinkota, Michael R., Pietra Rivoli, and Ilkka A. Ronkainen. *International Business.* Chicago: The Dryden Press, 1989.

Czinkota, Michael R., Ilkka A. Ronkainen, and Michael Moffett. *International Business,* update 2000. New York: Harcourt, 2000.

Davidson, William H. *Global Strategic Management.* New York: John Wiley & Sons, 1982.

Davidson, William H., and José de la Torre. *Managing the Global Corporation: Case Studies in Strategy and Management.* New York: McGraw-Hill, 1989.

Deloitte & Touche, *Leaders in Innovative Globalization Program,* report, London, 1998.

Dicken, Peter. *Global Shift: Industrial Change in a Turbulent World.* London: Harper and Row, 1986.

Douglas, Susan P., and C. Samuel Craig. *International Marketing Research.* Upper Saddle River, NJ: Prentice Hall, 1983.

Doz, Yves L. *Government Control and Multinational Management.* New York: Praeger, 1979.

Eccles, Robert G. *The Transfer Pricing Decision.* Lexington, MA: Lexington Books, 1985.

Enrico, Roger, and Jesse Kornbluth. *The Other Guy Blinked: How Pepsi Won the Cola Wars.* New York: Bantam Books, 1986.

Evans, Philip, and Thomas S. Würster. *Blown to Bits: How the New Economics of Information Transforms Strategy.* Boston: Harvard Business School Press, 1999.

Ferdows, Kasra. "Mapping International Factory Networks." In Kasra Ferdows, ed. *Managing International Manufacturing.* Amsterdam: Elsevier Science Publishers (North Holland), 1989.

Flaherty, M. Therese. "Coordinating International Manufacturing and Technology." in Michael E. Porter, ed. *Competition in Global Industries.* Boston: Harvard Business School Press, 1986.

Franko, Larry G. "Organizational Structures and Multinational Strategies of Continental European Enterprises." In M. Ghertman and J. Leontiades, eds. *European Research in International Business.* Amsterdam: North Holland, 1978.

Franko, Larry G. *The European Multinationals.* Greenwich, CT: Greylock Press, 1976.

Fuld, Leonard. *Competitor Intelligence: How to Get It—How to Use It.* New York: John Wiley & Sons, 1985.

Ghemawat, Pankaj. *Commitment: The Dynamic of Strategy.* Boston: Harvard Business School Press, 1991.

Ghoshal, Sumantra, Christopher A Bartlett, and D. Eleanor Westney, eds. *Organization Theory and the Multinational Corporation.* London: Macmillan, 1993.

Giddens, Anthony. *Runaway World: How Globalization Is Reshaping Our Lives.* New York: Routledge, 2000.

Grant, Robert M. *Contemporary Strategy Analysis.* Oxford, England: Blackwell Publishers, 1998.

Hamermesh, Richard G. *Making Strategy Work: How Senior Managers Produce Results.* New York: John Wiley & Sons, 1986.

Harrigan, Kathryn R. *Managing for Joint Venture Success.* Lexington, MA: Lexington Books, 1986.

Hatsopoulos, George N. "High Cost of Capital: Handicap of American Industry." Report sponsored by the American Business Conference and Thermo-Electron Corporation, April 1983.

Hax, Arnoldo C., and Nicolas S. Majluf. *Strategic Management: An Integrative Perspective.* Upper Saddle River, NJ: Prentice Hall, 1984.

Hertz, Noreena. *The Silent Takeover: Global Capitalism and the Death of Democracy.* London: William Heinemann, 2001.

Hofstede, Geert. *Culture's Consequences: International Differences in Work Related Values.* Beverly Hills, CA: Sage Publications, 1984.

Keegan, Warren J. *Multinational Marketing Management,* 4th ed. Upper Saddle River, NJ: Prentice Hall, 1989.

Klein, Naomi. *No Logo.* London: Flamingo, 2001.

Kotler, Philip. *Marketing Management,* 5th ed. Upper Saddle River, NJ: Prentice Hall, 1984.

Kotler, Philip, Liam Fahey, and S. Jatusripitak. *The New Competition.* Upper Saddle River, NJ: Prentice Hall, 1985.

Kozminski, Andrzej K., and George S. Yip, eds. *Strategies for Central and Eastern Europe.* Basingstoke: Macmillan, 2000.

Kozminski, Andrzej K., George S. Yip, and Anna M. Dempster. "Evaluating the Central and Eastern European Opportunity: Eastern Promise." In Andrzej K. Kozminski and George S. Yip, eds. *Strategies for Central and Eastern Europe.* Basingstoke: Macmillan, 2000.

Kyu-Won, Chang-Hoan Cho, and John D. Leckenby. "A Comparative Analysis of Korean and U.S. Web Advertising." Paper presented to 1999 Annual Conference American Academy of Advertising, Albuquerque, New Mexico (uts.cc.utexas.edu/~kwoh/3A/99AAA.html)

Lessard, Donald R. "Finance and Global Competition: Exploiting Financial Scope and Coping with Volatile Exchange Rates." In Michael E. Porter, ed. *Competition in Global Industries.* Boston: Harvard Business School Press, 1986.

Leung, Anthony, and George S. Yip. "Enter the Global Original Equipment Manufacturer: A New Type of Multinational Company," Working Paper, London Business School, October 31, 2000.

Lewis, Geoff. "Carlton & United Breweries." In Geoff Lewis and Peter Fitzroy, ed. *Cases in Australian Management.* Sydney: Prentice Hall, 1991.

Lindblom, Charles E. *The Policy-Making Process.* Upper Saddle River, NJ: Prentice Hall, 1968.

Lorange, Peter. *Implementation of Strategic Planning.* Upper Saddle River, NJ: Prentice Hall, 1982.

Malnight, Thomas W. "Toward a Model of Accelerating Organizational Change." In P. Christopher Early and Harbir Singh, eds. *Innovations in International and Cross-Cultural Management.* Thousand Oaks, CA: Sage, 2000, pp. 267–310.

Management Analysis Center/Paul J. Stonich, ed. *Implementing Strategy.* Cambridge, MA: Ballinger, 1982.

Markides, Constantinos C. *All the Right Moves.* Boston: Harvard Business School Press, 1999.

Mintzberg, Henry. *The Nature of Managerial Work.* New York: Harper & Row, 1973.

Morrison, Allen J. *Strategies in Global Industries: How U.S. Businesses Compete.* Westport, CT: Quorum Books, 1990.

Nohria, Nitin, Sumantra Ghoshal (contributor), and Cedric Crocker (editor). *The Differentiated Network: Organizing Multinational Corporations for Value Creation.* San Francisco: Jossey-Bass Business and Management Series, 1997.

Ohmae, Kenichi. *The Borderless World: Power and Strategy in the Interlinked Economy.* New York: Harper Business, 1990.

Ohmae, Kenichi. *Triad Power: The Coming Shape of Global Competition.* New York: Free Press, 1985.

Ohmae, Kenichi. *The Mind of the Strategist.* New York: McGraw-Hill, 1982.

Ouchi, William G. *Theory Z: How American Businesses Can Meet the Japanese Challenge.* Reading, MA: Addison-Wesley, 1981.

Pascale, Richard Tanner, and Anthony G. Athos. *The Art of Japanese Management: Applications for American Executives.* New York: Simon & Schuster, 1981.

Porter, Michael E. *The Competitive Advantage of Nations.* New York: The Free Press, 1990.

Porter, Michael E. "Competition in Global Industries: A Conceptual Framework." In Michael E. Porter, ed. *Competition in Global Industries.* Boston: Harvard Business School Press, 1986.

Porter, Michael E. *Competitive Advantage: Creating and Sustaining Superior Performance.* New York: Free Press, 1985.

Porter, Michael E. *Competitive Strategy: Techniques for Analyzing Industries and Competitors.* New York: Free Press, 1980.

Prahalad, C. K. "The Strategic Process in a Multinational Corporation." Unpublished doctoral dissertation, Harvard Business School, 1975.

Prahalad, C. K., and Yves L. Doz. *The Multinational Mission: Balancing Local Demands and Global Vision.* New York: Free Press, 1987.

Prestowitz, Clyde V., Jr. *Trading Places.* New York: Basic Books, 1988.

Quelch, John A., Robert D. Buzzell, and Eric R. Salama. *The Marketing Challenge of 1992,* Reading, MA: Addison-Wesley, 1990.

Root, Franklin R. *Entry Strategies for International Markets.* San Francisco, CA: Jossey-Bass, 1994.

Rugman, Alan M. *The End of Globalization,* London: Random House Business Books, 2000.

Rugman, Alan M. *International Diversification and the Multinational Enterprise.* Lexington, MA: Lexington Books, D. C. Heath, 1979.

Rumelt, Richard P., and Robin Wensley. "In Search of the Market Share Effect." *Proceedings.* Academy of Management Annual Meeting, pp. 2–6, 1981.

Segal-Horn, Susan, and John McGee. "Strategies to Cope with Retailer Buying Power." In Pellegrini & Reddy, eds. *Retail and Marketing Channels.* London: Routledge, 1989.

Singh, Kulwant, Joseph Putti, and George S. Yip. "Singapore—Regional Hub." In George S. Yip. *Asian Advantage: Key Strategies for Winning in the Asia-Pacific Region (Updated Edition—After the Crisis).* Cambridge, MA: Perseus Publishing, 2000, Chapter 7, pp. 155–79.

Skinner, Wickham. *Manufacturing: The Formidable Weapon.* New York: Wiley, 1985.

Steiner, George A. *Strategic Planning: What Every Manager Must Know.* New York: The Free Press, 1979.

Stopford, J. M., and S. Strange, with J. S. Henley. *Rival States, Rival Firms: Competition for World Market Shares.* Cambridge: Cambridge University Press, 1991.

Stopford, John M., and Louis T. Wells, Jr. *Managing the Multinational Enterprise.* New York: Basic Books, 1972.

Takeuchi, Hirotaka, and Michael E. Porten. "Three Roles of International Marketing in Global Strategy." In Michael E. Porter, ed. *Competition in Global Industries.* Boston: Harvard Business School Press, 1986.

Tallman, Stephen B., and George S. Yip. "Strategy and the Multinational Enterprise." In Alan M. Rugman and Thomas L. Brewer, eds. *The*

Oxford Handbook of International Business. Oxford, England: 2001, Chapter 12.

Treacy, Michael, and Fred Wiersema. *The Discipline of Market Leader.* Reading, MA: Addison-Wesley, 1995.

Vernon, Raymond. *Storm over the Multinationals.* Cambridge, MA: Harvard University Press, 1977.

Vernon, Raymond, and Louis T. Wells. *Manager in the International Economy.* Upper Saddle River, NJ: Prentice Hall, 1986.

Westney, D. Eleanor, and Srilata Zaheer. "Chapter 13: The Multinational Enterprise as an Organization." In Alan M. Rugman and Thomas L. Brewer, eds. *The Oxford Handbook of International Business.* Oxford, England: Oxford University Press, forthcoming 2001.

White, Roderick E., and Thomas A. Poynter. "Organizing for Worldwide Advantage." In Christopher A. Bartlett, Yves L. Doz, and Gunnar Hedlund, eds. *Managing the Global Firm.* London: Routledge, 1990.

Woo, Carolyn Y., and Karel Cool. "Porter's (1980) Generic Strategies: A Test of Performance and Functional Strategy Attributes." Working Paper. Purdue University, 1983.

Yip, George S. "An Integrated Approach to Global Competitive Strategy." In Roger Mansfield, ed. *Frontiers of Management Research and Practice.* London: Routledge, 1989.

Yip, George S. *Asian Advantage: Key Strategies for Winning in the Asia-Pacific Region.* Reading, MA: Addison-Wesley, 1998.

Yip, George S. *Asian Advantage: Key Strategies for Winning in the Asia-Pacific Region (Updated Edition—After the Crisis).* Cambridge, MA: Perseus Publishing, 2000.

Yip, George S. "Bases of Competitive Advantage." In Stuart Crainer and Des Dearlove, eds. *Financial Times Handbook of Management,* 2nd ed. London: Financial Times/Prentice Hall, 2001, pp. 253–63.

Yip, George S. "Do American Business Use Global Strategy?" Working Paper No. 91-101, Cambridge, MA: Marketing Science Institute, January 1991.

Yip, George S. "Global Strategy in the 21st Century." In Stuart Crainer and Des

Dearlove, eds. *Financial Times Handbook of Management,* 2nd ed. London: Financial Times/Prentice Hall, 2001, pp. 150–63.

Yoshino, M. Y. "Global Competition in a Salient Industry: The Case of Civil Aircraft Competition." In Michael E. Porter, ed.

Global Industries. Boston: Harvard Business School Press, 1986, pp. 517–38.

Yoshino, Michael Y., and U. Srinivasa Rangan. *Strategic Alliances: An Entrepreneurial Approach to Globalization.* Boston: Harvard Business School Press, 1995.

PERIODICALS

Advertising Age
Business Asia
Business International
Business Month
Business Week
Forbes
Fortune

Japan Times
Management Europe
Management Today
New York Times
The Economist
The Wall Street Journal

JOURNALS

Aaker, David A., and Erich Joachimsthale. "The Lure of Global Branding." *Harvard Business Review,* November–December 1999, pp. 137–44.

Baden Fuller, Charles W. F., and John M. Stopford. "Globalization Frustrated: The Case of White Goods." *Strategic Management Journal,* Vol. 12, 1991, pp. 493–507.

Bartlett, Christopher A., and Sumantra Ghoshal. "Managing Across Borders: New Strategic Requirements." *Sloan Management Review,* Summer 1987, pp. 7–17.

Bartlett, Christopher A., and Sumantra Ghoshal. "Matrix Management: Not a Structure, a Frame of Mind." *Harvard Business Review,* July–August 1990, pp. 138–45.

Bartlett, Christopher A., and Sumantra Ghoshal. "What Is a Global Manager?" *Harvard Business Review,* September–October 1992, pp. 124–32.

Behrman, Jack N., and William A. Fischer. "Transnational Corporations: Market Orientations and R&D Abroad." *Columbia Journal of World Business,* Fall 1980, pp. 55–60.

Berkowitz, Marvin, and Krishna Mohan. "The Role of Global Procurement in the Value Chain of Japanese Steel." *Columbia Journal of World Business,* Winter 1987, pp. 97–110.

Biggart, Nicole Woolsey, and Mauro F. Guillen. "Developing Difference: Social Organization and the Rise of the Auto Industries of South Korea, Taiwan, Spain, and Argentina." *American Sociological Review,* Vol. 64, No. 5, 1999, pp. 722–47.

Birkinshaw, Julian. "Why Is Knowledge Management So Difficult?" *Business Strategy Review,* Vol. 12, No. 1, Spring 2001, pp. 11–18.

Birkinshaw, Julian, and Nick Fry. "Subsidiary Initiatives to Develop New Markets." *Sloan Management Review,* Vol. 39, No. 3, 1998, pp. 51–62.

Boddewyn, Jean J. J., Robin Soehl, and Jacques Picard. "Standardization in International Marketing: Is Ted Levitt in Fact Right?" *Business Horizons,* Vol. 29, November–December 1986, pp. 69–75.

Buckley, Peter J. "The Theory of the Multinational Enterprise." Acta Universitatis Upsaliensis. Uppsala, Sweden: *Studia Oeconomiae Negotiorum,* Vol. 26, 1987.

Burggraeve, Chris C. "Meeting Product Standards in the Single Market." *The Journal of European Business,* May–June 1990, pp. 22–6.

Buzzell, Robert D. "Can You Standardize Multinational Marketing?" *Harvard Business Review,* November–December 1968, pp. 102–13.

Buzzell, Robert D., Bradley T. Gale, and R. G. M. Sultan. "Market Share—A Key to Profitability." *Harvard Business Review,* January–February 1975, pp. 97–106.

Campa, José M., and Mauro F. Guillen. "The Internalization of Exports: Firm and Location-Specific Factors in a Middle-Income Country." *Management Science,* Vol. 45, No. 11, 1999, pp. 1463–78.

Chakravarthy, Balaji S., and Howard V. Perlmutter. "Strategic Planning for a Global Business." *Columbia Journal of World Business,* Summer 1985, pp. 3–10.

Clee, G. H., and A. di Scipio. "Creating a World Enterprise." *Harvard Business Review,* November–December 1959, pp. 77–89.

Clee, G. H., and W. M. Sachtjen. "Organizing a Worldwide Business." *Harvard Business Review,* November–December 1964, pp. 55–67.

Conn, Henry P., and George S. Yip. "Global Transfer of Critical Capabilities." *Business Horizons,* Vol. 40, No. 1, January–February 1997, pp. 22–31.

Craig, C. Samuel, and Susan. P. Douglas. "Configural Advantage in Global Markets." *Journal of International Marketing,* Vol. 8, No. 1, 1999, pp. 6–26.

Daniels, J. D., R. A. Pitts, and M. J. Tretter. "Strategy and Structure of U.S. Multinationals: An Exploratory Study." *Academy of Management Journal,* Vol. 27, 1984, pp. 292–307.

Das, Gurcharan. "Local Memoirs of a Global Manager." *Harvard Business Review,* March–April 1993, pp. 38–47.

Davidson, William H., and Philippe Haspeslagh. "Shaping a Global Product Organization." *Harvard Business Review,* July–August 1982, pp. 125–32.

de Meyer, Arnold, Jinichiro Nakane, Jeffrey Miller, and Kasra Ferdows. "Flexibility: The Next Competitive Battle—The Manufacturing Futures Survey." *Strategic Management Journal,* Vol. 10, 1989, pp. 135–44.

Dess, G., and P. Davis. "Porter's (1980) Generic Strategies as Determinants of Strategic Group Membership and Organizational Performance." *Academy of Management Journal,* Vol. 27, 1984, pp. 467–88.

Dornbush, Rudiger, Stanley Fisher, and Paul A. Samuelson. "Comparative Advantage, Trade and Payments in a Ricardian Model with a Continuum of Goods." *American Economic Review,* Vol. 67, December 1977, pp. 823–39.

Douglas, Susan P., and C. Samuel Craig. "Examining Performance of U.S. Multinationals in Foreign Markets." *Journal of International Business Studies,* Winter 1983, pp. 51–7.

Douglas, Susan P., and Yoram Wind. "The Myth of Globalization." *Columbia Journal of World Business,* Vol. 22, No. 4, Winter 1987, pp. 19–29.

Doz, Yves L. "Managing Manufacturing Rationalization Within Multinational Companies." *Columbia Journal of World Business,* Fall 1978, pp. 82–94.

Doz, Yves L., Christopher A. Bartlett, and C. K. Prahalad. "Global Competitive Pressures vs. Host Country Demands: Managing Tensions in Multinational Corporations." *California Management Review,* Vol. 23, No. 3, 1981, pp. 63–74.

Dunn, S. W. "Effect of National Identity on Multinational Promotional Strategy in Europe." *Journal of Marketing,* October 1976, pp. 50–7.

Dunning, John H. "The Eclectic Paradigm of International Production: A Restatement and Some Possible Extensions." *Journal of International Business Studies,* Spring 1988.

Dyment, John J. "Strategies and Management Controls for Global Corporations." *Journal of Business Strategy,* Spring 1987, pp. 20–6.

Egelhoff, William G. "Strategy and Structure in Multinational Corporations: An Information Processing Approach." *Administrative Science Quarterly,* Vol. 27, 1982, pp. 435–58.

Egelhoff, William G. "Patterns of Control in U.S., U.K. and European Multinational Corporations." *Journal of International Business Studies,* Fall 1984, pp. 73–83.

Egelhoff, William G. "Strategy and Structure in Multinational Corporations: A Revision of the Stopford and Wells Model." *Strategic Management Journal,* Vol. 9, 1988, pp. 1–14.

Farley, Laurence J. "Going Global: Choices and Challenges." *Journal of Business Strategy,* Vol. 1, Winter 1986, pp. 67–70.

Fouraker, Lawrence E., and John M. Stopford. "Organization Structure and Multinational Strategy." *Administrative Science Quarterly,* Vol. 13, 1968, pp. 57–70.

Frazee, Valerie. "Tearing Down Roadblocks." *Workforce,* Vol. 77, No. 2, February 1998, pp. 50–1.

George, Abraham M., and C. William Schroth. "Managing Foreign Exchange for Competitive Advantage." *Sloan Management Review,* Winter 1991, pp. 105–16.

Ghoshal, Sumantra. "Global Strategy: An Organizing Framework." *Strategic Management Journal,* Vol. 8, No. 5, September–October 1987, pp. 425–40.

Goldhar, Joel D., and Mariann Jelinek. "Computer Integrated Flexible Manufacturing: Organizational, Economic, and Strategic Implications." *Interfaces,* Vol. 15, May–June 1985, pp. 94–105.

Gupta, Anil K., and Vijay Govindarajan. "Knowledge Flows Within Multinational Corporations." *Strategic Management Journal,* Vol. 21, No. 4, 2000, pp. 473–96.

Hamel, Gary, and C. K. Prahalad. "Do You Really Have a Global Strategy?" *Harvard Business Review,* July–August 1985, pp. 139–48.

Haspeslagh, Philippe. "Portfolio Planning: Uses and Limits." *Harvard Business Review,* January–February 1982, pp. 58–73.

Hedlund, Gunnan. "The Hypermodern MNC: A Heterarchy?" *Human Resource Management,* Vol. 25, 1986, pp. 9–35.

Heenan, David A., and Calvin Reynolds. "ROP's: A Step Toward Global Human Resources Management." *California Management Review,* Vol. 18, No. 1, Fall 1975, pp. 5–9.

Henzler, Herbert, and Wilhelm Rall. "Facing Up to the Globalization Challenge." *The McKinsey Quarterly,* Winter 1986, pp. 52–68.

Hill, J. S., and R. R. Still. "Adapting Products to LDC Tastes." *Harvard Business Review,* March–April 1984, pp. 92–101.

Hirschey, Robert C., and Richard E. Caves. "Research and Transfer of Technology by Multinational Enterprises." *Oxford Bulletin of Economics and Statistics,* Vol. 43, No. 2, May 1981, pp. 115–30.

Hout, Thomas, Michael E. Porter, and Eileen Rudden. "How Global Companies Win Out." *Harvard Business Review,* September–October 1982, pp. 98–108.

Hrebiniak, Lawrence. "Implementing Global Strategies." *European Management Journal,* Vol. 10, No. 4, December 1992, pp. 392–403.

Hu, Yao-Su. "Global or Stateless Corporations Are National Firms with International Operations." *California Management Review,* Vol. 34, No. 2, Winter 1992, pp. 107–26.

Huszagh, Sandra M., Richard J. Fox, and Ellen Day. "Global Marketing: An Empirical Investigation." *Columbia Journal of World Business,* Twentieth Anniversary Issue, Vol. 20, No. 4, 1986, pp. 31–43.

Jaikumar, Ramchandran. "Postindustrial Manufacturing." *Harvard Business Review,* November–December 1986, pp. 69–76.

Jain, Subhash C. "Standardization of International Marketing Strategy: Some Research Hypotheses." *Journal of Marketing,* Vol. 53, January 1989, pp. 70–9.

Jatusripitak, Somkid, Liam Fahey, and Philip Kotler. "Strategic Global Marketing: Lessons from the Japanese." *Columbia Journal of World Business,* Spring 1985, pp. 47–53.

Jeelof, Gerrit. "Global Strategies of Philips." *European Management Journal,* Vol. 7, No. 1, 1989, pp. 84–91.

Johansson, Johny K. "Determinants and Effects of 'Made in' Labels." *International Marketing Review,* Vol. 6, No. 1, Spring 1989, pp. 47–58.

Johansson, Johny K, and George S. Yip. "Exploiting Globalization Potential: U.S. and Japanese Strategies." *Strategic Management Journal,* Vol. 15, October 1994, pp. 579–601.

Kacker, M. P. "Patterns of Marketing Adaptation in International Business." *Management International Review,* Vol. 12, issues 4–5, 1972, pp. 111–18.

Kacker, M. P. "Export Oriented Product Adaptation." *Management International Review,* Vol. 6, 1975, pp. 61–70.

Kanter, Rosabeth Moss. "Change in the Global Economy: An Interview with Rosabeth Moss Kanter." *European Management Journal,* Vol. 12, No. 1, 1994, pp. 1–9.

Kashani, Kamran. "Beware the Pitfalls of Global Marketing." *Harvard Business Review,* September–October 1989, pp. 91–8.

Kashani, Kamran, and John A. Quelch. "Can Sales Promotion Go Global?" *Business Horizons,* Vol. 33, No. 3, May–June 1990, pp. 37–43.

Kester, W. Carl, and Timothey A. Luehrman. "Are We Feeling More Competitive Yet? The Exchange Rate Gambit." *Sloan Management Review,* Winter 1989, pp. 19–28.

Kogut, Bruce. "Designing Global Strategies: Comparative and Competitive Value-Added Chains." *Sloan Management Review,* Summer 1985, pp. 27–38.

Kogut, Bruce. "Designing Global Strategies: Profiting from Operational Flexibility." *Sloan Management Review,* Fall 1985, pp. 27–38.

Kogut, Bruce. "Joint Ventures: Theoretical and Empirical Perspectives." *Strategic Management Journal,* Vol. 9, No. 4, July–August 1988, pp. 319–32.

Kogut, Bruce, and Nalin Kulatilaka. "Operating Flexibility, Global Manufacturing, and the Option Value of a Multinational Network." *Management Science,* Vol. 40, No. 1, January 1994, pp. 123–39

Kogut, B., and U. Zander. "Knowledge of the Firm and the Evolutionary Theory of the Multinational Corporation." *Journal of International Business Studies,* Vol. 24, No. 4, 1993, pp. 625–45.

Korine, Harry. "Fresenius AG: High Speed Globalization." *Business Strategy Review,* Vol. 11, No. 2, Summer 2000, pp. 47–57.

Kotabe, Masaaki, and Glenn S. Omura. "Sourcing Strategies of European and Japanese Multinationals: A Comparison." *Journal of International Business Studies,* Vol. 20, No. 1, Spring 1989, pp. 113–30.

Kotler, Philip, and Ravi Singh. "Marketing Warfare in the 1980s." *Journal of Business Strategy,* Vol. 1, No. 3, Winter 1981, pp. 30–41.

Lazer, W., and E. H. Shaw. "Global Marketing Management: At the Dawn of the New Millennium." *Journal of International Marketing,* Vol. 8, No. 1, 2000, pp. 65–77.

Levitt, Theodore. "The Globalization of Markets." *Harvard Business Review,* May–June 1983, pp. 92–102.

Lewis, Geoffrey, John Clark, and Bill Moss. "BHP Reorganizes for Global Competition." *Long Range Planning,* Vol. 21, No. 3, 1988, pp. 18–26.

Malnight, Thomas W. "The Transition from Decentralized to Network-based MNC Structures: An Evolutionary Perspective." *Journal of International Business Studies,* Vol. 27, No. 1, 1996, pp. 43–66.

Malnight, Thomas W. "Globalization of an Ethnocentric Firm: An Evolutionary Perspective." *Strategic Management Journal,* Vol. 16, No. 2, 1995, pp. 119–41.

Markides, Constantinos C., and Norman Berg. "Manufacturing Offshore Is Bad Business." *Harvard Business Review,* September–October 1988, pp. 113–20.

Martinez, Jon I., and J. Carlos Jarillo. "The Evolution of Research on Coordination Mechanisms in Multinational Corporations." *Journal of International Business Studies,* Vol. 20, No. 3, Fall 1989, pp. 489–514.

Maruca, Regina Fazio. "The Right Way to Go Global: An Interview with Whirlpool CEO David Whitwam." *Harvard Business Review,* March–April 1994, pp. 135–45.

McCormick, Janice, and Nan Stone. "From National Champion to Global Competitor: An Interview with Thomson's Alain Gomez." *Harvard Business Review,* May–June 1990, pp. 127–35.

McGee, John F. "1992: Moves Americans Must Make." *Harvard Business Review,* May–June 1989, pp. 78–84.

Medina, J. F., and M. F. Duffy. "Standardization vs. Globalization: A New Perspective of Brand Strategies." *Journal of Product and Brand Management,* Vol. 7, No. 3, 1998, pp. 223–43.

Mirhan, Greg. "Advantage: Hewlett-Packard." *Global Executive,* March–April 1993, pp. 10–13.

Mitchell, Will, J. Myles Shaver, and Bernard Yeung. "Getting There in a Global Industry: Impacts on Performance of Changing International Presence." *Strategic Management Journal,* Vol. 13, 1992, pp. 419–32.

Montgomery, David B., and George S. Yip. "The Challenge of Global Customer Management." *Marketing Management,* Vol. 9, No. 4, Winter 2000, pp. 22–9.

Moore, Karl, and Julian M. Birkinshaw. "Managing Knowledge in Global Service Firms: Centres of Excellence." *Academy of Management Executive,* December 1998.

Morrison, Allen. J., David. A. Ricks, and Kendall Roth. "Globalization versus Regionalization: Which Way for the Multinational?" *Organizational Dynamics,* Vol. 19, No. 3, 1991, pp. 17–29.

Morrison, Allen J., and Kendall Roth. "The Regional Solution: An Alternative to Globalization." *Transnational Corporations,* Vol. 1, No. 2, 1992, pp. 37–55.

Morrison, Allen J., and Kendall Roth. "A Taxonomy of Business-Level Strategies in Global Industries." *Strategic Management Journal,* Vol. 13, 1992, pp. 399–418.

Motameni, R., and M. Shahrokhi. "Brand Equity Valuation: A Global Perspective." *Journal of Product and Brand Management,* Vol. 7, No. 4, 1998, pp. 275–90.

Murtha, Thomas P., Stefanie Ann Lenway, and Richard P. Bagozzi. "Global Mind-Sets and Cognitive Shift in a Complex Multinational Corporation." *Strategic Management Journal,* Vol. 2, No. 19, 1998, pp. 97–114.

Oliff, Michael D., and Donald A. Marchand. "Strategic Information Management in Global Manufacturing." *European Management Journal,* Vol. 9, No. 4, December 1991, pp. 361–71.

Perlmutter, Howard V. "The Tortuous Evolution of the Multinational Corporation." *Columbia Journal of World Business,* January–February 1969, pp. 9–18.

Pierson, Robert M. "R&D by Multinationals for Overseas Markets." *Research Management,* July 1978, pp. 19–22.

Porter, Michael E. "Changing Patterns of International Competition." *California Management Review,* Vol. 28, No. 2, Winter 1986, pp. 9–40.

Porter, Michael E. "New Global Strategies for Competitive Advantage." *Planning Review,* May–June 1990, pp. 4–14.

Prahalad, C. K., and Yves L. Doz. "An Approach to Strategic Control on MNCs." *Sloan Management Review,* Summer 1981, pp. 5–13.

Quelch, John A. "Global Brands: Taking Stock." *Business Strategy Review,* Vol. 10. No. 1, 1999, pp. 1–14.

Quelch, John A., and James E. Austin. "Should Multinationals Invest in Africa?" *Sloan Management Review,* Vol. 34, No. 3, Spring 1993, pp. 107–19.

Quelch, John A., and Edward J. Hoff. "Customizing Global Marketing." *Harvard Business Review,* May–June 1986, pp. 59–68.

Quinn, James Brian. "Strategic Goals: Process and Politics." *Sloan Management Review,* Fall 1977, p. 22.

Ramachandran, K., and George S. Yip. "It's Time to Globalise Now." *General Management Review* (Economic Times, India), Vol. 2, No. 1, 2000, pp. 40–7.

Rau, Pradeep A., and John F. Preble. "Standardization of Marketing Strategy by Multinationals." *International Marketing Review,* Autumn 1987, pp. 18–28.

Reeb, David M., Chuck C. Y. Kwok, and H. Young Baek. "Systematic Risk of the Multinational Corporation." *Journal of International Business Studies,* Vol. 29, 1998, pp. 263–80.

Ronstadt, Robert, and Robert J. Kramer. "Getting the Most Out of Innovation Abroad." *Harvard Business Review,* March–April 1982, pp. 94–9.

Roos, Johan, Georg von Krogh, and George S. Yip. "An Epistemology of Globalizing Firms." *International Business Review,* Vol. 3, No. 4, special issue on Organization's Knowledge, Knowledge Transfer and Cooperative Strategies, November–December 1994, pp. 395–409.

Rosen, Barry Nathan, Jean J. Boddewyn, Ernst A. Louis. "Participation by U.S. Agencies in International Brand Advertising: An Empirical Study." *Journal of Advertising,* Vol. 17, No. 4, 1988, pp. 14–22.

Roth, Kendall, and Allen J. Morrison. "An Empirical Analysis of the Integration-Responsiveness Framework in Global Industries." *Journal of International Business Studies,* Vol. 21, No. 4, Fourth Quarter 1990, pp. 541–64.

Roth, Kendall, and David A. Ricks. "Goal Configuration in a Global Industry Context." *Strategic Management Journal,* Vol. 15, No. 2, February 1994, pp. 103–20.

Roth, Kendall, David M. Schwieger, and Allen J. Morrison. "Global Strategy Implementation at the Business Unit Level: Operational Capabilities and Administrative Mechanisms." *Journal of International Business Studies,* Third Quarter 1991, pp. 369–402.

Rugman, Alan M. "The Corporate Performance of U.S. and European Multinational Enterprises, 1970–79." *Management International Review,* Vol. 23, No. 2, 1983, pp. 4–14.

Samiee, Saeed, and Kendall Roth. "The Influence of Global Marketing Standardization on Performance." *Journal of Marketing,* Vol. 56, April 1992, pp. 1–17.

Schlie, Erik, and George S. Yip. "Regional Follows Global: Strategy Mixes in the World Automotive Industry." *European Management Journal,* Vol. 18, No. 4, August 2000, pp. 343–54.

Schuh, Arnold. "Global Standardization as a Success Formula for Marketing in Central Eastern Europe?" *Journal of World Business,* Vol. 35, No. 2, Summer 2000, pp. 133–48.

Schütte, Helmut. "Strategy and Organisation: Challenges for European MNCs in Asia." *European Management Journal,* Vol. 15, No. 4, August 1997, pp. 436–45.

Segal-Horn, S., D. Asch, and V. Suneja. "The Globalization of the European White Goods Industry." *European Management Journal,* Vol. 16, No. 1, 1998, pp. 101–9.

Shanks David C. "Strategic Planning for Global Competition." *Journal of Business Strategy,* Winter 1985, pp. 80–9.

Sölvell, Örjan, and Ivo Zanden. "Organisation of the Dynamic Multinational Enterprise: The Home-based and the Heterarchical MNE." *International Studies of Management and Organization,* Vol. 25, No. 1/2, 1995, pp. 17–38.

Sorenson, Ralph Z., and Ulrich E. Wiechmann. "How Multinationals View Marketing Standardization." *Harvard Business Review,* May–June 1975, pp. 38–167.

Spence, A. Michael. "Entry, Capacity, Investment and Oligopolistic Pricing." *Bell Journal of Economics,* Vol. 8, Autumn 1977, pp. 534–44.

Spence, A. Michael. "Industrial Organization and Competitive Advantage in Multinational Industries." *American Economic Review,* Vol. 74, No. 2, May 1984, pp. 356–60.

Starr, Martin K. "Global Production and Operations Strategy." *Columbia Journal of World Business,* Winter 1984, pp. 17–22.

Taylor, William. "The Logic of Global Business: An Interview with ABB's Percy Barnevik." *Harvard Business Review,* Vol. 6, No. 2, March–April 1991, pp. 91–105.

Vancil, Richard F., and Peter Lorange. "Strategic Planning in Diversified Companies." *Harvard Business Review,* January–February 1975, pp. 81–90.

Vernon, Raymond. "The Product Cycle Hypothesis in a New International Environment." *Oxford Bulletin of Economics and Statistics,* Vol. 41, 1979, pp. 255–67.

Walters, Peter G. P. "International Marketing Policy: A Discussion of the Standardization Construct and Its Relevance for Corporate Policy." *Journal of International Business Studies,* Summer 1986, pp. 55–69.

Westney, D. Eleanor. "Research on the Global Management of Technology Development." *Business Review,* Vol. 46, No. 1, August 1998, pp. 1–21.

White, Roderick E. "Generic Business Strategies, Organizational Context and Performance: An Empirical Investigation." *Strategic Management Journal,* Vol. 7, 1986, pp. 217–31.

White, Roderick E., and Thomas A. Poynter. "Strategies for Foreign-Owned Subsidiaries in Canada." *Business Quarterly,* Summer 1984, pp. 59–69.

Yip, George S. "A Performance Comparison of Continental and National Businesses in Europe." *International Marketing Review,* Vol. 8, No. 2, 1991, pp. 31–9.

Yip, George S. "Gateways to Entry." *Harvard Business Review,* September–October 1982, pp. 85–92.

Yip, George S. "Global Strategy as a Factor in Japanese Success." *The International*

Executive, special issue on Japan, Vol. 38, No. 1, January–February 1996, pp. 145–67.

Yip, George S. "Global Strategy … In a World of Nations?" *Sloan Management Review,* Vol. 31, No. 1, Fall 1989, pp. 29–41.

Yip, George S. "Industry Drivers of Global Strategy and Organization." *The International Executive,* Vol. 36, No. 5, September–October 1994, pp. 529–56.

Yip, George S. "Patterns and Determinants of Global Marketing." *Journal of Marketing Management,* Vol. 13, 1997, pp. 153–64.

Yip, George S. "Who Needs Strategic Planning?" *The Journal of Business Strategy,* Vol. 6, No. 2, Fall 1985, pp. 30–42.

Yip, George S., and George A. Coundouriotis. "Diagnosing Global Strategy Potential: The World Chocolate Confectionary Industry." *Planning Review,* January–February 1991, pp. 4–14.

Yip, George S., Javier B. Gomez, and Joseph Monti. "Role of the Internationalization Process in the Performance of Newly Internationalizing Firms." *Journal of International Marketing,* Vol. 8, No. 3, 2000, pp. 10–35.

Yip, George S., Pierre M. Loewe, and Michael Y. Yoshino. "How to Take Your Company to the Global Market." *Columbia Journal of World Business,* Winter 1988, pp. 37–48.

Yip, George S., and Tammy L. Madsen. "Global Account Management: The New Frontier in Relationship Marketing." *International Marketing Review,* Vol. 13, No. 3, 1996, pp. 24–42, special issue on Global Marketing Implementation.

Yip, George S., Johan Roos, and Johny K. Johansson. "Effects of Nationality on Global Strategy." *Management International Review,* Vol. 37, No. 4, October–December 1997, pp. 365–84.

Yoffie, David B., and Helen V. Milney. "An Alternative to Free Trade or Protectionism: Why Corporations Seek Strategic Trade Policy." *California Management Review,* Summer 1989, pp. 111–31.

Yunker, Penelope J. "A Survey Study of Subsidiary Autonomy, Performance Evaluation and Transfer Pricing in Multinational Corporations." *Columbia Journal of World Business,* Fall 1983, pp. 51–64.

CASES

Aguilar, Francis J., and Michael Y. Yoshino. "The Philips Group: 1987," case No. 9-388-050. Boston: Harvard Business School.

Buzzell, Robert D. "Citibank: Marketing to Multinational Customers," Harvard Business School case No. 9-584-016, Boston: Harvard Case Services, 1984, revised 1/85.

Collis David J. "Saatchi and Saatchi Company, PLC," case No. 1-387-170, Boston: Harvard Business School, 1986.

Quelch, John A. "British Airways: Teaching Note," case No. 5-587-016. Boston: *Harvard Business School,* 1987.

Yip, George S. "Planning at Pepsi (B)," case No. 9-583-051. Boston: Harvard Business School, 1983.

COMPANY INDEX

Italicized page numbers refer to boxed text or illustrations.

SUBJECT INDEX

Italicized page numbers refer to boxed text or illustrations.

AUTHOR INDEX

Italicized page numbers refer to boxed text or illustrations.